MW00716784

the

scope of

astrological

prediction

BOOKS BY
MARC EDMUND JONES

HOW TO LEARN ASTROLOGY

THE GUIDE TO HOROSCOPE INTERPRETATION

HORARY ASTROLOGY, PROBLEM SOLVING

ASTROLOGY, HOW AND WHY IT WORKS

SABIAN SYMBOLS IN ASTROLOGY

ESSENTIALS OF ASTROLOGICAL ANALYSIS

THE SCOPE OF ASTROLOGICAL PREDICTION

OCCULT PHILOSOPHY

GEORGE SYLVESTER MORRIS

THE SABIAN MANUAL

THE SABIAN BOOK

IN PREPARATION

MUNDANE PERSPECTIVES IN ASTROLOGY

FUNDAMENTALS OF NUMBER SIGNIFICANCE

marc edmund jones

the

scope of
astrological
prediction

an introduction to the
dynamic horoscopy

sabian publishing society
stanwood, washington 1973

PRINTED IN THE UNITED STATES OF AMERICA
BY SCHNEIDEREITH & SONS, BALTIMORE, MARYLAND

proem

the

true function

of astrology

is to reveal

(1)

the nature of

human capacity and

(2)

the relative importance

of events

or their possibility

Foreword		ix
Introductory		3

ABRAHAM LINCOLN

One	The Basic Attitude	13
Two	The Natural Drive	60
Three	The Basic Sensitivity	70
Four	The Basic Excitation	82
Five	The Five Transcendencies	91
	The Nascent Consistency	93
	The Nascent Integrity	96
	The Nascent Independence	98
	The Nascent Responsibility	99
	The Nascent Enlightenment	100
Six	The Natural Involvement	102
Seven	The Transits	119
Eight	Life Recapitulation	133
Nine	The Primary Directions	143
Ten	The Tertiary Directions	157
Eleven	Horoscope Rectification	168
Twelve	Supplementary Background	178

ANNIE BESANT

One	The Basic Attitude	189
Two	The Natural Drive	212
Three	The Basic Sensitivity	225
Four	The Basic Excitation	237
Five	The Five Transcendencies	241
	The Nascent Consistency	241
	The Nascent Integrity	243
	The Nascent Independence	245

contents

	The Nascent Responsibility	246
	The Nascent Enlightenment	247
Six	The Natural Involvement	249
Seven	The Transits	271
Eight	Life Recapitulation	280
Nine	Horoscope Rectification	287
Ten	Supplementary Background	291

DYNAMIC ANALYSIS

One	The Basic Attitude	299
Two	The Natural Drive	326
Three	The Basic Sensitivity	333
Four	The Basic Excitation	344
Five	The Five Transcendencies	354
	The Nascent Consistency	356
	The Nascent Integrity	361
	The Nascent Independence	367
	The Nascent Responsibility	370
	The Nascent Enlightenment	371
Six	The Natural Involvement	373
Seven	Progressed Calculation	378
Appendix	Tabulation of Secondaries	390
	Essential Principles	394
	Primer of Calculation	403
	Components of the Horoscope	444
Index		449

SPECIAL SUBSECTIONS

Ordering of Variables	3
Bugaboo of Words	6

contents

Substance of Delineation	7
Horoscopic Aspects	21
Progressed Potentiality Distribution	22
Psychological Trend to Balance	23
Dynamic Activation	27
Nonfulcral Indication	29
Time Orb in Directions	30
Horoscopic Affinities	36
Qualities of Uniqueness	41
Fulcrum Indication	46
Challenge by Progressed Station	49
Lincoln's Intimate Involvements	52
Role of General Grant	114
Proliferation to Infinity	120
Progressed Horoscope	136
Planetary Differentiation	147
Mundane Astrology	154
Basic Rapport with Circumstances	307
Retrogradation	311
Rationale of Keywords	317
Cultural Matrix	334
Dynamic Nature of Myth	355
Problem of Fatality	362

HOROSCOPIC DIAGRAMS

Abraham Lincoln	12	Annie Besant	188
Stephen Douglas	37	Charles Bradlaugh	195
Mary Todd	40	Helena Blavatsky	208
William Herndon	51	Solar return	281
Solar return	135	Lunar return	283
Progressed chart	137	Diurnal chart	285
Lunar return	139		
Diurnal chart	141	Walt Disney	402

fOREWORÒ

Again it has taken an unanticipated sheaf of years to produce one of these projected basic textbooks of astrology. *Horary Astrology* came first in 1943, and out of turn for the reasons explained at the time. *Astrology, How and Why It Works,* properly the introductory volume, appeared in 1945. *Sabian Symbols in Astrology* followed in 1953. *The Essentials of Astrological Analysis* was published in 1960. Since the difficulties in creating the series have increased consistently, with a greater complexity of interweaving psychological and physical factors on each new plateau of concern, the completion of the two remaining volumes lies very much in the lap of the gods. Work is already under way, however, on the *Mundane Perspectives in Astrology.*

The preliminary mimeographed materials covering the present ground, the *Directional Astrology* lecture-lessons, were issued in 1932 from May 9th through October 17th. Their principal contribution was the stress of a progressive analysis in time rather than space, or a fundamental consideration of the characteristic significance of each planet separately. Emphasis was given to the particularity of any indication in the sequence of its special type of activity, instead of in its more superficial concurrence with other progressed testimonies coming to a common pertinence at some specific moment. Here was a simple insight. In not too dissimilar fashion or as the basis for sound judgment a man's business must be viewed primarily in its own largely self-maintaining chain of events or sequence of challenges and consummations, as must also and rather independently his psychological and philandering involvements or his recreational pattern or his health and so on through every varied avenue of his self-realiza-

ix

tion. The development of this procedure in its astrological form had only a groping exposition three or four decades ago, and what was accomplished was no more than a prestatement of the ultimate organization of the technique.

The initial attempt at an exposition of the directions in a more permanent form began at the Salisbury Hotel in New York City in mid-October, 1953, or at the time *Sabian Symbols* had been nursed through the successive stages of a first printing and binding. This effort was interrupted by a tentative preparation of the *Horary Handbook,* but the refinement of that manuscript and its definite publication as a third smaller manual has never proved practical. Instead, the major attention at that point soon turned to the analysis of natal astrology for the projected *Essentials.* The outreach for some adequately ordered presentation of horoscopic progression continued but in sporadic fashion through the author's move of residence to Washington State at the end of September, 1954, and on for a large part of 1955. Ultimately the earlier treatise once completed in its unedited or tentative form could be seen to be a very abortive effort, and it was abandoned in toto. A fresh start did not prove possible until June 1, 1965, or almost a decade later. The rough draft that then was prepared was definitely disappointing in cold perspective after its completion, but at long last there seemed to be real promise in the manner of treatment that had evolved and therefore a program of careful revision was worked out in early 1966 and actually begun with effective results in mid-December. The main text of the manuscript went to the printer on May 9, 1968.

The author from the beginning has been sensitive to the fact that the self-designated stellar science, from its ancient and quite precursory forms to the beginning of its refinement in a definite horoscopy by perhaps the third or second century B.C. and on through its subsequent sophistication in the medieval and early modern period, has made a most exceptional impact on the imagination of man. Nonetheless he has found that he cannot lean in direct or specific fashion on any of its major writings, and as a result none are cited in the bibliography of this text. In today's world a scholar might be regarded as decidedly incompetent if, in any area of scientific thought and accomplishment, he built his own contribution on an uncritical acceptance of what could well be unsubstantiated assumptions and conclusions on the part of those preceding him in his field a century or more or even as little as a decade or so prior to his own effort. In consequence the procedure in preparing these basic manuals has been to take the work of the early astrologers and, by a thoroughgoing analysis of their own account of their accomplishment or explanation of their techniques, to determine just what they were trying to do in their characteristic fashion and to discover just how it came about that their deductive insights did achieve significant correspondence to real events in their experience or observation. Each volume in this present series seeks to hold with utter faithfulness to the ageless genius of astrology, but not as this remains in a strait jacket of inadequate expression or is distorted in concepts that have become confusingly outdated.

The beginning task in the exposition of progressed analysis was to find adequate illustrative cases of its employment. Ideally this would mean individuals (1) who would be well-known enough to give delineation productive meaning or actually have it serve to exemplify any given detail of signification, (2) about whom there would be sufficient reliable information so that there would be a reasonably self-evident correctness in finding indication correlated with event, and (3) for whom there would be an available horoscope of almost unimpeachable validity. This in practical terms was asking the impossible. Any effective example case would be somebody who had lived long enough to provide a full calendar of personal eventualities for identification in horoscopic progression, and thus would be born back in an earlier era when little attention was paid to precise times of birth. Actually the overall unreliability of astrological data back in the nineteenth century is notorious, and the problem has been discussed in *Sabian Symbols.* An even more serious difficulty of general exposition in a textbook to be widely read or consulted is that the public image of any person of importance is quite likely to be different from the private and more genuine manifestation of himself that astrology measures fundamentally. Even in cases of no special prominence the inwardness or basic core of character may not really be known either by the individual himself or his intimates.

The author is under a weight of obligation to a larger host of students and friends, as well as contemporaries in the astrological field, than it ever would be possible to bring to specific mention. Robert Spencer, whose generous tender of his mathematical ability has resulted in vital contribution to the development of this text, began the search for the needed biographical material. This was to prove utterly frustrating until Annis Fromm discovered the two-volume biography of Annie Besant by Arthur H. Nethercot, published in 1961 and 1963. An examination of these beginning in November, 1964, revealed the possibilities of which advantage was taken at the end. An obvious initial reaction would be that this remarkable British iconoclast and indefatigable sociopolitical reformer might be an objectionable example because she had become more broadly known as a Theosophist and had been involved in most unfortunate miracle-mongering. Would an often notorious person living far out of the beaten path provide helpful illustration of horoscopic technique for an astrological student or practitioner functioning for the major part in contact with rather humdrum mediocrity?

As against this however was the voluminous wealth of competently documented material. Ultimately the challenge to interpretation in her case may have added more to the incisiveness of the text than could have been anticipated in early 1965. Meanwhile the author had long had in mind the superficially attractive possibility of Abraham Lincoln as an example, since Lincoln was the subject of an unusually large literature. To select these two individuals would give an exposition from masculine and feminine perspective in tandem. Standing against the selection of the American president however was the psychological mystery of the melancholia obsessing him through perhaps the whole of his adult years, and at the end in these pages at least the explanation of that phenomenon as well as of the final resolution of Annie Besant's life consummation in the private matrix of her own consciousness must remain a matter of the purest conjecture.

Helen Rentsch, the author's sister, has been tireless in her assistance whether in obtaining additional materials and verifying various points through her university resources or coming to Washington State during her vacations for all sorts of editorial chores as well as her professional reading of various versions of manuscript. James Givens Allen has given freely of his time for the drudgery of checking mathematics for the text, and has made many practical suggestions on the basis of his long experience as a professional astrologer. James and Helen Hill have read every page of manuscript in its versions beyond the mere rough-out stages, with a particular attention to literary criteria and clarity of presentation. Ruth Gerry with assistance from Alfred Jacob and others at Chaplin, Connecticut, has given generous and indeed yeoman service in reading proofs and checking astrological operations and explanations. Miriam Krause made the horoscope wheels, and in corrections and supplementations in this area the art department at Schneidereith & Sons has been unusually helpful. The co-operation of the printer in the whole spread of technical detail has been a most happy chapter.

As a curious example of minor co-operations, Bern Stave the proprietor of the only service station near the author's home and so a longtime and immediate resort in emergency happened to possess Carl Sandburg's *Prairie Years* of Lincoln's life. Thus the author had these out-of-print volumes on his shelf for all the span of the task, as an infinitely greater convenience than an interlibrary loan. The library staff of the Theosophical Society in America at Wheaton, Illinois, were extraordinarily generous in permitting the long possession of irreplacable materials. A real service was performed by workers at the headquarters of the Church of Light in Los Angeles, in the calculation of minor progressions in the life of Lincoln in proper accordance with the methods they employ and teach.

During the seven-year period embracing the early Nineteen-fifties when the author was at work somewhat concurrently on the several books already mentioned, he was operating under a grant from Arthur Middleton Young's Foundation for the Study of Consciousness. Mr. Young was not interested in publication, but he did give some help in the printing of both the *Sabian Symbols* and *Essentials,* and there was substantial financial assistence from a number of sources in 1953 and 1960 that were no longer available in 1968. For the production of this *Scope of Astrological Prediction* in hard-cover book form there has been generous help from quite a few contributors of the past, but this time a general appeal to the members of the Sabian Assembly has brought spectacularly gratifying support. A number of Sabian students who contribute regularly toward putting out the new titles may well have established the consciousness that under-girded the remarkable response to the present need.

When the manuscript had been shaped into a piece sufficiently to be typed in clean copies, and given to the several willing readers for textual criticism, a very serious issue emerged. While it was not exactly expressed in such a fashion, it was all too obvious that what the author was trying to say in his explanations of astrology and of the necessary nature of its operations did not have the fundamental clarity the book would need to serve its purpose. Behind the impasse was the fact, as noted in the text, that for a long while now the astrological metaphysics has remained hopelessly medieval or out of all connection with any cosmology of today's scientific community. In writing the exposition it had seemed advisable to disregard this whole speculative area as extraneous, or perhaps comprising too much to bring to the general attention of the average reader. But what had happened was that in the lack of a definite rational ordering for the underlying concepts in their application to delineative method the text, and particularly in its opening parts, was in a sense simply without cohesion as far as any logically disciplined mind might be concerned.

The principles the author was using quite habitually were part of the very fiber of his intellectual maturing since his curiosity as to the dynamic interrelations of things had been awakened at the World's Columbian Exposition in Chicago in 1893, or when he was living almost within a stone's throw of the grounds. Although a child he noted a striking gradation of difference in jewels on the one hand and in wood textures on the other, and to him this meant sequence as a living something. It was an insight for which he had no words to permit his rumination, and in consequence he was bothered and the matter made an indelible impress on his mind. He could not ask the questions nobody could have answered, but two decades later he encountered astrology which in unexpected fashion began to articulate it all for him. And now in 1968 and suddenly he needed to give a verbal expression to what had only developed as the structuring that his mind had employed continually without ever being led to stand apart from it in any metacomprehension of it. The essential principles of astrology formulated in this crisis and interlarded in the text at a very late stage, to give the exposition a needed intellectual competence, may be a very defective tour de force in their initial statement under these conditions. This book, however, pretends to be no more than an introduction to the dynamic horoscopy as it is ordered to a point of limit of capacity in the author's general clarification of astrological procedures.

Above all else the goal has been to provide the student or practitioner of astrology with an integrated series of techniques embracing the whole possibility of progressed or dynamic indication. The basis for this can best be found in the mathematics on which so much of astrological procedure must rest. Thus the fundamental requirement accepted for the writing of the book was to make sure that everything of mathematical nature should be done in essentially the same way, to the end that there would be constant realization of horoscopy as a unified way of thinking or of reaching conclusions. There is much in these pages that adds up to puttering or wearisome computation but, in the step-by-step mode of operation that has been kept the distinguishing characteristic of all the Sabian texts, everything is single-minded or held to a common center in comprehension.

In connection with the three and a half years of exhausting self-expenditure in the production of this exposition of progressed indications, the author above all else must pay tribute to Priscilla Jones for making it possible for him to complete this particular assignment. She not only shared the cost in physical stamina and psychological vitality through every minute of every day of this time, with the hand of a subtle strengthening never withdrawn, but she has helped in every practical fashion whether with idea or manuscript or with all the concomitant technical and business detail.

Norman, Washington, Thanksgiving, 1968

BIBLIOGRAPhY

Besant, Annie   *Autobiography,* London, 1893

Greenwalt, Emmett A.   *Point Loma Community in California,*
                             Berkeley, 1955

Lutyens, Lady Emily   *Candles in the Sun,* Philadelphia, 1957

Nethercot, Arthur H.   *First Five Lives of Annie Besant,*
                             London, 1961

                             Last Four Lives of Annie Besant,
                             London, 1963

Randall, Ruth Painter   *Mary Lincoln,* Boston, 1953

Sandburg, Carl   *Abraham Lincoln* (one-volume revision),
                             New York, 1954

Thomas, Benjamin P.   *Abraham Lincoln,* New York, 1952

introductory

THE DYNAMIC ANALYSIS

Most people are familiar with the conception of the world
as a stage, on which men and women must play their parts
through the course of their years. This is a way of looking at
life that Shakespeare has popularized most generally, but the
idea goes back to Pythagoras if not to others still earlier. What
is important however is the realization that not one but a
great many roles are assumed by each different individual, not
only every day but perhaps in every hour of conscious existence. Indeed, by the same token, each successive group in
which a person appears in common portrayal with his fellows
will prove to be equally protean in every successive manifestation. There is never a situation that does not have infinite
ramification in its possible significance, and so never a native
coming to astrological analysis who (1) in relation with the
continual shifting of things around him and (2) in very practical fashion because of his own make-up and individual
development is not revealing himself in illimitable potentials
in every variety of perspective provided by the many differing
eyes through which he is recognized or by the minds through
which he is known. Here is the baffling complex of reality in
which the astrologer must somehow find a means to center his
attention effectively, and thus to anchor judgment accurately.

The Ordering of Variables

A mere contemplation of complexity accomplishes nothing.
To overload the mind with more than it has been trained to

synthesize is to defeat its effective operation. Hence the necessity in any analysis is to identify and trace out the pertinent factors of the particular matter so that, when they are taken in proper connection with themselves or without extraneous complication, they can contribute to the understanding needed in each special instance. This of course is the manner in which all ordinary common sense comes to its conclusions. If in everyday business affairs a given activity must be administered, a screening of those who might possibly assume the responsibility is usually quick to reveal both the assets that would help and the handicaps that would hinder each candidate for the job. The consideration would be quite irrespective of the nature and scope otherwise of these elements of character or experience. Astrology to be effective must operate along precisely such lines, and this is possible because through the horoscopic charting the basic order of the cosmos itself may be employed as the screening agent able to establish the pertinence of virtually anything that comes to immediate and personal concern or needs attention as a potentiality in some given context of relationship. All astrological method adds up to an intelligent selection of significant indications, such as can be brought together in a logical pattern of judgment and so become a means for advisement.

By organizing this operation on a basis of initial consideration of intrinsically more simple or obvious factors, and thereupon ranging from them in any form of natural connection to the more complex and increasingly subtle ones, the interpretative task is greatly facilitated. Obviously what thus can prove particularly helpful in the employment of analytical skills should certainly be of great service in mastering the skills in the first place, and it was in realization of such a possibility that the author's *How to Learn Astrology* was written. The extent to which that little manual has proved its worth in more than a quarter century has suggested a repetition of the procedure in preparing this present text. At all points therefore in the presentation now of the dynamic horoscopy, or the analysis of the performance of the native in his living years as in contrast with the examination of his character or inherent potentials through the nativity, there is a sequence of convenience established primarily to contribute to a sound grasp of the fundamentals of the method.

The step-by-step exposition in these pages as in *How to Learn Astrology* is of a sort where from the beginning each factor of delineation may be (1) used as it is mastered and (2) employed with an effective reliability that cannot be contravened no matter how supplemented by further insight in either direct or remote connection. This procedure however does not involve any resort to an oversimplification that would only destroy any incisiveness of realization. As a necessity in dealing with elements in human life of extraordinary liquidity, varying perspectives of similar reference must be used in different places to hold understanding in the continuity of a pertinent consideration. This adjustment in perspective is the simple proposition illustrated when a father and a mother do not resort to the same action in their same response to sudden rain at a picnic. After all, it is only in the conception of an analyzing mind that existence in its kaleidoscopic phases can have a specific ordering in some unbroken intellectual validity of the moment. The astrologer, in his role of analyst and in his use of the horoscope, in a sense is centering the cosmos in himself as a means for screening his client's potentials. The latter individual of course or any layman for that matter would be quite confused by too much reference to the horoscopic technicalities, but they are the tools of the astrologer's analysis and to maintain his competence he must keep them well sharpened and be careful not to confound them with each other.

The Bugaboo of Words

Nobody is ever bothered by the fact that a physician or scientist will use strange or forbidding words in the technical area of his professional specialization. It is generally realized that they are needed in the abstruse processes resulting in some required judgment, and that this in due time and whenever necessary will be explained in ordinary and less precise fashion to anybody with less specialized concern with whatever may be at issue. In connection with astrology however it always has been assumed, and rather naïvely perhaps, that by the peculiar wonder of horoscopic art there is no necessity that anything of equivalent nature stand between the tyro and an actually skillful interpretation of a nativity. The reason for this assumption of course has been a general dependence on intuition or a dedication of soul rather than on the more conventional training or refinement of intellectual capacity. There are few who ever suspect that the long years of graduate discipline of mind on university levels required for an adequate qualification of a doctor might also be necessary for the making of the ideal astrologer. Certainly the largely self-taught practitioners of a present generation, no less than their academically certified compeers in other fields, must operate with a preciseness that can only be sustained by employing definitely technical terms. Some of these by their essential nature are a commonplace, as the names of the zodiacal signs for example, and so these pose no great problem. Others that are many in number and mostly important in facilitating the more definitive analysis are a genuine difficulty for beginners as well perhaps as for students of considerable experience. Often they are a principal bugaboo in defeating any real study or examination of astrology.

It all however is a matter of quite uncomplicated preciseness. The first relatively unusual word to be used in this text is *protean.* A popular and competent college dictionary defines it in toto if uncapitalized as "readily assuming different forms or characters; exceedingly variable." What could be suggested therefore might be the use of the word *changeable,* but the point in the opening paragraph is not an instability but rather a capacity for playing a role in life with convincing steadiness or total continuity of the moment and without interfering in any respect with the assuming of any number of other roles in an equal continuance. This was the gift of the god Proteus. To have used changeability would have been to imply the very opposite of what was meant. In the choice of terms through these pages the simplest ones are always used, and in the full of their variety, but cases of the inadequacy of the apparently much more simple ones as in this example will be found continually and in every such instance of their avoidance there is likely to be some subtle and illuminating insight that should have careful attention. Above all else it should be realized that the astrological terminology is something that sooner or later must be mastered through experience. The dictionaries when consulted without perspective can be as misleading as helpful.

The Substance of Delineation

These pages in no respect represent an attempt either to write history or to enter the area of historical criticism. While every effort has been made to conform to validated material in illustration of the horoscopic indications, inevitably some facts of broad acceptance will prove to be wrong. As becomes important in this exposition, such has been dramatically the case with Abraham Lincoln. The eventuality however is of minor if any significance, since the corrected information remains a valid illustration of the technique even if in somewhat altered fashion. The actualities of human performance taken for illustrative purposes are not necessarily presented here in a sequence of occurrence, but rather in the scattered form through which they best serve the basic purposes of an orderly presentation. The specific examples of delineation are generally sketchy and much explanation is syncopated, depending on the immediate point to be brought out. This is a practical necessity since any single dynamic interpretation carried out to its full would become a chapter by itself if not a whole book. The reader handicapped by overfamiliarity with the fortunetelling specifics, as "with Mars coming to square with the sun the house burned down" or "when Venus made its opposition with the moon the native began his affair with the woman next door," must understand that psychological analysis in any depth must avoid all such superficial simplification and the great unreliability characterizing it in advance expectation. In an effective comprehensive system of progressed analysis there can be no strait jacket of prescribed and literalistic ways of thinking or expressing things. Actually the formulas in constant repetition in these pages are no more than verbal guide lines, and the occasional long or marathon sentences serve fundamentally to hold ramification of relation at center in the mind's ordering. The summaries as convenient suggest application or expanded perspectives as well as provide the review or usual epitomization of ground covered.

The astrological data for example cases other than those represented by horoscopes printed in the text will be found in the author's *Sabian Symbols in Astrology*.

aʙraham lincoln

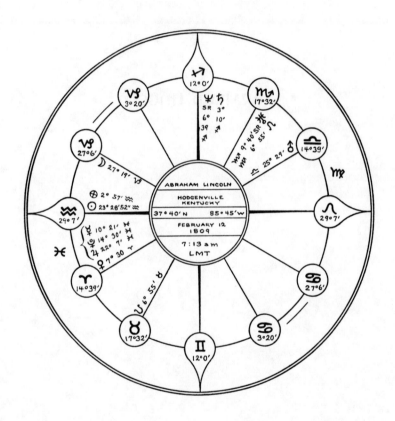

THE BASIC ATTITUDE

Abraham Lincoln was thirty-seven years old when the planet Neptune was discovered, and it was then that his life began to fall into place once and for all. This coming to common point in time of these two otherwise quite unrelated developments of respectively celestial and terrestrial circumstances, contributing to an illuminating understanding of the unfolding experience as well as the fundamental character of America's president, is striking illustration of the astrological principle of concordance or concomitance. A considerable number of these governing laws of horoscopic analysis can have definite formulation, and those of particular service to this present text are summarized in the appendix. This one of them now cited has a convenient brief statement in the fact that astrology fundamentally measures the constant repetition or reduplication, in both time and space, of any or all reality. It is obvious of course that elements of the real thus seen in repetitive or paralleling relation must be of comparable substance or have equivalent rank in significance. The problem of the shifting pertinence in the varying interconnections will need much further consideration but here, in dramatic epitome, is the very heart of a proper and effective dynamic horoscopy.

Many of the governing laws of astrology come to simultaneous emphasis at this starting point in exposition. Thus the essential principle of impartiality or adaptability dictates utilization of possible significators on the basis of convenience or pragmatic suggestiveness in every respect. The astrologer is charting physical cause and effect only most incidentally, and in actuality and indeed is concerned in toto with the meaning of material phenomena in a specific and individual pertinence. Thus gravity may hold a traveling bag on a station platform, although a porter can pick it up and take it away or a gust of wind can tip it over. In a fundamentally psychological perspective these are quite minor factors that seldom need attention on their own account. Until anything in question enters experience or has the possibility of doing so it is of no horoscopic consequence, as in the instance of the three major planets only identified by the astronomers in modern times or Uranus in 1781, Neptune in 1846 and Pluto in 1930 respectively. Because coincident with their discovery there have been new dimensions of human expression of no appreciable prior manifestation, the employment of these bodies in horoscopic analysis in conformity to the principle of equivalence or distinction becomes particularly effective in the indication in order of each such enlarged phase of man's self-realization.

Serving however as a vital check on all ramification of significators and signification is the important principle of selectivity or efficiency. This is the logical necessity, in every identification of pertinence in any given consideration, to favor as far as possible the fewer factors of greater significance. In a truly valid horoscopy there is no reason whatsoever to consider (1) the some two thousand asteroids so far identified and in orbit mostly between Mars and Jupiter or by the same token and on the other side of the coin (2) the illimitable trivialities of daily occurrence that with little consequence in any native's life would need correspondence with unusually petty elements of the nativity. Astrology at this point is thus revealed as a consistently empirical science. Horoscopic analysis moreover and under the governing law of convergence or convenience makes a continual adjustment to free will and chance or to the core of inherent discreteness in everything of concern. In consequence the competent astrologer is never under necessity to dismiss man rather willy-nilly to some supposedly inevitable manipulation of his destiny by wholly external factors, such as are subject to precise mechanical calculation in advance. In a universe of palpable flux the phenomenon of order is a concordance, and not a matrix of compulsion. The fundamental unpredictability of any native keeps all factors of any relevance to him in their own shifting or dynamic context as it happens to have immediate importance for him. What is fixed at birth, by a sort of quick-freeze in the form of a horoscope, is a pattern of individuality in its frame of circumstantial convenience and so never a strait jacket of immutabilities merely extended in time and space.

To be able to deal with the utter flux of all reality in any reliable perspective, astrology proceeds under its principle of incisiveness or consistency to formulate and maintain a fulcrum of mind or a logical immutability of reference established in its own special organon. Thus it achieves its effective realization by the use of concepts that (1) are not permitted the least change of implication in general and (2) are never subjected in any respect to any modification of meaning in consequence of any of their interweaving relations with each other. As a foundation for the dynamic horoscopy the progressed planets are kept distinct from each other as representing activity-facets of the native's self-expression, and thereupon considered separately in a fundamentally complete independence. In this fashion the role of Mercury, in the awkwardly-named secondary directions to which prime attention is given in this text, is the delineation of the development and manifestation of his basic attitude as of foundational import in his conscious self-realization. Here is his commonplace of easily observed approach to experience.

The progressions of Mercury in the life of Abraham Lincoln can involve only eight of the ultimately ten common significators by activation during his youth and early manhood or prior to 1846, but a deeper analysis in a frame of afterview and in the light of personal conditioning and performance is demanded under astrology's governing law of convergence or convenience and by the dramatic features of the dynamic horoscopy in his case. Under the essential principle of equivalence or distinction the uniqueness of patterning must be complemented, whether actually or potentially, by a self-manifestation of paralleling scope in life. Thus people are challenged by their very existence to a worthiness characteristic of them, but this of necessity is a relative matter and it can as easily be on the minus as on the plus side of things. Delineation can find itself charting rebellion. Significance can be purely psychological or fulfilled in fantasy. A frog may be big because the pond is small.

There is in Lincoln's basic attitude an extraordinary emphasis of Pluto that has no meaning whatsoever in connection with a conscious existence more than a century ago, but in view of his continuing immortal influence in American history the astrologer obviously has something to take into account. This is a proper start in the recognition of him as the very special myth figure in American history, as well as in the identification of elements in his own day that at this later time can be seen in their unsuspecting contribution to the apotheosis. To be especially noted is that progressions in this activity-facet reveal for the years of his maturity an exceptional arrangement of aspects much like Chinese boxes. Mercury's activations (1) by conjunction of undiscovered Pluto in 1829 and 1858 embrace (2) its conjunctions with its own natal position in 1833 and 1853 and then (3) its trines with Uranus in 1834 and 1852 and finally (4) its squares with Neptune in 1839 and 1847 as (5) it provides the center for the unique pattern with its station in 1843 or dramatically close to the discovery of Neptune. What is more, two preliminary quickenings of Pluto in similar fashion mark off the initial two decades of the actual physical life. If it were not for the three recently discovered significators, Mercury would have no progressed indication except of or with itself until less than a year before the assassination. Here is strong testimony or the stark astrological distinction demanding the unusual consideration. Abraham Lincoln must be seen as a loner at core from the beginning, or not to be fitted easily at any point into the conventionalities even of his own day and particular milieu. With so much of the emphasis of it coming to pertinence in afterview, it is not likely however that he was particularly sensitive to the fact of it in his lifetime.

Yet the question to be raised in the light of all this would be the extent to which an astrologer of Lincoln's generation as say the pioneer Luke Broughton might have been handicapped because unaware of Pluto, or perhaps more importantly whether in some like present case a practitioner might be operating inadequately through the lack of still newer significators not yet available. The answer under the essential principle of immediacy or relevance is an emphatic denial.

Astrology functioned very completely and for centuries with its original seven planets, and the new ones are not additions to compensate for a previous lack since such an assumption would establish an infinitely regressive deficiency ahead. In pattern with what happened dramatically in modern times with the acquisition of three extra major indicators, (1) any establishment of exceptional supplementary indication or special recourse to some otherwise neglected factor of normally lesser import in analysis must be recognized as a one-remove in the logical process and (2) correspondence thereupon must be with what can be identified as a significantly additive element of experience in connection with the issues or potentialities under consideration. The outreach of horoscopic insight is illimitable in successive removes of pertinence as long as these remain anchored at the self's center in its own background and personal development.

Especially important in this overall matter of scope is the complementing essential principle of definition or discrimination in its demand that judgment be sharpened in the context of actualities that can be identified and given obviously pertinent horoscopic significance rather than of what by necessity may remain speculative or mere assumption and so of dubious astrological import. Thus the horoscope taken wholly by and of itself reveals nothing, even the wholly primary fact of the native's continued existence or the fundamental certification that it is indeed the chart of a human being. Applied to life, it delineates the actuality that is brought to astrological comprisement. As erected for Abraham Lincoln the birth wheel and its progressions have extraordinary features that the native came to exemplify most signally in his own day and in the enduring myth figure, but in general there are always numberless others around the globe who will have nativities with increasing approximation to the occasional few natives of stark uniqueness such as the two principal examples on which this text is based in order to have here the broadest possible canvas for exposition.

Any spectacular revelation of potentials by astrology in consequence is never any guarantee of genius or fame or anything beyond the exceptional lean out of indistinction required by the particular make-up of the individual. Since human nature fundamentally centers in free will, a given person obviously may live up to his highest promise or sink to the lowest of life's permissions in his special case. By the same token he may select a frame of reality ranging from very broad co-operation with the more worth-while living at his place and in his times on to ways of existence of diminishing acceptance or even total repudiation on the part of his fellows. Thus it is necessary to examine the course of Lincoln's days to see whether he was moving to genuine greatness or is to be dismissed as no more than an eccentric or possibly even a perverted member of his cultural matrix.

The ultimate achievement of modern astrology is probably its effective reconcilation of material order and symbolical personification in such fashion that (1) neither is ever found in unrestricted or entrenched dominance in life and circumstances since (2) both rather are always charted in their frequently unsuspected but continual service or value to each other. This is the essential principle of dichotomy or identity utilized for the opening of the exposition in the author's *Astrology, How and Why It Works* in order to reveal the very structure of all astrological method and effectiveness. In overview the character analysis of natal interpretation holds a foundational reference on the side of natural order while the dynamic horoscopy primarily charts the personal focus of individual meaning and implication. This latter phase of selfhood takes wide-ranging form in a pyramiding experience that through the living years will follow its convenient and differing paths in execution of the natal pattern. These two completely basic techniques bring illumination to each other, but they necessarily are in total disconnection because of their polar opposition in logical nature and the astrologer therefore at no point should ever attempt to combine their operation in common insight.

This fundamental dichotomy of astrological structure and procedures can and should be established and maintained in the mind for a refinement or clarification of all practical judgment in the dynamic horoscopy. Under astrology's governing law of discernment or validation the recourse is to alternative techniques of progressive analysis as (1) an adjustment through varied perspectives to the fluid nature or the multiple variables of everyday experience and (2) a method of continual check on all conclusions. In a pattern of logical removes the three forms of the directions and the three types of cyclic returns can be taken variously as mutual correctives in the illimitable gamut of astrological relationship, ranging from the secondaries that in their outworking lean to the side of material order to the techniques that move toward the wholly symbolical horoscope given its special exposition in the author's *Horary Astrology.* A horoscopic symbolism in complete divorce from any immediacy of ordering structure in either time or space has long been provided by a specialized interpretation of the zodiac or a characterization of its individual degrees by suggestive picture, and the technique has a modern formulation in the author's companion *Sabian Symbols in Astrology.*

Horoscopic Aspects

The aspects in astrology are indications of stress in the cosmic mechanics as this is given symbolical representation in a convenient circle in the heavens. As against (1) the emphasis of the same place on its rim there can be (2) a balance provided with another point straight across, and to these possibilities can be added (3) middle points on the two half circles created by the balancing bisection of the whole rim or a subordinate reduplication of the significance under the essential principle of concordance or concomitance. Here are conjunction, opposition and square aspect in order as a delimitation of the structuring relationship in the fundamental horoscopy. Considered with these under the complementary principle of immediacy or relevance are the tripodlike relations of third segments of either the circle or semicircle with each or any two of the three points thereby marked out on the rim. They can be seen indicating a sort of kingbolt effectiveness in the characteristically freewheeling run of events in their own course. In this species of kingbolt application of stress relation the trine primarily and the sextile secondarily constitute the momentum aspects. Out of the interplay of all these factors of fundamental activity in their two disparate groups both the signs of the zodiac and the houses of the horoscope are created in the manner given its full explanation in *Astrology, How and Why It Works.*

For both the basic interpretation of a nativity and the dynamic horoscopy the two complementary families of astrological aspect are kept separate in a distribution respectively of (1) pure character in maintaining an enduring fiber of self and (2) the characteristic everyday manifestation of individuality through which the conditioned factors of self-realization may be dismissed to automaticity. In common practice these five major aspects alone have consideration, but the circle is subject to divisions of itself by all prime numbers beyond the two and three as here and in consequence there can be subdivision and combination of division on to infinity. Minor aspects thereupon developed may be very revealing in exceptional circumstances, but under the essential principle of selectivity or efficiency they are best ignored in general along with the parallels established in similarly subordinate relationship and produced by a variant mode of horoscopic measurement.

Progressed Potentiality Distribution

In the interpretation of the horoscopic progressions there is the fundamental factor of the aspect itself, irrespective of the planets it involves, as it charts the distribution of the dynamic relationship. The conjunction and sextile, differing from their more primary classification in basic families and in a special application of the essential principle of immediacy or relevance, have a common significance of immediate practical pertinence in contrast with the opposition and trine that correspondingly are linked through an idealistic or wholly mediated pertinence. In this particular dynamic symbolism the distinction is between the nearness to a point of origin or a directness of relationship on the one hand and the converse remoteness or contingency of relation on the other, and it permits the identification at times of a marked psychological trend in a native's progressive self-establishment. Special terms are needed to facilitate this first procedure of interpretation to which the attention now must turn, and the rationale of analysis may be suggested conveniently by table.

THE DISTRIBUTIVE MODE OF PROGRESSED ASPECT

| Practical | } { | ☌ Alertness | Idealistic | } { | ☍ Alertness |
| Immediate | } { | ⚹ Adroitness | Mediate | } { | △ Adroitness |

The square aspect has a special fulcrum role in the dynamic horoscopy and therefore has consideration in that different context.

In summary, the three planets undiscovered until the past two centuries have special significance relative to human developments corresponding to their location in the heavens. In an afterview they give dramatic testimony to the immortal stature of Abraham Lincoln. There would have to be countless horoscopes around the globe in increasing approximation to his, and it is necessary to check the events of his life for the particular capacities and moves on his part that carried him rather than these others to greatness. The astrologer must give essentially separate consideration to the natal horoscope and the progressive indications arising from it because a birth promise and a life performance will have widely differing manifestation in respect to each other. Astrology gains its power through its inescapably stereoscopic perspective, since its very structure leads the astrologer at all points to utilize two modes of comprehension in continuous mutual rectification. The progressed aspects are properly classified in a twofold manner, and this is done in two different ways with resulting valuable indication of a native's necessary ordering of his efforts in the various and essentially distinct channels of his self-expression.

The Psychological Trend to Balance

For its effectiveness the dynamic astrology holds to a systematic program for each particular detail of analysis and by

keeping basic reference immediate or relevant, in accordance with the fundamental principle, all eventuality is identified in chains of relationship carried from the native to the
elements of his private world of existence in terms of their
rank in significance or in a manner to defeat any unrealized
regression toward infinity. The interpretative rationale initially
recognizes the ten activity-facets or the immutably direct self-
activity differentiated conveniently by the progressed planets
and then follows four logical procedures for dealing with each
of these phases of the self's dynamic manifestation of itself.
The first is to determine if (1) during the life seen after
decease as a whole or (2) as far as lived when it is given
analysis or (3) in any subperiod marked off in the general
course by a change in the emphasis, the psychological slant is
toward either practical and immediate or idealistic and mediated self-orientation. This is charted in each activity-facet by
the major progressed aspects other than square. If they are
predominantly conjunction and sextile, the former tendency is
shown. If contrariwise the trines and oppositions predominate,
the latter lean is indicated. Within the frame of the overall
pattern, the first nonfulcral activation sets the nature of the
slanting preliminarily whether in the general or subordinate
case. Whenever the emphasis is brought to balance between
the two trends, the one continues either in neutralization or
recapitulation.

Abraham Lincoln has lived on in the immortal practicality
of American democracy as a wonderfully inspiring myth figure. With three progressed conjunctions to natal Pluto, the
emphasis in basic attitude of the practical over the idealistic
becomes very striking in the ultimately symbolical indication.
Aside from activations of the new planet the testimony is the

same for the actual career through three conjunctions and no sextiles against two trines and no oppositions, and the pragmatic orientation was significantly characteristic of his earlier years. A definitely idealistic but subordinate emphasis came into manifestation in the summer of 1852, or when in a sense the mantle of Henry Clay fell on his shoulders, and the impact of this carried him into the presidency and on through the Civil War up to the renewed and more immediate confidence in final outcomes with the fall of Atlanta just before his re-election in 1864.

A sheer practicality dominated his roots in every way. His father Thomas had settled down in Hardin County in Kentucky with Nancy Hanks as his bride, and there he supported himself by his skilled carpentry and various odd jobs. After the birth of their first child, Sarah, Thomas followed in the path of his immediate forebears by turning to the pioneer farming at which he would prove increasingly inept. He possessed moderate means during these early days since at one time he owned three small farms and two town lots and considerably later was still able to pay off the debts of the widow he persuaded to become his second wife. Nonetheless the log cabin on his place a short distance from Hodgenville, to which he moved shortly after his first marriage and in which Abraham was born, was the typical one-room affair with a dirt floor. This second child was ushered into the world in customary fashion with the aid of the neighborhood granny woman.

When the boy was two or three and his sister four or so the father moved again to a more promising location at Knob Creek on the main road from Louisville to Nashville, and then after five more years made another move from the fairly well-settled section of Kentucky to a region in Indiana where few settlers had penetrated but where land could be obtained cheaply from the government and title to it was much more sound. This change of base was in midwinter, and the inclement months were spent in a lean-to or half-faced camp until with clearing weather another log cabin could be built. Dennis Hanks, of dubious cousin relationship and who then was a happy-dispositioned and energetic youth, became the one real companion of the boy nine years younger than he was. The foster parents of Dennis had joined in the move to the anti-slavery North, but almost immediately they succumbed to the mysterious and fatal milk-sickness now believed to have been a result of cattle feeding on white snakeroot or rayless golden-rod, and the mother of young Abe very shortly afterward became another victim. Now there were three males wholly dependent on the efforts of a twelve-year-old girl to meet the exacting household demands of their rough-and-ready living. Thomas in the following year made the long trip back to Kentucky to marry the widowed Sarah Johnston who at an earlier time had rejected him in favor of a rival. From the start Abraham adored her.

Conditions while bettered remained primitive, with the crowding making its own added demands. The angel mother, as Abraham came to call her, brought three children of her own. There were a boy of the same age as the adolescent Sarah, and a girl and boy respectively two and five years younger than the future president. Eight people centered their days in the hand-hewn box of a dwelling. If privacy by modern standards was totally lacking there yet was a strict if implicit modesty and morality, and thanks to the inescapable simplicity of their existence the nascent myth figure was irrevocably stamped as of the soil above everything else. Astrologically this fact can be seen to be the true source of his ultimate influence.

In summary, the basic attitude of Abraham Lincoln is revealed with its overall trend to balance on the practical side. This indicates that his conscious approach to life most fundamentally was through the immediacies of experience and situation, but momentary idealistic orientation of subordinate nature that contributes most significantly to his immortal dimension is shown for the years 1852-64. His early development in emphasized exactions of pioneer hardship and continual stress of life's simplicities can be seen to have provided the effective frame for his gradual refinement of a myth-figure potentiality.

Dynamic Activation

A natal planet receiving a progressed aspect must thereupon play a different role from its representation of an unchanging potentiality in the nativity. This does not mean any modification of the fundamental concept such as an effective astrology disallows under its essential principle of incisiveness or consistency, and discourages by the establishment of a key-word of explicit implication for every particularized employment of each of the foundational building blocks in its logical structure. What is to be identified at this point in exposition rather is multiple significance or the phenomenon that actually is characteristic of all life, and that is taken into astrological account in the governing laws of concordance or concomitance and of discernment or validation on the sides respectively of material order and symbolical personification. What is to be seen activated in progression is the unconditioned or original promise in some wholly self-comprised phase of itself as this emerges in contribution to the chance-and-choice evolution of the dynamic individuality, and for identifying the planetary nature of the specific potentiality in activation in the case of each of the ten major significators the astrologer may well employ a technical term used for this purpose alone and adopted under the principle of definition or discrimination to help him keep matters at issue clear and distinct in mind. He must remember that there is no escape from a given life's overall pattern, but that this however is a flexible matrix and never any sort of strait jacket.

He must remember also that by the same token the illimitably ramifying relations that evolve out of the fundamental make-up of self are not to be escaped either, although an increasingly individual shaping of their course is possible as long as the world at large is characterized by the continual and universal shift of circumstances in and out of relevance. This of course is the phenomenon of the concordance or concomitance essential to the operation of astrology. Human effort may reach high or low in the development of what remains inescapably a personal opportunity at every point, and horoscopic judgment primarily is the recognition of tendency as leading to advantage or disadvantage. The astrologer is not dealing with heavenly entities actually able to do anything to specific people in particular detail, but is employing celestial symbols in a system of logical correlatives that on the dynamic side can help identify the manner and potential of act quite apart from the actor's characteristic capacity for action and so thereupon contribute to an increasing control by the actor of his own self-unfoldment or ultimate destiny.

HOROSCOPIC POTENTIAL IN PROGRESSED ACTIVATION

⊙ strength	♃ zest	♂ persistence	♅ release	☿ aplomb
☽ endurance	♄ concern	♀ realization	♆ acceptance	♀ probity

Nonfulcral Indication

PROGRESSED MERCURY IN CONJUNCTION WITH NATAL MER-
CURY, NOVEMBER 30, 1833, AND MAY 23, 1853   In deviation
from what this text will present as the normal schedule of
analysis for each of the activity-facets of self in the dynamic
horoscopy, the consideration of the nonfulcral progressed
aspects is taken here as the second instead of the fourth of the
four procedures. In addition there is variance in this case from
the usual approach to them in simple chronological order. The
progressive distribution of the nativity potentials as these tend
to become manifest through a regular flow of experience
grooved in a general milieu of circumstances has in the basic
attitude of Abraham Lincoln the unique arrangement to
which attention has been called, and to hold to the exceptional
pattern at this point can contribute to the broadest possible
understanding. An effective approach to the interpretation of
the progressed aspects is to state them first in a formula provided by the keywords for (1) the activity-facet plus (2) the
horoscopic potential activated plus (3) the mode of distribution in the activation and then to rephrase the testimony in
terms of the immediate situation as this will have the necessary
meaning for either astrologer or client.

Thus in 1833 when Lincoln was almost twenty-five years
old the indication in basic attitude of an activated aplomb
through a practical or immediate alertness charts his first real
overt expression of himself in his own strong individuality
when he gained his deputation as a county surveyor, and
qualified for the work through brutally exacting self-prepara-
tion. This accomplishment was his induction into public life,
and the repetition of the indication almost an even twenty
years later in 1853 corresponds to the events precipitating his

effective re-entry into politics in an entirely new chapter of self-assurance. The background for the development in the Eighteen-Fifties is vital to understanding at this point. His earlier ambitions as the politician of purely conventional stamp had been blighted when in 1849 it had been embarrassingly necessary for him to bury himself in his private law practice after his single term in the House of Representatives at Washington, and his maladventure in that minor chapter has attention under the proper progressive measure. Subsequently the maneuvering in Congress relative to slavery had erupted into real crisis with particular consummation in January, 1854, when the brilliant Stephen A. Douglas in a strangely feckless move brought before the Senate the Kansas-Nebraska Act with its express repeal of the Missouri Compromise of 1820 in an effort to reconcile Southern and Northern interests. It was with the passage of this act that the native finally was stirred as he had never been before, and overnight became an entirely reborn national personality thanks to his acceptance of a cause to which an immortal life's devotion could become possible if not virtually inescapable.

Time Orb in Directions

Orb or the sphere of planetary effectiveness in astrology is a matter of prime importance in delineation. In a nativity it is the permissible deviation from exactness of the aspects of the planets at birth, or is a determinant of the quality of pertinence to be accepted in what essentially is a spatial judgment. In the dynamic horoscopy contrariwise the exact culmination of an aspect is the fundamental focus of progression, and therefore what must be considered is the corresponding temporal compass of the progressed indication. The significance of the particular details in the make-up of human experience

may range from very narrow lineaments of immediate concern
in the mind on to very wide inclusion of virtually all the contingent factors in the given context, and the purpose of astrological charting is primarily to bring all salient elements of
necessary consideration to a point of comprehension or decision either in space or time or in both. Thus an accident as a
pertinent event is usually tightly defined in a close compacting
of circumstances whereas an illness by contrast tends to be less
a single eventuation than a circumstantial syndrome calling
for many variant types of realization such as (1) the inception
or the continuance and (2) the incapacity entailed or escaped
and (3) the ramifying secondary effects through concomitant
interrelations of personal or economic nature and so on almost
endlessly. In consequence the astrologer must learn to weigh
the pertinent latitudes of existence against the horoscopic relative encompassment under the governing law of convergence
or convenience and thereby avoid insignificance in analysis.

The ever present problem of time orb in the directions is
illustrated in Abraham Lincoln's two conjunctions of progressed Mercury with natal Mercury. By 1833 he had settled
down in the growing log-cabin community of New Salem on
the Sangamon River in Illinois twenty-five miles northwest
from Springfield in the same county. He had made his complete break with his father and family on coming to age,
shortly after Thomas Lincoln had migrated to this new state
from Indiana. While the start as a surveyor seems proper for
correspondence with the maturing of the Mercury direction
there is minor difficulty in the fact that the native's earliest
known report in that capacity was submitted on January 14,
1834, or six weeks after the aspect was exact. An alternate
choice of significant development might be his appointment as

postmaster on the preceding May 7th. This was an earlier achievement of sorts, but the responsibility was insignificant and the distinction virtually nil. It has been suggested that the young man saw the happy chance to read the newspapers before delivering them, and this may have been all the office meant to him. In any case a time orb of over six months would rule out anything as generally inconsequential even if it was a definitely prior factor in the emergence of the new aplomb.

Another possibility is even less promising. On returning in late July, 1832, from his eighty days of service in the opéra-bouffe Black Hawk Indian war he entered into an ill-starred partnership with William F. Berry to operate one of the three general stores and even to buy out one of the others. The heavy drinking of Berry, combined with his own temperamental unfitness for the bargaining routine of the times at a retail counter, apparently already or by late spring in 1833 had put the enterprise on the rocks. There was hardly any effective significance in an establishment of community position. The fact that he piled up debts that he was not able to pay off for years was an important development, but of no pertinence here. Thus what is accomplished in the balancing of considerations in this fashion is an identification of the dominant convergences in the life.

In 1853 the time orb accepted for indication has a spread in purely literalistic terms of the seven-odd months from the culmination of Mercury's aspect to the presentation of the Kansas-Nebraska Act to the Senate. Furthermore, Lincoln's positive stand was not evident until considerably afterward and may not have had real public manifestation until his Springfield address repeated and reported more fully at Peoria in October, 1854. Circumstances in the national turmoil were pyramiding around him all through the 1853 period and it certainly would be possible, with a thorough search of the contemporary records of political or legal or socioeconomic developments whether in Illinois or the country in general or the city of Springfield in particular, to select something with recognizable impact in the experience of Lincoln and more immediately in correlation with the May 23rd progression. Detailed research of such sort is seldom practical, and often it only contributes to superficiality. The purpose of the dynamic horoscopy is to identify elements of vital issue and actual or potential pertinence during periods of concern, and to chart their interrelations and their relative importance among each other as a guide to perspective and action. The astrologer however must avoid any greater effort toward establishing the fact of a correspondence between an indication and an event than in determining what genuinely significant testimony can be adduced from the possibility of the signification.

PROGRESSED MERCURY IN TRINE WITH NATAL URANUS, SEPTEMBER 4, 1834, AND JULY 10, 1852   This indication in basic attitude of an activated self-release through idealistic adroitness is found twice in an eighteen-year span, and in this text it provides the convenient introduction to the momentum type of progressed quickening of self-identity in everyday experience. What is or should be demonstrated by the native in correspondence with it is some salient participation in a definite chain of developments that contribute to his individual interest and tend to do so in an increasingly autonomous manifestation of themselves as far as he is concerned. On August 4, 1834, he was elected to his first term in the Illinois legislature and on July 16, 1852, he delivered his eulogy of

Henry Clay at Springfield. The former event launched him in his life-long political career however momentarily interrupted by the debacle of his brief experience as a congressman in Washington, and the latter marked the threshold of his idealistic subperiod in his psychological trend to balance. The activations of idealistic nature are of interests fundamentally mediated to self through others, and with Lincoln are well represented by his dedication to public life as the most vital factor in his presentation of himself to his generation. Contributing particularly to his progress was the fact that he was a Whig, and so ultimately a Republican and as such carried into the presidency.

Here originally was only one of many strands in his outreach for the definite place in life of greater fulfillment than the roustabout status that in spite of exceptional excellencies had remained his general lot at New Salem. At least the other accomplishments had meant little. He had been a candidate for the state legislature a term earlier, but participation in the Black Hawk War had interfered with any adequate campaigning and he had had no chance of election. More importantly for the moment however was the fact that he was captain of the volunteer company, and as an officer came into intimate association with John Todd Stuart or gained the contact that proved the beginning of his ultimate distinction. Here the momentum side of individual life is to be seen in operation. Through the sponsorship of this newfound friend he began the study of law, and won the election on his second try in 1834 all of a year after the earlier but more superficial break for him in his destiny when he became a deputy county surveyor.

The Whigs in the United States constituted a relatively

ephemeral political movement. The name had been established in England and originally was a term of abuse applied as a label in public life from the late seventeenth century, and it roughly indicated the more liberal point of view. The American counterpart had come forward as one of the two major parties for about two decades or on to 1856, and its lineage went back to the National Republicans of John Quincy Adams as well as to the Federalists headed by George Washington and Alexander Hamilton. The men who took the name in America had hoped in doing so to fasten the designation of Tory on the Jackson Democrats of whom Stephen Douglas became a shining light.

When Lincoln went to the legislature then meeting in Vandalia, he shared a large room with Stuart and this quickly became a Whig center. Now he began to meet men who would become governors, congressmen, United States senators and in general figures of power and influence. The representatives from Sangamon County all sharing tall stature came be known as the Long Nine, and the young giant from New Salem quickly began to dominate this delegation through the tacit recognition of his innate legislative skill. Among the rising politicians in Illinois to be met at this time was Douglas, who was four years younger than Lincoln and in 1834 had just been admitted to the practice of law. Ultimately the remarkable success of the Little Giant in getting his Kansas-Nebraska Act through Congress was the single event most responsible for bringing Lincoln back into the political arena, and the famous debates of 1858 between these most dissimilar individuals would have a principal result in giving the lesser known of them the national prominence that could lead to the presidency. The curious linking between them might seem a veritable tie of destiny such as was dramatized by the extra-ordinary efforts of Douglas despite ill health to help the new president when the Civil War broke out. In the record are two hours of intimate consultation in the White House. There was the senator's strong public declaration of support, and it is not altogether unreasonable to believe that it was Douglas who took Lincoln's hat and cane and held them during the inaugural address in 1861. Certainly the man of the far lesser prominence at the end had worn himself out trying to save the Union by one means if not another. With his death on June 3, 1861, it could be said that he no less than the great martyr had literally given his life for the common cause.

Horoscope Affinities

The comparison of horoscopes is of particular value in revealing the phases of general compatibility as well as potentials of particular rapport or antagonism between individuals whenever they are brought into any sort of intimate relationship. It is a technique for determining what adjustments to each other may be necessary or advisable if they attempt to work in team to common ends, and as an examination of character and its constant potentials or a consideration of the overall pattern of the natives at birth it has its detailed attention in the author's *Essentials of Astrological Analysis*. Only one of the seven steps in the procedure outlined in that text is of any pertinence in the dynamic horoscopy, and it involves the case when any natal planet of one chart lies in the zodiacal place of any natal planet of the other one or at a point directly opposite. This interrelation must be within sixty minutes of arc in exactness and it is not often found. The absence of it merely means that the scope of possible rapport is devoid of specific delimitation. Its presence however is testimony to

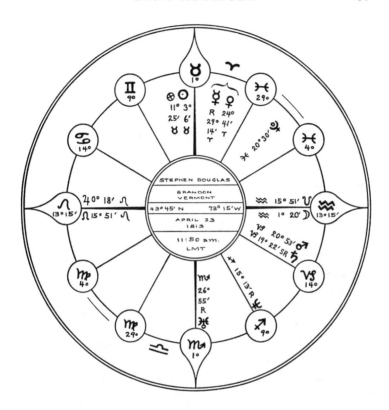

what can be the sharing of a highly significant potentiality of experience in common.

A single instance that should have attention in the exposition at the present point is the opposition of the natal Venus of Douglas with the natal Mars of Lincoln. These cross ties are actually the dynamic potential in the comparison of horoscopes and in this example case an idealistic alerting is indicated. In distinction from the basic weighing of factors of character in simple rapport it is important here to note that Venus is the applying planet, or is the one that must be moved forward in the zodiac to make the aspect exact, and that in consequence Douglas is shown to provide the ultimately positive role in the relations of Lincoln and himself. The Little Giant's sensitivity, or his passion for dramatic compromise in the shadow of Henry Clay, becomes the stimulus to the creative excitation that through the person of the martyred president led to the actual unification of the nation and to the substantiation of the myth figure that has helped perpetuate the national ideal. It was on the shoulders of the latter that the mantle of the Great Compromiser was to fall, but it was the former who precipitated the political developments or channeled the way for the more literal giant who superficially was his archrival.

In the ultimately dominant strand of Lincoln's outreach for position in his presentation of himself to life at large through his basic attitude, the men comprising the group into which he integrated himself very definitely from the days of the Black Hawk War on to his death by assassination had a much more immediate part to play than Douglas. When the Illinois state capital was moved from Vandalia to Springfield in 1838, as virtually the result of single-handed effort on his part, he had in the short two years since he had left New Salem been warmly embraced as a leading figure in the social and intellectual life of the new political core of things. His conspicuous eccentricities had not proved to be any particular handicap. The already well-established Little Giant was very much a participant in the gay affairs, and it was gossip although definitely denied by her that he had courted the future Mrs. Lincoln. He did not marry however until much later, when he had gone to Washington and was very well established.

The younger set that dominated Springfield society at the threshold of the Eighteen-Forties revolved around the Ninian Edwards and was known as the Coterie. Edwards himself was son of a former Illinois governor. He had campaigned with Lincoln, and was a faithful member of the Long Nine in the legislature. His wife was a sister of Mary Todd, who had come to live with them in the year the town became state capital, and John Stuart was a cousin of these thoroughly aristocratic young women. Thus the native had been brought almost inextricably into his tie with a family of very top rank in the southern blue blood now establishing itself in the Midwest.

The Kentucky home of the Todds was in Lexington, only some seventy-five miles from Lincoln's birthplace and the unquestioned cultural and financial center of the expanding and prosperous slave territory. Mary Todd had attended an exclusive finishing school directly opposite the Ashland estate of Henry Clay in Lexington, and had enjoyed a girlish intimacy with the famous Whig who curiously enough was Lincoln's particular political idol. Thus the dramatic convergences under the astrological principle of concordance or concomitance, that indicate his potential high significance, are seen in their dramatic pyramiding of themselves in space as well as time. What is almost inconceivable is the marriage and ultimately very congenial life together of close to absolute extremes of primitive ruggedness and simplicity on the one hand and exceptional education for a woman of that day in the instance of one with long-established social refinement in background on the other. Between their horoscopes there are no planetary cross ties to show any particularized delimitation of the great

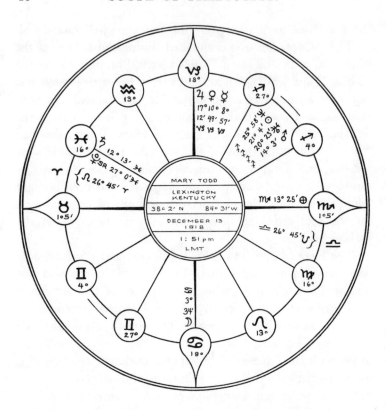

individuality or exaggerated independence characteristic of them both. The interrelation of the nativities taken in respect to the potentials of mutual impact of general makeup from birth, and quite a parenthetical matter in connection with the dynamic horoscopy, reveals that in the three normal areas of compatibility of (1) temperament (2) everyday practical livingness and (3) subconscious or instinctive rapport they are ideally complementary to each other. This should be noted in passing perhaps in view of the unfortunate but widespread misconception of the marital relationship through all the earlier years of Lincoln literature.

The Qualities of Uniqueness

The indication of Uranus is often oversimplified as personal eccentricity or revolutionary nature and conduct. Its real significance in an individual life is best suggested as an identification of the psychological as well as literal elbowroom coming to man with the development of the industrialized society and the emergence of a new form of democracy that together have general correspondence with its discovery in the heavens. The astrological principle denying it any signification of immediate import before 1781 does not deny the conventionalized form these new resources of humanity will have in the average instance, and it is the possibility of the release and not the nature of it that is revealed in the dynamic horoscopy. To be noted however is the particular strength of the initial impact of the planet in American destiny. There is remarkable convergence in the fact that the original era of the strong leaders in the republic had come to a climax with the celebrated senatorial trio of Henry Clay, Daniel Webster and John Calhoun. They were born within five years of each other and almost coincident with the discovery of Uranus. The linking had re-emphasis when all of them died within a span of less than three years. Whether Stephen Douglas sought consciously or subconsciously to step into a definite succession of leadership, he was second only to Clay in getting the Compromise of 1850 through Congress and redrawing the line between slave and free states. In all this there were the dramatic events in chain that are charted so particularly by the trine family of aspects in astrology.

It might be thought that because of the extent to which Abraham Lincoln was caught up in the general momentum of unfoldment in the new type of democratic society in the New World, there might be at least an overall explanation for the most puzzling feature of his eccentricity or his frequently almost obsessive melancholy. This recurrent and extreme moodiness, which had afflicted him from his New Salem days if not before, might by that hypothesis have been no more than a psychological reaction to the sheer pressures of the potentialities into which he was being carried by the very drift of circumstances. Here of course is something beyond specific horoscopic indication. Thus his physical abnormalities, including the length of the extremities and the heredity features of the Marfan syndrome that have been identified in other individuals in the Lincoln line, have no astrological implication any more than virtually all elements of purely family and racial inheritance. What is significant for the moment in the present exposition is that in 1852 the mysterious build-up or plethora of inwardness was at so great a peak that the native's law partner, William Herndon, reported the depression as literally dripping from him as he walked. For the phenomenon there was no obvious reason in superficial developments. The death of little Eddie Lincoln occurred in 1850, but Willie was born in that year as a measure of consolation. At the time of Herndon's comment the partners were enjoying a very successful practice since in 1850 they handled eighteen percent of all cases in the Sangamon County Circuit Court and by 1853 it was thirty-four percent. On the whole these seemed to be happy domestic years.

A common astrological misconception is to accept a mode of conduct as an inherent trait of character, or to fail to realize that it is the meaning of what is done and not the literal manner of doing or the material employed that alone has horoscopic indication. A broad and tolerant perspective is needed here as in any of the essentially therapeutic fields of analysis. Human uniqueness superficially is of necessity a repudiation of established standards and customs, and for the greater part is to be observed in (1) common dissipations as the least harmful or dangerous phenomenon and (2) criminality or extreme mental disorganization as the more serious threat to the general well-being. The pendulum of differentiation has a curious overswing, however, and with the development of an epochal deviate course in particular instance the sustainment of it comes through an increasingly greater number of individuals who in their mass tend to average out their own differentiae and find an almost intoxicating fulfillment in a shared revolt. It is thus that the demagogue gains a mob unity for his purposes on a lower or more destructive level, and that contrariwise a spiritually exalted individual can lift a whole segment of mankind into a transcendental state whether momentarily or in truly enduring fashion.

Here the myth figure is perhaps most signally presaged for Abraham Lincoln in the remarkable extent to which he was the loner and kept his thinking processes to himself or achieved his intellectual stature strictly on his own while yet almost universally accepted into the hearts of those with whom he had daily association. His extraordinary melancholy has led to considerable Freudian speculation and even acceptance of a possibility of abnormal sex. Not only is there no reasonable suggestion of deviation of such a sort in the known events of his life, but on the contrary the testimony is toward exceptionally normal capacity for fitting into the widest variety of situations and meeting the broadest spread of everyday experience in the prevailing conceptions of decency. His eccentricities probably stemmed mainly from a physique of which he was proud and from deficiencies of pioneer background that actually and early proved a political asset, and so to an unprejudiced eye they would have little if any appearance of a defense mechanism. Since most personal deviation is a matter of self-expression with perhaps widely varying acceptance in different patterns of society, astrology has no way to identify it except most indirectly or when it becomes significant as a case of warped norm in character or in the refinement of experience.

PROGRESSED MERCURY IN CONJUNCTION WITH NATAL JUPITER, JULY 28, 1864   This indication in basic attitude of an activated zest through practical alertness has significant correspondence with the fall of Atlanta on September 1st. The loss in the Civil War of this important industrial center of the South was a definite death blow to the Confederacy. The result in the North was an immediately revivified morale, as possibly the vital factor in the re-election of Lincoln. To be noted at this point is an extraordinary phenomenon in his secondary directions. For the most exacting years of his life, or from the late Fifties until his assassination, there are no major progressed aspects in any activity-facets with the exception of this conjunction of Mercury with Jupiter. In consequence he can be seen by the astrological testimony to be proceeding wholly on the momentum provided by capacities developed in his formative or earlier years, and the realization supplements the indication through Uranus of the dramatic circumstances bringing him into alignment with the sweep of events in American history. The single whiplash of encouragement to steady morale in the unusual activation of Jupiter to self-protection is further possible certification of the cosmic concordance involved.

PROGRESSED MERCURY IN SEXTILE WITH THE NATAL MOON, JUNE 13, 1868 The first progressed aspect following decease in an activity-facet of selfhood has no validity in connection with the actual or living years of a native, but it can give valuable suggestion of any possible continuing influence and by the same token perhaps offer a measure of crowning judgment on the given career. In the basic attitude of Abraham Lincoln the indication of an activated endurance through a practical adroitness is suggestion of the myth figure to be anchored challengingly in the modern world of everyday sociopolitical actualities.

In summary, the nonfulcral directions for the basic attitude of this native are important because of the extent to which their unique pattern charts his extraordinary potential. In their limitation to the activation primarily of only two of the natal planets they couple (1) his appointment as deputy county surveyor in 1833 and his effective re-entry into politics in 1853 as marking the exceptional aplomb he gained by climbing up in some two decades from little more than small-town roustabout to the stature of a statesman of national promise and (2) his election to the legislature in 1834 in an initial achievement of public office or a definite release of political capacities and the symbolical impact on him in 1852 of the death of Henry Clay when in a sense the mantle of the Whig patriarch fell on his shoulders and gave preliminary release to the transcendental elements of the myth figure in American history. Except for the 1864 activation of Jupiter in correlation with the fall of Atlanta, or the event that restored

Northern morale and probably assured his re-election, there are no major progressions whatsoever in the secondary system for the final epoch of his life. His destiny can be seen unfolding in an almost irresistible sweep of events in which he was linked closely with a vital group of men active in developing the Midwest, and including Stephen Douglas significantly as suggested by planetary cross tie in their horoscopes. The chain of events brought Mary Todd into his orbit and led to the outwardly incongruous union of a relatively unendowed scion of the soil with a highly cultured beauty of as proud a lineage as might have been found in the South.

Fulcrum Indication

PROGRESSED MERCURY IN SQUARE WITH NATAL NEPTUNE, JULY 23, 1839, AND JANUARY 29, 1847   In this third of the four normal procedures in analysis of an activity-facet in the dynamic horoscopy, but here following rather than preceding the delineation of the nonfulcral indications in deviation from the usual order of attention in the special case of Lincoln's basic attitude, the consideration is of the critical self-mobilization required by the native under the pressure of objective events especially revealed by the fulcrum aspects. These squares in the geometrical symbolism, that have been seen established at the mid-points in the celestial half circles through which all differentiation in experience has its fundamental charting in astrology, represent the factor of change or choice in its effective culmination both in time and event or in what most simply may be designated as crisis. This never presupposes ill result necessarily, but rather a heightened consequence of act or reaction. To be noted in the secondary directions of Abraham Lincoln is that the only instances of Mercury forming a square are the two activations of Neptune that first antedate its discovery by some seven years and then follow the astronomical event by about four months. Here is a building to climactic signification in the curious Chinese-boxes arrangement of Mercury's progressions in relation to the native's fundamental self-projection into life, but the signification as only partially inoperative during his lifetime is testimony to (1) the potential uniqueness of the career through the extraordinary correspondence of his activities in general with the emergence of the new horoscopic factor in human history and (2) the almost inescapable subjectivity of the personality at its best and as perhaps most dramatically manifest in his chronic melancholy to which the more essentially psychological clue has been provided by Uranus.

The fulcral coming to stress in 1839 of matters concerning the native's general acceptance or adoption of an individual destiny through the basic attitude has overall correlation with the moving of the capital of Illinois from Vandalia to Springfield, completed with the proclamation by the governor on July 4th. Since Neptune was not yet discovered, the consequence of this is shown as of minor significance to him at the time. Gratifying as the certification of his accomplishment must have been, his attention certainly would have been centered on his problems in getting his start in law practice under the weight of his New Salem debts. What came to crisis in early 1847 by contrast had immediate and sharp repercussions when seen in correspondence to his election to Congress on August 3, 1846. By that time he had become a successful lawyer. After a friendly dissolution of relations with John Stuart in early 1841 he had had nearly four years of rewarding partnership with the exacting Stephen Logan, and in 1844 he had opened his own office. He then was a married man with domestic responsibilities, and he had cleared away the lingering New Salem obligations with the punctiliousness that earned him his sobriquet of Honest Abe. Still lacking most fundamentally was the sophistication that would develop only when he was galvanized into a truly transcendental self-dedication a good eight years later.

At crisis in 1846 most significantly was his naïve assumption that his mere integrity at core was sufficient basis for his progress. He had yet to learn that merit in human affairs in the larger global perspective must have dramatization sufficient for the comprehension and acceptance of it by at least an appreciable part of those concerned. In Washington in concert with the liberals of the period he condemned the morality of the Mexican War as pure aggression and demanded that President Polk inform the House of Representatives precisely as to where the shedding of American blood by the Mexicans supposedly, in violation of United States territory, had precipitated the conflict. The political influence of the veterans was extensive and their reaction against Lincoln was violent. The association of ideas, linking his antiwar stand based on an identification of the exact spot of its starting with the spotted fever then prevalent in Michigan, gained him the damning designation of Spotty Lincoln. He actually was termed a second Benedict Arnold by the home press, but now he very definitely was enmeshed in the national destiny as foreshadowed even if for the moment embarrassingly and with every sense of futility.

In summary, the fulcrum factors of sharp crisis in Lincoln's developing basic attitude (1) in the larger perspective beyond personal significance of Neptune's indication before its discovery suggested that in local delimitation at Springfield the native might have the potential of significant involvement in the ever increasing drift of the nation to actual civil war and (2) with the planet's emergence into horoscopic effectiveness revealed how much more statesmanly acumen he would need than he had ever demonstrated in his earlier political experience.

Challenge by Progressed Station

PROGRESSED MERCURY STATIONARY TURNING RETROGRADE IN 1821   In deviation from the normal order of procedure in the dynamic horoscopy or as a fourth instead of a second step in analysis of the basic attitude of Abraham Lincoln, consideration is of the stations established when a planet by progression comes to rest in the zodiac and begins to move retrograde instead of direct or vice versa. If the change is to retrograde the indication is more personal or intimate and if to direct more impersonal or instrumental, but this distinction is wholly supplemental to the main issue of the moment and in general may be disregarded. The phenomenon in the secondary directions always identifies a subtle or psychological shift in the fundamental course of life, such as requires a critical regrasp of experience and often proves to be an adjustment over an appreciable span of time whether marked by some single sharp event of easy identification or by a complex syndrome of changes of less obvious interrelation. This 1821 station occurs during the native's thirteen-odd years at Little Pigeon Creek in Indiana, or when he was growing from not quite eight to just over twenty-one, and with the limited information available is beyond any certain correspondence with events. The existing record of these boyhood times is based mostly on scattered recollections of many individuals collected long afterwards.

A reasonable guess as to a significant occurrence would be some eventuality that gained the particular interest of James Gentry for the youngster in his twelfth year or so. Gentry was the largest land owner around, and the proprietor of the store in which Lincoln would spend much of his time and there demonstrate his mimic gifts and real flair for entertaining his fellow human creatures. He was seventeen when he became a helper for James Taylor, particularly in the operation of a ferry across the Ohio River sixteen miles from the Pigeon Creek cabin, and he then could become very familiar with the exciting river traffic on this mainstream of American expansion. He became acquainted with Justice-of-the-Peace Samuel Pate on the other side of the river in Kentucky, and was quickened to a first if wholly anticipatory and transient interest in the law. When he was eighteen he was engaged by Gentry to help construct a flatboat and was sent with Gentry's son to take a load of local produce down to market in New Orleans. Thus an international world was opened before his eyes, although there is no knowing to what extent, but certainly he would encounter the waterfront exploitation of human vice or at least the easily viewed brutality of the slave trade. In any case, when he was of age and on his own, he had another opportunity to take a cargo down the Mississippi by way of the Sangamon River in Illinois. It was the project of a wild-eyed promotor by name of Denton Offutt, and its end result was Lincoln's definite if originally very precarious settlement in New Salem.

PROGRESSED MERCURY STATIONARY TURNING DIRECT IN 1843   The critical regrasp of experience in basic attitude is here the challenge to the native to establish a firm pattern in his public representation of himself for once and all, and it has

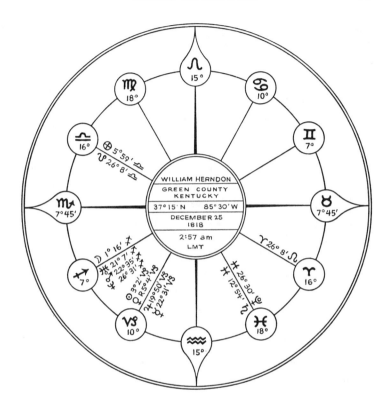

its key correlation with his marriage to Mary Todd. That event on November 4, 1842, was more or less concomitant with his opening in late 1844 of his own law office and his selection as a partner of William Herndon who was then a young man only just admitted to practice. Astrologically this station is central in the Chinese-boxes arrangement of the progressions of Mercury between 1821 and 1864, and in consequence the forming of the two close ties can be seen centering the whole of the life in very particular significance. Contributing further to the general context of convergences characteristic of unusual significance in a given life is the extraordinary fact that his wife and the fledgling lawyer were almost astrological twins. She was born on December 13, 1818, and Herndon on Christmas Day in the same year. Under the essential principle of concordance or convergence it can be noted that Lincoln's loss of his mother on October 5, 1818, has curious if remote relation with the birth of Mary Todd two months later. The arrival of Sarah Bush Johnston at Pigeon Creek in a little over a year afterwards or at the end of 1819, to become his angel mother in his own fond terms, meant that the only two women of enduring moment in his experience had interesting even if quite remote horoscopic linkage from the beginning. Wholly supplemental but perhaps worthy of notice is that in the course of clearing away his New Salem indebtedness he was able to purchase his permanent home in Springfield on January 7, 1844.

Lincoln's Intimate Involvements

In turning again to natal horoscopes in comparison for possible dynamic indication it can be seen that Herndon's sun applies by cross tie in opposition with Mary Todd's moon and that her sun similarly applies in conjunction with his Uranus, so that their active interrelation is indicated as wholly an expression of their respective unusually strong wills well revealed in life itself. The marked difference between them is a dramatic distortion of the alikeness shown as the moon in high focus in her splay typing has moved in with the other planets in his birth chart to permit a bucket classification and reveal his species of self-containment. He was a college dropout and while reared in Springfield by a politically prominent

father he yet chose to stand aside from the main course of
Midwest freewheeling individualism as a pseudointellectual.
The antithesis of Lincoln in perhaps as many ultimate respects
as proved to be the case with the irrepressible Mary, he yet
was as basically loyal to the senior member of the odd trio.
Unhappily the younger astrological near-twins utterly detested
each other, and managed a mutual mirroring for the very
worst. His manifestation of a distinction indicated by Uranus
completely outraged her, and she never welcomed him to her
house. He repaid her scorn in kind whether wittingly or not
when as a principal and rather privileged biographer of the
man who had held their common and unshakable regard,
and in the horoscopic impact channeled through her natal
moon, he blighted her image for years or was most responsible
for the distorted portrait generally accepted by history until
well into the Nineteen-Forties.

Abraham Lincoln was characteristically the man among
men, and in his day it was generally understood that he was
not too much at home with women although he had demonstrated himself capable of extraordinarily affectionate relations
as in the instance of his early idolized stepmother and in the
primitive or essential tribal concern over his own blood in his
violent reaction to the death of his sister Sarah in childbirth
and his unreasoning assumption that this was the fault of the
young husband. Probably what was observed by his contemporaries was no more than a natural shyness due to the failure
of his unschooled background to equip him with the more
sophisticated skills of social pleasantry. Certainly from the
record it can be seen that he found his genuinely intellectual
companionship in feminine company. In masculine areas west
of the Appalachians where most interest ranged from nation

building down to insensate personal aggrandizement, the more serious thinkers were likely to be either the high-purposed fanatics or the would-be pundits of whom young Herndon was a typical example and of no mental stimulus whatsoever for the future president. Between these two there was no planetary cross tie, and what horoscopic compatibilities existed were entirely superficial or on the side of casual everyday functioning.

In earlier New Salem days the native had boarded at a convenient tavern, and apparently had developed an unusually spontaneous companionship with a daughter of the proprietor. She was engaged to a good friend of his who was away on a protracted absence, and in consequence their relations could remain happily impersonal. Her father, Judge Rutledge, had had educational advantages and it is believed that he possessed a small private library such as would prove irresistible to the young man of twenty-three who notoriously was book hungry. Indeed, he is known to have walked eight miles to borrow one. About the sum of any valid historical record is that Ann Rutledge died in 1835 after a brief illness, and that the youthful Lincoln took her passing very hard. The magnification by various writers of his distress at losing a probably vivacious and stimulating partner in mental outreach of the moment into a great and tragic romance is now a misconception of the past. The most reasonable supposition is that this little miss four years his junior had introduced him to the camaraderie of mind that was to have an ultimate full flower in his marriage.

His relationship with a Mary Owens in his final New Salem days was hardly to his credit. She was another Kentucky girl of considerable social background and he not only had thought her attractive when she visited her sister in the little Illinois hamlet but from what he wrote later he had even entertained the notion of marriage, but nothing had come to any serious point. Three years later the sister in bantering fashion, when about to go off for a visit to the family home, had offered to bring this Mary back if he would agree to become a brother-in-law with all dispatch. He agreed, whether in the spirit of the badinage or with a resurgence of the earlier interest, but it was evident very quickly that there was no real rapport of mind to cement any tie between these two. Now on their second association he found her almost repulsive while she on her part rejected him for what she felt was his hopeless vulgarity. With his high sense of moral obligation he had been willing to fulfill his commitment, but his Rabelaisian humor when he put himself on record in the matter is certainly at least some confirmation of her verdict.

In Springfield the acquaintance between Abraham Lincoln and Mary Todd began in the winter of 1839-40, and by the end of 1840 they were engaged. Almost immediately however, in January of the next year, the engagement was broken under circumstances that can only be surmised. The likely presumption is that the Todd family through the Ninian Edwards raised the issue of Lincoln's social fitness, and that as instinctively the gentleman he was prompt in releasing the young lady. All evidence is against any possibility of a quarrel between them, and both were plunged into an almost irremediable misery. Unquestionably their minds of exceptionally seminal capacity had drawn them together, and the circumstances of their respective situations must have given them wide areas in which they could enjoy the magical release of self into fruitful and unrestricted discussion. Probably neither had ever encountered anybody else as a comparable peer in actual intelligence, and both ultimately gave testimony that theirs was the single love of their lives. With each of them insufferably lonely in mind and spirit without the other, and thus driven by stark mutual need and abetted by the physician who recognized the depth of their deprivation, they took the fateful step at last.

The marriage was remarkable because of the sheer intangibles in which it was grounded and through which it was held together. Children and domestic exactions in the earlier years of a near poverty for which she was utterly unprepared were the conventional factors that helped keep them close, but as a lawyer still struggling to get on his feet financially he was likely at the start to be away a full half of his time or through two annual periods of circuit court of three months each. What is more, even when with Mary and the children he might be just as far away from them psychologically in a characteristic concentration on some problem or perhaps lapsed into the general abstraction or spells of melancholy that were always baffling to those around him. Money continued the bête noire in their relationship since at the beginning he was still paying off debts, and there was appreciable drain on their slender means since at times they had to lend a hand to his people who by that time were hopelessly bogged down in ineptitude in nearby Coles County. Her father did provide some assistance, but this must have been an acute embarrassment to her. When all of two decades later she was given the task of refurbishing the White House, and did so with splendid taste, she exceeded the congressional appropriation and the fact of this made a bad impression in view of the deprivations suffered by the soldiers in the field. If a financial frustration came to obsess her on top of the pyramiding ordeals of the war years and the inhuman pressures on the man she loved, her mind in all other respects unquestionably was clear and competent to the end. Unhappily her well-meaning son Robert in 1875 sought to protect her resources and had her declared incompetent. The legal word for that at the time was insanity, and although the court action was soon reversed her public image had again been tarnished in an added injustice of a superficial history.

In summary the first progressed station in the basic attitude of Abraham Lincoln reveals the general circumstances through which the everyday flow of life was particularly dramatized for him in far more than usual dimension at the Ohio River and then on the waterfront in New Orleans. The second station in close correspondence with the discovery of Neptune identifies the permanent self-centering development when he consummated the two partnerships for the climactic years opening ahead. A happy and oddly sublimated marriage with Mary Todd was established in balance with the legal team of William Herndon and himself. There is no indication by natal astrology of planetary cross ties to show the husband and wife particularly linked, but they complemented each other rather in a unique intellectual need discovered by each of them and apparently never satisfied for either by anybody else. The two partners of the future president were almost astrological twins, but they mirrored each other for the worst and entertained a mutual and bitter hostility. In ultimate consequence of this the legal associate was responsible in principal part for the long accepted and distorted public image of the hapless wife even if his service to history was an exceptional and vital contribution.

Supernumerary Indication by Pluto

PROGRESSED MERCURY IN CONJUNCTION WITH NATAL PLUTO, MARCH 12, 1812   In a convenient supernumerary consideration of the planet as yet undiscovered in the lifetime of Abraham Lincoln, this first of its three foreshadowing indications in the basic attitude is of an activated probity through practical alertness at three years of age and has suggestive correspondence with the War of 1812 declared by Congress on June 18th. Here the general principle of concordance or concomitance has further illustration. Thanks to the conflict Henry Clay attained his national stature, and a sort of torch of astrological signification is lighted so as to be carried through the career of Clay on down until two decades later the native can be quickened to accept in effect the historical responsibility of the Whig patriarch.

PROGRESSED MERCURY IN CONJUNCTION WITH NATAL PLUTO, AUGUST 9, 1829   This repeated indication of an activated probity through practical alertness in the basic attitude and now an important framing factor in the Chinese-boxes arrangement for the major 1821-64 span of the native's life is at this initial point a certification of the transcendental importance of his coming to age and thus starting off on his own in a fresh and especially pregnant environment in New Salem.

PROGRESSED MERCURY IN CONJUNCTION WITH NATAL PLUTO, JANUARY 4, 1858   The third indication of an activated probity through practical alertness in the basic attitude and completing the delimitation of the unique patterning in the native's secondary directions has its correspondence to the culminative ordering of his career in its transcendent prefiguring. This perhaps was most marked in single focus when he made the attention-compelling "house-divided" address at Springfield on June 16th as prelude to the Great Debates with Douglas later this year.

In summary, the indications of Pluto in a perspective of afterview reveal the encompassing embrace of Lincoln's destiny in the potentials of the special role he actually has come to play in American history. Thus in his own day he can be seen moving however blindly into a line of immortal contribution to the democratic ideal thanks (1) to the ground broken by Henry Clay and (2) an arrival at maturity in uncompromising pioneer and individualistic self-assertion until (3) he could challenge his own and in passing all subsequent generations to the inescapable choice between genuine human reconciliation on the one hand and destructive allegiance to mankind's entrenched divisions and jealousies on the other.

THE NATURAL DRIVE

Continuing in the pattern of consideration in an order of logical importance of the elements of self-revelation examined by means of the secondary directions in the dynamic horoscopy, the turn in attention is from the activity-facet revealing the growth of individuality in its fundamental approach to experience in terms of a basic attitude to the equally vital factor of its continuing existence or to a natural drive that remains inherently unchanged throughout the years. Although a greater or lesser intelligence in its deployment is universally and often dramatically evident, this drive at core is essentially free will or the uninhibited choice exercised by any given person in response to the factor of chance that inheres quite as inevitably in (1) the general milieu of flux or cosmic illimitability as in (2) the unbroken manifestation of entity in the simple fact of selfhood. In the area of analysis now to be considered, what is charted is not as much the overall shaping or fundamental emergence of the personality in the frame of its potentialities shown by progressed Mercury as the pure or indomitably uninhibited and sovereign act of self as revealed by the sun in progression and shown as the self is specifically challenged to its opportunities.

In summary, for any understanding of the dynamics at play in any particular case of issue in human experience it is necessary to supplement the analysis of what life in general may help an individual create by way of his public image with an effective overall realization of what he has been able or may be able to do directly in his own behalf. The dynamic horoscopy facilitates this through the progressions of the sun, since these delineate the specific operation of his pure self-drive.

The Psychological Trend to Balance

In the normal pattern of analysis for each of the ten activity-facets of individuality charted in the dynamic horoscopy, the first of four procedures is to determine the extent to which the psychological orientation in the particular area of self-realization is likely to tend toward practical or idealistic ends. The natural drive of Abraham Lincoln is shown to have no overall emphasis of either extreme for his lifetime, but by bringing the one aspect with noneffective Pluto into consideration there is suggestion of the decidedly everyday practicality of the ultimate myth figure. A subsidiary ideal lean dominates his early years and is revealed perhaps most simply in his avid reading and curious and often moody self-sufficiency. It continues until his marriage to Mary Todd in 1842 and the concomitant developments at that time, and then there is a brief return to the idealistic dominance in 1852 when the death of Henry Clay in that year led however subjectively to the eventual high self-dedication or the substance of his very practical immortality.

In summary, Lincoln's early and instinctive outreaching to elements transcending his pioneer immediacies was the subordinate slanting in the overall indetermination of his psychological trend until he married and set up his own law office, and then it had a brief resurgence with the perhaps largely subjective impact of Henry Clay's death. An activation of Pluto in delayed manifestation several generations later identifies the truly practical influence of the myth figure ultimately.

Challenge by Progressed Station

Important in the dynamic horoscopy is the fact that the two lights or sun and moon of the astrologer's ten planets never have retrograde motion. While there can be no stations in their respective activity-facets, for consideration in normal course as the second procedure in analysis by secondary direction, the very absence of this fundamental shift here in self-act or its particularly critical regrasp of experience is valuable testimony to the utter stability of the natural drive at core irrespective of how irrational the conduct of some individuals might seem to be.

Fulcrum Indication

THE PROGRESSED SUN IN SQUARE WITH NATAL SATURN, SEPTEMBER 23, 1818   In the normal pattern of analysis for each of the ten activity-facets of self in the dynamic horoscopy the third of the four procedures is a consideration of any particularly critical self-mobilization required of the native and identified in the context of passing events by fulcrum square in progression. The elements coming to special stress in Lincoln's experience in the present instance are primarily an accentuation of his fundamental concern, and it is significant that this is the only indication of any such vital concentration of self-hood in the natural drive with actual horoscopic effectiveness during his lifetime. To be recognized is a driving power that once gaining momentum should be able to continue through the years with a single-eyed directness. This one basic crisis for the stability of his self-act came when he was not yet ten years old, and it obviously provided a particular possibility of gathering momentum toward ultimate accomplishment before his character had too conventional a set in the early Kentucky and Indiana matrix. The aspect corresponds within days of time orb to his mother's decease, and this suggests the extent to which the general impact of death may be a crucial factor in the unfoldment of his temperament. The loss of his baby brother Thomas in infancy could well have been prelude to the trauma at this point. Here horoscopically is suggestion of the depth in which his very being might come to be established, and hence also a partial explanation for the characteristic melancholy of his adult years.

THE PROGRESSED SUN IN SQUARE WITH NATAL NEPTUNE, MARCH 13, 1822 This indication of a fulcral coming to stress of matters concerning the general acceptance of an individual destiny in or through the natural drive, since it matures before the emergence of the planet into horoscopic significance, must be seen as providing light not on immediacies in an unconditioned outreach by the boy of thirteen but rather on the paralleling circumstances such as in the later view can be found in contribution to the greater dimensions of his more enduring involvement in a historical reality. Horoscopy here demonstrates the essential principle of equivalence or distinction in the manifestation of the universal concordance or concomitance since it can be noted that the Missouri Compromise became effective in all its ramifications with the admission of Missouri to the Union as the twenty-fourth state on August 10, 1821. The preservation in this fashion however of the balance of power between slavery and antislavery forces in the Senate only delayed the issue until Lincoln's time.

In summary, the one critical self-mobilization of individuality required of the native in natural drive in his lifetime is revealed when as a boy not quite ten the impact of his mother's death on top of a prior experience with the loss of a baby brother in infancy was probably in considerable part responsible for the depth of his effort to reach on and out of pioneer restrictions to some greater scope of self-realization. Emotional shock here perhaps also helps explain his exceptional inwardness and long-charactertistic melancholy, and in this fashion he may have escaped too great a set in the conventionalities of his Kentucky and Indiana years. An activation of an undiscovered Neptune reveals in afterview the possible extent to which his ultimate stature as a myth figure had significant framing in the actual history of his own living times.

Nonfulcral Indication

THE PROGRESSED SUN IN TRINE WITH NATAL MARS, FEBRUARY 10, 1811   In the normal pattern of analysis for each of the ten activity-facets of self in the dynamic horoscopy the fourth of the four procedures is a consideration of the nonfulcral aspects in simple chronological sequence as they chart the progressive distribution of whatever nativity potentials may become manifest through the regular flow of experience in the general milieu of circumstances. This initial indication in the natural drive when Lincoln was barely two years old was of an activation of the natal persistence through a necessarily nascent idealistic adroitness, and as the earliest major progressed aspect in any activity-facet in the important secondary system it suggests a primary role for the natural drive or an uncompromising and resourceful aliveness in his development. As a child he probably in consequence would exhibit a lively curiosity, but more vitally there would be every expectation of an essential purity or sheer decency and naïveté thanks to the grass-roots of his character. The progression corresponds by general time orb to his arrival at the Knob Hill farm, where he would spend some five formative years in typically frontier activity at the side of Kentucky's busy pike between Louisville and Nashville. He was free with a full rein of imagination to watch the procession by his very door of Conestoga wagons and various conveyances as well as driven stock. He could ask questions about the visiting peddlers of the goods and notions only sparsely available in the backwoods, or perhaps concerning the passing gangs of slaves on foot with their owner or overseer on horseback or about the occasional fine carriage in which people of quality might ride. While living here he would have some shreds of schooling with his sister Sarah, and in learning to write he would develop a love for forming the letters and according to surviving report persist doggedly in making them with charcoal or with a stick in sand or dust or even snow.

THE PROGRESSED SUN IN TRINE WITH NATAL URANUS, MARCH 19, 1825   This indication in the natural drive of an activated self-release through an idealistic adroitness is provided by the only aspect in the activity-facet made with this first-discovered of the three newer planets and of them alone horoscopically effective at the time. There is general correspondence to the onset of adolescence or perhaps specifically to the employment of the sixteen-year-old boy by James Taylor as a helper in operating the ferry across the Ohio River. Although indentured to his father and with no right to keep anything he earned, in accordance with the custom surviving among his people, the strapping young fellow could yet begin to feel very much on his own. Astrological testimony is to the importance of this psychological threshold in his development.

THE PROGRESSED SUN IN CONJUNCTION WITH NATAL MERCURY, NOVEMBER 17, 1825   This indication in the natural drive of an activated aplomb through a practical alertness corresponds of necessity to some next step in an establishment of an individual pattern for the current or relatively superficial continuities of American life as in contrast with the more psychological but isolated and preliminary quickening of the sense of self-momentum six months before. The thirteen-odd years at Pigeon Creek in Indiana, while posing the problem of identifying specific events because of the scantiness of surviving record, are shown astrologically to be exceptionally rich in opportunity for the self-discovery that of necessity unique with this emphasis would later have its manifestation in both general capacity and a soul-shielding eccentricity. To be noted is that four out of the ten progressions in the activity-facet effective during the native's lifetime, comprising both fulcral indications and the only quickening of Mercury and Uranus, occur in this particular span. With adultship the thoroughgoing loner can be assumed to emerge obviously and dramatically of a piece down deep in the depths of himself.

THE PROGRESSED SUN IN CONJUNCTION WITH NATAL PLUTO, JANUARY 11, 1830 This indication in the natural drive of an activated probity through a practical alertness while effective only in revealing factors going into the creation of the myth figure is yet confirmative testimony in its transcendental significance to what had superficial acceptance during Lincoln's actual living or the exceptional inner coalescence now seen to characterize his immortal make-up.

THE PROGRESSED SUN IN CONJUNCTION WITH NATAL JUPITER, AUGUST 30, 1837 This indication in the natural drive of an activated zest through a practical alertness shows the possible effectiveness of the native's gift for carrying others along with him in policy and accomplishment as he first established himself in his profession at this point and then ultimately makes his historical contribution in preserving the

Union. He had been licensed to practice law in 1836 and had been admitted to the bar in Illinois in March in 1837. Thanks to his resourceful maneuvers the legislature meeting in Vandalia voted in February, 1837, to move the capital to Springfield. At last it was possible for him to move down the twenty-odd miles from the deteriorating hamlet of New Salem into the community of better promise and there begin to build his real prestige as he entered into legal partnership with John T. Stuart on April 12, 1837.

THE PROGRESSED SUN IN SEXTILE WITH THE NATAL MOON, NOVEMBER 23, 1842   This indication in the natural drive of an activated endurance through a practical adroitness reveals the more completely independent establishment of its course with the buttressing of the native's nascent spiritual or deep inner and uncompromising incorruptibility in (1) marriage to Mary Todd on November 4th as most centrally important in the psychological rapport and followed in further substantiation of the lifelong thread of progress by (2) the purchase of a permanent home in Springfield a little over a year later and (3) the selection of William Herndon as a law partner some eight months after that.

THE PROGRESSED SUN IN TRINE WITH NATAL SATURN, OCTOBER 16, 1848   This indication in the natural drive of an activated concern for matters at hand through an idealistic adroitness has correspondence in the dynamic horoscopy to the superficial debacle of Lincoln's conscientious but politically unsophisticated performance in his single term in the House of Representatives at Washington. He suffered from a sort of lame-duck status in accepting a rotation-in-office arrangement with his rivals at home, and equally ill-advised was his part in the effort to discredit the Mexican War and undercut the policies of President Polk. What superficially was setback in forcing the native out of politics for the moment can be seen an actual and vital if inept stirring to the fundamental challenge of equity law. The importance of this emphasis in his rational orientation under a quickened Saturn is confirmed in his future career as statesman rather than merely politician.

THE PROGRESSED SUN IN TRINE WITH NATAL NEPTUNE, APRIL 26, 1852   This indication in the natural drive of an activated acceptance of greater self-responsibility through an idealistic adroitness is supplemental testimony to the actuality of a real quickening to the more enduring potentials of American destiny when with the summer of this year the mantle of Henry Clay in a sense fell on the native's shoulders.

THE PROGRESSED SUN IN CONJUNCTION WITH NATAL VENUS, MARCH 7, 1853   This indication in the natural drive of an activated realization through a practical alertness is of climactic significance in the charting of the larger course of the native's single-minded or happily naïve desire for eminence. Here is the only quickening in his lifetime by major progression of this particular planet, and in its identification of culminations of enrichment of experience and the like it shows in this case the building paradox in which one who is essentially a man of peace becomes an outstanding war president of the nation and in the suffering grounded quite objectively in this ambivalence submits willy-nilly to the refinement of the myth figure. Increasingly the loner under the necessity to surrender many of his Whig associations and to witness the death blow to the party's continued existence with the poor showing of Winfield Scott as its candidate for president in 1852, he was requickened to national potentials in his recognition of the emergence of the new Republican party early in

1854 as an ultimate and needed channel for his more significant efforts.

THE PROGRESSED SUN IN SEXTILE WITH THE NATAL SUN, JUNE 14, 1869 The first aspect of a particular progressed planet after decease has no validity in the actual living years of a native but it can give valuable suggestion of any possible continuing influence, and the indication in the natural drive of an activated fundamental strength through a practical adroitness is testimony to the building power of simple self-perpetuity of potentially immortal individuality and its capacity for the insemination of others as in the myth figure of Abraham Lincoln.

In summary, the nonfulcral directions for the natural drive in Lincoln's case show the heightening of an exceptional aliveness from babyhood, and an early exposure on through boyhood and adolescence to the widest possible spread of pioneer reality in its grass roots. Responsibility came to him as a youth, to the point of introduction even to an international world at New Orleans. Circumstances drove him more and more into himself, but in balance there was increasing recognition of his capacity by others and especially when he broke away from his family and its stagnations. In the Illinois legislature he early distinguished himself, and despite his lack of background he became a leading citizen of Springfield and not only married her most cultivated if visiting daughter but established what in time was the state's leading law office. Ahead of himself in national politics, he suffered an embarrassing setback in Washington that was a blessing in later perspective since when in a sense the mantle of Henry Clay fell on his shoulders he went on to significance in larger dimension and to final immortality as a myth figure of American democracy.

THE BASIC SENSITIVITY

Continuing in the pattern of consideration in an order of logical importance of the elements of self-revelation examined by means of the secondary directions in the dynamic horoscopy, the turn in attention is from the activity-facets of (1) the general maturing approach of the human individual to the circumstances of existence through the basic attitude in the development of a customary public image and (2) the concomitant manifestation of what by contrast is the essentially unchanging natural drive of the being at core to (3) the basic sensitivity as the creative self-refinement in experience of the particular skills and capacities through which a conscious rapport with life at large in its self-challenging immediacies can be maintained. Here is the definite quality of selfhood rather than the mere drift or purely repetitive continuance of necessary function such as most fundamentally distinguishes the lower living orders of nature. Individuality in this sphere of evolutionary expression is charted by progressed Venus as the private in balance with the public image of man, or as his ever-expanding dramatization of his own distinctiveness to-himself. What is revealed is the individual self-fulfillment in immediate consummation of effort toward the practical ends or useful facilitations of everyday necessity by which any or all potentiality will gain its foundation manifestation. This is plussage as the psychological phase of growth providing the added dimension of astrological delineation at this point, and represented quite uniquely by the curious eccentricity of Abraham Lincoln.

In summary, consideration turns from the basic attitude and the natural drive of the individual to the basic sensitivity that represents his private as in contrast with his public image and thus the progressive refinement of skills and capacities that creates the quality of his conscious existence and primarily distinguishes him from the lower living orders in nature. This is plussage in the projection of himself by man into reality, and it is at this point that a deeper understanding is provided for the exceptional eccentricity of Abraham Lincoln.

The Psychological Trend to Balance

In this first of the four normal procedures in analysis of an activity-facet in the dynamic horoscopy the indication for the basic sensitivity of Lincoln is again the lack of any overall particularity of lean to the practical or idealistic extreme of psychological trend except as the activation of the non-operative Pluto is taken into account in connection with the ultimate myth figure. In that case the dominant practicality buttresses the signification for the enduring contribution of the native in both basic attitude and natural drive. Here an initial practical slanting of his subjective self-dramatization becomes a natural development in the pioneer simplicities of life. With 1839 came an idealistic subperiod in a re-establishment of himself in the more generally sophisticated environment that could sustain and mirror the broader refinement in the depths of himself. He had moved to the future capital of Illinois two years earlier, but it was with its actual establishment as the seat of state administration that the idealistic expansion of his personal horizon gained its real significance. The final stage in the tempering of his potential in its immortal destiny came with the third subperiod or when in 1852 the decease of Henry Clay punctuated the course of history for him in highly symbolical fashion.

What comes to be revealed by this activity-facet is outwardly and superficially the common maturation of a given native through a refinement of aesthetic and artistic capacity or perhaps a marked functional ingenuity. More importantly it charts his particular delicacy of rapport with the standards or symbolized values of any given society whenever there is any evolution of these above the basic gregariousness, such as in the lower orders tends to limit any individual development to that bare convenience in division of labor which in the first place has created and maintained the general activities of the group. The subtle distinction to be recognized with this step in astrology's dynamic analysis is dramatized with unusual sharpness in Lincoln's career through the disparity in background and training of Mary Todd and himself. In his earlier frame of achievement at New Salem he had been attracted to the other Mary who had exhibited many of the advantages he was to find so much more enhanced in her counterpart of sorts in Springfield. Unhappily lacking however was the mental depth that later would meet his subjective hunger in terms of nascent sensitivity or private image. Meanwhile the leopard cannot change his spots and the lingering boorishness of Lincoln's roots had tragicomic manifestation in his new location when he wrote the second of some anonymous letters published in the *Sangamo Journal* in 1842, and assumed responsibility for the fourth that was written by the two merry mischiefs of whom one was the Mary to whom he would be married in a matter of weeks and on whom some of himself in this respect may well have rubbed off. In consequence he barely avoided a duel with the state auditor who was the victim of the last letter's tastelessly personal ridicule. These however were superficialities obscuring the main stream of events.

Marriage to Mary Todd must be seen to be a partnership in the curious but here heightened immediacy of the two basic cultural strands going into the make-up of the nation and thereupon strengthening the national sensitivity through which each type of potential, or an aesthetic flux and an untrammeled creativity on the one hand and an uncompromisingly pragmatic appreciation of work and accomplishment on the other, could have continual and mutual consummation as the basis of the new American democracy. Lincoln in the potentiality of the myth figure particularly dramatizes the reality and depth of development, and perhaps most strikingly toward the end of his actual lifetime in his immortal Gettysburg address on November 19, 1863. His remarks at that time followed the polished two-hour oration of Edward Everett, a staunch patriot and the North's finest speaker. The native's relatively extemporaneous contribution to history at the moment comprises less than three hundred words. Emphasizing the subtlety of what was gaining expression was the little appreciation of his brief eulogy by his contemporaries, who dismissed it as silly or ludicrous and the like.

Heightening the historical drama was the widespread conception of him as shoddily theatrical. There was quite common acceptance of the canard that in visiting the Antietam battlefield a year before he had indulged in obscene laughter at his own humorous stories and had asked the burly Ward Hill Lamon, an early Illinois legal associate who possessed a fine voice and who now was his most trusted intimate, to sing a cheap and shabby song. Apparently the committee making the arrangements in 1863 was under the necessity of inviting him but hoped he would not come and then perhaps play the fool and ruin the solemnity of the occasion. In private image he suffered no less than his Mary from the superficial public misconceptions that in reflection of their extreme sensitivity drove both of them so completely within themselves but gave them the compensating tie to each other.

In summary, the psychological lean in the basic sensitivity buttressed the testimony of the basic attitude and the natural drive to the definite practicality of the immortal contribution of Abraham Lincoln but in a much more significant way it charts through its subperiods the extraordinary fashion in which (1) the quality of character or the private image of the native and of Mary Todd was exceptionally intensified in the role of loner forced on each of them by the very press of circumstances so that the link between them became an almost inescapable necessity and also in which (2) the utterly disparate and individually unique strands of cultural development represented by them and providing the basic substance of the unfolding American democracy could be brought together through their union to establish the ultimate effectiveness of the myth figure.

Challenge by Progressed Station

In the consideration of the progressed stations as the second of four normal procedures in the dynamic analysis of the activity-facets other than the natural drive and the natural involvement, their occurrence is somewhat less frequent and a little more important for Venus and Mars than for the five slower bodies from Jupiter outward in their solar orbits where there is an annual regularity and for the faster Mercury in orbit next to the sun. The significance of the absence of the crucial regrasp of experience would show in the basic sensitivity, as here in Lincoln's case, an overall likelihood of fundamental emotional stability or a freedom from much external conditioning of the private image. Thus his attitude in connection with possible marriage to Mary Owens was due to the subconscious pioneer acceptance of the relationship as almost pure convenience or a necessary division of labor in primitive living with no thought of divorce or any juggling or abandonment of ties. In his extant letters he is shown to be concerned with his obligation or the honor of his word, and not with his feelings except most incidentally. With Mary Todd there was the same practicality of conduct and arrangement, but it was hallowed in special measure by the miracle of the deeper rapport.

Fulcrum Indication

PROGRESSED VENUS IN SQUARE WITH THE NATAL MOON, FEBRUARY 4, 1827   In the normal pattern of analysis for each of the ten activity-facets of self in the dynamic horoscopy the third of the four procedures is a consideration of any particular critical self-mobilization required of the native and identified in the context of passing events by fulcrum square in progression. A continuing example of the testimony to possible distinction in Lincoln's life through the multiplying syndromes of unusual planetary significance in his secondary directions is provided here by the dramatic fact that it is the two lights of the natal indicators and only the lights that are activated in fulcral emphasis in the basic sensitivity. The rallying in crisis to the potentialities of private image or the refinement of character in which man knows himself most thoroughly at core is shown in Lincoln's case to have its most important cradling in the wholly general factors of existence or the pristine substance of reality identified astrologically by the sun and moon. What comes to stress in correspondence to the activated moon can be presumed, in the frame of afterview on the life as a whole, to be the phenomenon of law in which through all his mature years he had unbroken and fundamental sustainment as legislator and lawyer and ultimately as president and myth figure. In 1827 after serving as ferry boy for James Taylor at the mouth of Anderson Creek in Indiana he had built himself a little boat at Bates Landing a short distance farther west and thereupon sculled passengers out to steamboats in the middle of the Ohio River or brought them back to shore. When he was served with a Kentucky warrant for his arrest, as allegedly operating a ferry without a license, he was able to prove he had never taken anybody farther than midstream. This incident led to his friendship with Squire Pate and to the many occasions when he rowed across to the Kentucky side to sit with this new friend on court days. Horoscopically this suggests a vital if preliminary fascination with the law that undergirded its definite study some seven years later under the encouragement of John Stuart and established it as the major element in his developing sensitivity.

PROGRESSED VENUS IN SQUARE WITH THE NATAL SUN, JANUARY 22, 1854 This indication of a fulcral coming to stress of matters concerning the native's inherent strength of an individual destiny through the basic sensitivity corresponds significantly to the introduction by Stephen Douglas of his Kansas-Nebraska Act in the Senate on January 23d and its railroading through that chamber on March 3d and the House eleven weeks later. News of the final passage reached Lincoln as he was attending court in Urbana, Illinois, and as he himself expressed it he was aroused as he had never been before.

The issue was law in its higher dimension or an effective equity in human relations. Here was the critical turn in his private image whereby he ceased to be the politician and emerged in practical self-refinement as the statesman. Deep in his consciousness was the realization that while slavery was an affront to the dignity of man the slaves yet de facto were property for which compensation should be made as they were freed.

In summary, the critical emphasis of the sun and moon and of no other natal planet is the unique feature of the fulcrum stress in the basic sensitivity and shows (1) that the native in the development of his private image or fundamental dramatization of himself to himself was unusually anchored in the general factors or pristine reality of existence as ultimate buttressing for the myth figure, and (2) that through contact at eighteen with Justice-of-the-Peace Pate he probably developed an early fascination with the law and through his outrage over the passing of the Kansas-Nebraska Act by Congress in 1854 he may well have intensified his conception of equity in justice as a principal factor in his final course.

Nonfulcral Indication

PROGRESSED VENUS IN SEXTILE WITH THE NATAL SUN, JUNE 30, 1823 In the normal pattern of analysis for each of the ten activity-facets of self in the dynamic horoscopy the fourth of the four procedures is a consideration of the nonfulcral aspects in simple chronological order as they chart the progressive distribution of whatever nativity potentials may become manifest in the regular flow of experience in the general milieu of circumstances. This progression in the basic sensitivity indicates an activated strength through a practical adroitness and it would seem most logically to correspond to the arrival of John Hanks, a cousin of Lincoln's mother, for his four-year stay in the crowded Indiana cabin. The supposition as necessarily a product of afterview is that his restless optimism and perhaps a penchant for tall tales and an outlook to the greener pastures at a distance was an important stimulation for the overgrown boy of fourteen with an exceptionally eager mind. When this newcomer at length pressed on west into Illinois, his enthusiastic account of the opportunities there led to the decision of the hardly less unstable Thomas Lincoln to pull up stakes once more. These were the eventualities through which young Abraham Lincoln was taken to an actual promised land for himself just as he happened to reach his majority. He began his independent career when with John Hanks and his stepbrother John Johnston he undertook to take produce to New Orleans by flatboat for Denton Offutt. Although the future ties with his increasingly shiftless relatives would prove a financial and psychological drain on his wife and himself at times it nonetheless was in this out-working of events with them that his private image got its foundation in the strengthened self-assurance for which the others hardly made more than a passing contribution.

PROGRESSED VENUS IN OPPOSITION WITH NATAL MARS, MAY 12, 1825   This indication in the basic sensitivity of an activated persistence through an idealistic alertness suggests the earlier and more solid contribution to his creative dramatization of himself to himself through his employment by James Taylor as ferry boy and general farm helper. This led directly to his construction of a boat of his own and in due course to his quickening to an interest in the law as a prime factor in his private as in contrast with his public image.

PROGRESSED VENUS IN OPPOSITION WITH NATAL URANUS,

FEBRUARY 4, 1839   This indication in the basic sensitivity of
an activated release of the more sophisticated potentials or
gifts of selfhood through an idealistic alertness corresponds to
the special validation of the native's private image with the
establishment of Springfield as the Illinois state capital and the
consequent buttressing of personal prestige. The outer manifestation of the quickened potentiality here for him occurred
when he became a trustee of the town within four months of
the progression's culmination.

PROGRESSED VENUS IN SEXTILE WITH NATAL MERCURY,
OCTOBER 10, 1839   This indication in the basic sensitivity of
an activated aplomb through a practical adroitness has a
very obvious correspondence with the beginning of intimate
acquaintance between Lincoln and Mary Todd, which as far
as can be verified was at about this time. Her vital intellectual
contribution to his life in lineaments of a genuine camaraderie
of spirit is thus revealed as very integral in the refinement of
his private image.

PROGRESSED VENUS IN SEXTILE WITH NATAL PLUTO, JAN-
UARY 23, 1844   This indication in the basic sensitivity of a
potentially activated transcendental probity of selfhood through
a practical adroitness is the only progression in this activity-
facet with particular reference to the myth figure to come or
with no significance at all in the native's experience in his
lifetime, but its correlation to his selection of William Herndon
as a law partner is testimony to the ultimate importance of
his extraordinary capacity for personal detachment and an
unimpeachable fairness in the delegation of responsibility. This
characteristic was dramatically evident when on achieving the
presidency he appointed some of his most bitter enemies to
key places in his cabinet. He did this because at that time they

seemed to be the ones who best could accomplish what had to be done, precisely as young Herndon seventeen years before promised to provide what was needed by way of everyday co-operation in the legal practice.

PROGRESSED VENUS IN SEXTILE WITH NATAL JUPITER, JUNE 14, 1852   This indication in the basic sensitivity of an activated zest through a practical adroitness corresponds to the death of Henry Clay on June 29th and reveals the deep and enduring nature of the buttressing of the private image through the transfer of the national Whig-become-Republican leadership to the native's unsuspecting shoulders.

PROGRESSED VENUS IN TRINE WITH THE NATAL MOON, SEPTEMBER 27, 1858   This indication in the basic sensitivity of an activated endurance through an idealistic adroitness has correspondence to Lincoln's famous Great Debates with Stephen Douglas of August into October of this year. Of primary importance in the dynamic horoscopy is the fact that this is the last major secondary direction in any of his activity-facets before the strange interim of almost six years in which he is shown in consequence to have been under the necessity of administering his own destiny and that of the country entirely on the momentum of the self-development that for better or worse has prepared him for his role. His untiring performance and surprisingly well-reasoned and eloquent presentation of his ideas on the platform in verbal combat with the better known and perhaps most worthy opponent he could have found in America brought him the initial country-wide attention he would need later even though in the immediate contest he lost the Senate seat to the Little Giant.

PROGRESSED VENUS IN OPPOSITION WITH NATAL SATURN, DECEMBER 22, 1866   The first aspect of a particular progressed planet after decease has no validity in the actual living years of a native but it nevertheless may give valuable suggestion of a possible continuing influence, and the indication here in the basic sensitivity of an activated concern through an idealistic alertness suggests the ultimate long-visioned and deep rapport of the myth figure with each developing and inspiring quality of the nation's existence. The immortal Lincoln challenges the country to the future rather than exalts any glory of the past.

In summary, Abraham Lincoln in his private self-dramatization is shown by the nonfulcral progressions to have been under unusual encouragement through the general flow of circumstances into the refinement of the potentials that might sustain him at core in his contribution to his fellows both in his lifetime and afterward as the myth figure. Beginning with what quite likely was a pivotal feeding of his imagination at fourteen by the restless and visionary John Hanks, there followed in train the practical stimulus to self-reliance in employment by James Taylor two years later as prelude to the self-realization achieved in his seven years at New Salem. Springfield widened his horizons as it became state capital, and Mary Todd there helped him deepen his psychological orientations. Henry Clay by the impact of his decease and Stephen Douglas by an extraordinary political maneuver and then in debate brought the native firmly and successfully into his own in very special and enduring sensitivity.

THE BASIC EXCITATION

Continuing in the pattern of consideration in an order of logical importance of the elements of self-revelation examined by means of the secondary directions in the dynamic horoscopy, the turn in attention is from the activity-facets of (1) the general maturing approach of the human individual to the circumstances of existence through the basic attitude and (2) the further manifestation of what by contrast is the essentially unchanging natural drive of the being at core on to (3) the basic sensitivity as the creative self-refinement of the particular skills and capacities through which a conscious rapport with life's self-challenging immediacies is preserved and so almost by necessity on now to (4) the complementary exercise or rehearsal of whatever skills and capacity may be enhanced through an exploratory self-expression identified by Mars in progression as the basic excitation of selfhood. This is the special quality that in man's self-act maintains the self-conscious distinctiveness charted fundamentally through his sensitivity. Excellence is always and peculiarly its own dynamic under the essential principle of equivalence or distinction, and its typically effective compulsion is dramatized at this point by Abraham Lincoln since as an example in astrological delineation of progressive indicators seeming to overshadow the natal ones it is possible to see how the horoscopy of performance at times may justify an exceptional latitude of interpretation of the nativity in any life of marked accomplishment. This does not mean that astrology's very different techniques of experience and character analysis ever at any point depend on or contravene each other in horoscopic judgment, but merely that one of them at times may provide the better approach to the salient nature of some particular individuality. Thus the former is dominantly illuminating in the case of the martyred president, and the latter in the differing instance of Annie Besant yet to be considered.

The interpretation of either natal or progressed indications is properly in the light of the actual life situation. The charlatans of every age however, in their effort to create the aura of magic that is their mainstay, have popularized the catch statement of tell-me-nothing-and-I-will-tell-you-all and legitimate astrologers in consequence are often expected to make their analysis without any adequate knowledge of the actualities in which a client has established himself. The problem is that an astrological chart in many instances may be interpreted in terms of a very marked plus or minus relative to the particular manifestation of its potentials. In the author's *Guide to Horoscope Interpretation* the presentation of Abraham Lincoln is on the normal level of natal judgment with a leading Mars of a bowl temperament in high focus seen triggering the moon in accurate signification of his exceptional resource in self-projection. That book was written well before the opening in 1947 of the Lincoln papers, and the resulting considerable clarification in Lincoln scholarship, but it remains fundamentally sound in its estimation of the native. In the *Essentials of Astrological Analysis* there is discussion of the deeper insight becoming possible through accepting wider orbs for natal aspects under astrology's governing law just cited, or when distinction in a career balances unusual horoscopic features.

What is important at this point in the present text is that in the basic excitation all four progressions of Mars for Lincoln's lifetime correspond to particularly pivotal events or to (1) his early quickening to an interest in the law identified as vital excitation by two of them and then (2) his consummation of the two enduring partnerships by which his life had its overall dynamic ordering and (3) his acceptance however symbolically of the mantle of Henry Clay as a species of cosmic energization. This is demonstration of the dynamic dominance of his life, and indication of his development out of his own self-act.

In summary, the consideration turns to the exercise or rehearsal of a native's potentials through his inherent effort to experience them in terms of self-refinement or the excitation of self that has its indication by progressed Mars. The dynamics of excellence has exceptional demonstration in Lincoln's case through the particularized emphasis of pivotal points of major self-unfoldment in the course of his actual life, and here astrology's entirely separate techniques of performance and character analysis are seen in the possibility of mutual validation although neither ever depends on or contravenes the other. The testimony of the former tends to be dominant with Abraham Lincoln and of the latter with Annie Besant.

The Psychological Trend to Balance

In this first of the four normal procedures in analysis of an activity-facet in the dynamic horoscopy the indication for the basic excitation of Lincoln is once more a lack of any particular overall lean to the practical or idealistic extreme of psychological trend. With no inoperative activations of Pluto there is no contribution to the ultimate make-up of the myth figure. A preliminary accentuation of the pragmatic tendency characterizes him for some forty-two years of growth and early accomplishment, and is represented by the exceptionally uninhibited outreach of the healthy boy and man both physically and intellectually. Superficial excellencies of every sort had a particular call on him. He mastered reading and writing with a dogged persistence that enabled him to educate himself quite fundamentally with but minor encouragement or formal schooling, and indeed in a matter of weeks at New Salem to qualify for surveying and then later and after an equivalent success in learning law on his own to press into Euclid if for no more than sheer relaxation. On the side of muscle there were few if any who could match him with an ax, and through a wholly amateur prowess at wrestling he won the core of his first political following from the obstreperous young men of Clary's Grove near New Salem. Here excitation is seen in stark pyramiding of itself, with the initial strong practicality first making the accentuation observable, and then toward the end the balance in this unusual stress of self-discovery came when he was quickened with the deeper grounding in the pattern of Henry Clay.

In summary, there is no overall lean to either psychological trend or toward any special potential of the myth figure in the basic excitation of Abraham Lincoln but an initial and long preliminary period of practicality charts the correspondence to his remarkable development of excellence of a physical and intellectual sort from childhood on through early adulthood. This built to the heightened quality of energized resource in psychological balance finally established in his lifetime in correlation with the impact of Henry Clay's death.

Challenge by Progressed Station

PROGRESSED MARS STATIONARY TURNING RETROGRADE IN

1827   In the normal pattern of analysis for each of the ten activity-facets of self in the dynamic horoscopy the second of the four procedures is a consideration of any essentially overall change that would require some sort of crucial regrasp of experience in the native's life. In all possibility this again would indicate the seminal nature of whatever fascinating hours may have been spent by the future president sitting in the Kentucky court of Squire Samuel Pate, watching the application of legal proscription and practice. The testimony of course is to the vital import of this in the molding of the significant individuality.

PROGRESSED MARS STATIONARY TURNING DIRECT IN 1906 The first progression of a particular planet after decease has no validity in the actual living years of a native but it does give valuable suggestion in this case of a possible continuing influence of which there is no other indication in the activity-facet. The nonsensical lapse of years in signification is seldom encountered in natal or dynamic horoscopy, but in horary art it commonly testifies to some pertinent illimitability and here it may suggest the long-range change in the complexion of law in American democracy or the shift toward a dominant emphasis on equity practice as was curiously instinctive in Lincoln's thinking and has come to have actualization in the historical transition from the Taney to the Warren Supreme Court. The fluidity of implication that always is characteristic of the time factor in astrology has particular consideration in the author's *Horary Astrology*.

In summary, the essential regrasp of experience in basic excitation in the case of Abraham Lincoln is shown to be most probably an adjustment in his sense of the overall balances of relation among his fellows as (1) he finds these ordered

traditionally in the phenomenon of law in the frame of everyday conflicts and transgressions but (2) instinctively grows to
the genuine feel of equity practice in curious anticipation of
the long-range transition in American jurisprudence.

Fulcrum Indication

PROGRESSED MARS APPROACHING ITS SQUARE WITH THE
NATAL MOON IN 1827   In the normal pattern of analysis for
each of the ten activity-facets of self in the dynamic horoscopy
the third of the four procedures is the consideration of any
particular critical self-mobilization required of the native in
the context of passing events by fulcrum square in progression. The single case in Lincoln's basic excitation fails of full
consummation by a mere five minutes of arc, but any such
incompleteness in astrology is testimony to the emphasis of the
potentiality over the actuality of the matters found at issue in
the given connection. The subquickening shown in this instance
is a proposition of endurance, or a ramifying on and out in
what ultimately through the myth figure is a possible strong
benefit from his early fascination with the law. That, in the
reasonable supposition of this text is seen indicated by the
progressed station in which the aspect culminates however
imperfectly.

Coming to concern at this point of general exposition is the
inexactness through which the general flux of reality has its
fundamental place in the cosmic concordance. The phenomenon is perhaps most familiar to the astrologer in the especially
effective correspondence of the 360 degrees of a circle with
365-odd days of the sun's annual circuit. What has become
horoscopically important in connection with Lincoln's immortal contribution is the concept of the loophole in jurisprudence,
or the irregularity in virtually all human relations that some-

how and sooner or later must be reduced to a mutual advantage rather than tailored to an impossible absolute justice. Here is astrology's essential principle of convergence or convenience in a special application, as well as needed light on the native's thinking in his own day or his realization that the wrongness of human slavery had to be equated with the rightness of property even when unhappily vested in slaves. As he saw the matter, compensation for their value was a necessity in the event of giving them their freedom. Not at all a factor in this view is the fact that he was inescapably conditioned in the overall preconceptions of his day and his cultural matrix, and hence like his fellow whites uncritically accepted the supposed intrinsical inferiority of the blacks.

In summary, the not quite completed square of progressed Mars with the natal moon primarily buttresses the testimony of the station to which the aspect is related, and strengthens the deduction that the first quickening of Lincoln's interest in the law was of supreme import in his life. The irregularity here faced is a quite proper component of the overall flux of reality of which astrology takes account, and it becomes an important basis of horoscopic significance. The native's intuitive recognition of the equity principle in law led him to feel that a freeing of the slaves would require compensation for their value, or that in the wrongness of slavery there was no lessened obligation to a rightness in property as such.

Nonfulcral Indication

PROGRESSED MARS IN CONJUNCTION WITH NATAL MARS, JULY 5, 1843   In the normal pattern of analysis for each of the ten activity-facets of self in the dynamic horoscopy the fourth of the four procedures is a consideration of the nonfulcral aspects in simple chronological sequence as they chart

the progressive distribution of whatever nativity potentials may
become manifest in the regular flow of experience in the general milieu of circumstances. This Mars progression indicates
an activated persistence in the basic excitation through a
practical alertness, and the correspondence is with Lincoln's
marriage by a time orb of seven months that in its lean from
superficial preciseness may well suggest the extent and depth
of the resulting partnership. What is important astrologically
is the retrogradation of Mars to its natal place after the inner
or psychological and fulcral excitation of the native in his
immortal outreach in preliminary or tentative form in 1827,
or the recapitulation of the overall development of energized
resource in the smaller compass of rehearsal and more definitive move to a given goal. Thus very shortly after he had
broken his engagement to Mary Todd in apparent acquies-
cence in the downgrading of his essential quality by the aristocratic and proud Kentucky family, he went ahead and
married her.

PROGRESSED MARS IN TRINE WITH THE NATAL SUN,
MARCH 31, 1851   This indication in the basic excitation of
an activated strength of self in depth through an idealistic
adroitness reveals a primarily subjective preparation for the
symbolic acceptance of the potentiality of immortal national
contribution in 1852 in the spirit of Henry Clay, through the
final severance of the umbilical cord of family origins and the
lingering tie to the unhappy ineptitudes of the Hanks-Johnston
clan with the death of Thomas Lincoln on January 17th in
1851. Signification by trine well identifies the subtle nature of
the loosening in circumstances, or the wide orientation of the
enlarged dimension of energy resources in development at this
crucial time, and the quickening of the native here at very

core is testimony to the continuing shaping of his life as the loner capable in his uniqueness of becoming the ultimate myth figure.

In summary, the indication by the nonfulcral aspects of the distribution of the nativity potentials in the general milieu of circumstances through the basic excitation of Abraham Lincoln shows the two particularly significant events to be his marriage and his release from the main drag of the Hanks-Johnston relatives through the death of his father. In the first instance he was at last asserting the particularly energized quality of his nature against the Todd snobbery and perhaps every persisting limitation of his own early roots as well, and in the second he can be seen making an asset of the role of loner enforced upon him as in a sense now and finally he was well integrated in an utter freedom of his marked individuality and could begin to grasp his national destiny.

THE FIVE TRANSCENDENCIES

Continuing in the pattern of consideration in an order of logical importance of the elements of self-revelation examined by means of the secondary directions in the dynamic horoscopy, the turn in attention is from the paired activity-facets of (1) the relatively uninhibited basic attitude and natural drive and (2) the more group-oriented quality of selfhood in basic sensitivity and basic excitation to (3) the definite manifestation of human individuality in its increasingly and inescapably personal experience of itself. In Jupiter and Saturn the early astrologers had their only two planets with a rhythm of an annual and easily observable swing from direct to retrograde motion and back, or a phenomenon that to them could represent a major surge and countersurge in human events whenever man sought to reproduce the cosmic ebb and flow in a course distinctively his own. Here would be a psychological distinctiveness, and the recognition of the consequent divergences within the encompassing universal orderliness would be an identification of what at the worst might be perversity but also at the best could be the characteristic nobility of an individualized entity. This is the age-old potentiality gaining dramatic enhancement with the emergence of a new and modern culture. The three additional planetary bodies employed in recent times, and as already pointed out, have been found to chart the remarkably expanded significations of the nativity and its progressions since fundamentally they must be considered in connection with the new dimensions of conscious human experience developing in correspondence with the discovery of the three of them in their respective order.

What astrology delineates through the now-five indicators collectively is the rational human creature in his effort to establish himself or to substantiate his desires and hold his advantages in the unending thrust and tug of overall reality in a world of flux. With modern life he must begin to exist as the conscious administrator of his own destiny whether in greater or lesser compass, and in this capacity in the extreme case he may be either the intellectual or the individual with strong but unreasoned opinions. The fundamental proposition is illustrated quite simply by the toddler who when taken for a walk will pull away from a guiding hand with all possible emphasis of his diminutive dignity in order to range free and wide and thus explore the phenomenon of existence by and for himself. But this is only to flee back in terror, and to regrasp the rejected sustainment however blindly, when there is sudden encounter with something beyond comprehension or ability for effective response. Any appreciably evolved selfhood in the emerging global society is inescapably experimental at every shifting threshold of self-expression. Problems in life become a primary challenge to the true individuality identified through the five transcendencies. Here is far more than mere stimulus and conditioned reaction, whether involving mind or muscle or both. To eat when hungry or make decisions instinctively under pressure is hardly to be dignified as a solution of difficulty. Consequently the planets out beyond Mars can never chart the trivial details of life that are easily dismissed to automaticity.

In summary, man is more than the mere member of human

society buffeted about by the exigencies of events, or the highly conditioned animal who continues to exist in inescapable bondage to the demands of his physical organism and his conventional situation. As the rational creature the native participates willy-nilly in the push and pull of reality in a world of flux, and his ultimate individuality is marked in experimentative capacities quite above what in the terms of fundamental character and performance will end up as no more than the general dismissal of life to automaticity.

THE NASCENT CONSISTENCY

The activity-facet of the expanding dimension of self-consciousness above a purely group-conditioned existence, and charted in the dynamic horoscopy by progressed Jupiter, reveals the motivated efforts of Abraham Lincoln toward special recognition or establishment of personal status as a rational creature. This always represents an alignment to idea rather than to fact, and fundamentally is the refinement of creative imagination. The probable origin of any transcendentality or particular psychological identity is in the phenomenon of dreams, where an individual's subsidiary reality exists however ephemerally in a completeness all its own and through which man early in evolution may have had intimation of his broader power of conscious discreteness. Dreaming as merely concomitant with sleep is illusory and has little practical continuation, but with the development of a human culture and of its illimitable divisions of labor the basic inward self-specialization in some doggedly maintained pattern becomes the prime characteristic of the species. Personality at root is a continuance in a cultivated distinctiveness, or is a steadfast adherence to the essentially dream realization of self

far above pure animal instinct or the commonplace conditioning of the unimaginative members of society. Here is the
nascent consistency of selfhood through which the individual
comes most definitely into his own.

The Psychological Trend to Balance

In this first of the four normal procedures in analysis of an
activity-facet in the dynamic horoscopy, and one of the only
two applicable in the nascent consistency of Abraham Lincoln,
the indication is a duplication of the testimony of progressed
Mars to (1) no special overall lean in the lifetime but (2) an
early subperiod of practical dominance that was balanced out
with his defeat in seeking a Senate seat when he re-entered
politics after the earlier debacle of his brief career as representative in Washington. His perhaps not fully realized compulsion toward transcendental achievement, as he remained
always and ever the loner, had its marked instrumentation in
circumstances at this point of balance in his ultimate orientation.

Nonfulcral Indication

PROGRESSED JUPITER IN SEXTILE WITH THE NATAL MOON,
MAY 6, 1831   In this fourth of the four normal procedures in
analysis of an activity-facet in the dynamic horoscopy the indication by progressed Jupiter in the nascent consistency of an
activated endurance through a practical adroitness is testimony
to the importance of Lincoln's settlement at New Salem
almost immediately on coming of age and thereupon striking
out on his own and in that pioneer community creating his
adult status in its earlier dimension. His ingenuity when he
was taking a loaded flatboat for Denton Offutt to New
Orleans on a second visit to that ocean-serving metropolis, in
getting it over the dam at the log-cabin hamlet, was demon-

stration of the uniquely imaginative capacity that characterized his expanding consciousness and enhanced his opportunity
at the moment.

PROGRESSED JUPITER IN TRINE WITH NATAL SATURN, JULY
31, 1855   This indication in the nascent consistency of an
activated concern through an idealistic adroitness corresponds
to the native's defeat in initially seeking a Senate seat in his
return to politics, and to the necessity in consequence to
interpret this as his fundamental lack of inner rapport with
lesser transcendentalities. Actually this second defeat for the
senatorship was further prelude to the almost magical developments precipitating him into the presidency less than six
years later. The potentiality revealed is of self-orientation in
some momentum of truly greater compass or cycle in circumstances.

PROGRESSED JUPITER IN TRINE WITH NATAL NEPTUNE,
JANUARY 29, 1870   The first progression of a particular planet
after decease has no validity in the actual living years of a
native but it does give valuable suggestion of a possible continuing influence as here in the indication in the nascent consistency of an activated acceptance of what would now develop
into the myth-figure role through an idealistic adroitness.
Self-orientation of an immortal or surviving livingness came to
accomplishment through the self-fidelity dramatized for the
nation by the martyrdom.

In summary, the nascent consistency of the native that
gained its principal manifestation in his single-minded struggle
toward a personal recognition established in a definite status
is shown by the practical emphasis of his living years up to the
final decade of his life and then as balanced by an increasing
deep compulsion from within himself to align himself with the

more enduring strands of national destiny. Beginning with his
New Salem days, the general course of circumstances definitely
helped facilitate the accomplishment.

THE NASCENT INTEGRITY

The activity-facet of the expanding dimension of self-consciousness above a purely group-conditioned existence, and
charted in the dynamic horoscopy by progressed Saturn,
reveals the rational efforts of the native to validate whatever
special recognition he might gain or what personal status he
might manage to establish. This means his identification of the
criteria or overall values to which he should attempt to conform in the world of idea in which he finds himself oriented
for better or worse, but in which he yet has every power of
creative judgment to use in bringing his destiny under some
appreciable control. Here is the operation of what (1) becomes
the relatively inexorable as life settles into its pattern but (2)
does not at all necessarily become the blind fate seen by the
early astrologers to be the particular manifestation of the ends
for humanity in general. In a sense their premodern insight
was a deification of time or of continuance in the fundamental
spread of experience. They took their seventh planet to be
the principal creator of the overall cycles or repetitive constants in human affairs through an astrological balance with
the moon in its establishment of cyclic dependabilities in life's
everyday or superficial manifestation, since these two planetary
bodies had closely corresponding periods although of years in
the one case and days in the other. In the more sophisticated
horoscopy of present times an individual's reaction to the outer
and more encompassing norms and meanings in the cyclic
distribution of the cosmic concordance becomes primarily a

matter of keeping his personal standards or values in convenient balance with universal necessity, and his fundamental and effective sensitiveness to the ultimacy in all things is identified as his nascent integrity.

Challenge by Progressed Station

PROGRESSED SATURN STATIONARY TURNING RETROGRADE IN 1838 In this second of the four normal procedures in analysis of an activity-facet in the dynamic horoscopy, and the only one applicable in the nascent integrity of Abraham Lincoln in his lifetime, the indication of essential change in his life requiring a crucial regrasp of experience has suggestive correspondence to his move from New Salem to Springfield and his part in the establishment of the latter and more considerable town as state capital concomitantly with his successful qualification as a lawyer and thus in general his achievement in putting down the real foundations for his career.

Nonfulcral Indication

PROGRESSED SATURN IN CONJUNCTION WITH NATAL SATURN, JULY 31, 1867 The first progression of a particular planet after decease and having no validity in the actual living years of a native, in its indication here of an activated concern through a practical alertness has valuable suggestion of the highly intensified dramatization of a nascent integrity in American democracy represented by the myth figure in process of evolution. In his lifetime, and above all else, Lincoln had demanded immediate validations in experience together with an equitable understanding as a basis for all human relations.

In summary, the nascent integrity of the native in his efforts to realize and express himself in proper orientation with the norms and values that came to be manifest in his destiny and concomitantly to create rational correctives in his own understanding is seen to come to significant focus when he makes the major transition from his earlier and self-discovering manhood while living at New Salem to the foundation for his whole subsequent career when he helped establish Springfield as the capital of Illinois and located his permanent home and legal practice there. Thereupon he began to function in a milieu gradually providing national and ultimately immortal dimension for his self-alignment.

THE NASCENT INDEPENDENCE

The activity-facet of the expanding dimension of self-consciousness above a purely group-conditioned existence, and charted in the dynamic horoscopy by progressed Uranus reveals the objectively personal stage of man's evolution into modern reality. This is a consciously transcendental orientation that was hardly possible in a primitive society with a necessarily provincial approach to everyday circumstances. Here is creative originality in contrast with the simple initiative that always has distinguished man most particularly from the lower orders of life. What is identified in the progressions is the capacity for invention in an expanded self-assertion rather than the practical adaptation to situation under necessity that is the more primitive basis of all conscious existence. Here is individual realization of a divinity or an immutable potency that in the modern age is to be seen filtering down at last into the most humble and least endowed segments of humanity. Individual difference can now be seen becoming a very special element in normal self-realization.

Challenge by Progressed Station

PROGRESSED URANUS STATIONARY TURNING RETROGRADE IN 1811 In this second of the four normal procedures in analysis of an activity-facet in the dynamic horoscopy, and the only one applicable in the nascent independence of Abraham Lincoln, the indication of essential change in the life requiring a crucial regrasp of experience for a child of barely two is significant in the fact that it coincides with the first major progressed aspect or the one that reveals an idealistic and adroit quickening of simple persistence or applied initiative in the natural drive. Thus there is an additional and strong certification of a distinctly single-purposed career irrespective of early gyrations or minor deviations, and a validation for interpreting both the immediate and immortal contribution of the native as grounded in the freedom of soul that found manifestation in his case in (1) the role of loner among his fellows and (2) the melancholy or gestative mood that plagued him on the introspective side.

In summary, the nascent independence of the native that enabled him as the loner in his generation to serve the destiny of his country dramatically unconditioned by prejudice or provincialism and then immortally to continue serving it as the myth figure astrologically is seen to be stamped in the very eccentricity of his make-up virtually from birth.

THE NASCENT RESPONSIBILITY

The activity-facet of the expanding dimension of self-consciousness above a purely group-conditioned existence, and charted in the dynamic horoscopy by progressed Neptune, reveals the subjectively personal stage of man's evolution into modern reality. This is a consciously transcendental orientation or a more broadly refined capacity for recognizing the strands of individualized and historically sharpened potentials in the cosmic totality of things. In effect it is the projection of selfhood to some one or several of these potentials through the responsibility assumed in the contribution to them by some extended manifestation of individual being.

Challenge by Progressed Station

PROGRESSED NEPTUNE STATIONARY TURNING RETROGRADE IN 1834   In this second of the four normal procedures in analysis of an activity-facet in the dynamic horoscopy, and the only one applicable in the nascent responsibility of Abraham Lincoln, the indication of essential change in the life requiring a crucial regrasp of experience has correlation with the general syndrome of events coming to center for him at New Salem and perhaps most particularly with his successful campaign for the Illinois Legislature. This entry into public life became a very actual acceptance of his destiny.

In summary, the nascent responsibility of the native that in its overall acceptance gave him an adequately conscious scope for his destiny is shown brought to issue and shaped by his first election to public office.

THE NASCENT ENLIGHTENMENT

The activity-facet of the expanding dimension of self-consciousness above a purely group-conditioned existence and charted in the dynamic horoscopy by progressed Pluto reveals the essentially impartial or in a sense impersonal stage of man's evolution into a consciously transcendental orientation to the greater and more comprehensive reality becoming available to humanity generally. Here is the capacity for extra-dimensional synthesis by which an individual (1) can consider himself and others simultaneously while yet preserving their distinctiveness and (2) can deal with overall or cosmic ramification of existence through a corresponding unconfused facility. There is no pertinent indication for Abraham Lincoln even as the myth figure.

THE NATURAL INVOLVEMENT

Continuing in the pattern of consideration in an order of logical importance of the elements of self-revelation examined by means of the secondary directions in the dynamic horoscopy, the turn in attention is from the paired activity-facets of (1) the relatively uninvolved basic attitude and natural drive and (2) the more group-oriented quality of selfhood in basic sensitivity and basic excitation and (3) the more rational self-determination in the nascent consistency and nascent integrity on through concern with the transcendental delimitation of man's behavior in terms of (4) nascent independence and nascent responsibility and now of what for present generations at least is a nascent enlightenment on further to (5) the utterly impartial convenience or chance presence in human affairs of general circumstances in their convergence to any immediacy of import. The indicator of this element in the progressions is the moon, and it reveals the short or transitory cycles of experience in distinction from the long or ultimately lifetime ones considered up to this point. Whereas the swiftest of the other nine planets in the extreme case can traverse barely more than three zodiacal signs to chart the living span of a native, the lesser light may circle the whole zodiac some three times in its corresponding indications. In this fact lies the possibility of horoscopic measure for the relative superficialities of conscious existence.

The more immediate eventualities indicated by the progressed moon develop in polar challenge to the ultimate world-facet established and continually confirmed for himself by the native in his own and inescapably individual case, and charted by Saturn. This constant balancing emphasizes the astrological symmetry noted by the ancients and preserved at perhaps a later period in a designation of the planetary hours, and it has been represented from earliest times by the establishment of seven days as the common unit of the week. The lesser light in the dynamic horoscopy identifies a phase of changeless manifestation closely akin to the natural or basic unconditioned drive in what may be described as a specific characteristic and continuing response to the steady overall or general drift of reality, to constitute an activity-facet of natural or equally unconditioned involvement. Every individual at birth acquires a momentum of being that must continue unbrokenly in its own discrete existence if it is to remain a core for the differences that permit the individuality its otherwise infinite ramifications. Man is an event in circumstances fundamentally because of the continuity in his immutable selfhood, and they must pivot around this in any relation with him. The lights as already explained have no retrograde motion to establish the progressed stations that thereupon would identify points of crucial regrasp of experience. The everyday kaleidoscope of events measured by the moon must be constant in a sheer variety, and in that they (1) sustain the illimitability of choice that is the very nature of consciousness because they (2) remain completely impartial relative to what may be chosen or avoided whether from whim or definite purpose.

Interpretation of the lunar directions must therefore recognize the almost paradoxical transiency of every practical application, since they always identify a choice facilitated in some fleeting rapport with chance in the overall matrix of change. This is a necessity of the universal flux, but also a basis for the concomitant cosmic concordance. Here is the ground for the essential principle of astrology, and the consideration is of no more than what proves to be or fails to be of service or value to the native at some given moment. What thus has attention now is actually the activity-facet of his ultimate disjunction, or of the expanding scope in life that must be possible for him at all points in the everyday business of preserving his individuality. Because any psychological trend to either pragmatic or idealistic orientation would be a superficiality difficult to identify with preciseness, or with much profit in understanding, the first procedure in dynamic analysis is here best disregarded. By the same token the fulcral squares show the coming to stress of general circumstances as more an intensification of potentiality in choice than a punctuation of planetary cycle of significance to itself, and in consequence it is better technique to delineate the moon's secondary progressions seriatim rather than in the more formalized fashion found helpful for the slower planets. In the case of Abraham Lincoln the period selected for illustration in these pages is the one of his unusually vital involvement in sheer circumstances, or the eight years from March in 1857 through the assassination on April 14th in 1865.

In summary, attention turns from the analysis of the native's self-revelation in the several basic dimensions of his evolution into his full creative stature and now gives consideration to the general developments in the immediate milieu of his everyday experience as this is charted by the progressed moon. Here in the astrological symmetry noted from the night of time is the factor of daily exigencies in continual if shifting balance with the world-facet he creates and holds for himself under the dynamic indication of Saturn. The lesser light also is seen charting the general course of events as a complementary phase of the unbroken continuity of cosmic concordance already encountered as the core of individual existence and found in its progressed significance through the greater light. The dependable if kaleidoscopic flow of circumstances is delineated in the limitless variety that provides similar balance with the illimitable scope provided for self in its capacity for choice or ability to preserve its individuality. With this activity-facet of ultimate disjunction in life's transiencies the determination of any psychological trend to balance becomes a superficiality not worth much notice, and by the same token the fulcral squares reveal what in practical terms is more intensification than punctuation of eventuality. In consequence the lunar progressions are best interpreted seriatim.

Fulcrum and Nonfulcral Indication

THE PROGRESSED MOON IN CONJUNCTION WITH NATAL MARS, MARCH 30, 1857 The activation facilitated through current affairs of the native's persistence in his own course is a circumstance contributing to a practical alertness of outreach into experience and is astrological testimony to the extraordinary importance to him of the Dred Scott decision. This Supreme Court ruling was delivered on March 6th by the venerable Chief Justice Taney, to the effect that since Negroes could not become citizens the Constitution had no reference to them and that they were property that legally could be held and therefore possession of them must be protected as by necessity under the law of the land. Lincoln made his only public address in 1857 on June 26th in reference to the epochal event and to the slavery stand of Douglas. The issue was joined very definitely as prelude to the Great Debates a year later.

THE PROGRESSED MOON IN SQUARE WITH THE NATAL MOON, MAY 14, 1857 The critical self-mobilization of the native's endurance demanded by exceptional pressure of circumstances in which he had come to be particularly involved has astrological identification at this point through the pivotal development on which the whole political course of affairs will turn ultimately, or the schism in the Democratic Party that paved the way to the presidency for Lincoln. It was on June 15th that the election in Kansas of delegates to frame a state constitution precipitated the personal conflict between Douglas and President James Buchanan.

THE PROGRESSED MOON IN CONJUNCTION WITH NATAL URANUS, MARCH 16, 1858 The activation facilitated through current affairs of the native's release of potentials is a circumstance contributing to a practical alertness to relatively transcendental elements of experience and is astrological testimony to the ultimate significance of his hurried trip to Chicago in February to consult with Norman B. Judd who was chairman of the state's Republican central committee and also of the political letters he wrote throughout the early part of the year as he began to shape his new political course in its expanded dimension.

THE PROGRESSED MOON IN TRINE WITH NATAL MERCURY, APRIL 2, 1858 The activation facilitated through current affairs of the native's aplomb is a circumstance contributing to an idealistic adroitness in the more significant elements of experience and is astrological testimony to the importance of these early 1858 activities and especially as leading to his famous clarification of the issue when on June 16th at Springfield and in application of the Bible dictum probably well known to his hearers he emphasized the impossibility of the house divided or of a nation half slave and half free. This was immediate prelude to the Great Debates that took place from August 21st through October 15th and gave Lincoln his initial national prominence.

THE PROGRESSED MOON IN TRINE WITH NATAL PLUTO, JULY 14, 1858   The activation facilitated through current affairs of the native's probity or the myth-figure potential that is evident only in later significance or afterview is here a matter of idealistic adroitness in ultimate human experience as having its astrological evidence at the actual time in his instinctive move to demand an adequate recognition for himself when in mid-July he challenged Douglas to the debates that would bring it to him.

THE PROGRESSED MOON IN TRINE WITH NATAL JUPITER, JANUARY 19, 1859   The activation facilitated through current affairs of the native's zest for the political battle is a circumstance contributing to the idealistic adroitness of his new projection of himself into experience and is astrological testimony not only to the significance of the ground swell of awakening to his potentialities as a candidate for the presidency but of the efforts of the influential Republican Jesse Fell to get him to supply biographical material for campaign purposes and of others to persuade him to organize a very definite bid for the high office. While he shrugged all this off almost laughingly he yet began to act under the compulsion of it.

THE PROGRESSED MOON IN SQUARE WITH THE NATAL SUN, FEBRUARY 22, 1859   The critical mobilization of the native's strength of character demanded by exceptional pressure of circumstances in which he has come to be particularly involved has astrological identification at this point through his efforts (1) to compensate perhaps psychologically in major part for his two-time defeat now for the Senate and his little-gratifying single term in the House of Representatives and incidentally but importantly (2) to recoup his personal finances after the political drain as in his lecture on this date at Springfield on inventions and discoveries.

THE PROGRESSED MOON IN SEXTILE WITH THE NATAL MOON, MAY 28, 1859   The activation facilitated through current affairs of the native's persistence in his course is a circumstance contributing to the practical adroitness of his basic political moves and is astrological testimony to the importance of his purchase of the *Illinois Staats-Anzeiger* in order to strengthen Republican influence in the state. This was a German-language newspaper published in Springfield, and of the foreign-born in the United States the Germans constituted the largest part and they had the greatest and indeed the most significant influence of all the minorities.

THE PROGRESSED MOON IN CONJUNCTION WITH NATAL SATURN, OCTOBER 21, 1859   The activation facilitated through current affairs of the native's underlying concern over national issues is a circumstance contributing to his practical alertness to the trends and is astrological testimony to what must have been the vital impact in his quickening to his destiny of the abortive slave rebellion launched at Harpers Ferry on October 16th by the insensately fanatical John Brown.

THE PROGRESSED MOON IN CONJUNCTION WITH NATAL NEPTUNE, JANUARY 16, 1860   The activation facilitated through current affairs of the native's acceptance of his destiny however unwittingly is a circumstance contributing to the practical alertness to it at least in potential and is astrological testimony to the significance of the efforts of the Illinois Republicans in obtaining the national convention for Chicago as a neutral place fortuitously removed from the bitter presidential rivalries in the East. At the moment, in thus leading to an honorary nomination of Lincoln for president and a vote for him as a favorite son on a first ballot on home grounds, he probably was aware that a possible future candidacy for the Senate would be strengthened by such a turn in events.

THE PROGRESSED MOON IN TRINE WITH NATAL VENUS, FEBRUARY 6, 1860   The activation facilitated through current affairs of the native's realization or developing sensitivity is a circumstance contributing to an idealistic adroitness in his experience and is astrological testimony to the actuality of arrival at a stage of true statesmanship potentiality as dramatically demonstrated in his Cooper Union address in New York City on February 27th and its actual scholarly approach to the issues of the day in a fashion quite free of either pioneer or Midwest provincialism.

THE PROGRESSED MOON IN SQUARE WITH NATAL MERCURY, APRIL 19, 1860   The critical mobilization of the native's aplomb demanded by exceptional pressure of circumstances in which he had come to be particularly involved has astrological identification at this point through the pivotal event on which national developments now would turn by necessity or his nomination for the presidency by the Republicans on May 18th.

THE PROGRESSED MOON IN SQUARE WITH NATAL PLUTO, AUGUST 2, 1860   The critical mobilization of the native's probity demanded by exceptional pressure of circumstances in which the myth-figure potential had come to be particularly involved, although only in later significance or evident except in afterview, has astrological identification at this point in

(1) the Democratic schism in the broader perspective of the ultimacies to which Lincoln contributed and (2) the emergence of John Hay in becoming his secretary following the nomination and subsequently in a significant political and literary career giving the martyred president a more immediate representation of the developing and immortal principles as a surrogate contributor to them by his preliminary demonstration of their soundness.

THE PROGRESSED MOON IN SQUARE WITH NATAL JUPITER, FEBRUARY 10, 1861   The critical mobilization of the native's zest for his new responsibility demanded by the exceptional pressure of circumstances as he entered the White House has astrological identification in his selection of his cabinet or the unprecedented nomination of virtually his greatest enemies in the Republican Party because of their promise of effective performance and in consequent disregard of personal feelings. Certified by the dynamic horoscopy is the high encompassment of his self-dedication as represented by his desire for overall accomplishment.

THE PROGRESSED MOON IN SEXTILE WITH THE NATAL SUN, MARCH 17, 1861   The activation facilitated through current affairs of the native's inner strength as he projects himself into his ultimate role in life is a circumstance contributing to the practical adroitness that from here on out to the assassination will characterize him almost completely and is astrological testimony to the genuineness of his capacity for decision when on March 29th he ordered the relief of Fort Sumter. To be noted again in significant correspondence with the overall indication of the major secondaries is that these final four years of Lincoln's life are a period in which history is unraveling the tangled skein of problems acquired with the Revolution and building to the inevitabilities of open conflict. Thus the new caretaker in the White House was charged with the custodianship of the enduring and original vision, and not with any positive establishment of some particular course ahead.

THE PROGRESSED MOON IN SEXTILE WITH NATAL MARS, MAY 7, 1861   The activation facilitated through current affairs of the native's persistence in the policies he has adopted is a circumstance contributing to the practical adroitness he needs and is astrological testimony to the significance of his proclamation of martial law on May 10th as the broader step following on his attempt in March to hold Fort Sumter by force if necessary. He was vested with war powers formally on July 22d and the struggle between the irreconcilables was irrevocably under way.

THE PROGRESSED MOON IN SQUARE WITH NATAL VENUS, MARCH 12, 1862   The critical mobilization of the native's realization or refinement of sensitivity demanded by exceptional pressure of circumstances in which he has come to be particularly involved has astrological identification at this point through the balancing of the disaster for the North at the battle of Bull Run the previous July with the check to the naval threat of the Confederacy in the encounter in Virginia's Hampton Roads of the *Monitor* and *Merrimac* on March 9th, and during the month before that in the emergence of Ulysses Simpson Grant with the decisive capture of Forts Henry and Donelson on the Tennessee and Cumberland Rivers in the Midwest. The wisdom of Lincoln's yielding in his strong sense of equity to the British stand in the Trent Affair and the release of the Confederate commissioners to continue their mission to the European powers at the threshold of this year, which at that time had seemed another setback, would soon result in a definitely greater advantage to the Union cause.

THE PROGRESSED MOON IN SEXTILE WITH NATAL URANUS, MAY 8, 1862   The activation facilitated through current affairs of the native's release of his enduring potentials is a circumstance contributing to the practical adroitness he needs and is astrological testimony to the importance of the occupation on April 26th of New Orleans and thus the loss to the Confederacy of its largest seaport in growing certification of the inevitabilities even if it meant no appreciable speeding of the end. A major objective was to open the Mississippi River and cut the Confederacy off from its western supplies, but the dynamic horoscopy identifies a more vital matter of bringing control completely to center as first marked by the success of Lincoln in relieving the immensely popular General John Charles Fremont from inept command at St. Louis without dangerous repercussions six months before and now as he began assuming charge of the military operations in the lack of otherwise adequately competent and available leadership.

THE PROGRESSED MOON IN SEXTILE WITH NATAL MERCURY, MAY 25, 1862   The activation facilitated through current affairs of the native's aplomb or ability to hold firm in the sheer essence of himself in crisis is a circumstance contributing to the practical adroitness especially characterizing his achievement in the White House and is astrological testimony to his military competence in the plan he laid down on May 24th at one of the times the safety of Washington was threatened and when it was the self-willed Frémont who while now in command in West Virginia was responsible for the failure in its execution.

THE PROGRESSED MOON IN SEXTILE WITH NATAL PLUTO, SEPTEMBER 11, 1862   The activation facilitated through current affairs of the native's probity or the myth-figure potential that is evident only in later significance or afterview is here a matter of practical adroitness in ultimate human experience as having its astrological evidence at the actual time in his preliminary emancipation proclamation issued on September 22d.

THE PROGRESSED MOON IN SEXTILE WITH NATAL JUPITER, MARCH 31, 1863 The activation facilitated through current affairs of the native's zest in pursuing his course is a circumstance contributing to the practical adroitness of act and decision and is astrological testimony to the successful manifestation of its solid independence by the nation as a promise for its future. Thus the offer of the French to mediate on February 3d was rebuffed, and on April 5th the building and equipping of Confederate raiders for their highly successful operation on the high seas was protested to the British although this had no immediate result.

THE PROGRESSED MOON IN SQUARE WITH NATAL MARS, JUNE 28, 1863 The critical mobilization of the native's persistence in his course demanded by exceptional pressure of circumstances in which he has come to be particularly involved has astrological identification at this point in the repulse of the Confederates at Gettysburg in the decisive battle of the war, together with the fall of Vicksburg to General Grant at almost the same moment in the first days of July to mark the vital turn in events.

THE PROGRESSED MOON IN CONJUNCTION WITH THE NATAL MOON, AUGUST 16, 1863 The activation facilitated through current affairs of the native's endurance in maintaining his course is a circumstance contributing to a practical alertness to the general trends in his experience and is astrological testimony to the historical importance of the political letter he wrote on August 26th to be read in lieu of the impossibility of his appearance on the election platform and known as his "last stump speech." In reply to bitter attacks and uncompromising antiwar efforts, it emphasizes the man as against the figure-in-office in this one instance in the lunar progressions for the White House period and dramatizes the measure of actual support that Lincoln was able to command from a public weary and suffering under the strain and cost of the struggle. It is striking prelude to the myth potential, and in the contemporary scene it was reflected in the surprising victories in the off-year elections in key states of the North.

THE PROGRESSED MOON IN SEXTILE WITH NATAL SATURN, JANUARY 19, 1864   The activation facilitated through current affairs of the native's underlying concern for the Union is a circumstance contributing to a practical adroitness in ordering military affairs effectively at long last and is astrological testimony to the significance of the revival of the grade of lieutenant general that only George Washington actively and Winfield Scott by brevet had enjoyed and the appointment of General Grant to it immediately after the authorization by Congress on February 22d.

The Role of General Grant

The ultimate importance of Ulysses Simpson Grant to the President in the days when the dramatic career comes to climax with assassination, and then in time with the emergence of a myth figure, suggests the value of supplementation for the progressive analysis through the horoscopic comparison that reveals potentials of active co-operation in living performance whenever these exist. There are two planetary cross ties in this instance and in the case of both the initiative or essential dominance rests with the elected civilian administrator rather than with the military man, but in that fact they show the extent to which the latter in terms of accomplishment could be an effective instrument for the former. The sun activation of Mars by opposition in the one detail of the dynamic mutuality indicates the idealistic persistence provided by the new commander in chief of all the armies as a climactic channelship for Lincoln's natural drive. The Jupiter quickening of Venus by conjunction in the other detail is testimony to the practical realization of an illimitable backing in pursuit of the envisioned ends that enabled Grant to complete his task in the immediate justification of the ultimately quite transcendental consistency of the country's chief executive.

Thus the great value of General Grant was his ability to maintain the pressure on the enemy at any and all cost. As the Confederacy weakened, the Southern forces had to surrender the initiative but they could hardly be expected not to expend themselves with continuing courage and faith in defense if not otherwise. The new man in command for the North reached the point where the price of forcing the firmly entrenched Confederates around Richmond became more than he could pay, or the free states in the light of the mounting casualties would tolerate much longer, but by forcing the struggle elsewhere without pause and through the unremitting attrition in all directions the South was brought to surrender at almost the last moment before the President might have been defeated for re-election. The role of the general in broad perspective would seem to be to provide the final and literal demonstration of the depths to which issues of the magnitude of human slavery must be carried if people generally are to learn the lessons that history at the best can teach. Had the Civil War ended early and easily, no matter which side was the winner, the sole gain might have been no more than a shuffling of the cards of destiny for a further deal of perhaps much pain but again little ultimate accomplishment.

THE PROGRESSED MOON IN SEXTILE WITH NATAL NEPTUNE, APRIL 24, 1864   The activation facilitated through current affairs of the native's acceptance of the price of the decisive move to final victory now under the direction of Grant is a circumstance contributing to the practical adroitness in the conduct of the war and is astrological testimony to the need for orientation in greater overall realities for progress on the lesser levels. With casualties mounting with the Battle of the Wilderness opening on May 4th the optimism of the North turned to resentment, and the degree of such revolt against the war was now the basic Confederate hope, but Lincoln stood firm in his acceptance of the necessary actualities and this if generally unappreciated was yet the corresponding hope of the North.

THE PROGRESSED MOON IN SEXTILE WITH NATAL VENUS, MAY 17, 1864   The activation facilitated through current affairs of the native's realization or developing immortal sensitivity is a circumstance contributing to his continuing practical adroitness and it had its probably great encouragement when in the national Republican convention in Baltimore on June 7th he was renominated for the presidency very decisively and in a period when a second term for a president was not common even for an incumbent.

THE PROGRESSED MOON IN SQUARE WITH NATAL URANUS, JULY 15, 1864   The critical mobilization of the native's release of potentials demanded by exceptional pressure of

circumstances in which he has come to be particularly
involved has astrological identification at this point through
his continuing firmness in adhering to the course embodying
the potentials that build to the myth figure and that has its
final and perhaps most spectacular challenge through the
uproar following his call on July 19th for half a million men
to be drafted in less than two months and the desperate but
nearly successful threat to Washington by the Confederate's
Stephen Early that had its climax on the 11th.

THE PROGRESSED MOON IN CONJUNCTION WITH THE NATAL
SUN, JULY 29, 1865   The first aspect of a particular progressed planet after decease has no validity in the actual living
years of a native but it may give valuable suggestion of any
possible continuing influence, and the indication here of an
activated fundamental strength through a practical alertness
in the natural involvement is suggestive of the effectively
simple insemination of circumstances by the myth figure to
come.

In summary, the secondary directions of the moon for the
final eight years of the native's life reveal a process of increasing involvement in the political circumstances through which
the slavery issue was coming to inevitable crisis. Challenged by
the tragic developments in Kansas, he was led to cross swords
with Stephen Douglas and through the ensuing debates he
gained national prominence. Defeated at the time for the
Senate, where he had hoped to have a chance to get into the
fight to limit the spread of slave territory, he intensified his
interest and activity in politics with his eye possibly on a later
try for a seat in the upper house of Congress. There were
many however who saw presidential possibilities for him in the
Republican Party, and as neutral among clashing factions he

was nominated and because of the schism among the Democrats for which Douglas was responsible he then was elected. He entered the White House on a program of preserving the Union at all costs and by force if necessary. For the four war years he struggled with an almost irresistible sweep of ineptitude, but gradually he got the reins in his hands and then delegated responsibility effectively and with unwavering adroitness brought the North to victory and in that established the young nation as indisputably a world power. The lunar progressions chart the key events in circumstances that facilitate these results.

THE TRANSITS

In the presentation of the dynamic horoscopy in these pages as a comprehensive predictive method the turn in attention from the activity-facets of the all-important secondary directions is first of all to the transits. This is not because they stand next in value, when it comes to charting the progress of life, but because they provide a particularly significant buttressing for the fundamental progressive interpretation and it is a simple matter to apply them. They consist of the geocentric planetary movements and configurations actually found in the heavens at any given time, in contrast with the motion or relationship that in the directional systems is wholly symbolical in its time measure. This fact of literal celestial position in a present moment may create the illusion of greater reality in what is indicated, but the fallacy of any such conclusion follows from a failure to take into account the extent of logical remove from the nativity and its dynamic evolution in progression or to hold to the principle of immediacy or relevance on which all sound astrological analysis must be based. Unhappily the popularized astrology that often ends up in a slipshod fortunetelling is very largely oriented in this area of horoscopic indication since (1) virtually no calculations are required once the nativity is established and (2) there are enough factors not only available to fit almost any conceivable conclusion but to be brought to such a superficially pat application with a very deceptive ease. While a blind intuition may

119

seem to be well served, by the same token a needless if unrealized bewilderment may preclude the well-reasoned deduction that alone can contribute consistently and reliably to a native's self-fulfillment.

Proliferation to Infinity

The transits actually can proliferate to an utter dilution of significance. The moon in not much more than a lunar month actually makes eight major longitudinal aspects in the heavens with each of the nine other planetary bodies, and also in every separate horoscope in the course of the circuit the similar but symbolical relations with all ten including itself when in an individual chart the ten are given natal fixity in the terms of which they may be quickened in dynamic interpretation. The concomitant case with the sun and its two closest satellites is about the same during a span of twelve months. The slower significators take increasingly longer time for their zodiacal circling but their more scattered contribution is far from inconsiderable. Additionally meanwhile there are minor aspects that fragment the circle on toward infinity and that may be taken into account, and an appreciable number of them are in common use. Also there are horoscopic elements often given planetary characteristics, as parts or nodes on the one hand and the cusps of signs in the zodiac and of houses in the nativity on the other. Actually the mere presence of any indicator in sign or house of transit may seem to be quite significant, especially in connection with the ingress. Thus very obviously the consideration must be narrowed to escape hopeless enmeshment in the jungle of ramification, and to facilitate the uncomplicated and sound ordering of the mind that is vital for any genuine competence or practical reliability.

What must be realized is that the transits of all the schemes of indication in progressive analysis have the least dependence on or modification by factors other than themselves. Although they are charted in geocentric perspective their movements in general are quite devoid of relation to the individual nativity except in the particular instance of their relatively casual or passing coincidence with the natal planetary positions by varying aspect that gives them their common signification, and this often is too undistinctive for much interpretative value. Any marked testimony of practical significance must result from an intensification of the earth's effect in the heavens since the terrestrial globe after all is the ground of tangible conscious existence. Retrogradation in the case of the planets capable of it is an example of the heightened possibility of pertinent testimony, and with the lights the phases of the moon gain special importance since the latter of these two bodies is an actual satellite of the earth. Thus in the transits in the dynamic horoscopy the most reliable procedure is to restrict consideration to the stations on the one hand and the lunations on the other. In respect to the latter, except perhaps in dealing with the special refinement of circumstances at some important point, the lunation is best not taken into account unless it is a solar eclipse.

When a station or solar eclipse in the transits occurs either at or opposite the place of a natal planet in the zodiac, a quickening of a particular potential of the nativity under consideration is indicated and interpretation is thereupon much the same as in the secondary directions. Because of the fact that in a sense divergent zodiacal planes are involved in transit indication relative to a natal chart, there is possibility of distortion in the geometric or true aspect as well as the additional remove in relationship and in consequence here as in the dynamic comparison of horoscopes the conjunction and opposition alone are considered significantly effective. No great time orb should be allowed in any instance, and the spatial or zodiacal orb should be limited at all times to sixty minutes of arc.

In summary, the transits are best considered with the secondary directions, although not ranking next to them in importance. They are often overemphasized in popular employment, since an endless proliferation of their possibility permits neat indication for almost any event. To avoid any encouragement of superficial fortunetelling, or any lean on blind intuition rather than forming sound and well-reasoned conclusions through strictly astrological means, the consideration is narrowed in this text to phenomena that occur with the least independence of the earth's influence in the celestial mechanism and therefore are most likely to provide reliable signification. This means most specifically the transit stations, the ordinary lunations and the solar eclipses all as employed in conjunction or opposition only and with no orb ever greater than sixty minutes of arc.

The Transit Stations

The transiting stations involving the planets other than the lights are primarily significant in the quickening of a native's more dynamic or overt activity, and for example in the life of Abraham Lincoln they are best taken in the case of the fifteen that became pertinent in the period of his definite establishment of himself in his ultimate destiny.

TRANSITING MERCURY STATIONARY GOING DIRECT IN OPPOSITION WITH NATAL NEPTUNE, JUNE 14, 1857 This station, indicating the critical regrasp of experience facilitated through current ultimacies of general development, identifies the importance to the native of the June 15th election in Kansas. It was the literal although remote precipitant of his new political career through a quickened acceptance of responsibility in basic attitude.

TRANSITING NEPTUNE STATIONARY GOING RETROGRADE IN CONJUNCTION WITH NATAL JUPITER, JUNE 29, 1857 This station, indicating the critical regrasp of experience facilitated through current ultimacies of general development, identifies the importance of the native's only political speech in this year on June 26th. It was his quickened zest in nascent responsibility as he began the immediate or actual formulation of his broader course ahead.

TRANSITING MARS STATIONARY GOING RETROGRADE IN CONJUNCTION WITH NATAL SATURN, APRIL 11, 1858 This station, indicating the critical regrasp of experience facilitated through current ultimacies of general development, identifies the importance of his lifelong loyalties at least in essence when the native dropped everything to defend a wild youth who had sprung from old New Salem ties and was to be tried for murder on May 7th. It was immediate quickening of exceptional concern in basic excitation.

TRANSITING URANUS STATIONARY GOING RETROGRADE IN OPPOSITION WITH NATAL SATURN, SEPTEMBER 13, 1858 This station, indicating the critical regrasp of experience facilitated through current ultimacies of general development, identifies the importance of the Great Debates with Stephen Douglas from mid-August to mid-October. There was the long range and dramatic release of genuinely universal potentials through the quickened concern in nascent independence.

TRANSITING MERCURY STATIONARY GOING DIRECT IN OPPOSITION WITH NATAL MARS, MAY 6, 1859 This station, indicating the critical regrasp of experience facilitated through current ultimacies of general development, identifies the importance at least to Lincoln of his purchase of the *Illinois Staats-Anzeiger* on May 30th. Whatever the value of this as a move it at least charts some long-range quickening in basic attitude of fundamental persistence.

TRANSITING URANUS STATIONARY GOING DIRECT IN OPPOSITION WITH NATAL SATURN, FEBRUARY 14, 1860 This station, indicating the critical regrasp of experience facilitated through current ultimacies of general development, identifies the importance of the native's epochal address at Cooper Union in New York on February 27th. In long-range impact this proved dramatic demonstration of his instinctive scholarship and statesmanly stature in the sophisticated East through the deeper concern quickened in nascent independence.

TRANSITING MERCURY STATIONARY GOING DIRECT IN CONJUNCTION WITH NATAL VENUS, APRIL 17, 1860 This station, indicating the critical regrasp of experience facilitated through current ultimacies of general development, identifies the importance of Lincoln's nomination for the presidency on May 18th. It was immediate quickening of realization through his basic attitude of the role to be played.

TRANSITING SATURN STATIONARY GOING RETROGRADE IN OPPOSITION WITH NATAL MERCURY, DECEMBER 21, 1860 This station, indicating the critical regrasp of experience facilitated through current ultimacies of general development, identifies the importance of Lincoln's fidelity to his personal roots at core as probably demonstrated over and over again in the month of preparation for the move to Washington. Especially characteristic if by very wide time orb was the considerable side trip down into Coles County to visit his beloved stepmother for a last time on January 31st, and here revealing an aplomb quickened for long range potential in nascent integrity.

TRANSITING SATURN STATIONARY GOING RETROGRADE IN OPPOSITION WITH NATAL JUPITER, JANUARY 1, 1862 This station, indicating the critical regrasp of experience facilitated through current ultimacies of general development, identifies the importance of Lincoln's replacement of Simon Cameron by Edwin M. Stanton in the war department on January 12th. This elimination of inefficiency and corruption in high administrative circles reveals the long-range encouragement of real zest in public service through its quickening in the nascent integrity.

TRANSITING VENUS STATIONARY GOING RETROGRADE IN CONJUNCTION WITH NATAL PLUTO, FEBRUARY 5, 1862 This station, indicating the critical regrasp of experience facilitated through current ultimacies of general development, identifies the importance of the fall of Fort Henry on the Tennessee River to the Union forces on February 6th but only with particular significance in the afterview of special dimension in connection with the myth-figure potential. The immediate quickening of immortal probity in the basic sensitivity was through the early emergence of competent generalship that while present as yet could not be enlisted in overall terms.

TRANSITING MERCURY STATIONARY GOING RETROGRADE IN CONJUNCTION WITH NATAL PLUTO, FEBRUARY 17, 1862 This station, indicating the critical regrasp of experience facilitated through the current ultimacies of general development, identifies the importance of the fall of Fort Donelson on the nearby Cumberland River to the Union forces on February 16th but again only with particular significance in the afterview of special dimension in connection with the myth-figure potential. The immediate quickening of immortal probity in basic attitude was repetitive indication of the early emergence of the military competence that could not yet be enlisted in the needed broader compass.

TRANSITING MARS STATIONARY GOING DIRECT IN CONJUNCTION WITH NATAL VENUS, NOVEMBER 7, 1862   This station, indicating the critical regrasp of experience facilitated through current ultimacies of general development, identifies the importance of the final removal of General McClellan from his command on this date. His failure to exploit the Union advantage after the pivotal battle of Antietam was immediate quickening of Lincoln's realization in basic excitation as the fortunes of war showed the possibility of a real turn at last.

TRANSITING MERCURY STATIONARY GOING RETROGRADE IN CONJUNCTION WITH NATAL MARS, SEPTEMBER 30, 1863   This station, indicating the critical regrasp of experience facilitated through current ultimacies of general development, identifies the importance of Lincoln's firm diplomacy following the Union victories at Vicksburg and Gettysburg in July. It was in an immediate persistence quickened in the basic attitude that brought the British government finally in October to seize the Confederate privateers building or being equipped in England to join in the near total destruction of the American merchant marine and thereupon bring the French to take similar action.

TRANSITING MERCURY STATIONARY GOING RETROGRADE IN OPPOSITION WITH NATAL NEPTUNE, MAY 12, 1864   This station, indicating the critical regrasp of experience facilitated through current ultimacies of general development, identifies the importance of the native's renomination for the presidency on June 8th. What had threatened to become repudiation by a war-weary public is seen countered in the long-range quickened acceptance in basic attitude.

TRANSITING NEPTUNE STATIONARY GOING RETROGRADE IN CONJUNCTION WITH NATAL VENUS, JULY 12, 1864   This station, indicating the critical regrasp of experience facilitated through current ultimacies of general development, identifies the importance of Lincoln's call on July 18th for an additional half million men to be drafted into military service. This immediate quickening of realization in nascent responsibility is the final regrasp of current ultimacies of circumstances in their cradling of his destiny.

In summary, the transiting planetary stations that quickened natal planets in the horoscope of Abraham Lincoln during the eight-odd years of his definite self-establishment in his destiny identify the points where the general circumstances of the world around him facilitated his development into immortal stature. Thus particularly important were the elections in Kansas bringing the slavery issue to fresh crisis, the Great Debates with Stephen Douglas that first gained him national attention, his Cooper Union address that revealed his real caliber to the sophisticated East, his nomination for the presidency by the Republicans, and then after inauguration the proving of his mettle when on the one hand he removed such individuals from office as General McClellan and War Secretary Simon Cameron and on the other dealt in adequate firmness with the British and French governments.

The Transit Lunations

The transiting lunations involving the lights rather than the eight other planets are primarily significant through a stimulation of the native's everyday functioning during the current and rhythmic punctuation of everyday circumstances when this may have particular impact on his individuality.

TRANSIT LUNATION IN OPPOSITION WITH NATAL SATURN,

MAY 23, 1857   The particular stimulation of experience in long-range terms indicated by this lunation is a quickening through the pulse of circumstances of the native's general concern, and is astrological testimony to the significance of the Kansas developments in the inauguration of the second great and immortally tinctured period of his life.

These ordinary lunations are seldom of sufficient import to warrant consideration, and may well be ignored in normal practice. This single illustration thus serves all purposes of the present text. But when a lunation is a solar eclipse it becomes quite a different story or a matter of marked intensification, and all fifteen of these natal impacts during Lincoln's lifetime can be given attention to advantage.

The Solar Eclipses

SOLAR ECLIPSE IN CONJUNCTION WITH THE NATAL SUN, FEBRUARY 12, 1812   The particular intensification of experience in immediate fashion indicated by this eclipse in a quickening of the native's strength of purpose even at three years of age through the current developments in everyday affairs is astrological testimony to the early significance of the refinement of his character in the tangible rigors of pioneer life.

SOLAR ECLIPSE IN CONJUNCTION WITH NATAL JUPITER, MARCH 13, 1812   The particular intensification of experience in immediate fashion indicated by this eclipse in a quickening of the native's zest or eagerness of response to the sheer challenge of living through the kaleidoscopic flow of everyday affairs is astrological testimony to the high significance of mere existence to him from the very start.

SOLAR ECLIPSE IN CONJUNCTION WITH NATAL MARS, OCTOBER 19, 1819   The particular intensification of experience in immediate fashion indicated by this eclipse in a quickening of the native's persistence in full sheer self-expression of himself even in his eleventh year is astrological testimony to the extremely fortuitous contribution to his emerging individuality when his father married Sarah Bush Johnston on December 2d and brought his new and in his own terms his angel mother into his life.

SOLAR ECLIPSE IN OPPOSITION WITH NATAL PLUTO, SEPTEMBER 7, 1820 The particular intensification of experience in long-range terms indicated by this eclipse is effective only in myth-figure delimitation or in afterview but the more symbolical activation of the native's probity is important testimony to the significance of the Missouri Compromise gaining passage under the leadership of Henry Clay early in this year.

SOLAR ECLIPSE IN OPPOSITION WITH THE NATAL SUN, AUGUST 16, 1822 The particular intensification of experience in long-range terms indicated by this eclipse in a quickening of the native's strength of purpose through the coming of the rather irresponsible John Hanks for his stay with the Lincolns in the Indiana period is astrological testimony to that individual's influence in encouraging big ideas in the mind of the boy now in his fourteenth year.

SOLAR ECLIPSE IN CONJUNCTION WITH NATAL NEPTUNE, NOVEMBER 29, 1826 The particular intensification of experience in immediate fashion indicated by this eclipse in a quickening of the native's acceptance of his pattern of life through such activities as working as farm hand and ferry helper for James Taylor at the mouth of Anderson Creek on the Ohio River is astrological testimony to the value of the thirteen-odd Indiana years despite the difficulty in pinpointing or identifying their major events.

SOLAR ECLIPSE IN CONJUNCTION WITH NATAL MARS, OCTO-

BER 20, 1827   The particular intensification of experience in immediate fashion indicated by this eclipse in a quickening of the native's persistence in his course of outramifying establishment of himself in life through such larger opportunity as taking a flatboat of produce to New Orleans and is further astrological testimony to the fruitfulness of the Indiana period on the Ohio River.

SOLAR ECLIPSE IN CONJUNCTION WITH THE NATAL SUN, FEBRUARY 12, 1831   The particular intensification of experience in immediate fashion indicated by this eclipse in a quickening of the native's strength of purpose through the demonstration in due course of his resourcefulness in mid-April in getting another flatboat bound for New Orleans over a dam at New Salem in Illinois and is astrological testimony to the importance of his consequent location in that hamlet now that he was of age and wholly on his own.

SOLAR ECLIPSE IN OPPOSITION WITH NATAL PLUTO, SEPTEMBER 7, 1839   The particular intensification of contribution in long-range terms through current developments to the ultimate myth figure is the establishment of Springfield as state capital as in large fashion a consequence of Lincoln's very individual effort, together with his acceptance in the local aristocracy in a facilitation of his ultimately almost transcendental tie with Mary Todd.

SOLAR ECLIPSE IN CONJUNCTION WITH NATAL PLUTO, MARCH 4, 1840   The particular intensification of contribution in immediate fashion through current developments to the ultimate myth figure is Lincoln's ripening acquaintance with Mary Todd leading to their formal engagement by the end of this year. Thus the event of this tie is shown astrologically to be ultimately more the combination of special symbols than mere personalities or a blending of significant endowments.

SOLAR ECLIPSE IN OPPOSITION WITH THE NATAL SUN, AUGUST 16, 1841   The particular intensification of experience in long-range terms indicated by this eclipse is a quickening of the native's strength of purpose through his several years of law partnership with Stephen Logan, beginning in mid-May, and is astrological testimony to the importance of the strict drill in legal practice that now would begin a vital new chapter in self-refinement as well as self-orientation in Springfield life.

SOLAR ECLIPSE IN OPPOSITION WITH NATAL MARS, APRIL 15, 1847   The particular intensification of experience in long-range terms indicated by this eclipse is a quickening of the native's persistence in his course through the opportunities he had as Congressman-elect to make contacts with leaders of national reputation, and is astrological testimony to the importance of the four-day trip he made by stage coach to Chicago in July to attend a convention and serve this end.

SOLAR ECLIPSE IN CONJUNCTION WITH NATAL PLUTO, MARCH 5, 1848   The particular intensification of experience in immediate fashion indicated by this eclipse is effective only in myth-figure delimitation or in afterview, but strangely curious is the fact that Mary Lincoln in boredom with Washington took the boys and returned to her family's house in Kentucky at this moment of key disintegration in the earlier and provincial chapter of the native's political ambitions and activities. Thus he was left alone in his futile tilting over the national war guilt in the Mexican conflict, since astrologically the strain for probity was a prematurely unfolding destiny.

SOLAR ECLIPSE IN CONJUNCTION WITH THE NATAL SUN, FEBRUARY 12, 1850   The particular intensification of experience in immediate fashion indicated by this eclipse is a quickening of the native's strength of purpose through the success of Henry Clay in gaining congressional acceptance of his compromise resolutions at this time, and thus is astrological testimony to the exceptional and pragmatically if not obviously effective closeness of link between the Great Pacificator and the rising Illinois statesman now at the threshold of his second and immortal chapter of life and career.

SOLAR ECLIPSE IN OPPOSITION WITH NATAL PLUTO, SEPTEMBER 7, 1858   The particular intensification of experience in long-range terms indicated by this eclipse is effective only in myth-figure delimitation or in afterview, but the quickening of the native's immortal probity is important testimony to the actually transcendental nature and implication of the Great Debates between Stephen Douglas and himself even as at the particular time and in their sharpening of the sincere convictions of the two determinedly honest men they helped clear the air in an era of intellectual confusions.

In summary, the transiting solar eclipses that quickened natal planets in the horoscope of Abraham Lincoln during his life identify the occasion and nature of definite intensifications of his everyday affairs through the tidal surges of general circumstances. At the start they reveal unusual challenge to his very awareness of existence and the rewards it may have for him. They verify the rightness of the primacy he gave to but two women in his life, or his stepmother and wife, and of the opportunities stemming from the river commerce in the Indiana years and his settlement at New Salem as well as the restlessness of the Hanks side of his heritage. Springfield is certified in its importance for him in two disparate chapters of his development, and the utterly intangible and psychological blood tie with Henry Clay has the strongest of validations.

LIFE RECAPITULATION

In the presentation of the dynamic horoscopy in these pages the turn in attention, after the consideration of the transits, is to a technique somewhat allied to them because it employs the transiting position rather than natal place and symbolical progression of the planets. The cyclic charts complete the comprehensive method recommended for the normal course of predictive analysis. The principle of concordance or concomitance, or the characteristic of all phenomena in their natural order to repeat or reduplicate themselves in their maintenance of the ultimate structure of reality, is the ground for these special horoscopes of life recapitulation. They reveal the rhythmic reinforcement of personal experience in circumstances through variation or variety in chance or choice, and by diminishing dimension of involvement through (1) the annual return of the sun to its place at birth where it indicates the current state of affairs with the individuality and (2) the moon's monthly re-emphasis of its natal position where it correspondingly defines the course of things in the more intimate nature of relation in self-unfoldment and (3) the ascendant's daily re-establishment of the distinctive horizon of selfhood in the general and kaleidoscopic shift of events to which some superficial adjustment must be made continually. Of these subsidiary astrological recapitulations the solar return can be of exceptional significance, and on the whole it ranks next in importance to the secondary directions.

SOLAR RETURN, WASHINGTON, D.C., FEBRUARY 11, 1861, 10:46 P.M. This supplementary horoscope, that does not necessarily coincide with the birthday, is interpreted in the same manner as the natal wheel but with much more attention to the houses in an approach to the specificity of horary astrology since under the principle of immediacy or relevance there is a one-remove toward the circumstances particularly revealed by the transits and that element of disjunction must of necessity be taken into account. Thus the indications of this subsidiary chart should never be progressed because under the governing law of selectivity or efficiency the recourse to progressions in what in no fashion is a nativity would be a calculation of wholly minor significations. What is brought out by repetition or recapitulation is not the time and nature of potential eventualities, which is entirely the concern of the directional systems and the transits, but rather is the quality of event likely to characterize the total of a fixed span of experience. As must be kept in mind at all points, the distinctly different techniques of character and performance analysis can never be combined with each other to any effective advantage.

The particular solar return selected for illustration in Lincoln's career embraces his assumption of the presidency, and to be noted at once is the significant emphasis of the angles by the positions of planets within sixty minutes of arc in orb on the cusps of the fourth and seventh. The first house is empty, in dramatic confirmation of the strangely impartial course at core in his fulfillment of his immediate destiny in the White House, and the elevated Jupiter dignified through standing alone in the tenth thus occupied in the important contrast with the first is testimony to his high dedication in his fundamental

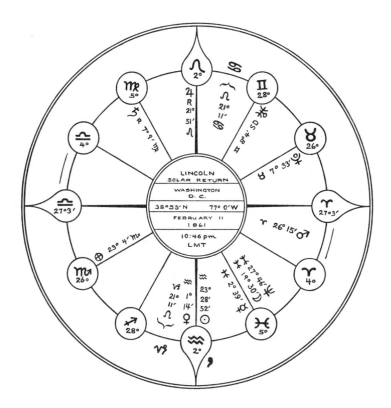

self-projection into experience. The pronounced skew of the seesaw temperament is indication of the exceptional individuality necessary at this point in his development if he is to grasp the explosive national situation, and the natal focus in self-act for this birthday year through the T cross in common signs is important clue through the focal Uranus to the possible release of human values and the better insemination of socioeconomic relations in the country at large for which as president he now will be horoscopic representative. The situation of Jupiter and Saturn apart from all the other planets in the seesaw typing is special emphasis of motivation as a factor of the balance now brought into the national administration, or is a special suggestion of the unusual moral nature of his role as chief of state and potential myth figure.

The Progressed Horoscope

A variant method for delineating the birthday year and one that has long been employed in astrological practice is the progressed horoscope. This is created by the hour and minute of birth taken on each proper following day in representation of the corresponding annual span of life, and it is a means for extending the secondary directions to a greater specificity. Since it charts the progression of the sidereal time of the natal wheel it in effect provides houses for the progressed sun, or the planet that establishes the terrestrial clock measure, and in consequence it has a subsidiary and superficial effectiveness akin to the popular sunscopes in natal analysis. Unfortunately however an undue importance is given to this particular technique in progressions because of a well-entrenched fallacy, or the assumption that any given moment in general duration is a sort of absolute reality in its own right, so that at say seven-thirteen in the morning when a native is born is ipso facto of significance in every following anniversary he may manage to reach. Modern science has been plagued by this obsession of the human mind with the supposed abstract absolutes of the temporal and spatial delimitations that while vital in virtually all practical thought and decision are yet no more than measurement and a basis of consciousness and thereupon a tool of judgment. The trained thinker is no longer worried over any necessity to find space filled with an all-pervasive something,

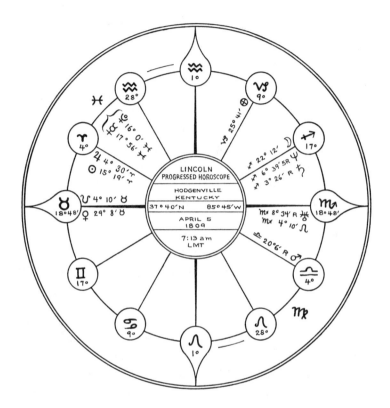

LINCOLN
PROGRESSED HOROSCOPE

HODGENVILLE
KENTUCKY
37° 40′N   85° 45′W

APRIL 5
1809

7:13 am
LMT

or to explain the lacuna of sleep as a species of vacuum. What primarily is significant in astrology in the yearly recapitulation of a person's own special experience is the return of the sun to its starting point in establishing his overall pattern and not the moment it happened to be there at the beginning of conscious existence.

An examination of Abraham Lincoln's progressed horoscope for the period embracing his assumption of his presidential responsibilities provides a convenient demonstration of the point that must be made here. Thus the first house has emphasis over the tenth in reverse of the situation in the solar return, and this suggests that the presidency is the culmination of personal ambition rather than the gain of public trust. However true this was in a sense it was not the real point in the development. The seesaw temperamental typing is repeated to emphasize the bridging nature of the new role, but the skew or indication of highly original expression is missing. A trigger configuration provides the dynamic focus in everyday activity as an application of mind to achieve ends and bring applause in place of the release of highly humanitarian potentials revealed in the corresponding chart for the repetitive buttressing of the natal sun. By and large the revelation of the native on the more superficial level is as the mere politician as against the statesman. What is lacking is the analysis in depth by which astrology has its ultimate justification.

LUNAR RETURN, SPRINGFIELD, ILLINOIS, FEBRUARY 7, 1861, 4:38 P.M.   This supplementary horoscope established by the return of the moon to its natal place by transit is indication of the astrological month of pertinence at any given point of the native's particularized involvement in current circumstances and is in correspondence to the basic horoscopic nature of the lesser as against the greater light. Interpretation is by natal rules with the modification already put down for the solar return, and consideration properly is of persons or things in representation of the factor of the generalized otherness in experience or of their definite mirroring at all times of the fundamental individuality in some immediately pertinent respect. Embraced in the lunar period from February 7th into March 6th in 1861 was Lincoln's final move of residence

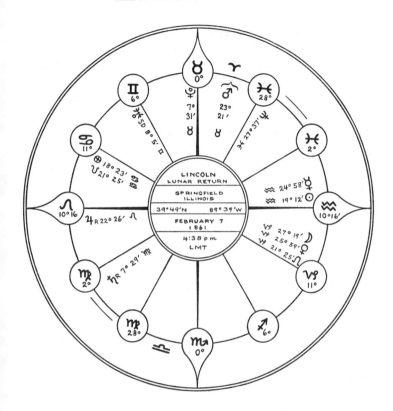

from Springfield to Washington and his inauguration as president. Marking the particularly psychological potential of this epochal point of transition in his life is Jupiter rising in solitary dignity in the first house and thus revealing the extraordinary impact of inwardness as perhaps most evident throughout his life in the mysterious melancholy. The unemphasized tenth angle is further stress of his nature as the loner when it came to this more psychological adjustment. The particular stress of the ninth cusp by Neptune, and the only case of such cusp emphasis, dramatizes his exceptionally conscious conception of his high responsibility as just about the whole of all matters for him in his emotional or personality expression for these few weeks. The lights in their curious special embrace of the seventh angle show an unusual strengthening by circumstances of the striking opportunity now brought to him.

DIURNAL RETURN, SPRINGFIELD, ILLINOIS, FEBRUARY 11, 1861, 7:15 A.M.   This supplementary horoscope established by the return of the ascendant to its natal place carries predictive indication to perhaps its greatest possible immediate specificity, and delineates the current elements of common reality in their sustainment of everyday experience. The February 11th selected for illustration saw Lincoln boarding the train for his final trip to Washington, and the diurnal wheel is remarkable for a congregation in or near the ascendant of six of the then nine planets in a curious approach to reproducing their arrangement in his original nativity. Superficially this suggests that he was holding very closely to his fundamental pattern. The focal emphasis is provided by Uranus, and its position close to the nadir show how subjective the release of potentials would be from the new starting point. This perhaps prefigures the ultimacy of the myth figure. Tangibles go largely unstressed since the tenth house is empty. Interesting above all else is the fact that all nine significators except Mars are either cadent or intercepted, and this reveals the overshadowing extreme measure of self-challenge on this threshold day of epic history in the making.

To be noted in connection with the diurnals is that the ascendant's return is only this conveniently in the early morning for a limited number of people. Any normal day however,

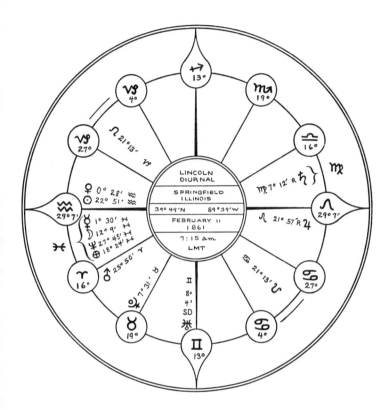

in its more active span of working hours, is usually kept a psychological unit by the weight of common activities of little essential interruption to their continuity. In a symbolism where cause and effect are never what actually is measured, the time orb is effective backward as well as forward and in consequence indication by a diurnal will tend usually to characterize a span of unfractioned daily experience. Thus what is moved into by way of indication may dominate what otherwise is more or less a drifting out of it.

In summary, since all reality is a repetition of itself or a recapitulation of accomplishment in fulfillment of existence the three more significant factors in horoscopy can have advantageous charting in any re-establishment of themselves. Thus the sun annually re-emphasizes its original role and so can be identified as revitalizing a native's life in terms of the indication through the solar return. Similarly the personal lunar month can help him understand and profit from the reordering of himself immediately and psychologically, and through the daily re-establishment of the ascendant he may have light on what in the more narrowed specificity may be converging to significance for him.

THE PRIMARY DIRECTIONS

In addition to the elements of the dynamic horoscopy presented in these pages as a comprehensive predictive method and consisting of (1) the secondary directions with (2) the transits as screened against their all-too-easy proliferation to inconsequence and (3) the cyclic charts for the regular return of the sun and moon and ascendant to their natal places, there are two supplementary techniques of occasional great value. They are closely related to the fundamental progressions or the important secondaries, but in the case of one of them an approximate four minutes and of the other a little over twenty-nine and a half days after birth are taken rather than a day to correspond to a year in the native's life. They are respectively (4) the primary and (5) the tertiary systems, and are so known because of the order in quickness with which progressive indications in general are established and not because this numbering in any way ranks them in importance. Neither technique is widely employed, largely because the calculations are tedious, but they chart the special significance of essentially mass development in human affairs in the one instance and an individual's psychological conflicts on the other and certainly are not to be ignored. In this text it is convenient to consider them with Abraham Lincoln as an example.

The primaries differ principally from both the secondary and tertiary directions in charting the dynamic elements of experience in the celestial equator rather than in the zodiac that astrologically is the representation of the ecliptic. Their progressed delineation is thus through that one of the two great heavenly circles in which the houses of the horoscope are established and this characteristic gives them (1) their methodological affinity with horary astrology and (2) their fundamental involvement with matters of distinctly chance impact in life. Since with measurement in terms of the faster or rotational motion of the earth there is under astrology's essential principle of immediacy or relevance a one-remove toward the significance of free-flowing circumstances, in their departure from the basic but more deliberate unfoldment of the nativity, the concern in primary directions therefore is with definitely general but concomitant phenomena in a native's ongoing. Most distinctive of the procedure in both horary analysis and this one of the three systems of progression is the fact that the planets are moved in purely symbolical fashion, either by the astrologer in forming his judgment in the one instance or by the turning of the heavens as a whole in the other. Employment of the significators in these two special techniques is kept in the equatorial perspective under the governing law of selectivity or efficiency. It would violate logical economy or introduce largely meaningless complication to attempt any adjustment to longitudinal shift in position or to actual movement of the heavenly bodies in their orbits, once they have been located and given their fixed or incontrovertible indication in the horoscopic schematism either at the moment of special inquiry or its precipitating event in horary investigation or at the occasion of physical birth in natal delineation and hence the dynamic analysis that can follow in due course.

The philosophy of time correlation is the same for the primary as the secondary system of progression, and it must have at least a preliminary attention at this point. A degree of the sun's zodiacal movement or in practical effect the calendar day represents the year of life marked off by its annual round, and in that correspondence establishes the secondaries under the essential principle of concordance or concomitance or as a matter of the interconnection of cycles measuring related phenomena in similar segments of human realization. Such units are man's waking-sleeping and nature's summer-winter. In extension of the symbolical correspondence in this case of the whole of one circle to a constituent single degree of an interconnected one, or of the twenty-four-hour day to the twelve-month year in a one-remove delineation of the latter through the secondaries, the similar day in its turn can be taken for an establishment of its four-minute or single-degree segments to provide the interpretation in the similar and supplementary signification of annual recapitulation in the native's life through the primaries.

There is a very different and fundamental remove in the logic of this shift from zodiacal to equatorial perspective, and again under the essential principle of immediacy or relevance the methodological gradation must have its manifestation in some variant or supplemental dimension of consideration such as in this instance becomes a particularized scope of specificity in identification. The reasoning at this point may well be specious, but its purpose is to explain a system of analysis and not to provide any verbally unimpeachable certification of its validity. The true justification of astrology is its performance in competent hands. In the matter of its inexactitudes, notoriously exemplified in the correlation of the degrees of a circle with the days of a year and commonly in orbs whether of position or time that are capable of infinite regression, there is the eventual averaging out of the divergent that not only is characteristic of all natural process but in all likelihood is the very essence of any ultimate reality. Meanwhile and under the governing law of convergence or convenience the whole basis of horoscopic insight is necessarily a delineation of the exceptional in experience as what inescapably is the basis of all immediate distinctiveness in the transitory and everyday reality.

Primary directions have been endlessly controversial, and they have suffered through both oversophistication and oversimplification. The first of these tendencies is an inheritance from the early Grecian and medieval world views. At the time the Ionian physicists were putting down the foundations for modern science, and the formal horoscope now known was probably having its evolution, the Pythagoreans and then Plato promulgated the conception of pure number as quite literally the basis of the cosmos. In due course and out of this conclusion came the fallacy that a ramification of precision is the final key to the structure of all phenomena. The remarkable medieval synthesis of a millennium or so later strengthened the accompanying and no less fallacious assumption of a self-contained cosmic completeness presumed to be quite within the range of man's comprehension. Consequently astrology's earlier practitioners came to accept the notion of a neat overall order that could be charted with absolute exactness. Cosmic forces in their interplay were seen creating and maintaining both the world at large and man as an integral part of it, and the expectation was that all things could be scaled out in terms of an inevitable cause and effect. Astrology was believed to have magical power because (1) it was a mathematical science and (2) mathematics was the root of everything. If all this now stands evident as strange naïveté, it yet has survived quite definitely in much of the established astrological literature.

Equally incompatible with the modern refinement of astrology has been the reduction of the primary directions at times to a virtual ineptitude through an uncritical oversimplification. A common example is the mere translation of the planetary positions into right ascension, or place in the equatorial circle, and the calculation of the progressions among them in the same fashion as in the secondaries or with even right-ascensional degrees taken to represent years at all points. Out of the same cloth and without the least basis in horoscopic logic is the occasional practice of amateur or intuition-oriented astrologers who take a difference in zodiacal degrees between any two factors of almost any sort in a natal horoscope, in what actually is an application of horary technique, and use the number of them as representing years in prediction.

Planetary Differentiation

It is very generally realized that astrology is based (1) on the movements of the nine planets that have major rank in the solar system together with the moon as a satellite of the earth to become a tenth planet for the astrologer but (2) as such motion is taken in strictly geocentric perspective so that as a result the sun replaces the terrestrial globe in the schematism and becomes a moving body instead of the latter and thereupon also has the convenient designation of planet. What does not have general understanding however is the inescapable circumstance that as astrological techniques gain their effectiveness in an advancing refinement or specialization of meaning through the various forms of remove in relationship they depart increasingly from the foundational or literal realities of the celestial mechanics. This shift to more and more symbolical designation is represented most familiarly and from the very beginning by the distinctive specificities with which the significators are endowed when placed in a geocentric structure. The process continues as symbols are established in layer upon layer of particular and varying but logically ordered context, as explained in this and the companion volumes, and while horoscopy in its illimitable range of analytical judgment is thus ever making use of the heavenly phenomena it actually comes to employ them only most incidentally in their original and material or least symbolical base. The most dramatic and almost arbitrary developments in this process are represented in horary astrology, where the genius of insight frequently depends on the use of significators stripped of all character except as lords of houses.

The planetary differentiation that becomes the basis of primary directions results from the dynamic part played in the formation of these progressions by the terrestrial horizon that has established the personal horoscope at birth in the first place. This ground plane of individual being in the astrological schematism is obviously the most important of all factors in horoscopy, and with the equatorial primaries it becomes the fundamental determinant of predictive indication. The zodiac, concomitantly, loses its relevance almost completely. With the daily rotation of the heavens the significators in the particular respect to the horizon come to be situated very differently from each other in comparison with the zodiacal aspects they form among themselves and with their natal places in the secondary and tertiary systems.

Administering the distribution of the relationships in the equator for indication by this special technique is the celestial point of pause or transition between the rising and setting phenomenon of any heavenly body in the course of any twenty-four hours. This creates the midheaven in the basic nativity, and it becomes the fulcrum point from which the indications of all the planets are determined in the primaries. Actually and also as a great convenience in calculation, there here is the least distinction among them in their possible relation with the horizon on the one hand and in terms of a potential common culmination in daily performance on the other. In practice none of them ever are precisely at apex in this manner but rather they are distributed into southeast and northwest or northeast and southwest right-ascensional quadrants of the natal wheel, i.e., in houses (1) 10-12 and 4-6 or (2) 1-3 and 7-9. If it is the former case of rising (houses 10-12) or investigating (4-6) potential the progressed aspect indicates a vivifying stimulus for the native's efforts, and if it is the setting (7-9) or germinative (1-3) complementation the indication is of external and superficial support or encouragement. This is the dynamic balance shown to characterize a given moment of relevance.

A further differentiation of planetary significance that is unique with the primary directions, and made possible because zodiacal motion is in no way a factor in the technique, reflects the different direction of normal turn in the two great heavenly circles as familiarly taken from a north-pole perspective. Thus clockwise movement or projection of relationship in the more tangible and narrow-scale context of the equatorial measurement as when a planet is said to be rising must always maintain a horoscopic balance with the counterclockwise movement or projection of relationship in the more intangible and broad-scale context represented in the familiar case of the formation of aspects in the zodiac. In general the primaries formed in the first instance have been known as direct. In this group the revolving heavens bring planets into aspect from greater to lesser degrees of right ascension as far as the basic nativity is concerned. In the other group of these progressions, that have been known as converse, the planets are seen in counteraction to the turn of the celestial vault or in a one-remove in preserving their natal position relative to the horizon with the consequent zodiacal shift of no dynamic significance in the primaries and thereupon carried into aspect from lesser to greater right ascension in the general fashion of the secondaries. Because this nomenclature has not been used consistently, and at best is confusing, it is avoided in the present exposition. Here is a distinction in psychological scope or the chance rapport of circumstances with the native's affairs that is heightened either tangibly and so of more obvious pertinence or intangibly and a matter of broader or more generalized importance.

Traditionally there are primary directions known as mundane, in distinction from the more widely recognized ones often termed zodiacal, and consisting of aspects formed as a matter of proportional place in the houses as for example a square from the middle of the tenth to the middle of the first. These may be dismissed as a case of the oversophistication that characterizes a great deal of the medieval refinements of horoscopy, or as an instance of inadequate application of the essential principle of immediacy or relevance.

In summary, there are two supplementary techniques of occasional great value in the dynamic horoscopy. Of these the primary directions stand apart from all other methods of progression because they are determined in the celestial equator, or great circle of the houses rather than in the zodiac of the signs, and because of that fact are particularly linked with horary astrology. In this perspective any actual zodiacal movement of the planets is inconsequential or virtually meaningless. The primaries, with their equatorial base, indicate the special significance to the individual of the mass developments in human affairs. A degree of turn of the heavenly sphere or approximately four minutes of time corresponds to a year of life. In this system each planet has a more particular differentiation thanks to the expanded variabilities with an anchorage of consideration in pure circumstances, and its role in this progressive analysis is determined fundamentally by (1) the quadrant of the equator it occupies in the natal horoscope with either a sharp vitalizing or a more neutral supporting indication in the dynamic horoscopy at this point and (2) whether in a given instance it is moved by the revolving heavens in a clockwise or counterclockwise direction as indicating respectively a tangible and narrow-scale or an intangible and broad-scale contribution of current eventualities to the personal ongoing.

The Lincoln Primaries

Illustration of these directions in the present text is confined to (1) three especially-linked indications in Lincoln's private life after an increasing activity in politics had led to his unsuccessful effort to win a seat in the United States Senate but also had precipitated the epochal debates with Stephen Douglas and (2) indication in two instances in his presidency when military action particularly advanced the Union cause. In this quite distinctive form of horoscopic progression the planets are given special keywords as each is seen operating in a zone of circumstantial rapport in which it charts particular and potential relevance in the general drift of everyday affairs. These zones are a precise equivalent of the less variant activity-facets

ZONE OF CIRCUMSTANTIAL RAPPORT IN
PRIMARY DIRECTIONS

☿	Empathy	Temperamental state of affairs
☉	Authority	Ordering of affairs
☽	Influence	General support by affairs
♀	Stability	Acceptance of standards
♂	Gamble	Trial-and-error accomplishment
♃	Gratification	Employment of potentials
♄	Justification	Depth of consideration
♅	Mutation	Exceptionality of significance
♆	Confluence	Overall integration
♇	Adjudication	Transcendent adjustment

identified in the secondaries, but the fundamental difference in perspective here is best served through separate designations. The adoption of terms of common usage to have key meaning in astrology has introductory explanation beginning on page 317. Because of the additional difficulty in any typification of freewheeling circumstances, as in this system of directions, qualifying phrases of supplementary suggestiveness can also be employed as is done for example purposes in these texts.

Because there are five variables to take into mind in contrast with the normal three involved in any statement of indication by secondary direction or transit, or the (1) dynamic significator forming its (2) aspect with the (3) basic horoscopic significator, the additional and more general two of the primaries are each given a preliminary simplified identification in these texts. This in a sense can lie in the background of analysis, perhaps almost subconsciously, in paralleling the more usual progressive judgments.

MARS BY PRIMARY DIRECTION IN COUNTERCLOCKWISE SEXTILE WITH NATAL MARS, FEBRUARY 7, 1858   Here circumstances are shown tending to supporting dynamism with broad-scale and intangible eventuation, or revealing for general perspective the fact of a trail-blazing sweep in Lincoln's progress and also the probability that the real fruits of his effort were ahead in developments quite beyond forecast. The drift of events is identified as a manifestation of persistence through practical adroitness in the mundane zone of gamble or trial-and-error accomplishment. Correspondence ultimately is to the epochal "house divided" address of the then-candidate for U. S. Senator at the Republican State Convention in Springfield on June 16th or when he was nominated for the office, but more generally to the building events perhaps coming to focus with his trip to Chicago in February to consult with the party chairman.

THE MOON BY PRIMARY DIRECTION IN CLOCKWISE CONJUNCTION WITH NATAL SATURN, FEBRUARY 22, 1858 Here circumstances are shown tending to vivifying dynamism with narrow-scale and tangible eventuation, or revealing for general perspective the additional factor of Lincoln's own immediate and self-dedicatory desire for the Senate seat as a step in his expanding but still wholly Midwest prestige. The drift of events is identified as a manifestation of concern through practical alertness in the mundane zone of influence or general support by affairs. Correspondence is to the growing necessity to recognize the real nature of the critical impasse in a nation half slave and half free.

SATURN BY PRIMARY DIRECTION IN COUNTERCLOCKWISE CONJUNCTION WITH THE NATAL MOON, MARCH 18, 1858 Here circumstances are shown tending to supporting dynamism with broad-scale and intangible eventuation, or revealing for general perspective the complementary and less effective proposition of the sheer earnestness represented by a Lincoln now brought all of a sudden face-to-face with the deeper issue over which the Civil War would have to be fought. The drift of events is identified as a manifestation of endurance through practical alertness in the mundane zone of justification or depth of consideration. Correspondence ultimately is to the curious fact that when the Illinois legislature failed to send him to the Senate in November he was almost immediately revealed as an ideal or politically unencumbered Republican candidate for the presidency.

Mundane Astrology

A major area of astrological interest that in earlier times was virtually a primary concern in the West, and that currently is very popular despite much controversy over method and a far from reliable performance, is given its extensive analysis in a companion volume or the author's *Mundane Perspectives in Astrology*. Momentarily important in this text however is the long-established principle of this mundane technique that the personal horoscope of the de facto ruler of a nation, or any unit of political sovereignty or similar organization, can be taken also as a horoscope for the latter in every respect as long as the individual with that general administrative responsibility remains in his position. In consequence the primary directions and indeed all progressive indications for Abraham Lincoln from the day he was sworn into office at Washington until his assassination or from March 4, 1861, to April 14, 1865, should be interpreted in their indications for the outworking destiny of the United States as well as for himself.

URANUS BY PRIMARY DIRECTION IN COUNTERCLOCKWISE SEXTILE WITH NATAL MERCURY, AUGUST 23, 1862   Here circumstances are shown tending to supporting dynamism with broad-scale and intangible eventuation, or revealing for general national perspective the beginning of the turn toward certain survival of the Union despite the lack of overall competence in the conduct of the war effort. The drift of events is identified as a manifestation of nascent aplomb or building morale of the North through practical adroitness in the mundane zone of mutation or exceptionality of significance. Correspondence is to the ultimately decisive but badly fought battle of the Antietam on September 17th with principal consequence that England and France, on the verge of recognizing the Confederacy, decided not to do so.

NEPTUNE BY PRIMARY DIRECTION IN COUNTERCLOCKWISE SEXTILE WITH NATAL VENUS, JULY 3, 1863   Here circumstances are shown tending to supporting dynamism with broad-scale and intangible eventuation, or revealing for general national perspective the definite turning point in the conflict itself. The drift of events is identified as the manifestation of dramatic realization for the North through practical adroitness in the mundane zone of confluence or overall integration. Correspondence is to the twin events on the 4th or the surrender of Vicksburg and the rolling back of the last possible real threat of the Confederates at Gettysburg.

It must be remembered that a change of no more than a single minute of arc in the horoscopic calculations can result at times in a difference of almost a week in the date for culmination of a primary indication, so that extreme time orbs can well be allowed. In the companion text on mundane astrology the primaries are calculated by computer, and different dates appear for the two examples above that are repeated there in the more complete analysis of the Lincoln presidency. Absolute preciseness in astrology is impossible, but bringing the various schemes of progression into a common approximation to actual events can be a great aid in rectification and this more circumstantial measure is especially valuable in carrying correspondences down to a fine point.

In summary, (1) three primary directions combine to delineate the dramatic unfoldment in public significance of Abraham Lincoln through the press of circumstances moving from mere local politician to national statesman through his struggle with Stephen Douglas for the United States senatorship in 1858 but thereupon becoming presidential timber and then (2) a pair of primaries delineate the special mundane importance respectively of the Battle of Antietam in 1862 and of the victories at Vicksburg and Gettysburg in 1863. Because the primaries move so swiftly in the culmination of each particular progression there is every justification for wide time orbs in their correspondences, and by the same token they can be very useful in rectification.

NOTE: For the 1973 printing, more significant illustrations of Lincoln primaries replace the original ones, and the table on page 384 has been calculated to a greater preciseness although not by computer as is the case throughout the companion text.

THE TERTIARY DIRECTIONS

The second of the supplementary and occasionally valuable techniques in the comprehensive predictive method presented in these pages is an expansion of the procedure given its extensive exposition in the form of the secondary directions. The secondaries have been found to be related fundamentally to the geocentric circling of the heavens by the sun, and a like zodiacal circuit of the moon can now have attention as a basis for the tertiary directions. In using this mode of envisionment for the heavenly mechanics of horoscopy, the primary directions can be seen to be provided through a similar circuiting of the heavens by the horizon although in the very short period of a day and in the celestial equator rather than the zodiac. Here is astrology's effective trichotomy of progressed measure with the three quite independent methods found to be respectively the dynamic potentials of indication of the three foundational elements in the establishment of a horoscope, or in the order of reference at this point (1) the sun and (2) the moon and (3) the horizon which usually and conveniently is identified in its positive significance as the ascendant. The moon is different superficially from the other two significators in the fact that a total circuit rather than a single degree of movement in progression represents a year of life, but degrees and whole circles of movement have been seen to be symbolically interchangeable in this creation of a native's progressions. Rather obvious in this connection of course is the fact

157

that the three forms of life recapitulation are provided by these same fundamental factors of the natal wheel, but it is most important to note that the directional systems employ planetary positions representing a direct sequence within the birth pattern whereas the returns present the significance established in a complete reorientation to momentary circumstances through the otherwise unrelated transiting places of the significators.

The role of the moon as coequal in horoscopic primacy with the sun and ascendant, with the consequent retreat of all other elements to subsidiary relationship, was well recognized by the medievals. The fixed relation between the lights in this pre-eminence in the nativity was thereupon taken to reveal the character of the psychological self-rehearsal of the native. In a sense the sun's nascency was seen to project itself from impartiality or relatively blind drive into the moon's actuality of a biased or characteristic emotional and at core ever fluid self-establishment in circumstances. This vital insight is preserved by the present text in its background dichotomy of self and the generalized otherness, and for practical purposes the fundamental balance in any personal existence is described as between a natural drive and a natural involvement. The distance at birth forward in the zodiac of the lesser from the greater light is thus found to chart the unchanging pattern of the characteristic temperamental fillip to experience in each given individual's case, and in an astrological usage of the term the configuration is known as the synodical lunation. A superficial phase of this consideration is to be seen in the common recognition of the moon as either increasing or decreasing in light and thereupon identifying (1) an inaugurative tendency in act or decision or (2) a complementary consummatory inclination respectively. More important however is the quality of rapport with circumstances in general, or the essential warmth or distinction in livingness with which an individuality actually reveals itself in any depth. In consequence the testimony through the month-for-a-year progressions can be of genuine service in all everyday matters of any special delicacy.

The tertiary directions are based of course on the synodical month of twenty-nine-odd days and not the sidereal month of twenty-seven-odd, and each period of progression is established when the moon comes again to the precise same relationship it had with the sun at birth. Thus a thirtieth recurrence of the phenomenon provides the directional threshold for tertiary indications for a native's thirty-first year. In this directional system a degree of the progressed moon's motions falls too far short in correspondence to a day in the given life to encourage any attempt at calculation to preciseness of indication, and the effort would have even less justification when the factor of time orb must be taken into account. However and by the governing law of selectivity or efficiency, any particular distinctiveness in the substance of analysis at hand should always have a principal consideration. Here it would be the matter of the lunar phases, as marked out in the irregularity of the planet's movement from slightly less than twelve to a little over fifteen degrees of daily mean motion in each month taken for the annual indications. Consequently the progressed synodical lunation properly is divided into four even quarters as represented by degrees and minutes moved. These will each indicate a three-months period of the life, and in that span the tertiaries can usually be determined with sufficient accuracy for normal purposes by eye inspection and mental approximation alone. When actual calculation seems necessary the operations are the same as performed for the secondaries.

A system of progressions of rather wide employment, and that takes the cycle of twenty-seven-odd days after birth to give progressed delineation for the given year of life, must not be confused with the tertiaries. Its indications are essentially a progression of the lunar return. They are known as minor progressions and the conception of which they are a part is that a syndrome of planetary factors in the heavens can be established as an overlay on any possible complex of man's existence for interpretive or predictive insight. In such a case these minors primarily would filter the dynamic testimonies down into more specific everyday realities.

In summary, the tertiaries stand apart from the other directional systems because they are based on the synodical lunation with a time measure of each of these following birth corresponding to a year of life. The moon is not always realized in its basic importance in horoscopy, ranking it with the sun and horizon. In both the nativity and the tertiary progression the lesser light reveals the native's fluid self-realization through his temperament, or in the emotional quality of his rapport with circumstances, and these directions in consequence can be of unusual value in matters of special delicacy.

The Lincoln Tertiaries

Abraham Lincoln is a case of the consummatory genius in emotional self-projection, and an individual of extraordinary reticence about whom no adequate information is available at this point. The extent of his standing off from his fellows is marked by the puzzling melancholia for which he was most distinguished as a fundamental psychological entity in the eyes of his close associates. Tertiary analysis in consequence will have to be by superficial straws in large part and of course on almost total presumption. The lunar directions of this system are nearly always omitted as too numerous for profitable consideration outside an extreme intimacy in horoscopic counselling. Attention here will be held to the fulcrum indications because in their instance the correlation with events is sharper, and the assumptions will have a greater chance of reliability. The period selected for examination embraces the two crucial years of 1857-8 in which there was intensive character adjustment, or in which he was quickened to an entirely new dimension of conscious selfhood.

VENUS BY TERTIARY DIRECTION IN SQUARE WITH NATAL MERCURY, EARLY SPRING IN 1857   This indication of crisis or accentuation through a temperamental fillip to experience is a matter of the native's aplomb in basic sensitivity. When the Dred Scott decision of March 6th brought him to the very radical realignment in his overall orientation there was a dramatic challenge to his psychological balance for the moment with the surprising and vociferous demand in the northern or free states for the secession from the Union that up to then had been the particular threat of the southern slaveholder. In political upside-downness a shoe however briefly was of a sudden on the other foot, and in coming at this time the phenomenon could have been a very valuable demonstration that there are never any easy answers in the hard realities of national life.

VENUS BY TERTIARY DIRECTION IN SQUARE WITH NATAL PLUTO, SPRING IN 1857   This indication of crisis or accentuation through a temperamental fillip to experience is one of two relatively concurrent fulcrum aspects for the native that are valid in identifying elements of the myth figure but are not immediately operative in personal developments. The matter of probity in the basic sensitivity, as important in Lincoln's immortal stature, has its probable correlation on May 29th with the insensate Pottawatomie Creek Massacre or the cold-blooded retaliatory butchery of five men at random in the night by the antislavery fanatic John Brown with the help of his four sons and two other men. It was high illumination in American history of the extreme lack of respect for personality with which Lincoln had been battling in small compass and in due course would be engaging in cosmic dimension. At the time the impact of the incident on him probably was indirect, or a detail of the whole Bloody Kansas chapter.

NEPTUNE BY TERTIARY DIRECTION IN SQUARE WITH NATAL PLUTO, MATURING IN 1857   This indication of crisis or accentuation through a temperamental fillip to experience was also inoperative at the moment but the matter of probity in the native's nascent responsibility has illumination as a corrective in afterview of the values in issue at the time. The immediate events of the summer provided Mary Lincoln with exceptional pleasure, since she was able to go along on a business trip to New York and have exciting encounter with the East and especially New York City. What came forward was her sense of the poverty she had entered willingly and with no subsequent regret when her husband led her by the hand to their first simple quarters in Springfield on the day of their marriage. Lincoln's fellow attorneys had long protested his low fees, and unlike most of his early contemporaries he had not grasped the pioneer opportunities that could have made him wealthy. Now he had just collected a spectacular five-thousand-dollar corporation fee that put him on even level with the best of Eastern legal talent, but while demonstrating his professional potential he would not be changing his ways.

Almost as if it were the sweep of destiny, he had escaped the limitations of a class-bound prominence. As within a year his defeat by Douglas would deny him the senatorship but bring him the White House, his homespun sympathies that had denied him clan status of the Todds had been keeping him clear for the immortal contribution.

VENUS BY TERTIARY DIRECTION IN SQUARE WITH NATAL JUPITER, SUMMER IN 1857   This indication of crisis or accentuation through a temperamental fillip to experience is a matter of zest in the native's basic sensitivity. It shows that the summer described as wonderful by Mary Lincoln in a surviving letter is testimony to a high spot in the marital relationship, and hence strong validation for the conclusion now that their life together in all normal respects was remarkably happy.

THE SUN BY TERTIARY DIRECTION IN SQUARE WITH NATAL MARS, MIDSUMMER IN 1857   This indication of crisis or accentuation through a temperamental fillip to experience is a matter of persistence in the native's natural drive. The sharp if brief financial panic precipitated on August 24th was sharpened dramatization of the economic considerations to which Lincoln came to pay increased attention.

MARS BY TERTIARY DIRECTION IN SQUARE WITH THE NATAL SUN, MIDSUMMER IN 1857   This indication of crisis or accentuation through a temperamental fillip to experience is curiously dramatic reinforcement of the sun's activation of Mars and reveals the extent to which the life of native and nation can become linked.

MERCURY BY TERTIARY DIRECTION IN SQUARE WITH NATAL VENUS, LATE AUTUMN IN 1857   This indication of crisis or accentuation through a temperamental fillip to experience is a matter of realization in the native's basic attitude. Senator

Douglas in the current session of Congress aligned himself with the Republicans, and prominent Eastern leaders in the new party suggested support for the Little Giant as he came up for re-election the following year. This was a challenge to any ultimate Republican integrity, or what to Lincoln was a moral issue he was quick to grasp.

VENUS BY TERTIARY DIRECTION IN SQUARE WITH NATAL VENUS, MIDWINTER IN 1857-8 This indication of crisis or accentuation through a temperamental fillip to experience is a matter of realization in the native's basic sensitivity. Lincoln was being edged into making the try for the Senate himself, and now far more for the sake of the cause than his own long-held senatorial ambitions. His broader sense of proportion may have been brought to issue.

THE SUN BY TERTIARY DIRECTION IN SQUARE WITH NATAL URANUS, LATE WINTER IN 1857-8 This indication of crisis or accentuation through a temperamental fillip to experience is a matter of release of political sagacity in the natural drive. Correspondence is to the matter of Republican support for Douglas. The native was keeping in constant touch with Lyman Trumbull, the junior senator from Illinois, and he had made a hurried trip to Chicago in February to strengthen support for himself. He was gathering psychological momentum in his course, such as would have fruits in the Great Debates if not in the ends he had more literally in mind.

MERCURY BY TERTIARY DIRECTION IN SQUARE WITH NATAL MARS, LATE SPRING IN 1858 This indication of crisis or accentuation through a temperamental fillip to experience is a matter of persistence in the native's basic attitude. Even as caught up in the details of his race for the Senate he was loath to surrender any phase of the wide spread of interest that

throughout his years has been evident in his omnivorous reading. In this month he lectured before a full house in Blooming-
ton on inventions and discoveries, and the occurrence under this
signification suggests a strand of his competence somehow
inadequately nourished since the lecture in repetition became
a dismal failure. It is likely that an opportunity was missed,
as perhaps not cultivating his scientific bent more assiduously
than he had.

VENUS BY TERTIARY DIRECTION IN SQUARE WITH NATAL
MARS, SUMMER IN 1858   This indication of crisis or accentuation through a temperamental fillip to experience is a matter of
persistence in the native's basic sensitivity. The circumstances
of his nomination for the Senate and his epochal statement of
June 16th would seem to suggest his development of his campaign as a species of holy war, and thus to characterize his
course as the manifestation of the almost inspired or prophetic
determination that at the end would carry him on to Washington.

MARS BY TERTIARY DIRECTION IN SQUARE WITH NATAL
MERCURY, SUMMER IN 1858   This indication of crisis or accentuation through a temperamental fillip to experience is a matter of aplomb in the native's basic excitation. Douglas opened
his campaign on July 8th, and Lincoln in responding was
accused of trailing the senator around in order to get an audience. This led to the challenge to the Great Debates through
which the native achieved a new maturity as well as the
national prominence he needed for next developments in the
sweep of destiny.

MERCURY BY TERTIARY DIRECTION IN SQUARE WITH NATAL
URANUS, LATE SUMMER IN 1858   This indication of crisis or
accentuation through a temperamental fillip to experience is a

matter of the further release of the native's potentials in his basic attitude. Thus the seven Great Debates of August 21st through October 15th are delineated astrologically in their deeper ultimate significance.

MARS BY TERTIARY DIRECTION IN SQUARE WITH NATAL PLUTO, AUTUMN IN 1858   This delineation of crisis or accentuation through a temperamental fillip to experience is a matter of the ultimate probity of the myth figure in the native's basic excitation as established preliminarily in the Great Debates or the whole context of his approach to the stability of the Union. Lincoln of course during his lifetime would have no conception of the immortal factor in his clarification of idea through the confrontation with Douglas, but in the dynamic horoscopy the ultimate or far later testimony is to the vital foreshadowing of the immortality.

THE SUN BY TERTIARY DIRECTION IN SQUARE WITH NATAL SATURN, LATE AUTUMN IN 1858   This indication of crisis or accentuation through a temperamental fillip to experience is a matter of the native's fundamental concern with his political future in his natural drive. The loss of the election to Douglas in the vote of the legislature on November 2d becomes a proposition of dimension, and thus in a sense the senatorship can be dismissed astrologically as too constricted for Lincoln's building destiny.

VENUS BY TERTIARY DIRECTION IN SQUARE WITH NATAL URANUS, LATE AUTUMN IN 1858   This indication of crisis or accentuation through a temperamental fillip to experience is a matter of a further release of the native's potentials in a basic sensitivity that by now is coming almost to guarantee the higher destiny. The first mention of Lincoln for the presidency on November 5th is the astrological straw, suggesting that the defeat of the moment is an escape from serious sidetracking in personal progress.

THE SUN BY TERTIARY DIRECTION IN SQUARE WITH NATAL NEPTUNE, EARLY WINTER IN 1858-9   This indication of crisis or accentuation through a temperamental fillip to experience is a matter of acceptance of almost obvious eventuality in the native's natural drive. The astute business promoter and Republican leader, Jesse Fell, at this time spelled out for Lincoln the practical possibility of election to the presidency as almost an obligation to the party, but it was too soon for the man of destiny to see it and so he shrugged it off.

MERCURY BY TERTIARY DIRECTION IN SQUARE WITH NATAL SATURN, EARLY WINTER IN 1858-9   This indication of crisis or accentuation through a temperamental fillip to experience is a matter of the native's deepening concern in his basic attitude, or is a reinforcing assurance to him of the presidential possibilities as a challenge for him now to develop the required public image through a fully articulate self-dedication.

In summary, the more inward or delicate indications of psychological stirring in the native's critical 1857-8 period show the gradual mounting of subtle impact (1) beginning with the Dred Scott decision and the shock of John Brown's massacre of five innocent men and then (2) as he had particular encouragement in his personal life with Mary Lincoln together with (3) the intellectual strengthening he gained in the debates with Stephen Douglas coming (4) to a peak in the mounting pressures on him to make the try for the presidency when the United States senatorship was denied him in the legislature.

HOROSCOPE RECTIFICATION

The most exasperating problem in astrology is the possibility of inaccurate data from which a personal horoscope may be calculated, and the process of correcting or verifying it is known as rectification. Many neat and seductive systems have been developed for accomplishing this result, but in general they must be dismissed on quite pragmatic grounds or for the reason that their basis is no more than metaphysical speculation. Perhaps the most ancient of them or the animoder of Claudius Ptolemy, who lived in the second century, presumed a necessary relation of the moment a child is born with the lunation preceding the event. The trutine of the astrologer Hermes of about the same period is of similar stamp, since it assumed a necessity of relationship between the moon at conception and the ascendant at birth and vice versa, and this latter theory has survived and in its modernized form as the prenatal epoch is still employed at times. Obviously however a reliability in rectifying a nativity requires a checking through known actualities in the given native's experience. The analyst who has established a sound orientation in past reality is certainly the only one equipped for conclusions of any appreciable correctness in his judgment of the future.

The rectifying procedure is a tentative turning of the horoscopic wheel one way or the other, like the knob of a safe or the dial of a radio set, until the zodiacal complex in the position it is given will correspond convincingly to the astrological

distribution of everyday affairs in both the natal and progressed patterns of the particular individuality. The determination of this correspondence requires a rigid logical discipline
of the mind, thanks to the numberless possibilities of gratuitous
assumption. Thus (1) because of the infinite variations in the
meaning of human experience, which of course is what astrology measures fundamentally, most definitive events can have
astrological indication in an almost illimitable variety of ways
and therefore cannot be attributed with surety to any single
accentuation and (2) in the secondary directions the significators other than the moon move very slightly in the twenty-four
hours that delineate a progressed year, and in addition must
often be given considerable time orb, so that any real pinpointing of circumstances in terms of progressive date is also
a rather speculative matter and moreover (3) this proposition
is no less true of the transits and the other directions and (4)
even the faster movement of the lesser light in the secondaries
is not enough to eliminate the difficulty of any scaling of life's
details in the handsome and superficial orderliness claimed for
astrology at times. Under the essential principle of selectivity
or efficiency the process of rectification must restrict itself to
considerations where analysis can operate with the strict delimitation needed for reliability of judgment of any sort.

The unique analytical genius of astrology has its formal
expression in its governing law of discernment or validation,
under which an operative dichotomy of techniques or perspectives is always established to the end that they may provide a
logical policing of each other. To effect this for the purpose of
rectification the two modes of approach should be as diverse as
possible, and their adoption under the essential principle of
dichotomy or identity could hardly be better than at the

extreme of external or material order on the one hand and psychological symbolization or personification on the other. This suggests (1) the moon particularly among the heavenly bodies with actual gravitational mass because it is the swiftest in zodiacal movement among them and hence the one most likely to move most specifically or obviously in rapport with the course of events and (2) the houses of the nativity since in any overall view they are wholly concerned with the free-wheeling swirl of circumstances that have no horoscopic pertinence except as selected or utilized in one manner or another and as thereupon established as symbols in the consciousness of some definite individual. The lesser light thus can represent cosmic order, and the horoscopic wheel the complementary and purely symbolized ordering of personal identity, as a convenient ultimate in polar opposition. By a concentrated attention to these factors the two great circles of the celestial vault, or the zodiac of the signs and the heavenly equator in which the houses lie, are brought to a special validation for each other.

The detailed procedure of rectification presented in this text is an adaptation of horary astrology, since in that wholly symbolical technique the cusps of the horoscope in a sense become deputy planetary entities capable of aspect and of the distribution of relationship in the illimitable removes of derivative correspondence. Here of course is accentuated departure from the employment of tangible bodies with motion in physical orbit. A first of two steps in adjusting a horoscope to a reasonable conformity to known events is to set up a subordinate dichotomy in the houses and make a sharp distinction between the fundamental indication of (1) the horizon as the actual plateau of existence and so the ground for any issue of pure personality or of the intimacies in which man mirrors himself most literally and immediately and (2) the midheaven axis as representing the determinate balance between the emerging and receding of all things that actually makes experience possible and thereupon provides a basic but subsidiary establishment of the practical but essentially symbolized substance and relations of everyday superficiality.

No rectifying value is to be found in anything lacking an unquestioned specificity, and as the progressed moon in charting general involvement passes over each angle or quadrant cusp of a nativity there should be correspondence to a situational development of an inescapably obvious but nonetheless fortuitous nature in such a case. The particularity of this is not the pertinent signification in rectification. The utilization is of current eventualities occurring very much in their own course in the overall or cosmic perspective, and hence coming to manifestation quite independently of the unfolding self-discovery and self-fulfillment of a native however much the phenomena of kaleidoscopic reality in the universal synthesis may have personally coincidental factors. The natal wheel should be located so that essentially unmotivated or unsolicited or unanticipated shifts in environment will have the greatest possible indication of individual pertinence through the successive conjunctions of the progressed moon with its angles. The strongest or most significant correspondence to the everyday manifestation of personal changes of special moment is likely to be at the ascendant, and then at the midheaven. The dramatic polarity to be recognized between these indications at the first and tenth cusps permits a refinement of analysis at this point, such as at times may involve the re-evaluation of some events as well as a special certification of the importance of others.

Second of the two steps in the application of horary astrology to natal rectification has a measure of connection with primary directions as does horary technique because all the operations here actually are in right ascension, but since (1) the manipulation of the indicators in signification is wholly symbolical or without any consideration of physical shift in planetary position and (2) the effectiveness of this step depends on restricting rectifying event to indication through the midheaven axis of the horoscope where the celestial longitude escapes all adjustment to the tilt of the horizon, all determination of aspect can be in zodiacal degrees. It is necessary in this procedure however to employ signification that can be found nowhere else but in the midheaven axis, and this need is met very conveniently by parents. It makes no difference which one of them is indicated by the tenth house and which by the fourth since effective aspect established from the one angle means an equivalent indication from the other. The nativity is placed in the heavens so that the midheaven point taken as a surrogate planet can be moved clockwise or counterclockwise to a conjunction, opposition, square, semisquare, sesquiquadrate, semidemiquartile or the never-named semidemiquartile from the opposition with certain planets in a number of degrees that correspond with years lived by the native at the time of some critical event in parental affairs that also has revolutionary impact in the lives of any children. Most typically this would be decease, and in such an instance the aspect normally would be with Mars or Saturn as the traditional anaretas.

In modern times the anareta role may also be given to Uranus or Neptune if the nature of the death justifies such an identification. Properly the same significator should not be taken for the passing of both elders, unless the two events are extraordinarily similar in a native's case. Any parental crisis can have rectifying value if the consequences are sufficiently crucial for the child and other planets may be seen receiving a rectifying aspect if the eventualities have sufficient significance, but such removes from the sharpness of shock at the loss of a mother or father may mean a regression to superficiality and hence an evaporation of pertinence. Because this second procedure can bring conformity to different if scattered points around the zodiac, it should always follow rather than precede the first or be used as a validation for what is revealed by the progression of the moon over the horoscopic angles.

The Lincoln Horoscope

There has been much difference of opinion concerning the hour and minute of Lincoln's birth. The astrologer L. D. Broughton some two decades after the assassination believed the time to be shortly after midnight with a consequent Sagittarius ascendant, and Evangeline Adams and others followed along. With information supplied at least as early as the publication of *Women Lincoln Loved* in 1927, the general wheel adopted for this text came into currency. Manly P. Hall after his own research in 1934 introduced a chart with an Aries ascendant. Now with Lincoln scholarship in its present state, after all restricted documents have been released and have had thorough examination, the data remain scanty but quite specific. The midwife or granny woman who brought the baby into the world, Aunt Peggy Walters, stated that this happened just after sunup. Sunrise was around five-thirty by local mean time on that day at that latitude. While she was questioned years afterward, and human memory in any case is fallible, the native's considerable prominence in early years could have helped sharpen contemporary recollections concerning himself.

In horoscope rectification it is vital to make sure in adjusting the wheel for analysis that no alternative possibilities are dismissed too lightly. The data actually provided should always be substantiated if possible. In the present instance the Sagittarius ascendants with their corresponding Virgo or Libra midheavens suggest the periods 1832-3 and 1827-8 respectively as peaks in the young man's outer and practical adjustments to the opportunities of his environment. This on the whole affords a distorted picture of the self-unfoldment, and a similar situation is found with the Aries ascendant and its related Capricorn midheaven. Thus the probabilities strongly favor the Aquarius ascendant with the Sagittarius midheaven and the first accentuation of the course of circumstances by the progressed moon under the hypothesis is in 1811. At that time the passing over the ascendant corresponds to the highly significant moving of Thomas Lincoln's family to the Knob Creek farm, which was accomplished in the following spring. The death within a few days of birth of a younger brother for the native may well have been the first vital trauma from this mysterious phenomenon even for a youngster turning three. In any case the tenor of events for the personality gains an early set for the life at this point.

The progressed moon under the hypothesis chosen here came to the nadir in October, 1819, and this of the four axial points in the houses is likely to be the least represented by some definite outer eventuality because of the fundamentally subjective nature of the house. In the lunar cycle of rectification however the progression to a fourth-cusp conjunction always reveals the start in an upward climb of twelve to thirteen years through circumstances to some sort of self-realization in a potentiality indicated at the midheaven. For Abraham Lincoln the nadir's precipitating event obviously was the marriage of his father and Sarah Bush Johnston in December of this year. Stress of the seventh cusp came next in October, 1825, and it quite likely was in this period that his interest in the law was first awakened. Midheaven emphasis in February, 1833, suggests the extent of everyday or conventional culminations when he obtained his appointment as a deputy county surveyor and for the first time in his life was able to lift himself above the status of mere common laborer for hire. If he had had recognition for many distinct skills, he yet had lacked any sort of establishment as a craftsman.

The pivotal ascendant accentuation in October, 1838, is a minor difficulty of rectification if worked out too superficially. Thus the event of marked change might seem to be when Lincoln rode into Springfield to make what was to be the state capital his permanent home on April 15th of the preceding year. As a move of residence however it was little more than coming from a suburb into town. If New Salem was sinking into the inconsequence leading to its disappearance, its reality yet survived in his consciousness in the form of the mountain of debt. The radical change in the life orientation obviously was psychological and beyond pinpointing in key event because of the lack of intimate and detailed information, but that is not to deny its signal importance. The nadir emphasis in February, 1847, can be found to correspond to his taking his seat in Congress in December. He had been elected to this in the August preceding. To identify the significant intermediary event is again impossible, but here actually began the final climb to eminence. The stress at the seventh cusp in April,

1853, has probable connection with the collapse of the Whig party and the extraordinary personal adjustment forced on both Mary Todd Lincoln and the native himself so very early in their marriage. The final accentuating of plateaus of personal experience at house angles by the progressed moon was in late May, 1860, and having high midheaven significance here was his nomination for the presidency by the new Republican party on May 18th.

Following this validation of the angles, justifying the acceptance of the particular Aquarius ascendant, should be confirmation of their positions through the aspects formed by the midheaven with the anaretic planets in correspondence to the decease of his parents. Quite fortuitously the case of Abraham Lincoln provides the most simple of examples, since the aspects in question are both conjunction. When Nancy Hanks Lincoln passed away he was nine and a half years old and Saturn lies forty minutes of arc over nine and a half degrees in longitude from the tenth cusp. Thomas Lincoln died when his son was forty-two years old and Mars lies in Libra within forty-six and a half degrees from the midheaven or in orb of four and a half degrees as generally acceptable for the late years of a native's life.

In summary, the rectification of a horoscope can hardly be by methods based on no more than metaphysical assumption. Rather there must be verification by known events, so that probability for the future is founded on actualities of the past. The difficulty in the employment of most circumstances for this purpose is that a given eventuality may be indicated in many variant ways in astrology, so that there can be little reliance on any single indication for a particular incident in the life. In the present text an adaptation of horary technique is used to surmount the difficulty. The progressed moon in secondary direction is taken in its role of identification of totally unconditioned involvement in general affairs, which it does not share with any other indicator, and the natal wheel is turned back and forth under the moon's progression over the shifting angles of the nativity until there is the best and most typical correspondence to unmotivated or unsolicited or unanticipated instances of great change in the general everyday orientation of the native's ongoing. To supplement and check on this result, the midheaven axis as the only signification of parents in horoscopy is brought to proper aspect with anaretic planets for correlation with parental crisis of exceptional impact in the lives of what children they may have. In the most usual case this is decease. The two tests are applied to the birth chart of Abraham Lincoln, in validation of the form in which it is presented in these pages.

SUPPLEMENTARY BACKGROUND

The natal horoscope of Abraham Lincoln shows no particular natural disposition at birth, and the absence of it indicates the extent of his nascent latitude in self-adjustment but also contributes to the possibility of dissociation as the loner in psychological make-up. His life actually becomes a classic example of the stretching of horoscopic potential that results from extraordinary interest or effort on the part of the native and thus brings a wide-orb aspect into effectiveness. In his case it was the eighteen-degree opposition of Venus with Mars. When he re-entered politics in the Eighteen-Fifties it was with a marked lean to the opportunism of a cardinal-sign emphasis, or the gift for extemporization that would prove responsible for his ultimate achievement. Thus it can be noted that, in view of this capacity of man to mold the everyday or transient signification of his birth wheel in very dramatic respect at times, the interpretation of a nativity cannot be assured of any competence in more than very general terms unless grounded in a case history definitive enough to permit rectification if necessary and to give practical substance to insight at all points.

The Lincoln chart in temperament type is a bowl, and this classification indicates the native's exceptional self-containment as a necessary realization at the start of analysis. Mars thereby brought into high focus shows the indomitability of his nature, and the fundamental emphasis of this quality warns the astrologer against any excursion up a blind alley of Freudian assumption in an effort to account for the strange melancholy that baffled Lincoln's associates in his lifetime as well as his biographers ever since. The emphasis of the first over the tenth house, in the form of horoscope adopted in this text, shows the highly personal manifestation of the deep-rooted honesty that often distinguishes the bowl temperament from the other six types. The striking cluster of planets at the eastern horizon magnifies the stress of pure personality in overall terms, and thus strengthens the possibility of the ultimate myth figure. The pronounced skew in the seesaw arrangement within the bowl adds to the strength of such a possibility.

The fact that there are no major aspects of normal orb between the significators in any of the four planetary departments is indication of the everyday detachment or inherent impartiality characterizing the life, with a result in the tendency to hold in general to existing patterns in self-expression. The mode of self-integration here determined by the two seesaw segments of the bowl pattern shows the necessity of disjunctive realizations as the basic substance of consciousness, or the need for a life of adventure through investigation or analysis or a breaking down of everything into its component parts for purposes of understanding or manipulation.

The technique of natal analysis presented in companion volumes of this series requires the identification of at least two determinators of focal emphasis in the case of any nativity, and here the trigger configuration provided by Mars in application to the moon is of first importance. In supplementing the testimony of Mars in high focus it shows the practical application of effort to be of necessity to the public, or in definite and immediate co-operation at all times with the generalized otherness of life. Thus it had to be a magnification of common issue to move Abraham Lincoln to any stirring concern. And so, if in triviality he might remain primitive almost to uncouthness, in ultimate crisis he could be superman. The required second focal determinator, in the recommended order of selection in these texts, would be the exceptional weighting of the ascendant to which attention already has been given.

By mental chemistry the testimony of the Lincoln horoscope is to normality, and thus there is no necessity for particular attention to the operation of his mind and thus again no justification for considering the melancholia as a psychological aberration or anything of pathological nature. The moon in oriental appearance identifies the great capacity of this native for the dramatic assimilation of himself into the collective ideal or aspirations of people at large, and hence suggests a vocational or avocational self-projection that at best can become a marked prophetic phenomenon. Particularly buttressing this characteristic would be the trigger square of Mars with moon, or the dynamic aptitude of the more direct or immediate sort.

In the author's 1941 *Guide to Horoscope Interpretation* the Lincoln horoscope accepted was the one most at variance with the chart rectified for the present text. Because it established the bowl configuration in a perfect squaring with the house axes it gave the native a much more conventional anchorage in life, and this earlier exposition in consequence emphasized a very distinctively outer or practical and objective existence in functional separation from quite as sharply delimited inner frustrations and subjective deficiencies. These latter were then dismissed to a silent and subconscious manifestation as in the puzzling melancholia. The total self-emptying arrangement of the planets was an indication of a lack of power to retain any of the fruits of self for the enjoyment of self, and was of a piece with the testimony to an ultimate personal detachment from everyday realities with unoccupied first and tenth angles. The author in further attention to Lincoln in his 1960 *Essentials of Astrological Analysis* not only was without access to the clarified historical materials relative to the native that had become available but indeed was quite unaware of them. To be noted is that with the shift in perspective after almost two decades the tendency to self-sacrifice on the native's part was still accepted rather superficially, and it is only the extensive investigation since 1965 that has provided the much more incisive understanding of that individual's psychological make-up. Highly exhibited however, even in view of the general adequacy of the prior delineations, is the inescapable necessity of proper case histories for any scientifically competent horoscopic interpretation.

THUMBNAIL BIOGRAPHY

Abraham Lincoln was born of good pioneer stock on February 12, 1809, in Kentucky about fifty miles due south from Louisville. The lineage of Thomas Lincoln the father has been traced back into England in the seventeenth century, but the antecedents of the mother Nancy Hanks are hopelessly obscure. Thomas had some means in 1809, since he owned several small farms and had earning capacity as a skilled carpenter. Neither parent could read, and the father was barely able to write his name. Schooling for the youngster amounted to less than a year, but he became assiduous in self-education at a very early age. His sister Sarah was two years older, but a third and younger child did not live very long. The elder Lincoln had persisting ill luck with his attempts at farming, compounded by continual difficulties over land titles in the state, and when the boy was seven he moved his family into Indiana where virgin territory was open to purchase with secure patents from the government The new location was some thirty-five miles east and slightly north from Evansville on Little Pigeon Creek, which emptied into the Ohio River to the southwest. As Abraham came of age a further move was made several hundred miles north and west into Illinois. It was to be the history of the restless father to go progressively down hill as his offspring climbed high, and the family tie between them apparently was none too strong. In these early days the living conditions were primitive, even to spending one winter in a lean-to and in the log cabins always occupying a single room with dirt floor in which at one time in the boy's life a total of eight individuals ate and slept together.

Spread out before him young Abraham Lincoln found in wonderful convenience a full panorama of American life west of the Alleghenies in the early nineteenth century, beginning with five years of impressionable childhood close to the well-traveled pike from Louisville to Nashville and continuing on through the whole of his adolescence within easy distance from the Ohio as the principal waterway of the nation's east-west commerce. His first job as distinct from casual hiring out was in Indiana as helper for James Taylor, who operated a ferry across the big river with its fascinating traffic. Here the well-muscled youthful giant caught the eye of James Gentry, and at nineteen he constructed a flatboat for that prominent citizen and with Gentry's son took a cargo to New Orleans. Later in Illinois when he was of age and free to go his own way he had another and similar opportunity to take produce down to market in the busy ocean port on the Gulf of Mexico, and there have additional exposure to human activities in wide dimension ranging from slavery to finance and from prostitution to the prodigality of entrenched wealth. In his own person however he retained almost puritanical insulation against the vices of his day, even as in contrast he was little attracted to religion or to intellectual abstraction with perhaps the single exception of the law and socioeconomic principle. His pragmatic slanting is well attested by his disinterest in his partner Herndon's transcendentalism. But he was not antireligious, as he was at pains to point out at a much later time in response to criticism in his political career. The fact that he never drank when virtually everybody living in the pioneer hardship did, and frequently to excess, is on the record not as a matter of moral conviction but wholly because he didn't like it. Presumably in much the same attitude he abstained from tobacco.

The foundation for his genuine opportunity followed his coming of age with settlement shortly thereafter in New Salem, a community established just north of Springfield on the Sangamon River. The hamlet was due to have a very short life, and he would go down into Springfield for the fulfillment of his destiny, but in the meanwhile he became postmaster and a deputy county surveyor and got down real roots as a personage. His acceptance of a wrestling challenge by the leader of the Clary's Grove boys, essentially a gang of roughs, led to a fine demonstration of his physical prowess and in rather ironic fashion got him his first political support when he was urged to run for office. From here on his progress in the public arena was fast, with a climax in actual election to the legislature. Since economic opportunity was then ebbing fast for him in New Salem, he enlisted in the insignificant little Black Hawk War and promptly was elected captain of his company. Out of this step came vital contacts. Through the friendship of the gifted politician and attorney John T. Stuart, who encouraged him to study law and then ultimately took him into partnership, it became possible for him to move to Springfield. His brilliant performance in the state legislature as a young man still in his twenties was the principal factor in his expanding good fortune. Indeed, it was almost wholly due to his leadership and in many respects singlehanded efforts that Springfield became the new capital of the state of Illinois.

Lincoln's personal life was actually about as uncomplicated as he himself regarded his individual history as a whole. Essentially the loner, and accustomed to bury himself in the reading to which he devoted himself assiduously or to relax into the abstraction that had so puzzling and morbid an appearance, he apparently took social and emotional matters in stride but as no more than the regular components of normal existence. With considerable talent as the mimic, he proved unusually able to entertain his companions in earlier years when he joined them in friendly intercourse. The beginning of the attraction between Mary Todd and himself somewhat later was in the sprightly insouciance of young people dependent on their own resources in a society of new and shifting roots. In his background however was the bawdy sense of humor of the primitive personality, and this had showed up earlier and in a way that in no respect was to his credit in his first romance of sorts when he became engaged to Mary Owens as a consequence of a prankish wager. While by all testimony never at ease with women in the sense of petty repartee, he yet was strongly attached to the older sister he had lost through her untimely death and he definitely idolized his stepmother. This however was in the familiar family pattern of his background. When he found personal companionship otherwise, as with the daughter of the tavernkeeper with whom he had boarded during his first months in New Salem, the reasonable suggestion was that the books they could share together was the basis of the camaraderie. At least with her he could be at ease since she was engaged to a close if absent friend of his. The fact that he was much upset when she died some four years later led tò the long and wide acceptance of an actually quite unsubstantiated account of this as a blighted romance.

Mary Todd was a thoroughgoing aristocrat with the best of Kentucky roots and connections, indeed, she may well have been the best educated young lady of the Midwest South of the time. Mary Owens of the abortive New Salem engagement was also born in Kentucky and perhaps no less cultivated in a shallow fashion, but she had offered no rapport of mind to the rising young man. Instead she was affronted by his utter lack of the superficial refinement she affected, while he in turn came to be repelled by a developing physical coarseness he had not detected when he first met her. In contrast and as even more outwardly disparate the emerging Lincoln and the more fine-fibered Mary might have seemed to be, they discovered a curious intellectual uniqueness they alone could share with each other. After an initial engagement was broken, presumably under family pressure on her side, their mutual deprivation brought them back together quickly enough and into their life of perhaps strange conditions but unquestioned happiness. His extraordinary prominence and influence at this time, when he was but thirty years of age, must be realized for any real understanding of his career. Inescapably eccentric in many ways, he yet moved in the best circles in Springfield. His complete lack of deviousness is shown in his intimacy for more than two decades with the other men who traveled the judicial circuit with him for the many months when it took them all far from home.

He and Mary Todd married in 1842, and in 1844 he selected his final law partner in William Herndon. These two ultimately closest associates of his had no love whatsoever for each other, but with his own incorruptible single-mindedness he did not permit the two areas of his concern to get unnecessarily entangled. When he was elected president he proceeded with much the same spirit of fundamental impartiality to select opponents and enemies for his cabinet because of their peculiar abilities in each instance. Gradually however he was drawn into the center of the inevitable open and armed conflict between the plantation and industrial patterns of life, and in the context of apparently hopeless irreconcilabilities he carried his destiny on down to the tragic end.

The assassination was April 14, 1865, in the native's fifty-seventh year.

ANNIE BESANT

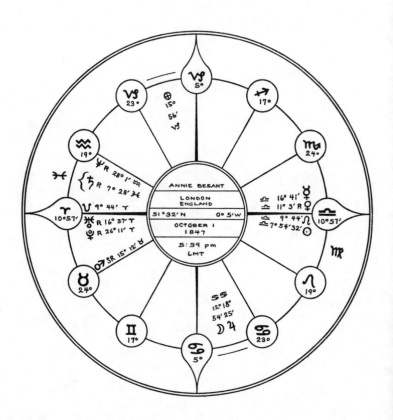

THE BASIC ATTITUDE

Annie Besant was a year old when the planet Neptune was discovered. In correlation with a fulcrum activation of this significator in basic attitude when she was twenty-eight, she made an effective start in the career in which in many ways she proved herself quite the most brilliant woman in the public life of her era. Two later fulcral activations of the same planet in this activity-facet correspond in order to her election as international president of the Theosophical Society in 1907 as she approached sixty and to the presidency of the Indian National Congress just before her seventieth birthday in 1917. Not only was her birth closely coincident with the discovery of this second of the three newly operative planets in astrology but her decease was within three and a half years of the identification of Pluto or the third of them. Uranus or the first is also exceptionally significant in her case, but more definitely from the complementary perspective of character analysis. Already noted has been the fact that it is the dynamic horoscopy that primarily charts the uniqueness of Abraham Lincoln and the basic nativity that provides the best astrological clue to her quite extraordinary potentials.

Like the case of the American president, in which the War of 1812 together with the Mexican War proved significant under the essential principle of concordance or concomitance, in hers (1) a crucial early sponsorship by Charles Bradlaugh was coincident with the founding of the Theosophical Society across the ocean or an event totally devoid of any immediate connection with her and (2) she not only was born at the threshold of the 1848 revolutions in Europe but the outbreak in 1914 of World War I in which the age-old institution of empire building and colonialism received its first death thrust was a marker for the impending collapse of the Krishnamurti messiahship developed all too prematurely in the outworn global pattern of a class-dominated human society. It might well seem that if in the New World a torch of light in man's evolution can be identified as carried from Henry Clay and dropped by Stephen Douglas to be picked up again and taken into enduring history by Lincoln in his survival as a myth figure, some sort of a similar bridging from what Neptune charts to what Pluto promises might also seem an ultimate contribution of Annie Besant in a more subjective immortality. Such at least is the hypothesis adopted in these pages in order to gain psychological substance for the interpretation of her life.

In summary, the life of Annie Besant like Abraham Lincoln's in astrological delineation is marked by exceptional emphasis of the three major planets of recent discovery. Thus again there is the possibility of a special historical significance, identified in the development of the American president into a definite myth figure and hypothetically assumed in this text to be her similar carrying of a torch of man's enlightenment in some less tangible ultimacy.

The Psychological Trend to Balance

In this first of the four normal procedures in analysis of an activity-facet in the dynamic horoscopy there is no certain indication of either extreme of psychological trend in the basic attitude of Annie Besant. At the start of her life there was an initial subperiod of strong idealistic orientation, and this prevailed uninterruptedly until her final four-odd years. At that time the potential of Pluto stood against what otherwise would have been the establishment of a fundamentally practical or immediate slanting in this area of her public image. Actually her early and highly imaginative self-projection even had a special instrumentation when she came under the tutelage of Ellen Marryat or the Victorian perfectionist who gave the childish world of near fantasy an expanded setting in social and cultural accomplishments, and this for a while provided an effective insulation against the more covert and far from admirable realities of British institutions. Effusive Annie was thirty-seven years old before George Bernard Shaw, and the group of men who generally were supplanting the more solid but thoroughly ideal influence of Charles Bradlaugh, had in a way begun to get her down on earth. But almost immediately she embraced Theosophy and thereupon perpetuated her own original otherworldliness with a different and immeasurably extensive transcendental orientation. It was in such a basically occult frame that she made her ultimately enduring and essentially practical contributions toward political independence and especially to higher education in India. The transcendental was long foreshadowed.

In summary, there is no overall psychological trend to balance in the basic attitude of Annie Besant, and this complicates the analysis of her public career because a subordinate and strong idealistic tendency dominated her life until her final very few years. Circumstances tended to bring her down on earth when she was thirty-seven, but she reached out to transcendental orientations in the frame of which she made enduring contribution to Indian education and independence.

Challenge by Progressed Station

PROGRESSED MERCURY STATIONARY TURNING RETROGRADE
IN 1893 In this second of the four normal procedures in
analysis of an activity-facet in the dynamic horoscopy the
critical regrasp of experience shown to be necessary for Annie
Besant at this point proved to be essentially intellectual. She
had come to the end of any possible challenge to her basic
self-projection in Victorian England, but in counter to this
there had been the opening up of wonderful new vistas with
the impact of Madame Blavatsky. A dramatic strengthening
of her self-assurance followed from her extraordinary success
in presenting Theosophy at the Parliament of Religions held
in connection with the World's Columbian Exposition in
Chicago in 1893, and a parallel event of ultimate high significance was her first effective contact with Eastern philosophy.
Professor Gyanendra Chakravarti, a Brahman mystic who
represented the Indian Theosophists at the Chicago exposition, served her most fortuitously by (1) providing her
through Hinduism with a corrective for the Buddhist claims
and assumptions that might more naturally have seemed to
fit in with her long-established socioeconomic evangelism and
(2) helping to open important educational doors when within
some two months she would be on her way to set foot in India
for a first time and thereupon to launch what in time became
her spectacular second chapter of secular and social reform.

PROGRESSED MERCURY STATIONARY TURNING DIRECT IN
1913 The critical regrasp of experience in basic attitude
shown here to be necessary for the native meant some very
definite choices if developments were to remain at all in her
control. On the objective side she launched the weekly *Commonweal* as a positive step in her plunge into the struggle for

Indian independence. The first issue was on January 2, 1914, and from her self-committal at this point would come her most distinguished achievements in the more conventional terms of history. On the subjective side and concomitantly, she was beset through most of 1913 by repercussions of the scandal of alleged sexual perversions that while not involving her personally yet tainted her sponsorship of Krishnamurti as a new world messiah and required a tolerance for which temperamentally she was not too well equipped.

In summary, the two points of critical regrasp of experience during her lifetime and necessary for the native in basic attitude are indicated by progressed stations corresponding to the years 1893 and 1913. In the first instance, when the challenge to her self-projection needed by her temperament had rather played out in her native England while vast new vistas of realization had been opened for her by Madame Blavatsky, she discovered the real range of her powers and achieved a needed fresh self-reassurance at the Parliament of Religions in Chicago. In the second case she launched the *Commonweal* in India and made vigorous advance toward the achievement of independence for her adopted new land, although by the same token she was too bewildered by the taint of scandal in connection with the anticipated messiahship of Krishnamurti to be able to handle her more occult potentials with equal facility.

Fulcrum Indication

PROGRESSED MERCURY IN SQUARE WITH NATAL JUPITER, OCTOBER 22, 1848   In this third of the four normal procedures in analysis of an activity-facet in the dynamic horoscopy the critical self-mobilizations required by the native under the pressure of objective events is here a pivotal quickening of the zest for life in the case of a babe hardly thirteen months old, and this first of all the secondary directions to culminate suggests actual response to a unique climate of reality. Jupiter as the planet so quickened suggests the presence in her make-up of her curiously innate sense of proportion or ease of self-projection into experience that may well have been her inheritance from the sheer and unbridled individuality of both her parents. Her father, William Wood, has been characterized as too versatile and accomplished but too volatile a half-Irishman to be able to settle at all steadily to anything. He died when she was five, and left his little family of a wife and a boy and Annie in serious straits. The mother, Emily Morris Wood, was the wholly Irish daughter of a gay and extravagant couple who in an earlier extremity had hardly even hesitated in permitting a maiden aunt to adopt their child. The strong-willed little beauty treated in such cavalier fashion had a remote royal heritage that she cherished very particularly, and she proceeded to justify her own conception of herself through uncompromising spunk when it became necessary to shoulder the responsibilities consequent on her husband's death.

PROGRESSED MERCURY IN SQUARE WITH NATAL NEPTUNE, DECEMBER 4, 1875　This indication of a fulcral coming to stress of matters concerning the native's general acceptance or adoption of an individual destiny through the basic attitude has overall correlation with the beginning of her eleven years of close association with Charles Bradlaugh. When she met him in 1874 he had recognized her exceptional capacities very quickly, and had given her a staff position on the *National Reformer*. This was the official publication of the National Secular Society, and her meteoric rise to prominence was

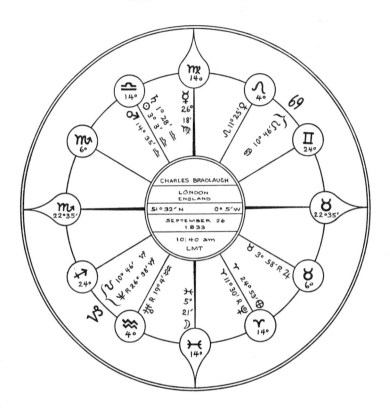

largely instrumented through her column "Daylight" written under the nom de plume of Ajax. Her first public lecture was within the month of meeting him, and on the following January 19th she gained an astonishing platform success as significant augury of her future as a public figure. With May she became a vice-president of the society, and the whole pattern of wide adoration that would mark her life in its happiest moments had emerged very definitely. Secularism was

anathema to Victorian righteousness, and to the smug her
success was sheer notoriety. With summer the strangely bigoted
husband from whom she had been separated legally for some
two years had begun the proceedings that would take her
two children away from her on the grounds that as an atheist
she like Percy Bysshe Shelley was a parent unfit to have custody of any of Britain's young hopefuls.

Charles Bradlaugh was a dedicated man, strong of mind
and body and with a rugged incorruptibility. His struggle for
human rights in the name of free thought had already begun
to have epic dimension, and he had achieved wide recognition
for better or worse in the English-speaking world. Living at
this time in crowded and frugal quarters with the two daughters who were his faithful co-workers, he soon would be
moving and therefore be spending the daytime in the nearby
and commodious house acquired by his new associate and
where they could give their attention to their separate tasks.
The simple camaraderie was an idyllic experience for both of
them, and Hypatia Bradlaugh the elder of his two daughters
believed they would have married except neither was free.
On his side and in carefully guarded secrecy he supported a
wife who had long been hopelessly alcoholic. The nativities of
the two outstanding individualists have no planetary cross
ties between them to indicate factors of dynamic impact in
the case of either native in respect to the other. Thus they can
be seen drawn together in a common convenience in meeting
a great humanitarian need, and so teamed more essentially
in a fight to be fought than in any special psychological fulfillment together. Theirs will be seen to be a happy platonic
intimacy fundamentally. To be noted is that their mutual
respect and appreciation continued without the least qualifica-

tion throughout the lifetime not only of Bradlaugh but of his two devoted girls after his decease in 1891.

PROGRESSED MERCURY IN SQUARE WITH NATAL SATURN, JUNE 29, 1884   This indication of a fulcral coming to stress of matters of the deeper and ultimate concern of the native's basic attitude has its most convenient correlation with the events marked quite dramatically or at least quixotically in her association with George Bernard Shaw. Close acquaint-anceship began on January 31, 1885, but she had taken note of him at a public meeting in London eight months before. She had been finding secularism rather sophomoric in its basic look to science for ultimate social reform, and had been drift-ing toward socialism although unable to stomach the extrem-ists. She ended up by joining the relatively moderate Fabian Society under Shaw's sponsorship, and her new camaraderie with the young Irish eccentric endured for some three years. Astrologically or in horoscope comparison he potentially could be of unique service to her, while her contribution to him was essentially casual, since his Mercury applies by cross tie in conjunction to her Jupiter. His unquestionable but as yet wholly unrecognized brilliance of mind brought her a new dimension of zest in basic outreach on a far higher level than the plane of the vital but purely material socioeconomic reform. Meanwhile and importantly she met his financial need in his days of early struggle in London through the magazine *Our Corner* she had launched in January 1883. In April, 1885, she published the first installment of a novel he had not yet been able to sell and shortly afterwards gave him the Art Corner in her periodical as a start in the critical career that before long would mean enduring recognition.

Annie Besant in her self-mobilization at this point was well on the way to lifting herself to new levels of understanding through her own intellectual bootstraps. During the close association with Bradlaugh she had felt the need of a greater compass of mind and had begun a process of formalized self-improvement when in 1879 she had entered London University under the new opportunity extended to women to earn a conventional degree. This was to prove a chapter of long-continuing frustration but she was able in August, 1884, to announce the enlistment of John Mackinnon Robertson as a staff member of the *National Reformer* and this was the significant event because he was the first genuine scholar with whom she had any working relationship.

PROGRESSED MERCURY IN SQUARE WITH NATAL SATURN, APRIL 14, 1900   This first repetition of a fulcral coming to stress of matters of the deeper and ultimate concern of the native's basic attitude has its most convenient correlation with the moving of the London headquarters of the Theosophical Society from her remodeled home on Avenue Road. The change was made on the grounds of expediency but it was significant for her because it meant abandoning Blavatsky Hall with its highly occult associations as well as the place of her happiest hours with Charles Bradlaugh. The farewell meeting of the Lodge was on September 21, 1899, or on the day preceding her departure to make her permanent home in India and there to inaugurate the second great chapter of her adult years. The prior charting of her basic presentation of herself in experience by this particular progressed aspect had its correlation with her momentary effort to assimilate some of Bernard Shaw's brilliance to herself as well as her endeavor to formalize her essentially self-instruction in the conventional university terms of the Western world, and in failing to establish such an anchorage effectively she had drifted toward substantiations through the dramatic organon inherent in Theosophy. Now and in broader lineaments on everyday levels she had begun to labor for the development of higher education in India. She had founded the Central Hindu College at Benares as a first step toward the greater literacy she envisioned for the Indian masses. It had opened on July 7, 1898, and it would become perhaps the core of her most enduring contribution of nonoccult nature.

PROGRESSED MERCURY IN SQUARE WITH NATAL NEPTUNE, NOVEMBER 5, 1907   This first repetition of a fulcral coming to stress in matters of the general acceptance or adoption of an individual destiny through the basic attitude has its most convenient overall correlation with the decease on February 17, 1907, of the co-founder and long president of the Theosophical Society and the consequent precipitation of the bitter power struggle that nearly fragmented the organization for once and all. Since Madame Blavatsky's death sixteen years before there had been continual dissension among the Theosophists under the formal leadership of Colonel Henry Steele Olcott but of Annie Besant in rather practical fact, and now the real conflict of loyalties developed with the American and British sections providing the greatest opposition to the latter in her election as the colonel's successor. The situation where Charles Bradlaugh had provided an entrance into an entirely new world of achievement in correlation with the indication in 1875 was repeated in the contribution to her career at this point by Charles Webster Leadbeater and the opening of the doors of infinite magic for her in a context of man's supersensual capacity. His advocacy of sexual practices for young boys that were wholly beyond Victorian acceptance had made it necessary for him to resign from the society in May, 1906. Untouched by scandal herself, Annie Besant came to accept his explanations by the end of the year and with his subsequent reinstatement she gradually established him in the creative intimacy that had been so very rewarding in her earlier camaraderie with Bradlaugh. Leadbeater's all-important vindication by the Theosophists themselves came at the American Convention on September 15, 1907.

PROGRESSED MERCURY IN SQUARE WITH NATAL NEPTUNE, JUNE 28, 1918   This second and final repetition of a fulcral coming to stress in matters of the general acceptance or adoption of an individual destiny through the native's basic attitude has its most convenient correlation with the consequences her election to the presidency of the Indian National Congress as a consummatory recognition of her sociopolitical achievement in the larger sphere of the East. The ratification was complete in mid-September, 1917. But the new horizons opening before her did not have clear enough definition in her mind to enable her to help carry India through the next steps. Her overall sympathy with the plight of the oppressed was not in the terms of the roots in which a heightened self-expression would be possible. Actually her intellectual slanting betrayed her since as the occultist she saw a transcendental ordering in the caste system and gave it a full and uncritical approval because of her failure to realize its hopelessly superficial crystallization. At the end it was Gandhi who made himself the living myth figure to which the Indian masses could assimilate themselves. The emaciated Mahatma traveled in loin cloth whereas she wore expensive clothes and displayed glittering jewelry. Against all advice she chose to make her

new office a basis for an aggressive instead of the more subtle
or occult influence of an honor bestowed, and thereby diminished its dimension. The course of the elections in England
after the armistice in 1918 destroyed all hopes of progress
through the course she was advocating. In the judgment of
Jawaharlal Nehru her ultimate political failure was not
because she was a Theosophist or a woman or particularly a
white woman as had been suggested but rather because she
was a politician who with splendid capacity was handicapped
by wrong principles.

PROGRESSED MERCURY IN SQUARE WITH NATAL SATURN,
MAY 13, 1927 This second repetition of a fulcral coming to
stress of matters of the deeper and ultimate concern of the
native's basic attitude has its most convenient correlation with
the definite revolt of Krishnamurti against the artificialities in
which his supposed avatarship had been cradled. Events
moved slowly, and it was August 3rd two years later when he
finally dissolved the Order of the Star that had been established to support his mission as the world's new messiah. In
the meantime on June 30, 1927, he had told a meeting at
the Star Camp in Holland that he was determined to be free
of the associations that had dictated his reality to him. A
month later he made it clear that for him the world teacher
was a transcendental entity that each person had to create
individually, and that in consequence he himself could be
such a myth figure for others only in the most symbolical
sense. The simplicity or spiritual integrity of the relatively
untutored young man was asserting itself, and this was something she caught and to which apparently she held very
steadily.

In summary, the critical points of self-mobilization in the

basic attitude of Annie Besant as indicated by the fulcrum
aspects of the progressions begin as early as her second year
with a special impact through her parental endowment and
reveal the extent to which she might become the uncompromising individualist in life. Thereafter the pivotal reorienta-
tions are charted by the dynamic horoscopy as she successively
became involved with (1) Charles Bradlaugh, (2) Bernard
Shaw, (3) Hindu higher education, (4) responsibility for the
Theosophical Society after the decease of its co-founder president, (5) responsibility for the Indian National Congress on
election to its presidency, and (6) responsibility to the essence
of herself following the disintegration of the grandiose plans
for the inauguration of an avatar.

Nonfulcral Indication

PROGRESSED MERCURY IN OPPOSITION WITH NATAL PLUTO,
AUGUST 29, 1853   In this fourth of the four normal procedures in analysis of an activity-facet in the dynamic horoscopy the single activation of this third of the new planets in
the basic attitude of Annie Besant, when she was not quite six
years old, supplements Mercury's progressed square in 1848
with Jupiter in the suggestion of an unusual set given to her
public presentation of herself from actual infancy. The prefiguring emphasis of Pluto more than half a century before
its discovery also strengthens the conception of the whole life
of the native as perhaps providing some as yet unrecognized
bridge from the horizons of human potential identified in
history as each of the two new significators have been located
by the astronomers. The progressed aspect has its inoperative
correlation with the death of her father near her fifth birthday
to testify to a transcendental significance over and above the
early traumatic effect of what to every child is the incompre-

hensible phenomenon of death, and this could be of an importance similar to the double impact on Abraham Lincoln with the passing of a baby brother when he was quite little himself and then of his mother by the time he was nine. A likely pyramiding of portents of no meaning to the little British miss at the moment, under the astrological principle of concordance or concomitance, was the sudden manifestation of a dramatic clairvoyance by her mother during the father's funeral.

PROGRESSED MERCURY IN TRINE WITH NATAL NEPTUNE, OCTOBER 28, 1854 This indication of an activated acceptance of a life destiny through idealistic flexibility in the basic attitude is the first of two progressions that reveal the setting of life's stage for the six critical self-mobilizations charted by these same two significators through the fulcral aspects to which attention already has been given. Here is symmetry in kind with the Chinese-boxes arrangement of indicators characterizing this activity-facet in Lincoln's secondary directions and so again a case, under the astrological principle of equivalence or distinction, of the matching uniqueness to be expected in horoscope and career in connection with marked achievement. The progressed trine here has correspondence to the surrender of eight-year-old Annie by her mother to the pedagogical mercies of Ellen Marryat. This benefactress was a financially independent spinster who joyed in a genius for teaching and welcomed a select little group out of her own and other families into her home for a proper conventional rearing.

PROGRESSED MERCURY IN TRINE WITH NATAL SATURN, JANUARY 19, 1861 This indication of an activated underlying concern for the norms and values of conscious existence through idealistic flexibility is the second identification of factors setting the stage for the native's critical self-mobilizations of basic attitude, and the superficial correspondence is with the opportunity for male attention that came in the spring of 1861 when Miss Marryat took her charges to the continent. In Annie's earlier years at Harrow where her mother in a courageous and successful manifestation of independence in particular had taken her older brother and herself for his educational advantage, she had been the tomboy and quite too self-centered or intense at core for contacts with others to be more than an impersonal camaraderie. Now and in this uniquely different context of experience as a thirteen-year-old adolescent, she had the very definite opportunity to discover herself as a personage and also as one of extraordinary protean characteristics. Always a thoroughly pious youngster, in Europe now she ricocheted from the chance to play the charmer in very serious fashion to grasp the opportunity to take the special confirmation class of an elderly American bishop of the Church of England who was visiting in Paris. In taking her first communion on Easter Sunday in 1862 she experienced an ecstasy that may have established the permanent set in her self-presentation to reality on the subjective side.

PROGRESSED MERCURY IN TRINE WITH THE NATAL MOON, OCTOBER 20, 1864   This indication of an activated endurance of capacity for a continuity of ongoing through idealistic flexibility is the first of three progressed aspects that while charting the everyday unfoldment of the native's basic attitude are not involved in the significant couplings provided (1) by the Neptune-Saturn delineation of crucial self-mobilizations in this activity-facet already considered in detail and (2) the

Sun and Venus signification that come to have special importance during the final five-odd decades of her life and to which attention must still be given. The quickening at this point reveals the high potential of public presence and exceptionally uninhibited initiative after her gradual but complete break with Ellen Marryat. Correspondences are hardly to be pinpointed as she plunged happily and wholeheartedly into social affairs and yet for the major part and even at seventeen enjoyed an intellectual exhange for which she prepared herself very effectively as she reveled in theology and read accounts of the Church Fathers and reports of the current discussions in Protestant circles.

PROGRESSED MERCURY IN OPPOSITION WITH NATAL MARS, MAY 24, 1866   This indication of an activated persistence of the native in basic attitude charts her nascent or still unconditioned self-expression in idealistic awareness at the threshold of maturity, but at eighteen she now was brought to face the more adult experience of living with crisis instead of flowing along in an unquestioning and simple self-intentness. At Easter on April 1st she met Frank Besant, and for her the occasion had a wholly adolescent halo of potential since she herself later unequivocally stated that she did not love the man she married but rather saw an opportunity for companionship in a life of service through the church.

PROGRESSED MERCURY IN TRINE WITH NATAL JUPITER, SEPTEMBER 10, 1868   This indication of an activated zest for life through an idealistic adroitness or capacity for adjustment has curious ultimate correlation with the greatest emotional shock of the native's life, and in that connection it charts the beginning of an actual appearance in the basic attitude of a more practical strand of her make-up as demonstrated dramatically in her fidelity to wifely duties and comprising competence in nursing and the superficial details of the domestic tragedy. The anesthetizing impact of utter outrage came in the marital bed after the marriage in December of the previous year, and she had to learn to insulate herself against the self-righteous cruelty of a young Victorian boor devoid of all sensitivity. In her despair of spirit and bafflement of mind she had recourse to the deeper core of the more subjective side of her nature, so wonderfully nurtured in her halcyon years, and thereupon she emerged for the first time in the strange dualism of her nature that now would distinguish her above all else and threw all her enthusiasm of livingness into her private intellectual world and into an amateurish authorship in which she had had fortuitous encouragement. Her definite start in her life career may well be dated by her first sale of literary effort on May 2, 1868.

PROGRESSED MERCURY IN SEXTILE WITH THE NATAL SUN, JANUARY 1, 1885   This indication of an activated strength of character as such or of integration of self in basic attitude through a practical adroitness of everyday adjustment has its convenient correlation with the start of the rather brief intellectual intimacy of the native with Bernard Shaw in what subconsciously at least was obvious rebound from what perhaps in her life may have been her closest approach to a sexual affair, with Edward Bibbins Aveling. There was nothing in her background of Victorian naïveté to make her any judge of men, but everybody else among the Secularists was equally blind to the fact that the newcomer in their ranks was a palpable scoundrel. Aveling had found the National Secular Society a quite happy refuge for the free display of his inherent scintillation of mind and wide virtuosity, and it had not been long before an effective triumvirate instead of the previous harmonious twosome of Bradlaugh and herself had come to dominate the movement. The episode began when she engaged Aveling in 1879 to tutor her for matriculation in London University, or perhaps before that when she had opened the columns of the *National Reformer* to him. It is possible that all unconsciously she had begun to tire of the rather stodgy Bradlaugh, and that the brilliance of the new Secular star began to meet the insatiable appetite of her own far from inconsiderable intellect. But in the summer of 1884 he calmly walked out of her life, and the blow to her esteem may have provided a considerable tempering of her character at core as the six momentum progressions begin to chart the overall turn to the development however subordinate of a practical lean in the activity-facet.

PROGRESSED MERCURY IN SEXTILE WITH NATAL VENUS, SEPTEMBER 29, 1889   This indication of an activated realization of the nature of the world of experience through a practical adroitness of everyday adjustment in basic attitude has its correlation with the native's meteoric rise in the Theosophy Society in significant duplication of her spectacular leap to prominence in the National Secular Society. Her actual contact with Madame Blavatsky was in March, 1889. She was elected to the presidency of Blavatsky Lodge in London less than a year later, or on January 17th. Probably altogether disillusioned by men in any conventionally romantic or idealistic sense at this point, with Aveling in one way and Shaw in another especially disappointing in an anticipation still heightened through the rose glasses of adolescence, she was coming however slowly and instinctively to disregard individual deficiencies of almost any sort in any fellow human if

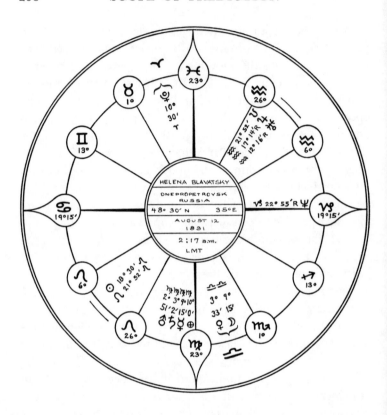

these proved to be balanced out by a higher-level merit or a transcendental promise. Thus she remained quite undisturbed by the idiosyncrasies of the Russian woman, whose studied offbeat genius gave modern Theosophy its enduring foundation, and she simply shrugged off the devastating report by the Society for Psychical Research of spiritistic trickery at the Theosophical headquarters in Madras.

PROGRESSED MERCURY IN SEXTILE WITH NATAL VENUS,

FEBRUARY 22, 1896   This indication of an activated realization of the native of the world of experience through a practical adroitness of everyday adjustment in basic attitude has its convenient correlation with her striking mastery of the genius of the Sanskrit language and her particular demonstration of this through the translation she completed and published in 1895 of the *Bhagavadgita* or cherished religious classic of the East. This was an additional achievement in her efforts to revivify interest in the ancient Hindu heritage.

PROGRESSED MERCURY IN SEXTILE WITH THE NATAL SUN, NOVEMBER 29, 1899   This indication of an activated strength of character as such or of integration of self in basic attitude through a practical adroitness of everyday adjustment has its convenient correlation with the closing of Blavatsky Hall in London after the last meeting there on September 21, 1899, and her permanent move of her base of operation to India. In her refusal to be bound by sentiment to her old home, she is more and more establishing the impersonality of her life work that in ultimate terms is needed to guarantee its immortality.

PROGRESSED MERCURY IN SEXTILE WITH THE NATAL SUN, SEPTEMBER 14, 1927   This indication of an activated strength of character as such or of integration of self in basic attitude through a practical adroitness of everyday adjustment has its correlation with the definitive self-assertion of Krishnamurti at the Star Camp at Ommen in Holland on August 2, 1927. In his clarification of the nature of his messiahship as the simple union of the self with its indwelling divinity he was able to accept his role as leader in the ultimate honesty of the insight. This conception Annie Besant accepted at once as the consummation of her own life pilgrimage, and in proceeding to tailor her course to the more solid and reasonable apotheosis she deferred to him for a first time on the public platform during the meeting at the Star Camp at Benares a few months later and at the Theosophical convention there she left the dais and sat on the ground with the rest of the audience during his talks. This self-abnegation, cheerfully accomplished according to the arcane injunction, was her final and presumably immortal strengthening.

PROGRESSED MERCURY IN SEXTILE WITH NATAL VENUS, FEBRUARY 3, 1930 This indication of an activated realization of the nature of the world of experience by the native through a practical adroitness of everyday judgment in basic attitude has its most obvious correspondence with the formal dissolution of the Order of the Star on August 3, 1929, and Krishnamurti's ultimately complete proscription of hierarchical trappings. The no less important correlation with the discovery of Pluto on February 18, 1930, shows the culmination in the building of the bridge from what Neptune charts to what the still newer planet may end up indicating even if the precise nature of this must remain indeterminate in the record.

PROGRESSED MERCURY IN TRINE WITH NATAL URANUS, FEBRUARY 13, 1934 This indication of an activated release of potentials through an ideal adroitness in basic attitude culminates after the native's decease and consequently is of no validity in connection with her living years, but it does give valuable suggestion concerning any possible continuing influence of her life and effort. Because this one of the new planets has its sole quickening at this point in the activity-facet, her presentation of herself in experience may be shown to have its greatest opportunity in some sort of an immortal continu-

ance. Actually the occultist's true role is that of the insemi-
nator in some special case of his species and times and
apparently Annie Besant as the most effective successor of
Madame Blavatsky may well be continuing the revelation and
refinement of the arcane organon in a way too subtle for any
present and everyday delimitation.

In summary, the nonfulcral aspects of basic attitude in
their progressive distribution of horoscopic potential chart the
course of the significant normal developments in the case of
Annie Besant. These are (1) the early family disruptions that
helped develop an independent and self-reliant individual,
(2) the unusual educational opportunity that buttressed a
happy and in its early phases a tomboy adolescence, (3) an
overidealized young womanhood that rushed her into a marriage she thought would be an exciting playtime of service
but that proved cruel torture as well as sexual outrage such as
in the one respect blighted the rest of her life, and (4)
recourse to a professional career of unexampled brilliance
marked by (a) activity in the National Secular Society in
idyllic camaraderie with Charles Bradlaugh and embracing
efforts to formalize her self-education, (b) intellectual outreach and ricocheting interest through various reform movements with the high point of brief association with Bernard
Shaw and in passing an emotional devastation through
Edward Aveling, (c) finding new frontiers in Theosophy
through Madame Blavatsky and fresh fields for her reformer's
zeal in India, and (d) adjustment with occult overtones as
yet beyond adequate assessment in the case of Jeddu Krishnamurti whom she had promoted as a new savior for the world.

ANNIE BESANT II

THE NATURAL DRIVE

Continuing in the pattern established for the delineation of the secondary directions in the dynamic horoscopy, attention next turns to the unchanging and fundamental drive that instruments all self-existence and is indicated by the sun. The life of Annie Besant as examined in the activity-facet of her basic attitude has been seen to be a development in an ultimate harmonious relationship of two very distinct strands in her make-up. These twin manifestations of her presentation of herself to her world of experience were most marked as she became and remained the uncompromisingly practical reformer on the one hand but yet in time also became and remained the strangely ingenuous but irrevocably dedicated occultist on the other. Necessary for consideration at this point are the indications of the power of choice or the exercise of free will in furthering the conscious or perhaps subconscious grasp of life's potentials.

The Psychological Trend to Balance

In the first of the four normal procedures in the analysis of an activity-facet in the dynamic horoscopy an overall idealistic and a preliminary practical slant in a way reverses the psychological situation in the basic attitude. Annie Besant in childhood is thus shown with a simple and pragmatic directness of free will and choice that served her halcyon years of adolescence very wonderfully and indeed on through her establishment of a comfortable London home and the happy

212

camaraderie with Charles Bradlaugh, but then she found she was asked to compromise a principle and thereupon she first really asserted herself and became in truth a leader on the basis of wide-visioned purpose.

In summary, the psychological trend to balance shows an early naïveté of directness in purpose emerging with maturity into a high capacity for impersonal dedication to wide-ranging ends. This supplements the slanting in basic attitude where an earlier uncritical idealism was finally brought to balance after long years of life by practical overall considerations and barely escaped yielding to their dominance.

The sun, never retrograding, has no stations in progression.

Fulcrum Indication

THE PROGRESSED SUN IN SQUARE WITH THE NATAL MOON, NOVEMBER 7, 1852   In the third of the four normal procedures in the analysis of an activity-facet the critical self-mobilization in natural drive required by objective events is here shown in the coming to special emphasis of matters concerning the native's endurance or what developed as a marked self-sufficiency. The correlation is with her father's death in early October and the spectacularly successful independent course pursued by her mother in assuming the larger responsibility and thus dramatizing the strength of purpose the little girl will grow up to emulate.

THE PROGRESSED SUN IN SQUARE WITH NATAL JUPITER, MAY 24, 1858   This indication of a fulcral coming to stress of matters concerning the native's zest for life or eagerness for experience in her natural drive has primary correlation with the valuable social and intellectual discipline that came when Ellen Marryat took over her education. The fact that this strong-minded patroness in one of her reports to the mother reported a lack of cheerfulness characterizing the young lady most recently known as Sunshine Annie is an indication not so much of a superficial sobering as the deeper enthusiasm for some potential and supreme self-dedication such as she failed to find in a shared ministry with Frank Besant.

THE PROGRESSED SUN IN SQUARE WITH NATAL NEPTUNE, DECEMBER 5, 1897   This indication of a fulcral coming to stress of matters concerning the native's acceptance or adoption of an individual destiny of fundamental consequence in her natural drive corresponds to a dramatic demonstration of her ultimately deep self-commitment. Up to this time the bitter power struggle among the Theosophists following the decease of Madame Blavatsky had not touched her because the clash of personalities may have seemed little different from the continual bickering with which she had lived among the Secularists, and perhaps had observed to some extent in ecclesiastical circles before that. She may have been quite insensitive to her eclipse of the society's president, Colonel Olcott, since she had been unblushingly favored by Blavatsky and for more than six years had certainly proved her exceptional value to the cause while he had begun to falter in holding the reins of administration.

The American Section had continued under the personal direction of William Quan Judge, the one in the background of an actual three original founders of the society who in a recent incident of vacillation by Olcott had been designated president-elect and who in consequence had expected to gain the position in time, but with the insensate wrangling over purported messages from the Masters and the like the section had withdrawn from the parent group in 1895 and he had passed away the following year. Emerging as leader in his place was Katherine A. Tingley, who had been a close companion and confidant of his last days, and in this flamboyant personality Annie Besant had found herself challenged by a rival of a mettle fully the equal of her own. At heart this more recent newcomer to Theosophy was more the humanitarian than the true occultist, and the Point Loma community she established in California was a significant achievement in its well-demonstrated but short-lived promise. In a comparison of the horoscopes of these two amazons the dynamic cross ties, of the Besant moon applying in conjunction with the Tingley sun and the Besant Neptune applying in opposition with the Tingley Venus, show the initiative to rest with the native and therefore in her natural involvement she not only could challenge the purpose of the other far-less-endowed exemplar of the occult principles in practical fashion but also in her nascent responsibility could call the other's realization to account in transcendent implication. In 1897 the redoubtable Annie had made her fourth trip to America in six years and after an exacting six months she settled the matter of ultimate dominance in the Theosophical movement at Chicago in mid-September. Her use in her lectures of colored stereopticon slides of auras and thought forms, as fruit of the clairvoyant investigation into which she had thrown herself at this time, was an important factor in her success.

THE PROGRESSED SUN IN SQUARE WITH NATAL SATURN, APRIL 13, 1907 This indication of a fulcral coming to stress of matters concerning the native's deep and ultimate concern for norms and values in her natural drive has convenient correlation with the death on February 17th of Colonel Olcott and her election to succeed him as international president on

September 15th. For better or worse she here would seem to become the ultimate hope of Theosophy.

In summary, the nascent driving force inhering throughout Annie Besant's widespread and tireless activities is seen in the dynamic horoscopy to have had an early twofold stimulus with (1) the death of her father at five years of age and the consequent emergence of the spunky self-sufficiency of her mother that she would begin to emulate and (2) the sobering realization of life's exactions in her eleventh year as Ellen Marryat began to prepare her for a more sophisticated grasp of everyday realities. Forty years later there was a one-two impact of challenge to her highly seminal independence when (1) at fifty she had to stir herself to dramatic effort to meet the sudden threat to the original Theosophical Society through the emergence of the flamboyant Katherine Tingley and then (2) at sixty was called to shoulder the full and official responsibility for its well-being.

Nonfulcral Indication

THE PROGRESSED SUN IN CONJUNCTION WITH NATAL VENUS, DECEMBER 11, 1850   In the fourth of the four normal procedures in the analysis of an activity-facet the progressive distribution of horoscopic potentials in noncritical course is here a practical alertness in the activation in the natural drive of the native's realization or assimilation of her experience to her own conscious selfhood even at three years of age. This first nonfulcral aspect of her major secondary directions has correlation with the move out from the grime of London to the initial happy place the native would be able to remember and where she gained the nickname of Little Pleasantina. There she knew a mother's bustling preparations for a father's return home to dinner, and enjoyed the special companionship with a brother two years her senior as they watched for the gentleman and anticipated the romp with him before the little family settled down to their evening meal.

THE PROGRESSED SUN IN OPPOSITION WITH NATAL URANUS, JULY 30, 1856 This indication of an activated release of potentials through an idealistic alertness in the natural drive has its correlation with the move by Emily Wood with little Henry and Annie into the delightful house at Harrow on the eighth birthday of the latter. The emphasis for the younger child, as in contrast with the mother's success in providing for the education of the older boy, was the vital interest soon to be taken in the little girl's schooling by Ellen Marryat who had met and been attracted to her in 1855.

THE PROGRESSED SUN IN CONJUNCTION WITH NATAL MERCURY, AUGUST 24, 1856 This indication of an activated aplomb or self-shielding insouciance through a practical alertness of everyday adjustment in the natural drive has its correlation with the definite surrender of Annie to the educational custody of Miss Marryat. Thus a very individual self-sufficiency is increasingly demanded of the high-strung child, confirming her as inescapably the individualist or very largely the loner among her fellows much as Lincoln became in different fashion.

THE PROGRESSED SUN IN OPPOSITION WITH NATAL PLUTO, MARCH 19, 1866 This indication of an activated probity or transcendental self-orientation through an idealistic alertness of everyday adjustment in the natural drive, of a sort not manifest before the discovery of the planet but perhaps highly significant in afterperspective, has correlation with the native's introduction to Frank Besant and hence to the circumstances that by completely cauterizing her rich adolescent bloom left her no course but the blind pursuit of the special destiny in which she alone could fulfill herself in the long-range view.

THE PROGRESSED SUN IN TRINE WITH NATAL NEPTUNE, JANUARY 17, 1868   This indication of an activated accept-ance or adoption of an individual destiny through an idealistic adroitness of everyday judgment in the natural drive has cor-relation with the native's turning her outrage of body and her numbing aesthetic disgust to whatever could be more promising channels for her purposed self-projection into experi-ence. Here at twenty begins her break with the entrenched Victorian establishment, and to be noted is that the astrological quickening at this point is through the one-two impact of the Neptune-Saturn combination that has such particularly unique significance in the fulcrum progressions of the activity-facet. There was intellectual recourse to serious reading in the theo-logical and philosophical materials easily available to her, but far more important was the dramatic introduction to the cur-rent sociopolitical ferment through William Prowting Roberts or the first individual she encountered with any actual or functioning dedication to the human masses.

THE PROGRESSED SUN IN TRINE WITH NATAL SATURN, JULY 12, 1877   This indication of an activated concern over norms and values of deeper or more ultimate nature through an idealized adroitness of everyday adjustment in the natural drive has its correspondence with her expanded interest in sociopolitical reform that as quickened for almost a decade was now brought to crucial self-assertion. Already an out-standing leader in Secularism, she had been a quiet advocacy of birth control as an essential feature of the freethinking movement. At this point a pamphlet advocating and explain-ing contraception, *The Fruits of Philosophy* issued originally in America forty-five years before and since printed and sold in England without stirring up any protest, was in 1876 dressed up with graphic illustrations by a Bristol bookseller, and this triggered legal attempts to suppress it. Its distribution and sale had been handled by the *National Reformer* and, while in the view of Charles Bradlaugh the material was rather innocuous and the book was not worth defending, Annie Besant would have none of that. Against the opposition of all the others involved, she demanded that it be defended in court. Emphatic enough to get her way, she emerges here at thirty in the full of her driving dominance.

THE PROGRESSED SUN IN TRINE WITH THE NATAL MOON, DECEMBER 23, 1882 This indication of an activated endurance or creative obstinacy through an idealized adroitness of everyday adjustment in the native's natural drive has correlation with her launching of her own literary magazine in January, 1883. *Our Corner* was a further mark of her expanding self-sufficiency and her desire to reach as broad a public as possible.

THE PROGRESSED SUN IN OPPOSITION WITH NATAL MARS, MARCH 25, 1885 This indication of an activated persistence of her assertive individuality through an idealistic alertness of everyday adjustment in the natural drive corresponds to her affiliation with the Fabian Society in late January. She had found her secularism increasingly barren in psychological depth, and in turning to others than Bradlaugh in rational outreach would more and more be demanding wider horizons.

THE PROGRESSED SUN IN TRINE WITH NATAL JUPITER, JUNE 6, 1888 This indication of an activated zest for life through an idealistic adroitness of everyday adjustment in the natural drive has correlation in long-range context but most specifically with the riot in London's Trafalgar Square in November, 1887, and the formation of the Law and Liberty League immediately after by the native and the crusading journalist William T. Stead. This new friend, who from 1883 to 1889 was the editor of the *Pall Mall Gazette,* gave her the two volumes of Madame Blavatsky's just published *Secret Doctrine* to review and as she devoured these she was virtually catapulted into Theosophy.

THE PROGRESSED SUN IN SEXTILE WITH THE NATAL SUN, SEPTEMBER 16, 1907 This indication of an activated strength of character or fundamental self-integration through a practical adroitness of everyday adjustment in the natural drive has correlation with the native's election to succeed Colonel Olcott as international president of the Theosophical Society, and testifies to its significant stimulation of her purpose.

THE PROGRESSED SUN IN SEXTILE WITH NATAL VENUS, OCTOBER 22, 1910 This indication of an activated realization or sense of culminations through a practical adroitness of everyday adjustment in natural drive has correlation with the first presentation to her in November, 1909, of the boy Jeddu Krishnamurti as the avatar to come. Because apparently the event did not register at all significantly in her consciousness, the matter if taken to be indicated at this point is therefore identified as a proposition of slow buildup. The single dynamic cross tie found in a comparison of his horoscope with hers shows his Mars applying by a conjunction with her moon that just possibly may be close enough to be considered. The initiative would be on his side as in his basic excitation he would quicken her endurance in her public image such as actually happened in this instance in her unwavering sponsorship of his messianic role once she had accepted it.

THE PROGRESSED SUN IN TRINE WITH NATAL URANUS, APRIL 19, 1916 This indication of an activated release of potentials through an idealistic adroitness of commonplace adjustment in the natural drive corresponds most significantly to the Benares Affair in early February or the unhappy public clash contributing to the bitterness between Mohandas Gandhi and herself. As the founder of Central Hindu College she was to have been the principal speaker at the climax of four days of elaborate ceremonies that had brought together a glittering assemblage of Indian and British personages for the laying of the cornerstone of the new Hindu University that would embrace the college. Unfortunately she had to take the platform prematurely thanks to Gandhi's late arrival, and his extemporaneous remarks following her led to the break-up of the meeting in a complete confusion that may well have symbolized the end once and forever of the rule by aristocracy in India. However unlikely it might seem for the native at the threshold of her sixties, the future is shown as yet opened up ahead for her.

THE PROGRESSED SUN IN SEXTILE WITH NATAL MERCURY, MAY 13, 1916 This indication of an activated aplomb or self-shielding insouciance through a practical alertness of everyday adjustment in the natural drive has correlation at this time with the interning of the native in June as virtually an enemy alien. She suffered no hardship other than the complete cancellation of liberty, and she maintained the morale worthy of her achievements. Three months later she was released, and her ordeal was largely responsible for her election to the presidency of the Indian National Congress.

THE PROGRESSED SUN IN TRINE WITH NATAL PLUTO, SEPTEMBER 10, 1925 This indication of an activated sense of probity or transcendental self-orientation through an idealistic adroitness of everyday adjustment in the natural drive, of a sort not effective before the discovery of the planet but significant in afterview, has its convenient correlation with the official Theosophical announcement in August, 1925, of the appointment by the spiritual hierarchy to which Theosophists give special allegiance of twelve apostles for the new savior. The miracle-mongering had indeed run riot. Here was the intemperance of idealistic outreach as inevitably self-defeating.

THE PROGRESSED SUN IN SEXTILE WITH NATAL NEPTUNE, JUNE 24, 1927 This indication of an activated acceptance or adoption of an individual destiny through a practical adroitness of everyday adjustment in the native's natural drive has (1) remote correlation with the summer of 1926 and the shock in a compulsion to entertain doubt of the validity of Krishnamurti's occult overshadowing, and (2) more immediate correspondence to his revolt against the strait jacket of a role forced on him in hopeless overritualization and almost ridiculously grandiose claims. The native is challenged to a more realistic hope, and it is the possibility of this that in the main is indicated.

THE PROGRESSED SUN IN SEXTILE WITH NATAL SATURN, OCTOBER 10, 1936 This indication of an activated concern for the ultimacies in the native's case through a practical adroitness in natural drive after her decease is without validity in her living years. The valuable suggestion it may give concerning any possible continuing influence of her life and effort is as the effective catalyst she actually had been in her human relationships in area after area of man's struggle to better his conditions. Astrologically she has been seen in definite progression to a universal realization devoid of all superficial embellishment, or what Krishnamurti finally defined for her in respect to himself. Above all else she gained a particular immortal stature in demonstrating what her innate purity at core could call out in all the stress and confusion of everyday conscious existence. Certainly there is no limit to what might be done in her spirit or name, whether in or out of the lineaments of the Theosophy to which she finally gave the totality of herself.

In summary, the nonfulcral aspects of the natural drive that chart the native's progressive distribution of horoscopic potentials in normal course emphasize (1) her endowment in self-reliance from her mother and in social competence from a childhood patron, (2) the outrage following on marriage and her recourse to intellectual outlet and gradual participation in the activity of sociopolitical reform, (3) the assumption of a dominant position among the Secularists and the publication of a personal literary journal in this self-establishment, (4) a transitional outreach to broader modes of human progress than mere sociopolitical protest, (5) a turn to Theosophy and in due course an achievement of dominance in the Theosophical Society, (6) an acceptance of Krishnamurti as the coming avatar and a long and whole-souled promotion of his mission, (7) a parallel and remarkably successful effort to further an interest in the great traditions of Aryan culture as marked particularly in an advancement of Hindu higher education, (8) an inspired entrance into the struggle for Indian independence in which she also made a significant contribution although unsuccessful in bringing her own measures to pass, (9) an unfortunately naïve and enthusiastic plunge into miracle-mongering occultism of the day with an ultimate disillusion of an extent perhaps never really to be known, and (10) the unexpected and total rejection by Krishnamurti of virtually everything that had been worked out for him and the consequent necessity for her to hold herself true to the young man's emerging insight as essentially a fulfillment of herself.

THE BASIC SENSITIVITY

Continuing in the pattern established for the delineation of the secondary directions in the dynamic horoscopy, attention next turns to the creative self-refinement in experience of the particular skills and capacities through which a conscious rapport with life at large in its self-challenging immediacies can be maintained. This is indicated by Venus. The harmonious relationship in the normal drift of circumstances of the two very different strands of Annie Besant's make-up has been found to be well-established in her life through her basic attitude, and then in her natural drive she has been seen developing her potentials to what in any fair view must be taken as their extraordinarily successful application. Now her career comes to astrological examination through her basic sensitivity or the definite quality of individual human expression as distinct from the mere move from one to another relatively material achievement. Her exceptional individuality must be charted through her private rather than her public image, or in her necessarily ever-expanding dramatization of her own uniqueness in some characteristic and fundamental fashion to herself.

The Psychological Trend to Balance

In the first of the four normal procedures in the analysis of an activity-facet in the dynamic horoscopy an overall idealistic and a preliminary practical slant here duplicates the indication in Annie Besant's natural drive and again gives testimony to the naïve directness of her childhood in the quality or deeper nature of her general rapport with reality. Far different however is the lack of any actual manifestation of the depth of her inner outreach to ultimacy until the last decade of her long life, or when the miracle-mongering began to defeat itself and in her own terms she acceded to the wish of her spiritual and invisible master to continue as leader of the Theosophical Society rather than follow her own desire to become a simple follower of Krishnamurti's final formulation of his own mission. Thus again the testimony is to an unknown future as far as her enduring significance is concerned, but obviously it is a salvage of the Blavatsky contribution.

In summary, the psychological trend to balance shows an almost lifelong practical or essentially conventional cast to her private as against her public image but with a sharp change in the decade of her last years she held allegiance to the movement through which her enduring and special immortality may actually become manifest.

Challenge by Progressed Station

PROGRESSED VENUS STATIONARY TURNING DIRECT IN 1870 In the second of the four normal procedures in analysis of an activity-facet in the dynamic horoscopy the single critical regrasp of experience in Annie Besant's basic sensitivity gives important emphasis to the extraordinary extent to which her life would have its depths cradled almost without break in inescapable personal responsibilities. In correspondence to the station her second child was born prematurely on August 28th of this year, and thereafter and for long the delicate daughter would need special care. It was through the native's use of her influence in October the next year that the struggling family obtained the Sibsey parish in Lincolnshire, and Frank Besant's insensate resentment that he should owe this financial rescue entirely to her was no help to her lot. The fact that the two children, Arthur Digby now three and baby Mabel, were delighted in the new location and apparently were quite unaware of the parental conflict was rare tribute to her fundamentally unwavering good will as too was the later circumstance that when in time they would be taken away from her as an unfit mother they yet would leave the father and return to her the very moment they were old enough to be free to do so. Through all this however her deeper sensitivity had no actual outlet in its own special quality, and again the testimony is to the almost tragic fashion in which the young woman was thoroughly sealed up within herself at the very threshold of her maturity.

In summary, the extraordinary sensitivity that enabled Annie Besant to stand up under the continual buffeting in personal circumstances for virtually the whole of her years in one way or another or the exceptional purity or almost naïve good will innate in her make-up had its eventual recompense in the uncompromising devotion of her children. The unremitting calls on her capacities are seen to choke off rather than facilitate any effective expression of the real depths of her sensitivity.

Fulcrum Indication

PROGRESSED VENUS IN SQUARE WITH THE NATAL MOON, NOVEMBER 27, 1896   In the third of the four normal procedures in analysis of an activity-facet the critical self-mobilization in basic sensitivity required by objective events on the first of two occasions in the native's case has general correlation with the quick rise of Katherine Tingley as her very real rival following the death on March 21st of William Quan

Judge. Annie Besant in the emphasis of her endurance or ultimate morale maintained her dominance very largely by the
employment of highly occult and speculative information as
in connection with auras and thought forms and the like, and
in this she revived in fresh form the catering to a wonder-
loving public or the policy of Madame Blavatsky that the
Russian seeress seemingly came to regret and to seek to rele-
gate to the background. Astrologically it is rather obvious that
the native was establishing an alignment with what she could
accept as the greater depths or more enduring reality of
existence, and in that she was meeting the unsated hunger of
the deeper side of her basic sensitivity that had so great a need
for a functional or effective outlet. Here is where any real
battle for her self-fulfillment may well have been joined.

PROGRESSED VENUS IN SQUARE WITH NATAL JUPITER,
OCTOBER 17, 1903   This indication of a fulcral coming to
stress of matters concerning the native's zest for life or eagerness for experience in her basic sensitivity has correlation with
her black depression for more than a year at this time. A
revealing correspondence with longtime friends, Mrs. Jacob
Bright and her daughter Esther Bright, asks the hypothetical
question about a really good man who commits acts unworthy
of him. It was a problem of ambivalence to which apparently
she was unable to make her reconciliation until three years
later. Presumably in the pressure of the inner hunger she
could make no choice but to hold to the vast spread of super-
physical planes and events, and in her own naïveté at core
to conclude that the apparent transcendental merit of necessity must justify even the most extreme deviation of character
and conduct from the accepted norms. She did not have the
philosophical background to recognize the casuistry in the

point of view she accepted finally in a hope of meeting her deeper need.

In summary, the great need of the long-suppressed depths of her basic sensitivity led Annie Besant at the two points of fulcral coming to stress in her reach to the quality of her self-fulfillment in the activity-facet to two important choices however subconsciously or otherwise. In 1896 she definitely adopted the program of miracle-mongering that in getting out of hand brought a particular chapter of Theosophy to a dead end, and in 1903 she managed to achieve a tolerance at least of sorts for whatever deviations of human nature might be taken to be balanced by excellencies of accomplishment. Here she may have depreciated her potentials and postponed the ultimate contributions shown as possible by her horoscope.

Nonfulcral Indication

PROGRESSED VENUS IN CONJUNCTION WITH THE NATAL SUN, NOVEMBER 29, 1852, AND JULY 16, 1889   In the fourth of the four normal procedures in analysis of an activity-facet the progressive distribution of horoscopic potentials in nonfulcral course in the basic sensitivity is here found to be an activation through a practical alertness of the strength of character or nascent impulsion in two stages of the tentative stirring of the native to her definite quality of self-fulfillment. The repetition of this particular progression is a result of the single station of the planet receding from and returning to the aspect in the secondary directions, and it fundamentally delineates (1) the impact of the death of the father and little brother in 1852 and 1853 as the manifestation of immutable higher forces in life to which even a child can become agonizingly aware and (2) in 1889 the first contact in the flesh with Madame Blavatsky as facilitating a different and fascinating

rather than fear-inspiring orientation to such transcendentalities.

PROGRESSED VENUS IN CONJUNCTION WITH NATAL VENUS,
APRIL 2, 1894   This indication of an activated realization or
sense of culminations in the basic sensitivity through a practical alertness of everyday adjustment has correlation with the
native's selection of Charles Leadbeater for the post of assist-
ant secretary of the European Section, and his resultant move
into residence in the London headquarters and thus close
intimacy with the leaders. He had taken orders in 1878, and
been active in the Episcopalian priesthood for six years. He
had joined the society in 1883, and had left the church shortly
afterward. Following Madame Blavatsky to India, in Ceylon
he had become a Theravada Buddhist as she and Colonel
Olcott had done before him. He was invited back to Europe
as a tutor by A. P. Sinnett, and at a meeting of the London
Lodge on an unremembered date in 1890 he and Annie
Besant had first met face to face although not then particularly drawn to each other. Their close and long association
apparently stems from their participation together in the
psychic research that soon would add an entirely new dimension to Theosophical thinking. Sinnett probably was responsible for the development since he had been particularly
drawn to the dramatic phenomena.

The curious circumstance that the native together with
Katherine Tingley and Charles Leadbeater were all born in
the year 1847 has a general significance under the essential
principle of concordance and concomitance because of correspondence to the discovery of the planet Neptune. Except
that the slower planets remain in much the same place over
some eight-odd months, the nativities of these individuals have

little in common. The dynamic cross ties between **Annie Besant** and her new associate show the initiative vested in her because it is her Neptune that by conjunction quickens his Neptune as well as his sun and Mercury and also her Venus that similarly by opposition provides a long-range activation of his Uranus. In her nascent responsibility she thus buttresses his particular acceptance as well as his aplomb and purposed expression, and perhaps more importantly in her basic sensitivity she contributes to the release of his unique powers. Since all this would have transcendental implication very fundamentally in the Theosophical context, it seems odd that by the record she should have tended to defer quite completely to her clairvoyant protégé in these matters of higher dimension in consciousness. As between them, the flow would have to be from her to him, but perhaps she would be unaware of this. The astrological testimony in such a case would be to a constant draining away of elements of her own unlocked depths. As a species of vampirization the process would only be checked as the inevitable disillusionments swept in upon her, and led to the self-reordering marked in the courage with which she held to center in herself in accepting the insight through which Krishnamurti gained his own release from the psychic bondage.

PROGRESSED VENUS IN OPPOSITION WITH NATAL URANUS, SEPTEMBER 23, 1901   This indication of an activated release of potentials in the basic sensitivity through an idealistic alertness has correlation with the native's book and lectures on Esoteric Christianity. Here is a phase in her broadening encompassment of prior intellectual exploration in the essential reference at this point to the early reading in theology to which she turned particularly during the psychological tragedy of her marriage. Her new course now may have been a matter of Leadbeater's influence, or precursory of the Christian sacerdotalism he in principal part would engraft on Theosophy some two decades later, but to be noted is the firmness with which she held to the sound frame of her Hinduism in her conscious intellection in contrast with the Buddhism that had been adopted by most of the non-Orientals in the ruling ranks of the society. Throughout her life in actuality there was never any dominance by others in her fundamental quality of realization.

PROGRESSED VENUS IN CONJUNCTION WITH NATAL MERCURY, OCTOBER 4, 1901   This indication of an activated aplomb or self-shielding insouciance of the native in her basic sensitivity through a practical alertness has its correlation with the strange social cradling of her outreach in the quality of her realization coming to particular emphasis at this moment of history. Under the essential principle of equivalence or distinction she always was drawn into association with individuals or events of prominence as characteristically in her Episcopalian confirmation in 1862 and now becoming significantly evident a half century later. Pinpointing correlations are difficult and with the subtleties involved might not be too rewarding, but it can be noted that Jawaharlal Nehru attended her lectures in 1901 and for a brief time was a member of the society and that Mohandas Gandhi who had been befriended in London earlier by the Theosophists had on his return to India at this point hurried to make a courtesy call on her.

PROGRESSED VENUS IN OPPOSITION WITH NATAL PLUTO, JUNE 17, 1912   This indication of an activated sense of probity or transcendental self-orientation in the basic sensitivity through an idealistic awareness of everyday adjustment, not effective before the discovery of the planet but significant in afterview, has correlation with the loss of fifty-five out of fifty-nine lodges of the German Section of the society by revocation of their charters for refusal to permit their members to affiliate with the Order of the Star or to participate as Theosophists in the promotion of Krishnamurti as the coming messiah. Thus Rudolf Steiner was led to reconstitute these expelled groups as the Anthroposophical Society, and the new organization became willy-nilly almost as great a threat to the parent society as the Universal Brotherhood of Katherine Tingley fifteen years before. Annie Besant and the German scholar had found no basis for particular rapport in their first contact a decade earlier. The cross ties between their horoscopes show the Besant natal Mercury applying by conjunction and her natal Uranus by opposition with the Steiner natal moon, so that any initiative had to be hers. Through her basic attitude she could have quickened his endurance on the practical side and in her nascent independence she could have also quickened his corresponding long-range endurance or administrative creativity and thus perhaps brought Theosophy more effectively to its principal task in one way or another. Unhappily she was too well in groove in both fundamental facets of her nature to be able to stop for any review or evaluation of her course. Here moreover all implication is in afterview. Only in her final years or after her decease could there be likelihood that the story might be different, thanks perhaps to an immortal assist from the Anthroposophical accomplishment.

PROGRESSED VENUS IN TRINE WITH NATAL NEPTUNE, MAY 11, 1914 This indication of an activated acceptance of an individual destiny by the native in the basic sensitivity through

an idealistic adroitness of everyday adjustment has fundamental correlation with the outbreak of World War I, and
the complete alteration in the global concordance enforced
by events as well as indicated by astrological factors. Now
she becomes completely dissociate, but with in due course the
falling away of her influence in the Indian struggle for independence and the revolt of Krishnamurti against the entangling superficialities imposed on him as the outer substance of
his mission she gradually gains the freedom to discover and
develop her immortal quality of realization irrespective of
what this may prove to be ultimately.

PROGRESSED VENUS IN TRINE WITH NATAL SATURN, OCTO-
BER 20, 1923 This indication for an activated concern for
deeper and ultimate norms and values in the basic sensitivity
through an idealistic adroitness of everyday adjustment has its
most suggestive correlation with (1) what after a momentary
resurgence in 1924 will prove the irrevocable rejection of the
native's leadership in Indian politics and (2) the celebration
of her fifty years in public life in 1924 that as an emotional
consummation of a very tangible sort is a challenge to a
needed inward survey of her career to identify what ultimacies
may yet be seen as significant and potential.

PROGRESSED VENUS IN TRINE WITH THE NATAL MOON, JAN-
UARY 10, 1929 This indication of an activated endurance or
morale of creative stubbornness in the basic sensitivity of the
native through an idealistic adroitness of everyday adjustment
has correlation with Krishnamurti's disbanding of the Order of
the Star that has been a principal agency in promoting the
overliteralized and miracle-mongering messiahship he himself
no longer could countenance. Thus Annie Besant is dropped
to nadir in the spiritualistic playacting that has held such high

hopes for her, but even in this she is quickened to a courageous continuance in all it represented in a more solid or genuinely immortal reality.

PROGRESSED VENUS IN OPPOSITION WITH NATAL MARS, FEBRUARY 25, 1931   This indication of an activated persistence of the assertive individuality in the basic sensitivity through an idealistic awareness of everyday adjustment has correlation with the native's letter of January 30th in which she reported the fact that although she had asked the permission of her unseen master to resign from the society to follow the simple insight to which she now was clinging she was acting as he wished and was remaining on in office.

PROGRESSED VENUS IN TRINE WITH NATAL JUPITER, FEBRUARY 7, 1934   This indication of an activated zest for life through an idealistic adroitness in basic sensitivity is after her decease and in consequence of no validity in connection with her living years, but the valuable suggestion it does give concerning any continuing influence of her life and effort is that since she almost single-handedly sparked a second virile chapter of Theosophy's contribution to the world she may yet in some perhaps very subtle fashion precipitate an even more productive third one.

In summary, the nonfulcral aspects of the basic sensitivity that chart the native's progressive distribution of horoscopic potentials in normal course emphasize (1) her vital quickening to external powers beyond everyday comprehension through the phenomenon of death encountered sharply as a child and even more dramatically in ultimate contact with Madame Blavatsky, (2) the invitation into organizational familiarity to Charles Leadbeater that resulted in her enthrallment to his psychic capacities, (3) her effort to bring her interests into a piece by fitting her early excursions into Christian theology into the encompassing frame of her Hinduism and her widening circle of significant associations around the globe, and (4) her extreme measures in support of the claims for Krishnamurti revealed in afterview to be a closing off of potentials of corrective judgment that might have spared her the later tragic disillusions but then might have denied her the priceless insight dramatized through the very miracle-mongering that in its superficial collapse along with the fading out of her role in the achievement of Indian independence left her frustratingly dissociate in her declining years.

THE BASIC EXCITATION

Continuing in the pattern established for the delineation of the secondary directions in the dynamic horoscopy, attention next turns to the explorative self-expression or exercise of the individual quality of skill and capacity as the basic excitation indicated by Mars. This creative self-stimulus in the instance of Annie Besant is marked by (1) a progressive distribution of its potentials rather restricted in effect to the preparation for her public career rather than the half century of actual great accomplishment and (2) a single conscious regrasp of experience through her own decision and effort when she delivered her ultimate hope or irrevocable spiritual anchorage into the uncertain and overguided hands of Krishnamurti. Under the essential principle of equivalence or distinction, and in the light of the life performance in the pattern of the nativity, there again is testimony to the necessity of a post-mortem significance in culmination of what otherwise might justifiably be summed up as tragic futility. By deduction there is testimony in consequence to the immutable naïveté that while giving her utter latitude in act yet always protected her from unnecessary involvement in the more common divergencies of everyday experience.

The Psychological Trend to Balance

In this first of the four normal procedures in the analysis of an activity-facet in the dynamic horoscopy a lifelong practical slant shows the complete lack of idealistic ordering of her creative self-stimulation and thus stresses her inability to match her overall enthusiasm in the various causes emerging in the struggle of man toward his own betterment with any nurture of a cause of her own or as offspring of her innate genius and a matter of the quality as beyond the dull fact of conscious existence to give the needed point to her career. Hence the possibility of this is pushed ahead, and even on beyond her decease, as a potential in no way diminished. The apotheosis of Krishnamurti offered her a surrogate for her need, and may well have made a significant contribution to the ultimacies as yet beyond envisionment.

In summary, Annie Besant's wholly pragmatic basic excitation gave her a great capacity for furthering the causes in which her interest was awakened, but in depth she needed a self-stimulus of the sort for which there was no dynamic indication in her lifetime and in consequence she had to grasp a substitute.

Challenge by Progressed Station

PROGRESSED MARS STATIONARY TURNING DIRECT IN 1911 In this second of the four normal procedures in analysis of an activity-facet in the dynamic horoscopy the critical regrasp of experience indicated for the basic excitation has correlation with the founding on January 11th in this year of the Order of the Star in the East. In 1927 it became the Order of the Star but at this point the elaborate hierarchy of ranks was inaugurated with uniforms and passwords on down to an array of geegaws including those that could be specially blessed and sold to the faithful. Thus under the principle of concordance or concomitance the regression to practical trivialities however fortuitously in this connection yet reflected the native's dynamic delimitation in the activity-facet and hence provides astrological testimony to the extent of the transcendental linkage with her at core.

In summary, the most crucial manifestation of Annie Besant's creative self-act in the quality of her skill and capacity was her establishment of her ultimacy as far as it rested in her hands to do so in the now well-ordered or ritualized conception of the new messiah for mankind.

No fulcrum progressions are formed in the native's basic excitation, and the absence during her life of any critical self-mobilization in the activity-facet contributes to her continuing and characteristic naïveté.

Nonfulcral Indication

PROGRESSED MARS IN SEXTILE WITH THE NATAL MOON, APRIL 4, 1860   In the fourth of the four normal procedures in the analysis of an activity-facet the progressive distribution of horoscopic potentials in nonfulcral course is here an activated endurance or creative obstinacy through a practical adroitness, and it has correlation with what she remembered in the afterperspective of her *Autobiography* as a phase of morbidness in fretting over the times of separation from her mother during her private schooling with Ellen Marryat. In the flow of circumstances an initial quickening of her deeper or qualitative and exploratory self-expression was in process of taking her very dramatically into a practical reality far removed from the fantasy realms of her childhood and one in which she would have to take her own stand and persist in her going with the doggedness that would be her own.

PROGRESSED MARS IN SEXTILE WITH NATAL SATURN, FEBRUARY 28, 1877   This indication of an activated concern over deeper and more ultimate norms and values through a practical adroitness in the basic excitation has correlation with the emergence of the native's inflexible determination to assert herself in the quality of her skill and capacity in whatever area of life may enlist her interest. Marking this was the stand she took in bringing Charles Bradlaugh and the other Secularists involved to rally to the legal defense of the *Fruits of Philosophy* and in passing of the birth control program the book was advocating.

In summary, Annie Besant began the exploratory self-expression of her individual quality of skill or capacity when (1) in her thirteenth year she managed to break out of a childhood world of relative unreality but fascinating camaraderie with her mother and (2) approaching thirty she found she could assert herself among her far more experienced colleagues and obtain her own way by the very persuasion of her sincerity and incorruptibility.

THE FIVE TRANSCENDENCIES

Continuing in the pattern established for the delineation of the secondary directions in the dynamic horoscopy, attention next turns to the five more slowly moving and regular performing planets that chart the individuality in its inescapably personal experience of itself and reveal the elements of human life in the social and symbolical significance that enables man to transcend his purely animal nature and essentially material conditioning.

THE NASCENT CONSISTENCY

The activity-facet of the expanding dimension of self-consciousness above fundamentally conditioned existence, and charted in the dynamic horoscopy by progressed Jupiter, indicates the consciously motivated efforts of Annie Besant toward special recognition or the establishment of personal status that gained an utterly gratifying consummation in the winning of the great central battle of the Secularists to which she had dedicated herself in first branching out on her own in public life. This can be seen to set the pattern for all her subsequent struggle to consummations that might be more particularly her own.

The Psychological Trend to Balance

In this of the normal procedures of analysis of an activity-facet in the dynamic horoscopy the single nonfulcral progression in nascent consistency is indication of an overall practical

241

emphasis without subordinate contrast as in the basic excitation, but it did not have its definite set until she severed all connection with her Indian political ties and came out in open and bitter conflict with Mahatma Gandhi on the one hand and almost simultaneously in England gained wide recognition as a faithful Briton. While caught up in all the historical crosscurrents she was handicapped in basic motivation by the lack of a sufficiently clear idealistic light toward which to move.

Challenge by Progressed Station

PROGRESSED JUPITER STATIONARY TURNING RETROGRADE IN 1886   In this of the normal procedures of analysis of an activity-facet in the dynamic horoscopy the critical regrasp of experience indicated for her nascent consistency has correlation with the seating of Charles Bradlaugh in the House of Commons in January after six years of refusing to admit him despite his continued election. Now she no longer would be sustained by his struggle against the political outrage to which he had been subjected as an avowed atheist, and with his triumph there was an end to the initial chapter of her life that had been given its form through the crusading efforts that in the earlier phases had brought her notoriety but later a very appreciable fame. Her ultimate justification would have to be a very appreciably larger dimension.

Fulcrum Indication

PROGRESSED JUPITER IN SQUARE WITH NATAL MERCURY, FEBRUARY 19, 1936   In this of the normal procedures of analysis of an activity-facet in the dynamic horoscopy the critical self-mobilization in nascent consistency is not required by objective events in Annie Besant's case since the aspect in maturing after her decease indicates postmortal potentials.

The activation of aplomb or self-shielding insouciance suggests the continuance of her underlying purity at core or characteristic naïveté in the future manifestation as it develops its actuality.

Nonfulcral Indication

PROGRESSED JUPITER IN CONJUNCTION WITH NATAL JUPITER, DECEMBER 10, 1921   In this of the normal procedures of analysis of an activity-facet in the dynamic horoscopy the progressive distribution of horoscopic potentials in nonfulcral course in the nascent consistency is here an activated zest in correlation with the native's definite severance of her connection with the Indian National Congress on January 11, 1921. The literal break was not complete, since there was an upsurge of her influence in 1924, but the significance in general is in the astrological certification of her ultimate self-direction in total alignment from now on with the occult tradition represented for her by Theosophy.

In summary, the nascent consistency of Annie Besant as wholly oriented in practical considerations was brought to dramatic maturity in the long struggle to gain political acceptance for Charles Bradlaugh but thereafter was unable to justify itself through the larger goal as possible architect of Indian independence. What increasingly became her greater concern in a more occult achievement ended up as a potential that would have to gain actuality after her decease in some manner beyond present envisionment.

THE NASCENT INTEGRITY

The activity-facet of the expanding dimension of self-consciousness above fundamentally conditioned existence, and charted in the dynamic horoscopy by progressed Saturn, indicates the consciously critical effort of Annie Besant to (1) gain an overall comprehension of the general world of which she was a part and (2) also achieve a concomitant wisdom or sense of proportion in establishing her integrity or gaining effectiveness in her self-realization. At all points in consequence she is seen very personally concerned over the role she plays and the spotlessness of her reputation.

The Psychological Trend to Balance

In this of the normal procedures of analysis of an activity-facet in the dynamic horoscopy a single nonfulcral progression again reveals the practical emphasis under which the native operates in virtually all phases of her life, but it really only gains its set with what became the key event for Krishnamurti himself in the dramatic collapse of the psychic house of cards.

Challenge by Progressed Station

PROGRESSED SATURN STATIONARY TURNING DIRECT IN 1890 In this of the normal procedures of analysis of an activity-facet in the dynamic horoscopy the critical regrasp of experience shown to be necessary for the nascent integrity has correlation with the remodeling of the native's London home to become the Theosophical headquarters in England, since the arrangement symbolically and perhaps quite subconsciously marked the transfer of the movement into her hands. In close connection with the event, Charles Bradlaugh died on January 30th of the next year and Madame Blavatsky immediately following on May 5th.

Nonfulcral Indication

PROGRESSED SATURN IN CONJUNCTION WITH NATAL SATURN, JANUARY 5, 1926 In this of the normal procedures of analysis of an activity-facet in the dynamic horoscopy the progressive distribution of the natal potentials in nonfulcral course in the nascent integrity is here an activated concern for the deeper and more enduring norms and values through a practical awareness and it has correlation with the sudden illness and death of Krishnamurti's brother Nityananda in the preceding mid-November. Here was a portent too clear to ignore, since a disciple for a new messiah just appointed by omniscient masters of wisdom would hardly be expected to decease before the high spiritual manifestation really began.

In summary, the nascent integrity of Annie Besant received high symbolical certification in the circumstances through which (1) the Theosophical movement was delivered into her hands for its principal development in her generation and (2) her practical slanting in this activity-facet finally gained its set when the miracle-mongering in connection with Krishnamurti arrived at an inevitable self-defeat and thereupon projected her into a potential of genuine immortality of her own in an unenvisioned future.

THE NASCENT INDEPENDENCE

The activity-facet of the expanding dimension of self-consciousness above fundamentally conditioned existence, and charted in the dynamic horoscopy by progressed Uranus, indicates factors only coming to effectiveness in human realization with the discovery of the planet and hence here the exceptional skills and capacities of Annie Besant for self-fulfillment in the pioneering originality opened to man's accomplishment in 1781. Thus occultism alone, and eventually, would seem to provide the scope for which she reached.

Challenge by Progressed Station

PROGRESSED URANUS STATIONARY TURNING DIRECT IN 1931
The critical regrasp of experience indicated in the nascent

independence shortly before decease has correlation with what Annie Besant believed to be the desire of her master that she continue on toward an ultimate significance within the distinctly Theosophical scheme of things.

In summary, it becomes obvious astrologically that through Theosophy as a definite organon or a body of insights of great validity and power the native must survive either in realizations that exalt her memory or in developments that carry further and more impersonally whatever has been the basis of her dedication for the whole latter half of her years.

THE NASCENT RESPONSIBILITY

The activity-facet of the expanding dimension of self-consciousness above fundamentally conditioned existence, and charted in the dynamic horoscopy by progressed Neptune, indicates factors only coming to effectiveness in human realization with the discovery of the planet in 1846 and here the exceptional capacity of the native for assimilating herself into the functional processes and developments of greater cosmic scope provided by the new epoch in man's accomplishment and history. In time she is found however to be ever more if perhaps quite subsconsciously disillusioned with the politically oriented social reform in which men sought to engineer their own salvation or protect their personal security in continual conflict with each other, and hence she was prepared very thoroughly for her outreach to the absolute impersonality she saw open to mankind in the higher realms of the occult.

Challenge by Progressed Station

PROGRESSED NEPTUNE STATIONARY TURNING DIRECT IN 1886 The critical regrasp of experience indicated in the nascent responsibility has correlation with the culmination in the rewarding chapter of her association with Charles Brad-laugh, in supplementation of the station of progressed Jupiter in this year but with the more transcendental implication. The new chapter in terms of challenge is of necessity in astrological indication an enlargement not only of dimension in motivation through greater range in the broadened world she must find for herself but of dimensional expansion in the quality of her self-dedication. Her increasing skills and capacities have every need for a more extended cause and a much more hopelessly caste-bound country to serve.

In summary, the end of her rewarding chapter of life pivoting on the career of Charles Bradlaugh is not only challenge to broader self-projection in her characteristic dedication to varying causes of human welfare but to an increasing transcendental ordering of skills and capacities as opportunity for greater achievement and immortal potentials that can be realized more deeply or perhaps at the core of history itself in times to come.

THE NASCENT ENLIGHTENMENT

The activity-facet of the expanding dimension of self-consciousness above fundamentally conditioned existence, and charted in the dynamic horoscopy by progressed Pluto, indicates factors only coming to effectiveness in human relations with the discovery of the planet in 1930 and here hardly anything other than the exceptional skills and capacities that may become manifest in the immortal potentiality in which the native would continue to serve her fellows in necessarily subjective fashion and in the pattern of her nativity. A progressed station of the third of the new significators in 1939 has correlation after her decease with the outbreak of World War II, and under the principle of concordance or concomitance there is at least some specific validation for the concept of her life providing a vital bridge in history from the transcendentals of Neptune to those of Pluto.

THE NATURAL INVOLVEMENT

Continuing in the pattern established for the delineation of the secondary directions in the dynamic horoscopy, attention next turns from the activity-facets of (1) the relatively uninvolved basic attitude and natural drive and (2) the more group-oriented quality of selfhood in basic sensitivity and basic excitation and (3) the inescapably personal administration of itself by the conscious individuality that in nascent (a) consistency and (b) integrity and (c) independence and (d) responsibility and (e) enlightenment must ultimately transcend man's purely animal nature or his essentially material conditioning to (4) the utterly impartial convenience of chance presence of particular phenomena in general human context as they converge to immediacy of import and have indication in the progressions by the moon. The lesser light charts the short or transitory cycles of everyday reality in distinction from the long or ultimately lifetime ones considered up to this point, and establishes the activity-facet of natural involvement. The measure is of man as an event in circumstances in the various ways his fundamental continuity of an immutable selfhood compels them to pivot around him in any relation with him. The indications in their correlation will always identify a choice whether overt or indirect in respect to some fleeting potential of change in the infinite flux of the cosmos.

In the case of Annie Besant the period selected for illustration of the natural involvement ranges from her irrevocable entrance into public life in England to her setting foot in India for the first time and launching her contribution to what in time would be her adopted land.

Fulcrum and Nonfulcral Indication

THE PROGRESSED MOON IN CONJUNCTION WITH THE NATAL MOON, JANUARY 27, 1875   In the current drift of affairs the activation facilitated through practical awareness of the native's endurance or creative obstinacy is manifest in her emergence on January 19th from her anonymity behind the nom de plume Ajax in the *National Reformer*. She would now stand on her own feet as essentially the loner she has been seen to become in quite dramatic fashion.

THE PROGRESSED MOON IN SEXTILE WITH NATAL MARS, MARCH 30, 1875   In the current drift of affairs the activation facilitated through practical adroitness of the native's persistence or assertive individuality is manifest in the flowering of the simple and unexacting camaraderie of common dedication with Charles Bradlaugh. Their association gained its full effectiveness on his return from his American lecture trip in mid-March, and this was what in her remarkable and underlying naïveté she had anticipated as fruitage of her marriage to Frank Besant.

THE PROGRESSED MOON IN SQUARE WITH NATAL RADICAL URANUS, MAY 8, 1875   In the current drift of affairs the self-mobilization that under accentuated pressure is required of the native's release of potentials is manifest in the key event of her dramatic emergence into public life, or her election on May 16th as one of the five vice-presidents of the National Secular Society of which Bradlaugh was president.

THE PROGRESSED MOON IN SQUARE WITH NATAL MER-

CURY, MAY 10, 1875   In the current drift of affairs the self-mobilization that under accentuated pressure is required of the native's aplomb or self-shielding insouciance is manifest as she developed her veritable quixotic assaults on whatever besetting evil came to her attention in this period of early enthusiasm. Indeed, she actually launched a series of attacks on nothing less than the British Parliament.

THE PROGRESSED MOON IN CONJUNCTION WITH NATAL JUPITER, JUNE 26, 1875   In the current drift of affairs the activation facilitated through practical alertness of the native's zest for life is manifest when in the early summer in the discussion period following a lecture at Leicester she was attacked for supposedly writing and promoting a book of which she had never even heard, although Bradlaugh had praised it for its sincerity in the *National Reformer*. In ranging wide in her efforts to ameliorate the limiting conditions of mankind, she was finding herself taken by assumption as encouraging sexual promiscuity or the very reverse of any possible intent on her part. Here was something that within two years would have dramatic repercussion in her life, and out of the incident she came to be challenged to a far more genuine depth of interest in her causes.

THE PROGRESSED MOON IN SQUARE WITH NATAL PLUTO, FEBRUARY 1, 1876   In the current drift of affairs the self-mobilization not actually required of the native's probity in any fashion in her lifetime but evident in afterview is manifest in her complete if only ultimately realized alienation from her Christian roots under the increasing virulence of the criticism she invited from an entrenched orthodoxy at its worst.

THE PROGRESSED MOON IN SEXTILE WITH THE NATAL SUN, JANUARY 4, 1877   In the current drift of affairs the activation facilitated through practical adroitness of the native's strength or nascent impulsion is manifest in her special buttressing of the psychological rapprochement with Charles Bradlaugh. On February 11th he announced his move to the London house that would long be his personal and business address, and this was a convenient less than a mile's walk from her more comfortable home where for the years of vital self-discovery in her case they could work each at his own task in her sunny study.

THE PROGRESSED MOON IN SEXTILE WITH NATAL VENUS, APRIL 6, 1877   In the current drift of affairs the activation facilitated through practical adroitness of the native's realization or sense of culminations is manifest in her quickening to the importance of defending the book *Fruits of Philosophy*. This was the crisis that suddenly forced Charles Bradlaugh and herself into their own publishing business, which in turn thereupon provided them with an appreciable factor in their economic stability.

THE PROGRESSED MOON IN SQUARE WITH NATAL MARS, AUGUST 6, 1877   In the current drift of affairs the self-mobilization that under accentuated pressure is required of the native's persistence or assertive individuality led to the ultimately striking but ambiguous victory for the cause of birth control in the original trial beginning on June 18th for the distribution of allegedly obscene literature. She now wrote *The Law of Population* for its serialization in the *National Reformer*, and as a published pamphlet it became a best seller throughout the English-speaking world and she began to be a genuinely authoritative voice of her generation in more than the limited sphere of the freethinkers.

THE PROGRESSED MOON IN TRINE WITH NATAL URANUS,

SEPTEMBER 17, 1877   In the current drift of affairs the activation facilitated through idealistic adroitness of the native's release of potentials is manifest in the issue forced on her when during this summer after the annual visit of their seven-year-old daughter with the embittered husband under the terms of the legal separation he determined to take the custody of the child away from her. Her unique contribution as the end result of her long and losing fight was to make it quite impossible for the government to be able again to deprive a parent of any children on the grounds of no more than pure bigotry.

THE PROGRESSED MOON IN SEXTILE WITH NATAL MERCURY, SEPTEMBER 19, 1877   In the current drift of affairs the activation facilitated through practical adroitness of the native's aplomb or self-shielding insouciance is manifest in the concomitant and considerable contribution she made to woman's rights in the rather spectacular historical precedent established when she determined, although of feminine sex and a layman, to act as her own counselor in court.

THE PROGRESSED MOON IN TRINE WITH NATAL PLUTO, JULY 30, 1878   In the current drift of affairs the activation facilitated through idealistic adroitness of the native's probity while not actual in any fashion during her life was manifest as seen in afterview in the unhappily naïve anti-Semitism revealed in her *Autobiography* in connection with Sir George Jessel. The actually very prejudiced jurist who ruled against her in the case of the custody of her children was none other than the Master of the Rolls and presiding judge of the Court of Appeal, and he had regarded the proceedings as important enough for him to conduct personally. Here was evidence of a caste consciousness indicated ultimately as a vital factor in the possibility of contribution whether to India or Theosophy.

THE PROGRESSED MOON IN OPPOSITION WITH NATAL NEP-
TUNE, AUGUST 24, 1878   In the current drift of affairs the
activation facilitated through idealistic alertness of the native's
acceptance or adoption of an individual destiny is manifest in
her definite move to formalize what started as private tutelage
and continued as essentially a self-education. In January of
this year London University had been chartered to confer its
degrees on women and by July, 1879, Bradlaugh was able
to announce that she had matriculated.

THE PROGRESSED MOON IN OPPOSITION WITH NATAL SAT-
URN, JUNE 9, 1879   In the current drift of affairs the activation facilitated through idealistic alertness of the native's
deeper and ultimate concern for norms and values is manifest
in her courageous renunciation of what slender rights of contact with her children the court had given her finally on April
29th, mainly because the impact of a milieu of hopeless conflict was crucially upsetting to the sensitive Mabel in particular.

THE PROGRESSED MOON IN SEXTILE WITH THE NATAL
MOON, NOVEMBER 24, 1879   In the current drift of affairs
the activation facilitated through practical adroitness of the
native's endurance or creative obstinacy is manifest in her
uncritical welcoming into warm camaraderie of the gifted
scoundrel, Edward Aveling. She had been impressed by his
obvious talents when he obtained an introduction to her, and
first had arranged for him to write for the *National Reformer*
and then in February had engaged him to tutor her for her
matriculation at the university. By the time the progression
culminated there developed the very effective triumvirate of
Bradlaugh-Besant-Aveling engaged in presenting secularism to
the public through both the written word and on the platform.
Not too widely evident was the fact that this also was a quasi-

romantic triangle such as in a sense encompassed an emotional rebound from the surrender of her children. In any case her new associate was of particular importance at the threshold of a decade of complete reorientation in her career.

THE PROGRESSED MOON IN TRINE WITH NATAL MARS, FEBRUARY 2, 1880   In the current drift of affairs the activation facilitated through idealistic adroitness of the native's persistence or assertive individuality is manifest (1) more objectively in the chance encounter for the first time with Herbert Burrows who later would offer the camaraderie her essential naïveté made more and more necessary at all times and who would be her companion in entering Theosophy but (2) more subjectively and importantly in the injury to her knee that in plaguing her for the rest of her life would come to be considered of particular occult significance.

THE PROGRESSED MOON IN SEXTILE WITH NATAL JUPITER, MAY 12, 1880   In the current drift of affairs the activation facilitated through practical adroitness of the native's zest for life is manifest (1) by repercussion in the almost incredible victory of Charles Bradlaugh at the polls in Northampton in early April as the first election of a freethinker to Parliament and as the great milestone of his career and ultimately the principal justification for his life and the uncompromising devotion of his daughters even if the actual seating was to be long delayed while (2) the freeing in a fashion of Annie Besant to her own path of a very different fulfillment was now under way.

THE PROGRESSED MOON IN CONJUNCTION WITH THE NATAL SUN, JANUARY 5, 1882   In the current drift of affairs the activation facilitated through practical alertness of the native's strength of character or nascent impulsion is manifest in a measure of encouragement in the program for conventional scholarly recognition and professional scientific employment when the two Bradlaugh girls at least were accepted as authorized teachers some weeks before the maturing of the aspect, even though Annie Besant herself would never be able to win this particular battle.

THE PROGRESSED MOON IN CONJUNCTION WITH NATAL VENUS, APRIL 13, 1882   In the current drift of affairs the activation facilitated through practical alertness of the native's realization or sense of culminations is manifest in the move of business quarters in order to dramatize a complete dissociation from the scurrilous *Freethinker* that to this point had been printed on the same presses as the *National Reformer*. Charles Bradlaugh and Annie Besant in a trend that would prove to their economic advantage now established themselves at 63 Fleet Street where she henceforward would spend most of her working time in London until his decease in 1891.

THE PROGRESSED MOON IN SQUARE WITH THE NATAL MOON, JUNE 10, 1882   In the current drift of affairs the self-mobilization that under accentuated pressure is required of the native's endurance or creative obstinacy is manifest here in the final cancellation of all hope for the cherished B.S. degree when in late July at a special meeting of the university council her qualifications after four years of effort and the winning of special honors in her work were voted inadequate and the less conventional course of her life was made inevitable.

THE PROGRESSED MOON IN OPPOSITION WITH NATAL URANUS, OCTOBER 2, 1882   In the current drift of affairs the activation facilitated through idealistic alertness of the native's release of potentials is manifest in her initial and serious attention to Theosophy as a possible threat to freethought rather than the complementation it offered for the latter's fundamental opposition to the literalistic Christian orthodoxy and the well-entrenched intellectual bigotry she had been fighting since her first awakening to their enslavement of the modern mind. Her warning at length in her "Daybreak" column for June 18th against an other-world-ism and vagueness of principle in the new movement brought her into the personal touch with Madame Blavatsky if here only through the printed word, but yet a start in opening vast new doors of self-realization at the time when the older and more narrow ones were closed in sharp finality.

THE PROGRESSED MOON IN CONJUNCTION WITH NATAL MERCURY, OCTOBER 4, 1882   In the current drift of affairs the activation facilitated through practical alertness of the native's aplomb or self-shielding insouciance is manifest in the conception and publication in January, 1883, of her own sixty-four-page magazine *Our Corner* in which to give herself the opportunity in a developing and characteristic effort to bring all the various threads of experience into a common fabric of reality. Here was her immediate and pragmatic response to the devastating rebuff through the bigotry at London University.

THE PROGRESSED MOON IN SQUARE WITH NATAL JUPITER, NOVEMBER 27, 1882   In the current drift of affairs the self-mobilization that under accentuated pressure is required of the native's zest for life is manifest in the subjective flow of her interests betrayed in the "Young Folks" corner in the first issue of her new periodical through a story she had written and entitled "A Hindu Legend" and then, although concurring in the secularist disapproval of anything spiritualistic, in the printing a few months later of "A Curious Ghost Story" for the truth of which she vouches with no equivocation.

THE PROGRESSED MOON IN OPPOSITION WITH NATAL PLUTO, JULY 24, 1883   In the current drift of affairs the activation facilitated through idealistic alertness of the native's probity while not actual in any fashion during her life was manifest as seen in afterview in the curiously occult recognition of her capacities in one of the mysterious Mahatma Letters received in the summer of 1883 by A. P. Sinnett, and by which he was instructed to make every effort to develop relations with her. A notation by him that he did so is not matched by any record of any result as far as she was concerned. He had lost his journalistic position in India through his overzealous promotion of Theosophy, and was now in London and caught up in spiritualistic experimentation. Interest along such lines was running high and the formation of the Society for Psychical Research at this time was a consequence. Within two years came their investigation conducted by Richard Hodgson of the spiritistic phenomena at the Theosophical headquarters at Madras, and this irrespective of Hodgson's competence or lack of it should have been salutary warning against clairvoyant excesses that in due course would create yet another and far more serious crisis in the history of the movement.

THE PROGRESSED MOON IN TRINE WITH NATAL NEPTUNE, SEPTEMBER 18, 1883   In the current drift of affairs the activation facilitated through idealistic adroitness of the native's acceptance or adoption of an individual destiny is manifest in the need she faced if she were to surmount the semantic difficulties at the root of the final strained relations between the Secularists and the Theosophists. At the end of this year the *Theosophist* made the dichotomy an irrevocable distinction of materialists and freethinkers versus occultists and metaphysicians. Astrologically this is shown to serve Annie Besant well because leading further in her case to her orientations in the social reform that of necessity must be administered right down on earth.

THE PROGRESSED MOON IN TRINE WITH NATAL SATURN, JULY 4, 1884   In the current drift of affairs the activation facilitated through idealistic adroitness of the native's deeper and ultimate concern over norms and values is manifest in the impact of the elopement of Edward Aveling and the daughter of Karl Marx in this month, or their open display of their free-love relationship as a needed final catharsis however slow in coming, after Annie Besant's psychological ravishment. Her hurt at the hands of the unprincipled libertine, who in characteristic Victorian fashion might well have had more satisfaction in probing the restraints of the famous lady than in possessing her, added a second trauma to the simpler one engineered in boorish innocence by Frank Besant and can be interpreted as helping signally to steel her inner resource against the abrasions of an often quite unreasonable world.

THE PROGRESSED MOON IN TRINE WITH THE NATAL MOON, DECEMBER 17, 1884   In the current drift of affairs the activation facilitated through idealistic adroitness of the native's endurance or creative obstinacy is manifest in her acquisition of John Mackinnon Robertson whom she had approached in Edinburgh in July and asked to join her staff permanently. He was the first real scholar she had known, and now in replacing the faithless Aveling in the literary and publishing side of her activities he spared her ultimately embarrassing emotional concomitants and left her the more free to order her public self-presentation.

THE PROGRESSED MOON IN OPPOSITION WITH NATAL MARS, FEBRUARY 24, 1885   In the current drift of affairs the activation facilitated through idealistic alertness of the native's persistence or assertive individuality is manifest in the inauguration of her camaraderie with George Bernard Shaw. She invited him to her house on January 31st and in April began to publish his writings in *Our Corner*. This became a chapter in which she had a fresh and somewhat more sophisticated dimension in her career, in contrast with the sharp and simple directness of her association with Bradlaugh.

THE PROGRESSED MOON IN TRINE WITH NATAL JUPITER, JUNE 1, 1885   In the current drift of affairs the activation facilitated through idealistic adroitness of the native's zest for life is manifest in a short period of channeling talents and energies into the program of the Fabian Society. This group offered a socialistic gradualism more palatable for her than the Marxist program of violent revolution, and in her growing sense of need for dimension in effort she is turning from essentially passive protest or fundamentally rationalistic revolt to an activism ultimately more compatible with her own nature and due before too long to characterize her whole career for all its intellectual overtones.

THE PROGRESSED MOON IN SQUARE WITH NATAL NEPTUNE, MARCH 15, 1886   In the current drift of affairs the self-mobilization that under accentuated pressure is required of the native's acceptance or adoption of an individual destiny is manifest in what in a final if symbolical sense cuts her wholly free from Charles Bradlaugh with his actual seating in the House of Commons in January and facilitates her next steps in larger overall orientation.

THE PROGRESSED MOON IN SQUARE WITH NATAL SATURN,

DECEMBER 21, 1886   In the current drift of affairs the self-mobilization that under accentuated pressure is required of the native's deeper and ultimate concern for norms and values is manifest in her organization in midyear of the Socialist Defence Association or a group of well-to-do individuals willing to provide bail either day or night when anybody was taken into custody for participation in public protest. Here is Annie Besant's fulcral turn from theoretical manipulation of ideas to down-to-earth action in connection with practical problems.

THE PROGRESSED MOON IN SEXTILE WITH THE NATAL SUN, JANUARY 3, 1887   In the current drift of affairs the activation facilitated through practical adroitness of the native's strength of character or nascent impulsion is manifest in a coming to a full of her camaraderie with Bernard Shaw, and as highly intellectual or pseudosophisticated on the one hand and without the libertine aura of Aveling and the possessiveness of Bradlaugh on the other it again may have seemed the essence of what she always had envisioned as the ideal association in common effort between the sexes. If a persisting naïveté it apparently remained a protection for her purity at core.

THE PROGRESSED MOON IN SEXTILE WITH NATAL VENUS, APRIL 6, 1887   In the current drift of affairs the activation facilitated through practical adroitness of the native's realization or sense of culminations is manifest in her attendance at the annual meeting of the Malthusian League in May of this year, to deliver an address. Here was the cause she had first risen to defend in the full stature of her emerging powers, and through all her years she never failed to comprise the goals of her earlier struggles in the overall pattern embracing those of later quickening in her interest. The astrological testimony here is to the essential self-sufficiency of her basic commitments.

THE PROGRESSED MOON IN TRINE WITH NATAL URANUS, SEPTEMBER 16, 1887   In the current drift of affairs the activation facilitated through idealistic adroitness of the native's release of potentials is manifest in her participation in the London riot of November 13th or the "Bloody Sunday" in Trafalgar Square when the reform groups made their dramatic protest in the place where they always had been permitted free speech. Annie Besant played a valiant part in this largely futile endeavor, but Bernard Shaw held back discreetly in what may well have been key disillusion for her as well as a further development in the circumstances that catapulted her into new avenues of much greater ultimate distinction.

THE PROGRESSED MOON IN SEXTILE WITH NATAL MERCURY, SEPTEMBER 18, 1887   In the current drift of affairs the activation facilitated through practical adroitness of the native's aplomb or self-shielding insouciance is manifest in her founding of the Law and Liberty League on November 18th as an aftermath of the violence in Trafalgar Square and in particular cooperation with the well-known crusading editor William T. Stead of the *Pall Mall Gazette*. Here began a new if somewhat brief camaraderie, and it was Stead who in some six months would bring for her to review the two volumes of the just published *Secret Doctrine* of Madame Blavatsky and thus be responsible very directly for her complete intellectual reorientation through her whole-souled embrace of Theosophy.

THE PROGRESSED MOON IN TRINE WITH NATAL PLUTO, JUNE 22, 1888   In the current drift of affairs the activation facilitated through idealistic adroitness of the native's probity, while not actual in any fashion during her lifetime was manifest as seen in afterview in her lightning-like grasp of the significance of the Blavatsky volumes or perhaps more specifically of the extraordinary organon emerging in the arcane tradition and given its dramatically effective if erratic exposition in this major work of the Russian seeress.

THE PROGRESSED MOON IN SEXTILE WITH NATAL NEPTUNE, AUGUST 12, 1888 In the current drift of affairs the activation facilitated through practical adroitness of the native's acceptance or adoption of an individual destiny is manifest in her climactic achievement in socioeconomic reform in England as precursory indication of what she will be able to accomplish in India. In camaraderie now with Herbert Burrows, and in championship of the ultimate unionization of miserably exploited girls in a chain of match factories, the gains were spectacularly successful with far-reaching constructive results.

THE PROGRESSED MOON IN SEXTILE WITH NATAL SATURN, MAY 10, 1889 In the current drift of affairs the activation facilitated through practical adroitness of the native's deeper and ultimate concern for norms and values in every walk of life is manifest in her grasp of new potentials in her overall pattern and her affiliation with the Theosophical Society on this date to instrument the new dimension of her efforts.

THE PROGRESSED MOON IN SQUARE WITH THE NATAL SUN, MAY 22, 1889 In the current drift of affairs the self-mobilization that under accentuated pressure is required of the native's strength of character or nascent impulsion is manifest in her high-visioned attempt to bring about some measure of unified front for the British liberal and reform forces through the great international socialist congress planned for mid-July in Paris, in connection with the universal exposition opening there on May 6th. Again the astrological testimony is to her fidelity to whatever she may devote herself irrespective of whatever else she may embrace in the increasing dimensions of her consciousness.

THE PROGRESSED MOON IN SQUARE WITH NATAL VENUS, AUGUST 19, 1889   In the current drift of affairs the self-mobilization that under accentuated pressure is required of the native's realization or sense of culminations is manifest in her initial psychic experiences as against some earlier super-physical incidents perhaps magnified in later recall. In July of this year, after the socialistic congress in Paris, she and Herbert Burrows went to visit for a day or two with Madame Blavatsky who for reasons of health and seclusion for writing was spending a few weeks at Fontainbleu. This unhappily was help to the drift to the later miracle-mongering.

THE PROGRESSED MOON IN OPPOSITION WITH THE NATAL MOON, OCTOBER 11, 1889   In the current drift of affairs the activation facilitated through idealistic alertness of the native's endurance or creative obstinacy is manifest in the extent of her hardly fortuitous new leading toward supernatural phenomena when at this time she joined William Butler Yeats, then a fellow-member of the Esoteric Section of the Theosophical Society, in the demand on Madame Blavatsky to give exhibitions of her occult powers. Thus Annie Besant was setting her public image in canons of past popularizations rather than in more seminal potentials of the future.

THE PROGRESSED MOON IN TRINE WITH NATAL MARS, DECEMBER 14, 1889   In the current drift of affairs the activation facilitated through idealistic adroitness of the native's persistence or assertive individuality is manifest in the dispatch with which she became an almost indispensable right hand for Madame Blavatsky and in particular began to meet the considerable need created when Mabel Collins was lost to the Society. By September in this year she had become co-editor of Blavatsky's magazine *Lucifer*.

THE PROGRESSED MOON IN SQUARE WITH NATAL URANUS, JANUARY 22, 1890 In the current drift of affairs the self-mobilization that under accentuated pressure is required of the native's release of potentials is manifest in her election in mid-January to the presidency of the Blavatsky Lodge in London. This was history in recurrence and astrological indication in repetition when seen in connection with her election to a vice-presidency in the National Secular Society fifteen years before.

THE PROGRESSED MOON IN SQUARE WITH NATAL MERCURY, JANUARY 24, 1890 In the current drift of affairs the self-mobilization that under accentuated pressure is required of the native's aplomb or self-shielding insouciance is manifest in the loosening of the more superficial bonds she had established in the British reform movements of the late eighteen-eighties as prelude to her self-orientation in greater dimension. When Charles Bradlaugh returned from the visit to India that he had hoped would help his recovery from serious illness in close correlation with this progression, and held to his decision to resign from the presidency of the National Secular Society, Annie Besant followed suit by withdrawal from her vice-presidency. Then and in due course they announced the dissolution by mutual consent of their Freethought Publishing Company.

THE PROGRESSED MOON IN OPPOSITION WITH NATAL JUPITER, MARCH 14, 1890 In the current drift of affairs the activation facilitated through idealistic alertness of the native's zest for life is manifest in a particular case of officiousness or the maneuvering through which her home at 19 Avenue Road in London was remodelled into more adequate headquarters for the Theosophical Society in England as well as more fitting facilities for Blavatsky Lodge. The project when completed in July had added not only a commodious hall for public meetings but for the Esoteric Section a large chamber connected with Madame Blavatsky's bedroom by a secret passage together with hidden and much smaller quarters restricted to a special inner elite. This of course was continuing the not-too-happy but sharp swing in the society to the phenomena side of the occult as essentially the most popular and perhaps at its best the most effective form of the antirationalism to which Theosophy fundamentally if not explicitly had been dedicated at the start.

THE PROGRESSED MOON IN SQUARE WITH NATAL PLUTO, OCTOBER 16, 1890   In the current drift of affairs the self-mobilization that under accentuated pressure is required of the native's probity if not actually in any fashion during her life was yet manifest as seen in afterview in the remarkable coming to center of almost the whole personal fabric of her being, and at what was a greater point of transition than she might ever realize. As in a sense the whole Theosophical movement was now delivered into her custody, her brother Henry Trueman Wood and only close tie in her own generation was knighted for his services as British Commissioner at the Paris exposition and after eleven years her two children returned to her entirely of their own volition. Here is horoscopic testimony to exceptional fulcral convergence as demanding almost by necessity an unusual self-manifestation or achievement under the essential principle of equivalence or distinction, even if an indication of later and broader overall perspective in which a myth-figure potential could take shape.

THE PROGRESSED MOON IN TRINE WITH THE NATAL SUN, SEPTEMBER 3, 1891 In the current drift of affairs the activation facilitated through idealistic alertness of the native's strength of character or nascent impulsion is manifest in her response to the challenge sharpened in high dramatic convergence through the impact of the death of Charles Bradlaugh in January and of Madame Blavatsky almost immediately afterwards in May. Now she stood alone and self-responsible in the bridging from Neptune as having vital summation in the former to Pluto as having more intangible preview in the latter, and of course as certified in the afterperspective of the dynamic horoscopy.

THE PROGRESSED MOON IN TRINE WITH NATAL VENUS, NOVEMBER 27, 1891 In the current drift of affairs the activation facilitated through idealistic alertness of the native's realization or sense of culminations is manifest in her dramatic valedictory address on August 30th under the auspices of the National Secular Society in London at the Hall of Science, where she has been speaking on freethought for sixteen and a half years. In the statement of her credo she began by first declaring that she was as much an enemy of a conventional Christianity as ever and that she was not in any way surrendering her adherence to modern science but rather was accepting greatly enlarged dimensions for its application.

THE PROGRESSED MOON IN SQUARE WITH NATAL MARS, MARCH 19, 1892 In the current drift of affairs the self-mobilization that under accentuated pressure is required of the native's persistence or assertive individuality is manifest in her editorial in the initial 1892 issue of *Lucifer* in which she begins to speak with the characteristic authority of the uncompromising occultist and to put down very specific predictions.

THE PROGRESSED MOON IN SEXTILE WITH NATAL URANUS, APRIL 27, 1892   In the current drift of affairs the activation facilitated through practical adroitness of the native's release of potentials is manifest most importantly in general fashion as with the Theosophical reins in her hands in de facto if not official fashion she begins to affirm her dedication. Of perhaps symbolical significance to her at this point is her daughter Mabel who with a young husband will go to Australia where he has a position and where the two of them will labor for Theosophy.

THE PROGRESSED MOON IN TRINE WITH NATAL MERCURY, APRIL 28, 1892   In the current drift of affairs the activation facilitated through idealistic adroitness of the native's aplomb or self-shielding insouciance is manifest in her uncritical or naïve rapprochement with William Quan Judge as the international president-to-be of the society after a petulant and later withdrawn announcement of resignation by Colonel Olcott. Actually the much jockeying for position now building to a bitter power struggle in the Theosophical Society was probably of no interest to her since she has been seen going her own way always and calmly enough while also inclined to yield an unquestioning trust to anybody with whom she might labor in common effort.

THE PROGRESSED MOON IN SEXTILE WITH NATAL PLUTO, JANUARY 6, 1893   In the current drift of affairs the activation facilitated through practical adroitness of the native's probity while not actual in any obvious fashion during her lifetime was manifest as seen in afterview in the vital orientation in Eastern philosophy and entrée to significant circles in Hindu education provided for her through Gyanendra Chakravarti. In afterview this is the horoscopic certification of the importance of her embrace of Hinduism rather than the Buddhism of most of her associates in the society.

THE PROGRESSED MOON IN CONJUNCTION WITH NATAL NEPTUNE, FEBRUARY 23, 1893   In the current drift of affairs the activation facilitated through practical alertness of the native's acceptance or adoption of an individual destiny is manifest in her leading role in the exposition of Theosophy at the World Parliament of Religions in Chicago in August as a climax to long and intensive travels and lectures to advance the greater scope of Theosophy in America. By gaining a special individual classification at the parliament, which was an integral part of the great Columbian Exposition, the movement achieved world rank it had never known before. Thus she no longer would be under necessity to make her presentations through the facilities of local lodges, or on some platform open to her through her prominence in social reform.

THE PROGRESSED MOON IN CONJUNCTION WITH NATAL SATURN, OCTOBER 28, 1893   In the current drift of affairs the activation facilitated through practical alertness of the native's deeper and ultimate concern for norms and values is manifest when on November 16th she first set foot on Indian soil and almost immediately gained her long and firm intellectual camaraderie with Dr. Bhagavan Das. He was one of the finest scholars in India, and of great help in the intensive study of languages into which she plunged at once.

In summary, the secondary directions of the moon for the first of the two chapters of Annie Besant's public life chart the circumstances of the opportunity for her self-realization and independence provided by Charles Bradlaugh and the National Secular Society and of the steps in her outreach to it until when she changes base to India she is a seasoned reformer and has become the de facto leader of the Theosophical Society and the ultimate successor of Madame Blavatsky. Her progress is marked out in close association with various individuals who assist her unfoldment or posit a threat to it as the case may be. These progressions indicate the particular importance in this respect and in successive order after Bradlaugh of Edward Aveling, George Bernard Shaw, William T. Stead, Herbert Burrows and especially Helena Blavatsky. The native is delineated in her transition from an interest in ideas and an assumption that the regeneration of society can be brought about through their manipulation to a turn to direct action believed by socialism to be necessary for the gaining of human rights and then a further turn in recourse to subjective factors as presented dramatically in occultism or specifically through Theosophy. She is revealed as somehow always succeeding in building each earlier cause for which she labors into each later one in an effective comprisement in her own mind at least. Shown as important in the steeling of her character is the surrender of her children to her embittered husband, and the reward for considering their interest first with their subsequent return to her of their own free will on growing up and able to do so.

THE TRANSITS

Continuing in the pattern established for the delineation of the native's performance in life through the dynamic horoscopy, attention here next turns from the three basic directional systems of which consideration is limited to the secondaries in the case of Annie Besant on to the transits or the significance of the planets in their actual geocentric movements and configurations at any given time. The possibilities of such signification can ramify to infinity, with progressive loss of any meaningful indication, but when these heavenly bodies are seen as acting most directly in consequence of the earth's own immediate participation in the celestial mechanics they gain import of marked value in astrological analysis. This means primarily (1) the stations where in terrestrial terms they pause for a shift in motion and thereupon emphasize direction in event and (2) the lunations established by an actual satellite of the earth or most particularly the solar eclipses through which the lunar phases in everyday functioning are marked out in their measure of the momentary set of the background for conscious experience in its own special context. As has been explained in connection with Abraham Lincoln, the quickening by transit to general circumstantial involvement of a natal significator is properly by either conjunction or opposition within an orb of sixty minutes of arc.

Because of the extraordinary subjectivity of the Besant horoscope, and of her life if it is viewed in any depth at all,

271

the illustrations of the transits in her case are best held to a few select years in which her rapprochement with circumstances is unusually accentuated in one way or another. Five of these moments of pivoting punctuation in her experience are convenient in this respect. Transiting Pluto is disregarded since the extent of remove from reality in this area of the analysis would hardly permit any definable significance in her peculiarly self-centered development even in afterperspective, but activations of natal Pluto can be noted as usual.

1867: The Adolescent Outreach

Annie Besant herself recorded the fact that she was not in love and knew she was not in love with the young and bigoted perfectionist she married, but rather had envisioned the opportunity for a rosy-hued camaraderie of service to a congenial little group of parishioners under the benign auspices of the church. Here was early and dramatic revelation of her naïveté as seen framed in one of the unusually radical transitions characterizing so much of her life.

TRANSITING MERCURY STATIONARY GOING RETROGRADE IN OPPOSITION WITH NATAL VENUS, MARCH 18, 1867 This station, indicating the critical regrasp of experience facilitated through current ultimacies of general development, identifies the importance of the pleasant and relaxing circumstances in which the happy chapter at Harrow that provided the education opportunities for both the native's brother and herself was ended with the move to London and in which her realization was given its broader dimensions in new association. This all was in such fashion that the girlish fantasies of her basic attitude were undisturbed, and her immature intellection was even encouraged in its own self-ordering. At the start the year was not brought to immediacy by any drift in things.

TRANSITING JUPITER STATIONARY GOING RETROGRADE IN CONJUNCTION WITH NATAL SATURN, JUNE 28, 1867 This station, indicating the critical regrasp of experience facilitated through current ultimacies of general development, identifies the importance of the summer in bringing everything down to a practical point after the psychological set encouraged in the realization. In nascent consistency there is now the arousal of concern for the issues of the day as the native is challenged to this by William Prowting Roberts.

TRANSITING URANUS STATIONARY GOING RETROGRADE IN CONJUNCTION WITH THE NATAL MOON, OCTOBER 20, 1867 This station, indicating the critical regrasp of experience facilitated through current ultimacies of general development, identifies the importance of the hanging of Irish patriots in Manchester in November as climax in the crucial awakening in the native's nascent independence or transcendental uniqueness of the endurance or public manifestation of a selfhood now never again to be able to live in a private unreality.

TRANSITING JUPITER STATIONARY GOING DIRECT IN CONJUNCTION WITH NATAL NEPTUNE, OCTOBER 25, 1867 This station, indicating the critical regrasp of experience facilitated through current ultimacies of general development, identifies the importance of the marriage finally solemnized in December as the acceptance of the sharpened or essentially tragic destiny in climax of the native's manifestation of her nascent consistency and its buttressing naïveté in the blind movement through these final months of the year in the life that would come to belong more and more to the world at large than in any real respect to the Annie Besant shorn of all happy innocence. Events in her twenty-second year are very much at an immediate center for her.

1874: Secular Horizons

The legal separation from Frank Besant, followed by the death of her mother who had been the one close tie that never had failed her, gave Annie Besant a freedom at the price of almost impossible responsibility. She had some assistance from her minor earnings in preparing a number of popular pamphlets, and then with midsummer in 1874 she happened on a copy of the *National Reformer* and this led to an irresistible desire to join the National Secular Society and to her meeting Charles Bradlaugh in August.

TRANSITING NEPTUNE STATIONARY GOING DIRECT IN CONJUNCTION WITH NATAL PLUTO, JANUARY 7, 1874 This station of no significance in the native's lifetime, indicating a concentration of experience to be seen in afterview as facilitated through current ultimacies of general development, identifies the historical importance of her association with Bradlaugh and the move toward the eventual probity of her contribution through the immediacy of her nascent responsibility in its gradual drift into consummation of the relationship.

SOLAR ECLIPSE IN CONJUNCTION WITH NATAL PLUTO, APRIL 16, 1874 The particular intensification of experience in immediate fashion indicated by this eclipse in what in afterview is a quickening of the native's probity is added testimony to the eventual high significance of the sweep of events in her life as she consummated the contact in due course with Bradlaugh.

SOLAR ECLIPSE IN CONJUNCTION WITH NATAL MERCURY, OCTOBER 10, 1874 The particular intensification of experience in immediate fashion indicated by this eclipse in a quickening of the native's aplomb is astrological testimony to the extraordinary self-establishment now provided for her.

THE SAME ECLIPSE IN OPPOSITION WITH NATAL URANUS
The particular intensification of experience in more long-
range fashion indicated by this eclipse in a quickening of the
release of her potentials is supplementary testimony in the
dynamic horoscopy to the importance of the development.

TRANSITING MERCURY STATIONARY GOING DIRECT IN OPPO-
SITION WITH NATAL MARS, NOVEMBER 25, 1874   This station,
indicating the critical regrasp of experience facilitated through
current ultimacies of general development, identifies through
the exceptional closeness of the aspect the remarkable fashion
in which in her basic attitude she now had stimulus for the
persistence of outreach that would carry her far and enable
her shortly after the new year to emerge from her nom de
plume of Ajax and stand forth on her own feet in her own
true identity.

1886: Rational Disillusion

According to Annie Besant's own account, the loss of her
faith in social reform by means of rational enlightenment
began in 1886 although she continued in her efforts to
broaden the thinking of people generally. But Edward Aveling had hurt her and Bernard Shaw had heightened her
disillusion in the liberal movement. With the seating of Bradlaugh in Parliament finally she found herself afloat for lack
of a truly moving cause, and events had become a real threat
to her self-sufficiency.

TRANSITING URANUS STATIONARY GOING RETROGRADE IN
CONJUNCTION WITH THE NATAL SUN, JANUARY 14, 1886
This station, indicating the critical regrasp of experience facilitated through current ultimacies of general development,
identifies the importance of the final admission in this month
of Charles Bradlaugh to the House of Commons. In the

native's nascent independence her strength of being is given an immediate stimulus for whatever may be the next step in her ongoing.

TRANSITING VENUS STATIONARY GOING RETROGRADE IN CONJUNCTION WITH NATAL SATURN, JANUARY 30, 1886 This station, indicating the critical regrasp of experience facilitated through current ultimacies of general development, gives additional identification of the importance of Bradlaugh's acceptance by Parliament at last as precipitating the subtle delivery of the native through this event to her own essentially greater career ahead. Her basic sensitivity is sharpened to an immediate and increasing concern over ends in view or deeper needs of personal existence.

1889: Occult Horizons

As the horizons of secularism had enabled Annie Besant to see and labor on beyond blind provincial orthodoxies that had begun to offer nothing but hopeless limitation with the destruction of her original adolescent dream, so now her introduction to vast new realms through Madame Blavatsky's *Secret Doctrine* seemed an equal escape from what had come to seem an equally hopeless constriction of spirit in the endless proliferating ideas and reform programs coming ever closer to ineptitude through unyielding conflict with each other.

TRANSITING MERCURY STATIONARY GOING DIRECT IN OPPOSITION WITH NATAL URANUS, OCTOBER 25, 1889 This station, indicating the critical regrasp of experience facilitated through current ultimacies of general development, identifies the release of new potentials of selfhood in the basic attitude as starting with the personal blessing of Madame Blavatsky on May 10th and continuing with spiritualistic experiences at Fontainebleau in July up to a climax of sorts for the native in the demand on the Russian seerness by William Butler Yeats and herself for more phenomena and thus indicating how she had begun to ground the whole of her self-acceptance in the remote orientations of the occult side of life.

THE SAME STATION IN CONJUNCTION WITH NATAL MERCURY The identification in this quickening is the importance of the immediate and meteoric rise of Annie Besant in the Theosophical Society in duplication of her prior swift achievement of place and prominence in the National Secular Society. By September in this year she had become coeditor of the magazine *Lucifer,* and shortly after the holidays she became president of Blavatsky Lodge.

1893: The Cosmic Potential

Annie Besant now can reach out as far as the mind of man may project his reality, into realms of subjective as well as objective tangibility, and the ultimate mark of her life will be established as she makes full use of all the elements of high significance she has gathered quite completely in her own hands.

TRANSITING MERCURY STATIONARY GOING RETROGRADE IN CONJUNCTION WITH NATAL URANUS, MARCH 23, 1893 This station, indicating the critical regrasp of experience facilitated through current ultimacies of general development, identifies the importance of the startling and unexpected recognition of Theosophy as a world movement in its own unique right at the Parliament of Religions in connection with World's Columbian Exposition in Chicago. The climax came at the actual sessions, and in their dramatic success, and the release of potentials in the basic attitude had an added manifestation in immediacy when the native set foot in India for the first time in November and began the new chapter of her life.

THE SAME STATION IN OPPOSITION WITH NATAL MERCURY
The identification in this quickening of the aplomb in the
basic attitude is the line of achievement of more remote or
long-range nature represented by the interest in education that
will lead to her more solid and continuing contribution to her
adopted land in the East, and to her development of her
Hinduism in the rejection of Christian bigotry as a basis of
her psychological poise in this new chapter.

SOLAR ECLIPSE IN CONJUNCTION WITH NATAL PLUTO,
APRIL 16, 1893   The particular intensification of experience
in immediate fashion indicated by this eclipse in what in
afterview is a quickening of the native's probity is additional
testimony to the importance of developments climaxing in the
unexpected wide recognition for Theosophy and the circumstances taking her to India and contributing to her ultimate
contribution through her determined validation of the Hinduism ordering her later alignments.

SOLAR ECLIPSE IN CONJUNCTION WITH NATAL MERCURY,
OCTOBER 9, 1893   The particular intensification of experience in immediate fashion indicated by this eclipse in a repetitive quickening of the native's aplomb is astrological testimony
to the extraordinary self-establishment now provided for her
in the compass so much larger than in 1874.

THE SAME ECLIPSE IN OPPOSITION WITH NATAL URANUS
The particular intensification of experience in more long-
range fashion indicated by this eclipse in the repetitive quickening in the release of potentials for the new or second chapter
of the native's life in comparison with the first is thus astrological testimony to the exceptional potentialities lying ahead.

In summary, the transits in Annie Besant's life can be
taken in a few particular years of transition in her affairs to

gain an overview of the current ultimacies of general development as they give particular facilitation to her progress and achievement. Thus her naïve entrance into marriage in 1867 is shown leading to her struggle to make a place for herself that in its pressures led the way to Charles Bradlaugh in 1874, and through her experience with what seemed the futility of reform by a mere manipulation of idea brought about the disillusion of 1886 and her freedom from bondage to the essential limitations of the course she had been following. In 1889 vast horizons were opened for her by Theosophy, and in 1893 she again but in larger dimension was as poised for high achievement as she had been nineteen years before.

LIFE RECAPITULATION

Continuing in the pattern established for the delineation of the native's performance through the dynamic horoscopy, attention next turns from the three directional systems and the transits to the cyclic recapitulations that complete the comprehensive method recommended in this text for the normal course of predictive analysis. As has been explained in connection with Abraham Lincoln, these subsidiary horoscopes reveal the rhythmic reinforcement of personal experience in circumstances through the return of the sun annually and of the moon monthly and of the ascendant daily to the zodiacal places they occupied at birth and the consequent establishment of the solar and lunar returns and the ascendant's diurnals that thereupon provide as essentially specific if transitory charting of the individualized life unfoldment.

SOLAR RETURN, LONDON, SEPTEMBER 30, 1888, 4:12 P.M. The illustrative cyclic returns in the case of Annie Besant are selected because in her autobiography she identified May 10, 1889, as the most pivotal moment of her life. The subsidiary horoscope for the sun lacks the special cusp emphasis found in connection with what has seemed to be the equivalent vital year for Abraham Lincoln, and this fact suggests her essentially lesser rapport with her immediate circumstances. Too, the important first and tenth angles are wholly empty in her solar return, with consequent suggestion of the covert nature of the 1889 transition for her in a

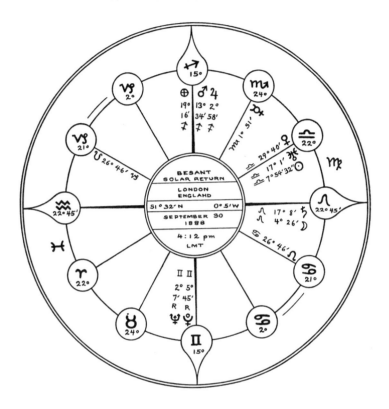

measure of similarity to the remarkably subjective change
identified in the instance of the American president. This is
far from a matter of tweedledum and tweedledee. There is
no particular indication for her to match the striking motivation stress indicated for him through his paired Jupiter and
Saturn in the temperament typing, but for her there is a planet
in high focus as there is not for him and it is Neptune and an
important clue to the strength of the fundamentally trans-

cendental responsibility characterizing her entrance into the infinitely ramified final chapter of her life.

The bowl typing of her return by slightly wide orb testifies to the significant fullness she must share with her fellows if she really is to fulfill herself, and accentuating this is a natural disposition shown by positive common-sign stress to call for the particularly humanitarian self-expression. Here first of all in 1888 would be a solution to her momentary need because of what had become the great loss of steam in the earlier chapter in a life of dramatically brilliant achievement. The strong emphasis of the midheaven axis, as against the horizon dominance of the birth chart together with the essentially empty eastern hemisphere, reveals the likelihood of encompassment in what in her case could be a species of cosmic womb in which to engender the larger dimension of her remarkable overall potential. The mode of self-integration re-emphasizes her intuitive gifts, since through subjective function in her new sense of fullness for these twelve months she is called by circumstances to challenge her fellows along the lines quickened for her by her encounter with Madame Blavatsky's *Secret Doctrine*. This could well be capstone to a whole adult life devoted thus far and with great dedication to distinctively everyday social reform. The repetitive appearance of the moon as the vocational planet is astrological certification of her prophetic role as now greatly expanded.

LUNAR RETURN, LONDON, MAY 5, 1889, 8:58 A.M. This lunar month including Annie Besant's spectacular conversion to Theosophy, and providing the context of her general involvement in circumstances pertinent to the significance of a step dividing her years into what superficially were strangely irreconcilable halves, is shown by the subsidiary horoscope of

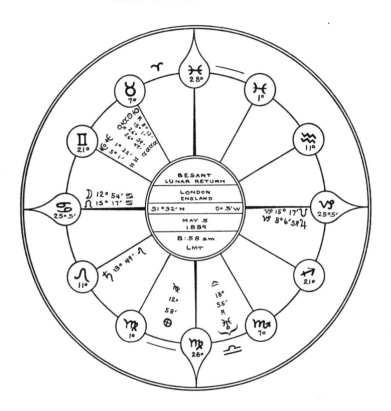

the moon's return to its natal place as indeed a most covert or occult matter. The chart itself has a strong emphasis of inwardness since the first and tenth angles once more are empty and the only angular planet is both intercepted and retrograde. The dragon's head and tail are lying close on the horizon, and this in the astrological tradition stemming from the medievals is testimony to particular spiritual protection for her at the ascendant and either exceptionally exalted opportunity or self-undoing at the opposite cusp. While these nodes are geometric points in the heavens that cannot be treated as planets or taken in aspect, they reveal the intersections of planes of reference in the manner of the equinoxes in the ecliptic and in this unusual case show the overall lunar orientation in circumstantial involvement to be self-confirming or self-challenging. The moon itself lies in the twelfth house of hidden things or of subjective sustainment, and since it is lord of the ascendant there is suggestion of particular and personal manifestation of transcendental considerations during the four weeks. A satellitium of five planets in the eleventh house, with Pluto an inoperative sixth, gives dominant testimony of vital objectives brought significantly to the fore and hence likely to help shape the lasting direction of the life.

DIURNAL RETURN, LONDON, MAY 10, 1889, 3:05 A.M. The horoscopic figure here superficially differs from the solar and lunar returns relative to the native's epochal transition because there is strong planetary emphasis of both the first and tenth angles. None the less it continues to emphasize the overall covert nature of the day's events since all angular planets capable of the phenomenon are retrograde while no others are. The fact of Jupiter in an angle with Saturn in strong square with the sun and rising Venus meets a traditional medieval dictum that would endow the native with a special priestly role as a birthright, and it is interesting that on this day when she took her step formally into Theosophy she had a personal blessing from Madame Blavatsky herself. The lord of the first house in the second suggests that Annie Besant may indeed have had the resources necessary for achieving the end to which she was called or for which she had volunteered. Uranus in the house of opportunity reveals

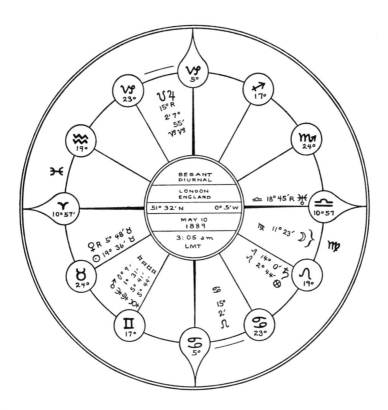

the value of her individual uniqueness in the readjustment she is making in her life. The splay pattern in temperament typing is suggestion of potential genius, and Jupiter in high focus shows how personal this must be.

In summary, the three subsidiary horoscopes charting the epochal transition through which Annie Besant divided her life into approximate halves of dramatic contrast with each other are strikingly in accord in showing the covert nature of the new major period in her experience. The solar return certifies the overall importance of the impact of the *Secret Doctrine* and the embrace of Theosophy. The lunar return reveals the scope of the occult organon that would now provide the major orientation for her aspiration and effort. The diurnal return presents a curious certification by medieval tradition of the general priestly function she could accept for herself in these trancendental areas.

ANNIE BESANT IX

HOROSCOPE RECTIFICATION

In her *Autobiography* Annie Besant states that according to what to her was credible information her birth occurred precisely at 5:39 p.m. on October 1, 1847. This can be presumed to be on astrological grounds. Through the Theosophical Society she had contact with two of the most famed astrologers in the West in her generation, Walter Old who wrote under the pen name of Sepharial and Alan Leo, as well as every opportunity to consult living individuals who might know of the events of her infancy at first hand. Alan Leo reports that she herself "said many years ago that she was born between 5:00 and 5:40 p.m." Her nativity in the author's *How to Learn Astrology* and *Guide to Horoscope Interpretation* was taken from Alan Leo's *A Thousand and One Notable Nativities* (second edition, 1917, p. 125) and is erected for 5:29 p.m. In his *Sabian Symbols in Astrology* the author adjusted the data to the tabulations in the projected *A Time To Be Born, Accurate Birth Data of 3000 Notable Persons and Events* by Lilian Polk or to 5:20 p.m. These are not appreciable variations, but they change the signification of the house cusps and dramatize the importance of rectification. It is to be noted however that the delineation of the native in *How to Learn Astrology* is in no way invalidated in the light of the present and far more thorough analysis, thanks to the techniques of primacy indication presented here and in the companion expositions.

With rectification in this case probably a matter of verification or of no more than minor adjustment, the procedure with the progressed moon in secondary direction is not a proposition of tentative assumption at the beginning. With the greater span of years there is less reason for attention to the fourth and seventh angles, where subjective factors may predominate. The midheaven was crossed first in mid-December, 1861, and this corresponds to the initial breakthrough into a larger dimension of life than the wholly provincial environment of her upbringing in England. Through expansion of her religious contacts there was a preliminary grasp at adultship. Permission had been given for European study early in the year, leading to intensive practice in French together with lessons in German, and in the following spring she received confirmation in Paris at the hands of an illustrious Anglican bishop visiting from America. The ascendant was crossed first in mid-March, 1868, corresponding to her first appearance in print in May as a personal breakthrough of epochal import in respect to her whole career. This had come as a means for a surrogate self-expression when her marriage in the preceding December had been traumatically disillusioning, and it may well have served to preserve her actual sanity.

The next progressed lunar passage over the midheaven was in early February, 1889, in correspondence with an epochal expansion in the whole frame of her life when she entered into the illimitable dimensions of occultism. Affiliation with the Theosophical Society was on May 10th. The next passage over the ascendant was in mid-April, 1896, and it corresponded with a complex of occult developments inaugurated perhaps most definitely when she brought Charles Leadbeater to residence in the London headquarters of the society or under the same roof as herself in the preceding August and in that month began a long and dramatic chapter of clairvoyant investigation. Here all unfortunately she picked up the course of the miracle-mongering such as possibly had brought Madame Blavatsky to needed or adequate general notice but at the same time has clouded the very genuine contribution of the Russian seeress.

The midheaven had its progressed lunar accentuation for a final time in early June, 1916, when the native rose to her peak as a public figure and her political career had culmination in her election to the presidency of the Indian National Congress. The ascendant had its final accentuation in early August, 1923, coincident with the bursting of the Krishnamurti bubble or the collapse of the overliteral and ultimately ridiculous conception of his mission. Here well may have been born, out of the very need of her immortalized sincerity, the curiously delimited or inescapably transcendental myth figure assumed in the present analysis to be the promise of her survival in some endless service to occultism in general.

In continuing the verification of her nativity, it is to be noted that Annie Besant's father died when she was almost exactly five years old and the midheaven axis moved to Gemini-Sagittarius 29°-odd is almost exactly within a semisquare with Mars to indicate his passing. Her mother deceased when she was twenty-six and a half, and the midheaven-axis regression to Gemini-Sagittarius 8°-odd is close to a precise square relationship with natal Saturn.

In summary, the horoscope of Annie Besant has no real need for rectification since in her own lifetime her association with prominent astrologers led to apparent validation through their offices. The time she records as precise checks out very satisfactorily under the procedures recommended in these pages.

SUPPLEMENTARY BACKGROUND

The normal course of precedure in natal analysis should never disregard a proper alertness for exceptional features such as stand out in a nativity and perhaps demand a primary attention even at first glance. There are two particular instances of the sort in the horoscope of Annie Besant. The opposition of Uranus with Mercury, exact to within four minutes of arc, is spectacular indication of her brilliance of mind and hence of the necessity to give some unusual account of her intellectual potentials in the development of her career. The presence of all but three of the planets in a cardinal T cross is striking testimony to the unbridled opportunism of her nature, but even more remarkable is the fact that the moon as not the focal planet in spite of its many squares can with a high significance be considered very curiously apart from the character-establishing configuration and thereupon be seen in a trine-type emphasis that is supernumerary in respect to it and that embraces all the other planets since the conjunction of Neptune with Saturn involves the former by a translation of light. Here is an overlay of transcendental implication that not only marks the most outstanding characteristic of the native in her uncompromisingly universal scope of interest but identifies the two strangely discrete sides of her nature. This is not the phenomenon of split personality but rather is the case of a multipersonality in which one phase of her being may provide a very practical complementation of another and without prejudice or psychological disturbance. Planetary indications of course do not distinguish between these often quite independent manifestations, since she is a single person and it would hardly be possible to identify them apart from each other too literally or specifically, but she has been described as one of the most protean individuals ever coming to such overall prominence.

Her natural disposition is cardinal as an emphasis shown also by the T cross and the focal determinator of preponderance, and so she is not the intellectual for all her facile use of her mental powers nor by the same token is she the humanistically-minded individual despite her long devotion to socioeconomic reform. Indeed, in the latter area she lost supremacy to Mahatma Gandhi in the struggle for India's independence because he assimilated himself to the masses and she remained condescendingly apart in her luxurious habiliments of mind and person. The temperament type is splay since she never exerted herself sufficiently at core, as proved the case contrariwise with Abraham Lincoln, to be able to bring Mercury to trine with Neptune and produce the locomotive pattern and thus instrument the key achievement as perhaps also a myth figure developed in a significant chapter of conventional history. Genius was evident and effective in her life, but her quite signal accomplishments were scattered or casual in the sweep of the times.

The emphasis of the first house over the tenth is testimony to the dominance of individuality over social instrumentation, and this has strong buttressing in the mode of self-integration determined by the two-configuration focus in Jupiter and the moon as well as confirmation if a single extra degree of orb is allowed for a trine of Saturn with Jupiter. Of necessity, by

all these significations, she functioned completely as a creature
of circumstances and remained unbendingly personal in what
Madame Blavatsky identified as a Luciferian pride. Of focal
determination chosen in familiar course, the cardinal T cross
first and the cardinal-sign preponderance secondarily have
had consideration in other connection. The mental chemistry
is of the order of whole-insight immediately realized, and thus
she was self-sure in virtually every phase of her activities. Like
Lincoln, the planet of oriental appearance is the moon and
the necessity for the public career or some equivalent has
basic indication.

THUMBNAIL BIOGRAPHY

Annie Wood, of three-quarters Irish stock, was born under
conventional middle-class circumstances in London on October 1, 1847. Her rather impractical father died when she was
five, and he left the little family in precarious condition. Her
mother, an independent and strong-willed person with whom
she would keep the closest of ties for more than twenty-six
years, found a way to support herself and two children by
opening a boarding house for boys at Harrow. This took care
of the schooling for Annie's brother Henry, who proceeded
on to distinguish herself quite appreciably in later life. Annie's
own education, in a smug age when there was very little of
this for women, was taken over by an eccentric woman of
means who was drawn to her at Harrow. The result was a
thorough grounding in French and some mastery of German,
facilitated by considerable broadening through time spent on
the Continent and climaxed of course by a rigorous drilling
in etiquette and the permissible graces.

In the frame of all this she also had encouragement for

marked tomboy proclivities. Frank Besant, as the young curate, at first offered real companionship for the hoyden in her. In complete Victorian innocence of the stark facts of life she saw the opportunity for a glorious service to her fellows in the union with him, but the traumatic experience of the marital bed when she was barely twenty together with the following years of a continuing horror resulted in an effective sealing off of a core of steeled purity in the depths of her nature. Thus began the two-strand development, so that a lingering adolescence could serve to keep her insulated from contamination through all the periods in which she would buffet the waves of humanity's feckless deviations or insensate bigotries when they threatened to sweep over her. Her first self-protective recourse from surrender to hypocritical conventionality and domestic submergence was to an immature authorship that really presaged the whole of her later and ultimate pragmatic career. Through William Prowting Roberts she was led into the areas of British social protest and reform, and this led to Charles Bradlaugh and the National Secular Society and thus to what in many respects was the happiest or at least the most simply structured chapter of her ongoing.

With her restless disposition primarily, and the inevitable thinning out of the sense of a holy warfare in the context of a world moving to total readjustment with the discovery of Pluto not too far ahead, she ricocheted from one social program to another in perhaps subconscious disillusion with the effectiveness of it all. Gradually her recourse was to the sealed-up side of herself and this led to Edward Aveling or the unprincipled sophisticate who proved a real threat to her core purity. That experience left the vacuum to be filled by Madame Blavatsky and Theosophy, and thereupon and in due time resulted in the long chapter in which Charles Leadbeater was the seminal factor and in which the excitements and scandals of the miracle-mongering took place and in which finally the evolution of Krishnamurti and his eventual reconciliation gave her a terminal anchorage in what was largely the apotheosis of her own unsullied and still adolescent aspiration. In general her service to Theosophy has been a major achievement in the revivification of the Theosophical Society and its establishment on a very solid foundation. On the other side of the coin was the happy accident of Gyanendra Chakravarti, who protected her from the orthodoxy of the Theravada Buddhism that in respect to the Christianity that had so outraged her would have been altogether a case of more of the same even though this earlier tradition in Eastern faith had served most of the other Theosophical leaders quite adequately. Through Chakravarti very largely she gained entrée to the Indian elite and the chance with the founding of Central Hindu College and the concomitant developments to make a wonderful contribution to the land of her adoption.

She never married a second time. She had two children, Arthur Digby Besant, who grew up to give an excellent account of himself, and the younger and more frail Mabel who matured and had her happy self-fulfillment at the end. Frank Besant with unbending viciousness succeeded in taking her children away from her for many years, when the court decided that as an atheist she was an unfit mother, but she lived to see both return to her and to have both become Theosophists.

She passed away peacefully in her sleep on September 20, 1933, at Adyar in India where the Theosophical Society had long had its headquarters.

dynamic analysis

THE BASIC ATTITUDE

The dynamic horoscopy, in fundamental feature and competent practice, is by far the simplest of the astrological techniques. Contributing to this fact is that, except in the subsidiary procedures, the planets and their immediate mathematical relations are all that is involved. The signs of the zodiac and the houses of the horoscope simply do not enter the picture at the outset. Concern moreover is restricted very properly to the ten significators that have common employment, including the sun and moon which in astrology assume regular planetary roles or are in no way distinguished from the actual solar satellites. For the progressive analysis each of these ten factors is taken in turn and examined in the pattern of the heavens established on a given natal day through various types of symbolical measure, or has a significance stemming in principal part and in varying fashion from its actual geocentric motion in the zodiac from the moment of birth. Its consideration is in terms of the aspects it forms with the original places of itself and the other nine planets in the basic nativity.

Any individual who has learned to erect a horoscope is equipped for the calculations required by the dynamic analysis, and detailed instructions follow in due course. No departure from their fundamental simplicity is ever necessary. Indeed, the most common cause of inaccuracy or incompetence in horoscopic interpretation is the tendency of the poorly grounded or less experienced practitioners to make astrology impossibly difficult or in effect to demand tasks of their minds that might well need an electronic computer. Actually there always are illimitable astrological factors that can be taken into account, but the fallacy contributing to logical handicap is the widespread assumption that as more and more details can be embraced in a given consideration the likelihood of sound judgment is greatly increased. Contrariwise, and especially under astrology's essential principle of selectivity or efficiency, the basis of intelligent conclusion whether through common sense or disciplined insight is not so much what can be comprised as what in much more pertinent fashion can be disregarded. It has long been noted in everyday reality that the most frequent cause of breakdown in mental balance of either momentary or continuing manifestation is almost inevitably some overweight of complication crowded in on the mind.

What is required in the dynamic analysis is not an all-too-easy fragmentation of pertinent considerations in the thinking process, as in the pattern of the faculty psychology dominating English thought at the time modern horoscopy had its principal development, but rather is an uncompromising centralization of reference from which judgment may operate both conveniently and accurately. A remarkable feature contributing to astrology's particular uniqueness under the essential principle of concordance or concomitance is that it provides testimony to anything of given issue in a quite unlimited variety of forms or measures, whether as a matter of repetitions or alternatives. This in an abstract way of looking at it is the phenomenon of universal circularity, or is the fact that there is absolutely nothing that in some fashion does not inhere in everything else through the varying common continuities of existence. Thus no materialistic or literal atomism is involved, but rather an operating division of labor in all instances of connection or relation. When attention is held to factors of core pertinence at every point of astrological delineation, the converging elements of lesser import have little chance to distract or confuse the judgment. Regression of concern to subordinate detail is needed only when some specific phase of significance or marked immediateness of crisis justifies the particular consideration in the limited context.

In order to keep analysis simple and accurate, the dynamic horoscopy operates under astrology's essential principle of incisiveness or consistency by which every indication must mean precisely what it means no matter what connection there may be with other indication. For effective reasoning it is necessary that meaning while subject to supplementation or variety in application must never have any modification in basic implication. Thus the natal technique has been clarified most fundamentally by recognizing the absolute independence in respect to each other of (1) the horoscopic houses and (2) the zodiacal signs and (3) the planets as these three distinct instrumentations of astrological measurement thereupon provide the rigorously discrete significations used for the measure of circumstances, function and activity respectively. This is the foundational approach to delineation explained in the author's *Astrology, How and Why It Works*. There can be any sort of connection between these houses, signs and planets without the combination in any fashion changing their real service to each other in the identification of the divisions of labor constituting life or reality at all points. What often is hard to understand however in this connection is that while horoscopic significators have their immutable distinctiveness yet each comes to chart specific actualities of the widest variation.

A classic example of the resolution of the age-old intellectual problem of unity in diversity is supplied by the evangelist Paul in *Romans* when he refers to the members of the human body as adding up in their varying and separate responsibility to a very simple completeness. In the frame of this encompassing unity of the individual are psychological elements of sharp differentiation in man's character, such as can be identified in a marked self-sufficiency of operation without any necessary by-your-leave on the part of any of them in respect to each other no matter what the mutual convenience might be. Indeed, any one or several of them may have particular emphasis in the given life without the slightest dependence on any factor not inhering in itself. In the unity of selfhood in the larger or social dimension it is possible to conceive of a person who is a linguist, an industrialist, a musician, a mechanic, a sportsman, a scholar, an inventor, a sociologist, an ambassador and a property holder and to realize that the fact that he is any one of them does not prove the least necessity that he be any of the others. A hand is a hand, no more and no less, but what it may do or what may involve it can range to infinity. Thus the activity-facets of a particular native in the dynamic analysis are each able to chart one special area of his effective or operative psychology very completely.

What constitutes a dynamic horoscopy fundamentally is the projection of the planets, either by purely symbolical motion or by employment of their actual movements, to establish their significant relations with the various positions of themselves and the others. The progressed aspects so created are taken in correlation with the moment of events in experience, and the procedure by which they are determined in their most familiar form is to equate a day in the celestial phenomena with a year in the native's life. Such a correspondence in a sense permits two motions of the earth to define each other with an astrological effectiveness, since the axial rotation creates the one and the ecliptical revolution the other of these important temporal units establishing man's waking and sleeping cycle and the similar seasonal rhythm of nature respectively. The astrologer's assumption is that the days following birth represent the years lived by the given individual in a corresponding succession.

The rather elaborate hypothesis here is that (1) the phenomenon of bare existence in conscious being can be identified astrologically through simple circumstances such as would be charted by the equatorial factor of the horoscope's houses created by the more intimate or self-contained motion of the earth, and (2) the manifestation of this basic existence through a personal continuity in the more complex individual experience marked by distinctive and repetitive functions can be delineated effectively through the zodiac or the more social action of the globe charted by the ecliptical factor. The shorter cycle of immediacy in its consistent if lesser rhythms would thus be taken as building into the greater ones in which an individuality becomes an expression of the encompassing cosmic potentiality in some significant specificity. The mathematics of this is inexact but as employed is purely symbolical with 360 degrees representing 365-6 days. At best however all such occult or wholly metaphysical explanation is of dubious validity, as far as presenting any literal account of reality. Astrology is curiously insusceptible of proof in any academic sense, or apart from the actuality of its practice and the pragmatic value of its performance, since in structure it is no more than a manipulation of ultimately elusive abstractions in their contribution to insights of characteristically and highly generalized nature.

The planetary interrelationships principally constituting the dynamic horoscopy are known in actual usage quite interchangeably as progressions or directions. In their most general employment as now to have an essentially analytical exposition, they are identified as the secondary directions. This unhappy designation arises from the fact that the so-called primary directions equate equatorial degrees instead of days of motion with the years of life following birth, and that in consequence they are established more quickly after a native's advent.

In summary, the dynamic horoscopy is the simplest of the astrological techniques fundamentally because its main concern is with the planets and their active interrelations and its attention to houses and signs is minimal and wholly subsidiary. Only ten basic significators are taken into account. Each of them has an absolute identity, or is considered entirely in its own self-sufficiency whether providing or receiving a progressed aspect. Thus analysis can be simple and direct in terms of the activity-facets that chart individuality in quite particular divisions of labor. The earth's motions provide the two heavenly circles that create the horoscope, and the various interactions between the cycles they establish and that in a sense define each other are the basis of progressed time measure as at the present point each day after birth taken in correlation with each year of life in corresponding sequence. The basic astrological assumption is that man's waking and sleeping cycle is anticipatory recapitulation for him at least in essence of the seasonal rhythm yet to be lived, but this is metaphysical theorizing and astrology is not susceptible to proof in any academic sense and thus has its justification in its performance in competent hands. To be avoided is the attempt to take in more detail than the mind could possibly synthesize. Restriction of consideration to clear-cut and immediate pertinences does not risk any neglect of anything of importance since astrology has a peculiar capacity to produce testimony such as confirms itself continually in a great breadth of varying perspective.

THE BASIC ATTITUDE

Mercury in the dynamic horoscopy localizes the first of ten distinct types of activity characterizing conscious individuality because it is the planet traditionally charting (1) the greatest discrete variability to be found in the human entity and (2) by the same token and in general the bottommost fluidity of potential of any immediate pertinence in astrological analysis. This smallest of the true solar satellites is only a little larger than the earth's moon and it has an eccentricity exceeded by Pluto alone, and because of its nearness to the sun it has the greatest amount of change from direct to retrograde movement and back again in the zodiac that instruments the geocentric perspective necessary in astrology. Such exceptionality from normal planetary performance, in the celestial scheme established with its pertinent earth center, provides a measure of logical support for its designation as the horoscopic significator of mind or of what might be symbolized as the quicksilver point of everyday reality. It must be remembered however that in all these explanations there is the convenient rea-

soning after the fact that may give graphic and valuable aid
to understanding, but that in any genuinely scientific perspective remains wholly speculative and in consequence has no
reliability in and of itself.

The characteristic of mind fundamentally is its ease of
change, but also and of the most practical importance is its
capacity in consequence to establish and perhaps maintain the
special sets or tendencies of act and reaction that constitute
the foundation factors of a maturing personality. It is through
this manifestation of self in tentativeness that real fulfillment
takes place, and that individual skills develop and refine themselves. For a long while an emerging modern psychology
entertained the notion of mind as a sort of wax tablet on
which the elements of character were imprinted, there to
persist for better or worse, but the concept was an over-
literalization of the proposition. In the dynamic horoscopy the
operation of this self-molding of individuality is recognized
primarily in terms of the basic attitude of a native, or his general presentation of himself to the world of experience at large.

Here is the distinctive activity-facet of growth or (1) the
general alignment of the conscious individual to his inner
realization of his own mercurial individuality and (2) his self-
establishment outwardly as a dweller in the tangible realities
in which he must of necessity function if thereby to preserve
and fulfill himself. In no other phase of his make-up is there
this almost primitive fluidity of potential ever remaining in
abeyance for him, and in consequence a first consideration in
the dynamic horoscopy must be given to progressed Mercury
in counselling a given person. It is a beginning at core in any
examination of the critical issues arising in a life, and is therefore a start in any holding of reference to pertinent sim-

plicities while seeking answers in the baffling complexity of a personal existence as a whole.

The Basic Rapport with Circumstances

As introduced in the analysis of Abraham Lincoln, the five traditional major aspects of common employment in astrology have been seen to classify into two markedly distinct groups of structural and momentum indication in the case of four of them while the fulcrum square or the fifth stands particularly apart in the special function that becomes an important feature of the dynamic analysis. The logical factors involved in the evolution of these relationships, and comprising minor variations that range to infinity, have a full exposition in the author's companion volume on *Fundamentals of Number Significance.* For the charting of the progressed indications it is possible to go further in the establishment of dichotomies in the nonfulcral aspects with representation not only of the two basic families of the active relationship but of a difference in mode of pertinency in each family pairing, and these subordinate pairings already have been presented and employed in connection with Lincoln and Annie Besant. However, the vital and more subjective distinction between alertness and adroitness was not stressed since the superficial contrast between the mere responsiveness to stimulus and more sophisticated capacity for intelligence in reaction serves all general purposes. Interpretation in greater depth can take account of the underlying difference between (1) noninvolvement or focus in pure chance or change as what in the surface view is the mere alertness and (2) involvement or corresponding focus in some phase of the established momentum of individuality in what is inhering personal responsibility but in external perspective is the mere challenge to possessed skills in

THE DYNAMIC PAIRING OF PROGRESSED ASPECTS

Immediate Direct Practical	$\big\}\big\{$	♂ Alertness in noninvolvement ✳ Adroitness in involvement	Mediated Contingent Idealistic	$\big\}\big\{$	☍ Alertness in noninvolveme △ Adroitness in involvement

a transient adroitness. The expansion of indication into greater depth can have tabulation at this point.

In the basic attitude of Annie Besant there was an exceptional dominance of the operative progressions of involvement against those of noninvolvement, and nothing was more characteristic of her career than the extent to which she was caught up and carried through a veritable labyrinth of concerns from almost humorous development in reflection of her extreme naïveté to the marked achievement stemming from her utterly selfless dedications. In the activity-facet of Abraham Lincoln contrariwise there were three operative aspects of noninvolvement against two of involvement to indicate the stark self-sufficiency in his refinement of his public image, and this was greatly reinforced by the three testimonies by Pluto to the particular freedom from conventional delimitation that characterize the ultimate myth figure. Advisement from the beginning and throughout the Besant lifetime would have been toward a proper disciplining of the urge to self-dedication that some critics of her course have identified as a martyr complex, but in the instance of the American president the analyst would have had to caution him very particularly against any surrender of his ultimately vital uniqueness of character when developments in connection with the slavery issue in Kansas brought him back into politics.

In summary, Mercury in the dynamic horoscopy charts (1) the most distinctive variability exhibited by the human entity as well as (2) the greatest fluidity of individual potential. This characteristic of the indication is accepted because it is the planet that changes direction in the zodiac most frequently, and that in general has high astronomical eccentricity in comparison with the other fundamental significators employed in progressions. It is taken to reveal the development of mind as instrumenting change in human experience and thus facilitating the establishment of the elements of act and reaction represented most primarily by the basic attitude. The aspects may again be seen, with added perspective at this point, in the special pairings that reveal the native's mode of basic rapport with circumstances and hence the possibility of advisement in the light of this.

The Psychological Trend to Balance

The first of four normal procedures of dynamic horoscopy employed in the determination or astrological prediction of tendency or potential in the basic attitude charted by progressed Mercury is to see whether there is any marked swing to either of two possible extremes in the self's public manifestation of itself in alignment with the practical immediacies of life on the one hand or with the more essentially remote potentialities of individual development on the other. The principles in determination of this have been explained in the analysis of Abraham Lincoln.

In summary, and in an expansion of application the psychological lean of the mind in each activity-facet is to be seen of particular importance because it shows whether a particular individual can be advised advantageously toward direct and immediate or long-range and more subjective self-presentation to the world at large. Thus if what may be of issue for a given native is a matter of embarking in a business or accepting social or economic responsibility of some sort, and he is inclined to the former of the extremes, it decidedly is best that he steer clear of everything not completely definite down to the last pertinent detail. Contrariwise, with the inclination for the more indefinite contingencies he certainly should sidestep anything not providing limitless elbowroom for his skills and so a genuine call to the potentials of principal interest to him.

Challenge by Progressed Station

The second of four normal procedures of dynamic horoscopy employed in the determination or astrological prediction of tendency or potential in the basic attitude charted by progressed Mercury is to see whether this planet changes direction of zodiacal motion from direct to retrograde or vice versa in any of the days after birth corresponding to years of life during the span of the astrologer's consideration. As has been seen with the analysis of Abraham Lincoln and Annie Besant, this phenomenon indicates the critical regrasp of control in experience such as is compelled from the native or needed in his affairs. Likelihood of the occurrence in this activity-facet is in perhaps a third of all possible cases. It appears more frequently in the progressions of the five planets occupying the outlying orbits of the solar system, but only in this area of the self's everyday presentation of itself in experience is there any appreciable expectation of its appearance twice.

Demanding attention at this point are two contrasting patterns in the unfoldment of human potentiality, and they may be recognized with differing importance in all activity-facets of self-expression. The simplest and most generally evident of these is the persisting struggle forward to self-realization on a single line of sequential effort in a given strand of dynamic existence, or where the consequences of act and reaction succeed each other in natural order, and this can be taken as the fundamental nature of all experience and it needs no special exposition. Against this relatively normal expectation is the alternate and at times dramatic case where an individual evolution moves to a point of critical self-extension in some channel of manifestation, and then as in a sense overrunning the basic momentum is suddenly under the necessity of regrasping the particular potential in perhaps a greater realization or at least of moving forward with fresh impetus in a more adequate dimension of self. Thus the difference in each activity-facet is between (1) a mere acceptance of the self-actualization as it happens to unfold itself and (2) a coming up to some point in life where the individual must meet radically shifting or enlarged demands on himself and thereupon is enabled at the best to proceed more successfully along the characteristic but newly adjusted line of definite self-manifestation in the particular area of conscious existence. To be noted in this connection is the vital turn in basic attitude consequent on Abraham Lincoln's taking Mary Todd as his wife and accepting William Herndon as legal partner for the rest of his years, and the epochal firming of Annie Besant in her destiny as a result of her participation in the Parliament of Religions in Chicago.

Retrogradation

Since it is the position of a planet in a symbolical scheme of relationship rather than its true movement in the ecliptic that is the primary basis of astrological significance, the latter is essentially a contributing and never an originating or modifying factor in astrology. Actually all horoscopic relations are controlled in one way or another by the earth, as must follow by necessity with the compression of the solar mechanics into a geocentric perspective. Nothing dramatizes the fact of this more strikingly than the reduction of a significator to apparent motionlessness in its celestial course, and the phenomenon might be expected to have high importance in the dynamic horoscopy. The zodiacal point at which the planetary motion reverses is identified as a station, and it is seen to represent a punctuating ascendancy of the factor of circumstances in individual affairs since the terrestrial element evident in the very structure of the houses is overriding for the moment the normal sequences charted in the signs. This is due to the pause in the concomitant general activity of which the significator itself is representative. Thus the stations in progressions, however symbolically the matter may be explained, show the possibility of a native's completely unconditioned regrasp of the control of his experience in some particular area. In a sense he stands at center in the context of his reality, and acts or reacts at core in selfhood.

When there is no progressed station in an activity-facet, the more usual course of things may be expected to prevail. When stations are found they may be identified according to the type of motion they inaugurate. It is to be noted parenthetically that the common consideration of retrograde and direct motion as of subjective and objective indication respectively is correct enough, but this can be misleading because to many people the former term means intangible rather than closely tied to the subject himself or characterized by definitely personal relationship. The distinction at times may not seem significant, but yet Mercury went direct to emphasize 1843 for Abraham Lincoln and he changed from the man largely buried in himself and his melancholy to the public figure assimilating the totality of his countrymen to himself. The planet went retrograde to emphasize 1893 for Annie Besant, and she began to orient herself more as an instrument of her own envisioning in her pioneer work of quickening India to its dramatic heritage of a most remote past and in her concomitant projection of herself into the largely intangible genius of Theosophy and its dream of a world messiah.

When certain events are found by an astrologer to be major punctuation of the life in the particular activity-facet, he can identify valuable elements of personal intensification on which to build in his counseling. Here is where the progressed stations have their supreme value. A categorical imperative for advisement is to remember that if the native fails to supply or emphasize the characteristic lines of his own continuance, the overall order at large will do so and perhaps not so happily for him. Reality to have potential must be sustained in the cosmic flux, and the phantasmagoria of events is uncompromising challenge to distinctiveness in existence as well as to continuity in experience. Actually the more a given person will himself line out and follow his individual way, the more he will be found functioning effectively in a pattern of his own with which circumstances can co-operate. This can be so because it is the characteristic of all nature for developments in form or function to hold to established grooves in their evolutional emergence. This is very evident in anatomy and physiology, and human beings from earliest times have estimated any future potentialities of their kind on a basis of past performance. There is the familiar aphorism that criminals return to the scene of their crimes, and even children early discover that the misbehavior that may be a test of their delimitations can gain appeal through its repetition. Quite different of course is the exercise of a more productive self-discipline and the pyramiding of worthy and gratifying skills of mind and body.

When progressed stations already have occurred in a particular instance, the horoscopic necessity in any counsel of the moment is toward the intelligent acceptance of whatever may have taken place in the life as (1) an asset of some sort on which to capitalize or (2) as a basis for reapplication or reinterpretation in ultimate significance. At the least a past indiscretion can always be incorporated as a further component in the human wisdom that very necessarily must be grounded in the actualities of experience whether it be good or bad. Sins of omission can be as productive of understanding as the consequences of more dynamic fault in act or judgment. Unfriendly circumstances can usually be seen as those improperly or inadequately taken into account.

When stations lie ahead in progressions there is the necessity (1) of avoiding encouragement of act or commitment such as obviously would have disadvantageous results in the light of the general likelihood of the coming radical self-reorientation or reorganization of effort but (2) of furthering every immediacy of outreach to the possible consummations ahead. In some overall fashion there is the need to consolidate gains and conserve resources for the sake of the very probable regrasp of control in experience ahead. Any guess concerning the nature of an anticipated punctuating event can be a great mistake if it should warp the native's outlook and so hinder rather than advance his ongoing. Perspective in advance at this point should lie uncompromisingly in the ultimate flux of circumstances.

In summary, the progressed stations of the planets will chart the cases where eventualities are not likely to follow along in a general and relatively normal course and so will indicate a critical regrasp of control in experience that may be compelled from the native or at least be needed in his affairs. The phenomenon of retrogradation involved at this point in analysis is of particular importance because it brings about an unusual emphasis of circumstances at a time of potential personal crisis. There is a likelihood of an overriding of the normally rather automatic basis of the native's self-expression, such as will facilitate some unusual change or shift in the pattern of his efforts. The great cosmic flux of events comes to an individual pertinence of which he can take advantage at the best and further every interest or remain unaware at the worst and so perhaps suffer setback.

Fulcrum Indication

The third of the four normal procedures of dynamic horoscopy employed in the determination or astrological prediction of tendency or potential in the basic attitude charted by progressed Mercury is to interpret the fulcrum squares or through them, as they come to their significant stress in the immediate context of each special instance, identify the vital transition points of structural development in the native's character. Here is the critical self-mobilization required by events that in crisis may have very constructive potential but also quite destructive threat at times. At this point an additional factor comes to be included in the analysis since the individuality of the planets brought into progressed aspect must be given attention in their reflex or wholly contingent significance. Such instance of activation of a natal significator remains a simple matter however because whatever event or contingency comes to be charted in this manner must be seen to possess an inherent self-reference or to be without the slightest dependence of any immediate pertinency on anything other than what inheres in itself.

There is no complicated thinking process involved in the unfolding astrological or schematism but rather a proposition of ready acceptance everywhere as a matter of no more than common sense. Thus a man eats and suffers sharp upset. This establishes a syndrome of considerations, each of which must not only be handled separately by the mind but in the terms of its own logical functioning and in the light of the conclusions sought. There is what was eaten, and what was wrong with it, and the why and how of the eating, and the stage of bodily fitness for dealing with the untoward material taken into the digestive system and so on through every possibility of pertinence. Indirectly if perhaps not immediately the relations with physician, dietitian, hostess or cook, supermarket perchance, social obligation maybe and heaven knows what else may be concerned. Most people cut the Gordian knot without fuss or worry by simple and immediate reference to whatever in their experience has convenient application, such as taking an alkalizer. In this of course is illustrated what must be characteristic of all sound thinking, or a reaching out to understanding from whatever immutable and essentially private or personal center of reference may be available in any given instance. A more studied or logically ordered realization differs in its resort to epitomization, or to a generalization of relevance to facilitate any given balancing of concomitant factors for the purpose of judgment, and this is accomplished through tools of thought such as are represented most commonly in language itself. In astrology the need can be met most effectively through the establishment of keywords.

The Rationale of Keywords

Simple cases of the epitomization in horoscopic indication have long had a familiar acceptance. Thus the numbered houses of the astrological chart have meaning quite different from the mere sequence of them in the circle, and their traditional rulerships must be learned at the start. Aries is much more than the name of a constellation. Actually the star pattern artificially described or selected to serve as a sort of ephemeris in the sky at about the time of Hipparchus in the second century B.C. no longer corresponds to the segment of the zodiac it charted originally. Mars by the same token has broad ramification of horoscope signification with which neither the physical planet in its make-up apart from its motion in its orbit nor the Roman god as a supposed factor of supernatural influence has anything in common. Horoscopy in effect is a language. The beginner by a labor of understanding must translate his houses and signs and planets and aspects into the insights he may build up with the help of the indications listed for him suggestively in the astrological textbooks, and at the beginning the process may prove quite laborious or even at times completely misleading if he merely juggles the words around in superficial patterns. The skilled practitioner by contrast has a sort of special encyclopedia of pertinencies opened up in his comprehension all in a flash when he hears or sees a reference to the first house or Aries or Mars or a conjunction and the like, simply because his attention is brought to far more than the mere word triggering his response.

The dynamic horoscopy at points where it is vital to maintain its marked distinction in type of perspective from the character analysis, makes continual use of the triggering

SUMMARY OF FULCRUM INDICATIONS

Scope of activity-facet indicated by the progressed planet	in square aspect with	Natal planet and nativity scope	Nature of activation	Typical character of dynamic crisis
☿ The basic attitude — Manipulation of experience		☉ Vitality	Strength	Upsurge of energy
☉ The natural drive — Established course of existence		☽ Vitality	Endurance	Energy under strain
♀ The basic sensitivity — Enrichment of experience		♃ Motivation	Zest	Upsurge of interest
♂ The basic excitation — Expansion of experience		♄ Motivation	Concern	Interest under strain
♃ The nascent consistency — Response to potentiality		♂ Efficiency	Persistence	Overeagerness
♄ The nascent integrity — Response to actuality		♀ Efficiency	Realization	Overintensity
♅ The nascent independence — Psychological freedom		♅ Significance	Release	Rebellion of spirit
♆ The nascent responsibility — Psychological dependence		♆ Significance	Acceptance	Realignment of spirit
♇ The nascent enlightenment — Manipulation of potentiality		☿ Efficiency	Aplomb	Overcompensation
☽ The natural involvement — Established course of experience		♇ Significance	Probity	Overjustification

designations represented by the important activity-facet or a specific ordering of highly discrete channels of self-manifestation such as the basic attitude. Special keywords for the natal planets in their reception of a quickening in dynamic aspect were introduced in connection with the activations by Mercury in the delineation of the Lincoln nativity. In the cases of Abraham Lincoln and Annie Besant the total for both of them of these fulcrum aspects by progressed Mercury is nine, and five of that number show Neptune quickened if the one culminating seven years before the discovery of that planet is included. Of the ten significators charting progression, this particular one has been found to be of primary import in both lives when viewed in an overall or ultimate perspective, and in consequence it is particularly suitable for illustrating the effectiveness of astrology's verbal symbols or tools of thought.

The keyword for Neptune is acceptance. This does not so much imply a conscious or recognizable act or reaction as it identifies a generally irreversible move or drift for better or worse into the essence of something of vital consequence. The subtle ramifications are limitless, and would indeed have been beyond normal grasp prior to the middle of the nineteenth century. Any initial understanding of the term demands an approach to its implication through the specific instance or by observing the tenor of event such as at this point in the dynamic analysis would involve a critical self-mobilization in the face of developing actualities in circumstances. Both the two fulcrum progressions in Lincoln's basic attitude were a quickening of Neptune. In 1839 he saw the Illinois state capital moved to Springfield, largely as a result of the individual effort on his part, and in 1847 his election to Congress took him to Washington where his attempt to demonstrate that the Mexican War was pure aggression led to his elimination from the prevailing low-level politics of his day. He himself did not see the significance of the events that brought him into the orbit of the Todd family in the first instance, when the planet was inoperative, but in the second he well understood the necessity for a complete new grasp of any destiny he might encompass in political rather than legal circles. The three Neptunian quickenings in the basic attitude of Annie Besant were out of a total of seven fulcrum aspects of significance in connection with her public image, and it already has been seen that they were of deeper significance than the three involving Saturn and the very early one involving Jupiter. In 1875 she attained remarkably quick stature through her pen and on the platform among the Secularists, in 1907 she succeeded Colonel Olcott as president of the Theosophical Society of which he was a founder and in 1918 she became president of the Indian National Congress. These were her key points of eminence or general acclaim.

In summary, with fulcrum indication in the secondary directions a critical self-mobilization is required by events and the nature of its probable manifestation is indicated by the particular natal planet activated in the activity-facet. Each specialized phase of self-being as stabilized at birth has a distinct expression of its own with every capacity for acting in unimpeded accordance with its own genius, and the keywords for the planets in receiving the progressed quickening help the astrologer identify the particular specificity of self-assertion on which the life for the moment is pivoting. What is important is not any charting of the fact of the eventualities of the moment but rather the recognition of the overall significance in the given immediacy of things. Thus Lincoln could somehow have been shown in any counseling (1) that Springfield was a place of fulfillment for him and that the Todd-related individuals from John Stuart to the Edwards and plump little spitfire Mary as well as Stephen Douglas of the fun-loving Coterie were the principals with whom he should be associating and (2) that Washington and conventional political advancement were not for him at any price in the light of his real potentiality. In corresponding if not similar fashion it might have been brought home to Annie Besant that it was (1) the idealized cause of which Charles Bradlaugh was a minor myth figure and not the Edward Avelings or Bernard Shaws and (2) the arcane tradition for which Madame Blavatsky played myth mother with strange and erratic fidelity and not the William Judges and or Katherine Tingleys or Charles Leadbeaters and Jeddu Krishnamurtis and (3) the revivifying of the most important Indo-Aryan racial heritage long bound in the strait jacket of passive resistance to the waves of conquest and not herself or a Mahatma Gandhi that were the measure of her enduring contribution in the terms of her public image.

Nonfulcral Indication

The fourth of the four normal procedures of dynamic horoscopy employed in the determination or astrological prediction of tendency or potential in the basic attitude charted by progressed Mercury is to interpret the nonfulcral aspects that up to this point in each activity-facet are usually considered only as they reveal the psychological trend to balance, and thus to identify the points of stimulus in the progressive distribution of the natal potentials in the frame of the more particular immediacies of conscious existence. The difference

SUMMARY OF NONFULCRAL INDICATIONS

Activity facet of progression	in ☌, ☍, ⚹ or △ with	Natal planet in activation	The fillip by progression	The circumstances of stimulation by aspect		
☿ The basic attitude		☉ Strength	Vitalization	Uninvolved alertness	☌ direct	☍ contingent
				Involved adroitness	⚹ direct	△ contingent
☉ The natural drive		☽ Endurance	Recuperation	Uninvolved alertness	☌ direct	☍ contingent
				Involved adroitness	⚹ direct	△ contingent
♀ The basic sensitivity		♃ Zest	Morale	Uninvolved alertness	☌ direct	☍ contingent
				Involved adroitness	⚹ direct	△ contingent
♂ The basic excitation		♄ Concern	Tact	Uninvolved alertness	☌ direct	☍ contingent
				Involved adroitness.	⚹ direct	△ contingent
♃ The nascent consistency		♂ Persistence	Initiative	Uninvolved alertness	☌ direct	☍ contingent
				Involved adroitness	⚹ direct	△ contingent
♄ The nascent integrity		♀ Realization	Enjoyment	Uninvolved alertness	☌ direct	☍ contingent
				Involved adroitness	⚹ direct	△ contingent
♅ The nascent independence		♅ Release	Advocacy	Uninvolved alertness	☌ direct	☍ contingent
				Involved adroitness	⚹ direct	△ contingent
♆ The nascent responsibility		♆ Acceptance	Conviction	Uninvolved alertness	☌ direct	☍ contingent
				Involved adroitness	⚹ direct	△ contingent
♇ The nascent enlightenment		☿ Aplomb	Adjustment	Uninvolved alertness	☌ direct	☍ contingent
				Involved adroitness	⚹ direct	△ contingent
☽ The natural involvement		♇ Probity	Perspective	Uninvolved alertness	☌ direct	☍ contingent
				Involved adroitness	⚹ direct	△ contingent

from what are characterized as crises in life is what has the greater appearance of the normal course of things, and this on the average has three times as frequent a quickening as in the fulcrum case or when a progressed station occurs. In consequence these dynamic aspects become a particular charting of the actualities in any fulfillment of the general natal potential. The events here shown at focus in experience are a very practical index of personal accomplishment.

Hence the success of Abraham Lincoln in gaining his first responsible position as a deputy county surveyor when his basic attitude had a practical alerting to an aplomb in his public image is significant testimony to a capacity and determination to express himself at the height of his promise at any given time. The directness and competence of his effort to get the appointment, and the extraordinary energy expended in preparing himself for handling it, are the certification by the event under the astrological correlation to the inherent quality of the selfhood seeking to fulfill itself. This and this only is the role of events in horoscopy. Progressions do not precipitate anything. Rather they provide dramatic illumination for the current act or reaction of a native in a convenient and sharply defined channel of his own special reality. Counseling that is a matter of proper adjustment to crisis to be expected, or of adequate capitalization on critical shifts already experienced in correspondence with fulcrum indication and progressed stations, is now a more tangible checking upon everyday potentials in the light of nonfulcral signification as perhaps supplemented by such subsidiary techniques as commonly the solar returns and horary astrology. Annie Besant could have been well advised in 1868 to throw the whole focus of her interest into her first and amateurish literary effort that actually was prelude to the whole course of her desperate self-buttressing at this point through the surrogate zest to which she was turning in escape from the boorish tyranny in her home life.

A first effective step toward solution of a crime is often known as breaking the case, and akin to this in a sense is the necessity for the astrologer to break the horoscope and so have a competent and whole view before venturing the interpretation that can bode for much good but also much harm in a given life. The author's *Guide to Horoscope Interpretation* dramatizes one particular method for accomplishing this breakthrough with the natal chart, and the special approach to the analysis of Abraham Lincoln in the present text is dramatization of the possibility of a similar accomplishment in the dynamic horoscopy through an exceptional but primary attention to the nonfulcral aspects. In his case the curious Chinese-boxes arrangement of the indications in the basic attitude offered significant clue to the life developing in a straight line out of unusually primitive immediacies to an end culmination in the symbolical apotheosis. Annie Besant is better approached in the usual pattern of dynamic analysis, but with her it is instructive to note that the three stages of her rise to eminence that have just been summarized in connection with the fulcrum indications have corresponding testimony through the unusual three pairs of sextiles in progression in this same activity-facet to the essentially psychological developments with (1) the 1885-9 Aveling trauma building to her meeting with Madame Blavatsky and (2) the 1896-9 windup of her British orientation with the closing of Blavatsky Lodge and the move to India and (3) the 1927-30 surrender of Krishna-murti to his own leading as in a sense her life came to the transcendental climax suggested by the discovery of Pluto.

In summary, the nonfulcral secondary directions beyond their incidental usefulness in delimiting any psychological trend to balance are the ones that chart the everyday manifestation of a native's potential most frequently and essentially. In consequence they are most useful as (1) a current index of his effort to achieve his promise and (2) a basis of advisement on very specific levels of opportunity at hand as well as of the act or reaction of greatest possible effectiveness. Intelligent initial approach to the horoscope may often be greatly facilitated by the perspective afforded through these immediacies of emphasis.

THE NATURAL DRIVE

The sun in the dynamic horoscopy localizes the second of ten distinct types of activity characterizing conscious individuality because it is the planetary body traditionally charting the greatest invariant element of simple human existence. Here is an indication in polar contrast with Mercury's, and the consideration is transferred from (1) a never-ceasing and creative self-assertiveness to (2) the more subjective but core manifestation of pure selfhood in the everyday time-and-space reality. What has analysis at this point is the personal identity as it persists in its own changeless essence during the rather baffling elusiveness of the basic attitude. If Mercury has charted the protean public image of the social creature capable either of growth and achievement or frustration and defeat in association with its kind, this significator reveals the inherent and uncompromising dignity of self-consciousness at root. An absolute integrity appears as the ultimate basis of any genuine experience of an individual nature. Thus the will to live has long been recognized as the final recourse of man and indeed of all living species. Whereas there may be the abnormal embrace of suicide, the most lowly of creatures when trapped or at a threshold of nothingness can turn suddenly and for the moment at least become the peer of a knight in armor.

The sun is considered a planet in the astrological language because in the geocentric perspective it assumes the zodiacal motion of the earth, and in consequence it also provides the measure or indication of all possible reference at center for man on his terrestrial globe precisely as in the actuality of the solar system it continues to center the whole complex of celestial energy. This transfer of character in the two heavenly bodies is no misapprehension of the regular balancing of gravitational forces, such as in terms of tangible cause and effect are treated in proper fashion by astronomy, but rather is the quite legitimate employment by astrology of the heliocentric energy factors in a geocentric patterning in order to establish the convenient correspondence between (1) the completely predictable or wholly physical phenomena in the skies and (2) what in human or wholly psychological constitution are rather the characteristically nonspecific predictabilities of consciousness or the personalized constants of pure contingency. Here is selfhood of necessity holding the reins in the special or private world it creates for itself, and this fundamentally inescapable self-administration is represented in the natural drive as the uncompromisingly distinctive continuance of individuality in its self-act.

In summary, the sun in the dynamic horoscopy charts (1) the immediate effectiveness of a native's fundamental stability of character or persisting self-anchorage at the core of his own individuality and (2) the consequent if potential persuasiveness of his personality or weight of his underlying morale in the current circumstances into which perforce he maintains himself. In this activity-facet a positive advisement for individuality in action must add up in general to encouraging the native to be true to himself above all else, and thereupon and in the face of all specific issues to preserve the fundamental and straight lines of his going in whatever manifestation of steadiness may prove to contribute to this.

The Psychological Trend to Balance

First of the four normal procedures of dynamic horoscopy employed in the determination or astrological prediction of tendency or potential in the natural drive charted by the progressed sun is to see whether there is any marked swing by the native to either of two possible extremes of deployment of his nascent store of energy in the course of his simple forging ahead in his accustomed fashion. Here the factor of psychological lean differs from the more mercurial shifts in the dependence of conscious expression on commonplace external factors as characteristic of the establishment and maintenance of a public image, since an inflexible although largely subconscious self-sufficiency of act and reaction is involved. If there is no testimony to particular psychological trend the indication is of a relatively relaxed manifestation of the native's everyday course in familiar grooves of his ongoing. This was the horoscopic situation with Abraham Lincoln in overall perspective in connection with his actual living years, although the earlier practical and later more generally idealistic subperiods have been noted. The dynamic impetus in the case of Annie Besant had an initial and uncompromising anchorage in her immediacies or in a strengthening of her marked naïveté as again a subperiod of importance, but then circumstances challenged her to assert herself in wider and more ultimate perspectives as she reversed her lean and rose to her true stature in taking her own stance on her own feet and forcing the Secularists to defend the book on birth control.

In summary, an effective first step in analysis of the natural drive is to determine if there is a psychological lean in the fundamental energies of the native either to an unusually literalistic and matter-of-fact development of selfhood or to a tentativeness of outreach to potentials in an essentially imaginative realization of self in the basic flow of experience. Horoscopic advisement should encourage any emphasis of either tendency, as helping to strengthen the manifestation of selfhood at the core of itself. With no trend toward the one or the other orientation in natural drive there is the more simple case of a potentially consistent self-realization through accustomed grooves, and astrological counseling should be directed to furthering the consistency of self-act at core.

Challenge by Progressed Station

Second of the four normal procedures of dynamic horoscopy employed in the determination of astrological prediction of tendency or potential is never possible in the natural drive since in the case of the lights no retrogradation can occur. The sun in astrology is wholly surrogate for the earth, since its geocentric movement in the orbit of the terrestrial globe endows it with the signification of a potentially crisis-free control of experience in the necessarily simple or basic ongoing of the conscious selfhood. There may be a lack of effective direction, but there can be no problem of the fundamental capacity to act in any fashion whatsoever.

In summary, there is in the natural drive an innate morale that always will be evident in courage or decency if not in blind or insensate self-assertiveness. The astrologer should be able to distinguish between the various manifestation of this uninhibited self-act, and thus be in a position to make constructive suggestion relative to the effectiveness of the native's primary act or reaction.

Fulcrum Indication

Third of the four normal procedures of dynamic horoscopy employed in the determination or astrological prediction of tendency or potential in the natural drive charted by the progressed sun is to give a particular and specialized attention to the squares or the fulcrum relationship that reveals either the advisability or necessity of maintaining morale and exercising a fundamental stability under circumstances of challenge through relatively untoward elements coming to crisis or sharp realization in personal affairs. General dissociation or breakup in a current situation may occur or be imminent or appear likely, and advisement must (1) demand some sort of capitalization on the actual experience of the moment or (2) must suggest some sort of strengthening of self-confidence if consideration is in advance of the culmination of the fulcrum aspect.

Self-analysis by astrology has its obvious dangers, since with any pyramiding of self-concern there is increasing defeat of perspective through the normal trial and error of the logical process. Against this however is the obvious fact that the best of all ways to learn astrology is for the neophyte to become familiar with his own nativity and those of his intimates. The author in full awareness of the possibilities of warped judgment, but yet as a matter of common sense in taking account at least in overall fashion of his own indications, can offer a clean-cut example at this point in the exposition. The two fulcrum aspects of his progressed sun matured in the mid-Twenties within eight months of each other in a quickening of his natal moon and Saturn. Some time before this his military service had uprooted him from a rather haphazard self-unfoldment characterized by some appreciable success, but it was not until this crucial period that his efforts gained an overall purpose in a larger dimension of the natural drive. The significant and concurrent events were (1) the publication of

Key Truths of Occult Philosophy, (2) the cabalistic break-through with the Ibn Gabirol magic squares, (3) the start toward a complete Bible commentary in the frame of the arcane tradition, (4) the inauguration of a Solar discipline under the Sabian name and (5) an enduring marriage.

In summary, an effective third step of analysis of the activity-facet is to consider the indication of any critical self-mobilization required by events through the progressed squares and to determine what likelihood there may be of qualities of self-potential subject to possible activation in challenging fashion for the ongoing of the individual at core. Any tendency toward ego dissociation should be countered in advisement by suggestion for strengthening the general course of the life, and every possible self-dignification should be encouraged.

Nonfulcral Indication

Fourth of the four normal procedures of dynamic horoscopy employed in the determination or astrological prediction of tendency or potential in the natural drive charted by the progressed sun is to give a special and particular attention to the nonfulcral aspects in the secondary directions. These have their vital part in a revelation of the usual course of things in everyday personal experience, and it is convenient to continue illustration from the author's own progressions. The total activations of both his natal moon and Saturn exceed those of any other planet and show (1) in the completely practical four-odd decades prior to the fulcral self-mobilizations, an initial emphasis that had principal instrumentation through an early and closely knit threesome of boyish playmates of which he was the center one in age and thanks to which he developed a great spread of concern and endurance as background for his later career. Then in the subsequent four-odd decades with important idealistic ferment in the Forties but without diminution of the exceptionally dominant practicality of purpose the same two planets chart (2) the full sweep of the publishing project with the issue of the *Sabian Manual* and the definite stage in preparing the *Essentials of Astrological Analysis*.

In summary, an effective fourth step of analysis of the natural drive in the dynamic horoscopy is to determine what indication may be provided by the nonfulcral aspects for a proper understanding or directing of the course of experience in the everyday affairs of the native. The activation of concern and endurance in the author's case not only marks out the exceptionally definitive change in the whole pattern of his life but identifies an earlier and a subsequent shaping of the course of events such as always can be helped very effectively through competent horoscopic advisement.

DYNAMIC ANALYSIS III

THE BASIC SENSITIVITY

Venus in the dynamic horoscopy localizes the third of ten distinct types of activity characterizing conscious individuality because it is the planetary body traditionally charting the inward immediacy or personal culmination of man's act and reaction. Establishing its role is the fact that it shares some of the special limitation of movement and resulting irregularity of zodiacal conduct characteristic of Mercury in progression, and that its next position of orbit on the inner or inferior side of the earth in the astronomical arrangement of the solar system conveniently symbolizes the common human tendency to pre-empt various elements in experience as of necessity. While this is explanation of the sheer ruthlessness or insensate selfishness it can signify at times, the normal indication is no more than the instinctive effort of a social animal to (1) draw whatever may seem to be the substance of a need toward the center in selfhood that is represented by the sun circling the ecliptic as surrogate for the earth and (2) hold in definite personal intimacy whatever factors of existence it finds it must keep in this association or in subservience to itself in one form or another in order to maintain its conscious continuance. Here is the familiar urge toward both survival in time and fulfillment in space particularly dramatized in the exaltation and worship of love or simple privileged relations on the one hand and of money or power and a sense of security in pyramiding individual advantage on the other.

333

The Cultural Matrix

The turn in consideration is to the inescapably complex socioeconomic identity of the native as revealed in sharp contrast with his essentially simple manifestation of himself through his basic attitude and his natural drive. There is nobody who in this connection does not realize the vast difference between a savage and a savant, and yet there is no more indication in the horoscope as to which an individual might be than there is any clue to whether he is male or female or much of anything of total specificity. Advisement must differ very radically for the aborigine and the modern sophisticate, even if they have practically identical nativities. The factor coming to pertinence at this point is the cultural matrix, or what universally constitutes and sustains the added dimensions of individual existence that differentiate man from all other animals whether to greater or lesser extent. Particularly characterizing him is the fact that both objective things and distinctive entities come to have a continuing significance of their own in his awareness of them, in contrast with their merely momentary importance or necessarily taken-for-granted place in his more fundamentally close to solipsistic and consequently uninhibited realization. There is of course much attribution to living entities of every sort from domesticated pets even on to deity of the strictly human qualities now to have attention, as they emerge in increasingly transcendental phases of nature at large, but this is relatively harmless and supernumerary manifestation of the anthropomorphizing proclivity of mind on which any self-awareness depends. Conscious identity thus maintains its inevitable reflection of itself or co-operation with itself in everything other than itself with which it is involved in expressing itself.

Social existence is the continual sharing by man and his particular world of the factors of fundamental interchange that instrument individuality in distinctions of public or general as against merely private or essentially dissociate realizations. The more complex but not necessarily complicated elements of cultural self-establishment are fundamentally (1) possession on the one hand and (2) proclivities or adaptations on the other. What any one person may have or be facile in doing, anybody else conceivably could possess or be able to do in virtually the same fashion, and out of exchanges and co-operations leading to a division of labor in common cause comes the very possibility of a society. Theoretically it is inconsequential which one of the many may possess what the others might gain or covet individually, or by the same token who develops a given capacity for performance irrespective of the particular importance it might have for the whole. The social insects dramatize the potentials of a cultural matrix as in a sense frozen in a subindividualistic evolution, since as an example any appreciable discreteness among the drones of the honeybees is apparently nonexistent although the single queen when needed apparently can be manufactured in a rather literal sense from an egg that normally would produce one of the indistinguishable workers of the hive. With man however a continuing process of high individualization, both for the species and for every single person as well, is virtually a *sine qua non* of any truly human existence. An illimitable variation in the divisions of labor between self and an illimitable variety of other selves must be taken into particular account in the dynamic horoscopy.

In summary, Venus in the dynamic horoscopy charts the distinctive efforts of man as the genuinely social animal (1) to draw whatever may seem to be the practical substance of his needs toward a centering in selfhood and (2) to maintain the intimacy with the elements of existence he must hold at least in symbolical subservience to himself as a fundamental condition of his enlarged dimension of self-awareness. Thus the consideration turns away from the relatively solipsistic problems of basic attitude and natural drive to the social matrix or private world into which the native inextricably is framed. He now must have analysis in connection with his possessions or resources whether these are potential or are in definite manifestation, and as they come variously to issue or crisis in his continual actualization or justification of himself in an everyday reality shared with his fellows in a conscious division of labor. Advisement in the perspective of this activity-facet must deal primarily with the relations established or possible of establishment with particular things and specific people, and it always should seek to further a profitable or self-fulfilling participation in whatever adds up to developing and sharing immediately and personally challenging elements of reality brought to common significance or found conveniently at hand through the cultural matrix.

The Psychological Trend to Balance

First of the four normal procedures of dynamic horoscopy employed in the determination or astrological prediction of tendency or potential in the basic sensitivity charted by progressed Venus is to see whether there is any marked swing to either of two possible extremes of overemphasis of the cultural matrix in which the native sharpens his particular individuality among his fellows by (1) pursuing or assuming or crowding the promise of everyday human interrelationship in exceptional idealization or metaphysical exaltation and theoretical detachment or by (2) developing a feckless devotion or what may be an exaggerated practicality in emphasis of the intimacies or special privileges and heightened indulgences of life. The contrast is between what at the best can be poetic insight on the one hand and political sagacity or business genius on the other, and at the worst between possibly unwitting viciousness or fanaticism as against the myriad of seductive and self-degrading dissipations.

An excellent example of extreme psychological orientation in this activity-facet is provided by Walt Disney, the creative genius of the animated cartoon of motion pictures and his ultimate more general accomplishments. Progressed Venus makes a total of six nonfulcral aspects of which four are trines and two sextiles, and the fact that one trine has delayed significance does not upset the testimony. The idealistic sensitivity of his early years is shown when in World War I he drove an ambulance in France. He was just eighteen when, with signification taking momentary practical dominance under the indication of the second and final sextile, he became a cartoonist for a motion-picture publication in Kansas City. This opened the way for his happily pragmatic experimentation in the world of films. The overall idealistic slanting was again established after he made his place for himself in feature-length production.

Sensitivity as a common English word has gained an added and highly sophisticated meaning such as for lack of any other available term must have here a precise and technical employment, and in consequence cannot be used otherwise in this text. Unfortunately it is in general use as the equivalent of sensitiveness, and there is the possibility of considerable confusion against which to guard since the latter is the basic keyword for the planet Saturn in the author's clarification of natal astrology. The nearest to an alternative for sensitivity is sensibility, but sensibility in equally unhappy case however preferred by some authorities for conveying the meaning desired in the dynamic horoscopy is yet not as suitable because it carries the stronger nuance of mere response to stimulus and would not escape confusion with the general sensitiveness. Astrology is virtually a language on its own account, as must be kept in mind at all times, and analysis is not helped by trying to compromise with the meaning of the terms employed in its specialized usage. In the simplest of explanation the basic sensitivity of the native is no more than the common manifestation of his purely personal relationship with his particular cultural matrix, or what usually can be identified even if somewhat unprecisely when he is said to be cultured. This fundamental refinement of character may range from an aborigine fidelity to tribal taboos on to every delicacy of rapport with civilized niceties. Here is self-fulfillment as definitely individual plussage or as an added dimension of being properly indicated astrologically through this activity-facet.

Advisement on the basis of the secondary directions at this point, beginning with progressed Venus, requires equal attention to (1) the potentialities of the nativity as the changeless pattern of the life and so constituting the underlying immutability on which to build competent judgment, and (2) the actuality of the cultural matrix in which the native has developed his everyday character or established his place among his fellows and through which in consequence and of necessity he must express himself in a continuing revelation of his creative livingness. Thus it is vitally important to note his actual realizations and accomplishments prior to the time of

consideration of his case. Walt Disney could have been told
very early that his self-fulfillment as the artist would have to be
grounded in the humanistic emphasis marked in his World
War I participation, and given expression in the realm of
motion pictures where he gained a first opening as cartoonist.
The spectacular expansion of his gifts could be found later or
when he grasped the opportunity to produce the films of
multiple-reel length and scope.

In summary, an effective first step in analysis of the basic
sensitivity is to determine if there is any extreme lean in
psychological orientation as an overemphasis of the cultural
matrix in poetic or idealistic insight if not its perversion in
bigoted egomania or fanaticism on the one hand or in political
sagacity or practical genius if not its dissociative counterpart
in dissipation on the other. Astrology is essentially a language
that cannot compromise the meaning of its terms by seeking
to fit them too literally to vernacular usage. Thus sensitivity
is used to identify an individual's wholly personal relationship with the special world of his own experience, and this is
a factor inescapably present in the totality of himself as a
living creature. Proper advisement involves a recognition of
actualities of realization and accomplishment out of which the
native refines his character in the larger dimension of his
ongoing as the social entity, and of which there is initial
horoscopic indication in his basic sensitivity, all to the end
that he may be helped to achieve the plussage of the truly
human creature.

Challenge by Progressed Station

Second of the four normal procedures of dynamic horoscopy
employed in the determination or astrological prediction of
tendency or potential in the basic sensitivity charted by pro-

gressed Venus is to give a particular or special attention to any station established by this planet and thereupon to identify a critical regrasp of experience needed or achieved in this activity-facet. The chances are a third less than in the case of the superior planets lying out from Mars in the solar system, and not much more than a quarter of the frequency of expectation with Mercury, and therefore the occurrence can be more significant. The challenge to self-plussage can reveal the native's accentuated capacity for self-refinement in his cultural matrix, and concomitantly a possibly exceptional co-operation from his circumstances in the details of life coming sharply to issue. Personal resources may have rather vital manifestation or there may be marked intensification of individual skills. Some dramatic enhancement of life's promise is likely, if only on a quite minor plateau of being.

When there is no signification of this sort the native generally proceeds in relatively unbroken course in his cultural self-refinement, and advisement here would be toward care in (1) avoiding the precipitation of crisis of any unusual sort in the larger compass of social relations but rather holding to the values that have proved themselves and (2) refraining from the initiation of needless change in the private patterns of self-enhancement or self-enjoyment. In the career of Walt Disney a station of Venus in progression culminated in 1953 and had correspondence with the probable planning and building of Disneyland. That now famous playtime attraction opened to the public two years later, and the enterprise is excellent example of an expansion of basic sensitivity in dramatic diversification or as a product of aesthetic outreach in an utterly fresh and hence continuing true self-fulfillment.

In summary, an effective second step in analysis of the basic sensitivity is to determine if any special punctuation in the refining of the self in its cultural matrix is charted by a progressed station of Venus at some special point in the native's life. When anything of the sort is lacking, as is quite often the case, he can be advised to develop as great a consistency as possible in his relations of the more subtle or aesthetic sort with his general environment while at the same time developing his personal plussage by holding to the essential pattern of his self-gratifications. When a station occurs the advisement contrariwise should attempt to recognize and exploit every significant expansion or extension of sensitivity in the given case in both any general and particular move to the possible heightened refreshment of act or reaction in the larger dimension.

Fulcrum Indication

Third of the four normal procedures of dynamic horoscopy employed in the determination or astrological prediction of tendency or potential in the basic sensitivity charted by progressed Venus is to give a particular and specialized attention to the squares or fulcrum relationship that reveals either the advisability or necessity of a critical self-mobilization in response to some developing stimulation through the cultural matrix or what would be a definite quickening of self-potential in continuing expansion of rapport with the immediate environment. During the lifetime of Walt Disney the one fulcrum progression of Venus matured in September, 1934. This approximates the start in the four years reported as embracing the production of his *Snow White and the Seven Dwarfs*. The film had public release in 1938 and was significant as the first feature-length animated cartoon in motion pictures. In a sense this can be accepted as a crest of his career, when it comes to the achievements in animation for the screen. The activated natal planet was Mercury, and since the quickening was of his aplomb it was necessary for him to deal with the cultural matrix in total self-assurance or in virtually a dictatorial conformity to his own artistic insight or judgment. Advisement might well have been that for what turned out to be a final thirty-two years or almost precise second half of his life, and for his own complete self-fulfillment, he properly should refuse to cede any authority whatsoever in his own creative world of reality to anything or anybody at all centered exterior to himself.

In summary, an effective third step of analysis of the basic sensitivity is to determine what indication of necessary critical self-mobilization is provided by the progressed or fulcrum squares. In this activity-facet the testimony is to possible special exactions developed in the cultural matrix or private world of the native, such as would demand a manifestation of personal potentials with likelihood of significant contribution to the pertinent scheme of things whether in large compass or in some relatively intimate context. Advisement at this point has double reference as (1) encouraging what may increase individual stature in its move to ultimate best self-fulfillment and (2) suggesting what reciprocally would mean some measure of contribution to the enduring benefit of the general milieu of concern.

Nonfulcral Indication

Fourth of the four normal procedures of dynamic horoscopy employed in the determination or astrological prediction of tendency or potential in the basic sensitivity charted by progressed Venus is to give a special and particular attention to the nonfulcral aspects in the secondary directions. These have their vital part in a revelation of the probable general course of things in everyday personal experience, and again it is convenient to turn to Walt Disney's case at this point to note the value at times of the seldom employed basic rapport with circumstances explained in connection with the basic attitude in the general exposition of the dynamic analysis. All six nonfulcral progressions in this native's life are of the involvement focus in some phase of the established momentum of individuality, and his spectacular achievement can be found to be an unswerving adaptation and expansion of the potentials lying at his hand in the milieu into which he gravitated and in which he grew into his own real stature. Thus Disneyland in a sense can be seen to be no more than a motion picture production in carnival rather than theater lineaments.

In summary, an effective fourth step of analysis of the basic sensitivity in the dynamic horoscopy is to determine what indication may be provided by the nonfulcral progressions for a proper understanding of the course of experience in the everyday affairs of the native. His opportunistic if leisurely development of his individual potentials in the special cultural matrix that had offered a haven for his talents is convenient illustration of the basic rapport with circumstances that complements the psychological trend to balance.

THE BASIC EXCITATION

Mars in the dynamic horoscopy localizes the fourth of ten distinct types of activity characterizing conscious individuality because it is the planetary body traditionally charting the outward immediacy or personal initiation of man's act and reaction. Establishing its role is the fact (1) that it is close enough to the sun in its astronomical placement to be held to the irregularity of zodiacal movement it shares with Mercury and Venus to perhaps a less obvious extent but with a possible greater individual difference in its case, and (2) that its next position of orbit on the outer or superior side of the earth in the actual arrangement of the solar system conveniently symbolizes the common tendency of humanity to explore and manipulate the elements of its existence as of necessity in a dispassionate complementation of its concomitant clasping and retention of the substance of its experience in its selfhood under the signification of Venus. These concurrent phases of the primitive organic and social self-realization are particularly evident in the infant who must kick out or throw off or reject no less than appropriate or assimilate or adapt, but the twin processes while serving each other in passing are in no way related in any fixity of cause and effect. They are respectively the objective and subjective activity-facets of self-actuality in the cultural matrix. Thus violence in the indication of Mars has polar rapport with the ruthlessness that can be shown by Venus, and these extreme manifestations are superficially quite indistinguishable. Here are ardor and hunger as the most simple forms of life in its purely psychological foundation, and events can now have analysis as they are experienced in the personal halo provided by the essential quality of human existence.

Excitation to act or reaction of itself however is irrevocably neutral. The more an individual's simple eagerness is free or unencumbered in the cultural matrix, as is the case no less with nascent acquisitiveness, the more it is the indistinguishable characteristic of everybody. When humanity is viewed from the perspective of its foundational alikeness in quality of existence represented most commonly by basic hunger and ardor, the sating of the former is no more than amelioration in the general lot in life on any or every level but at the best this will lead to aesthetic enrichment or some admirable development of social self-presence while the latter as of necessity and for the major part is an uncompromising struggle against any averaging out to relative nondistinction in the scheme of things and will be marked on the better side in an achievement of excellence or of some genuine quality of refinement in skills. With the progressions of Mars and the five other superior planets there is greatly diminished indication because of successive slower average motion in the zodiac, but there is heightened signification with the rarity of secondary direction and in consequence the natural and inescapable if at times repressed fervency of the native may have unusually important measure in the dynamic horoscopy at this point.

What perhaps is the most difficult realization in its astrological importance is the absolute equality of all people in their capacity for the social act and reaction that as end result is so largely responsible for distinguishing them from each other. The potentials of primary initiative are identical for everybody because of (1) the common possession of the mammalian organism the human spirit in the course of evolution can be assumed to have specialized for its own use and (2) the no less common functioning of everything at hand in the single great closed system of energy that has come to be established in the solar system. This universal but completely dynamic unity of all men at core creates the necessity for an uncompromising respect for personality as the *sine qua non* of any intelligent psychological or ethical interpretation of a horoscope. No matter how much distortion or abuse the physical body or the psychological and spiritual endowment of a given self-existence may suffer, the individual continuity of a native continues as what it is in its own evolving genius of distinctiveness and the astrologer most properly must reach his conclusions in the frame of the characteristics provided by the native's particular balance between the potentials of the organic differentiation and the necessary conformities to the cosmic order. Any basic excitation is actually no more than effort to maintain the balance, and ardor in life is a sense of excellence in performing the task. And here of course is the ground for all psychological understanding.

It must be remembered that circumstances of necessity work out so that when a person falters in self-realization, nature thereupon can take over in averaging him to the most convenient concordance. This is a process that to the unthinking might seem to be an intervention of destiny, but actually it is merely a sort of simple gravity or the tendency of all existence to come to balance. Thus when life itself ceases the organic aggregate employed for the physical continuance of the conscious entity is promptly embraced by natural forces, in order that decay may release the materials for fresh utilization in other forms of the common reality. It is in this cosmic economy that when the average individual builds up his particular matrix, and retains sufficient interest in it to maintain it, he is likely to be swept on to quite satisfactory fruitions. In his case any advisement should therefore bring reassurance in the course of his ardor, together with help in deciding on relatively convenient moves or acceptances. When a native in the exceptional instance seeks to cut sharply across the lines of some existing sweep of time and space, he can expect any reasonable possibility of success only as long as the upsurging energies needed for the ends in view have their continued application. If the unique self-projection loses momentum, events then in startling fashion will tend to snap back into the pertinent trends in the way a stretched rubber band will contract the instant it is let go. And of course as diversity becomes greater drama it very possibly may have rather spectacular horoscopic indication. At the opposite extreme an absence of signification by progressed Mars may reveal a basic dominance over personal excitation by the general drift.

In summary, Mars in the dynamic horoscopy charts the characteristic individualization by which the native's inherent ardor may direct itself to the exceptional career or to the more conventional self-fulfillment. As a creature capable of self-act he exists in a balance between the two primitive factors in which he and his fellows share an absolute alikeness at core or (1) the mammalian organism used by the human spirit and (2) the cosmic order in which all existence is embraced. The possibilities of his choices depend on his particular maintenance of relations with the general organic and material reality. In this activity-facet the indications begin to lessen sharply with slower zodiacal movement, but the horoscopic testimony to unusual self-potential starts to increase by inverse proportion. The relative dominance of a native over the elements of his cultural matrix, or his essential subservience to them, is revealed at this point by the grim necessity that if he continues to exist as the conscious entity he must resist any averaging out of his fundamental discreteness in a common nondistinction. Advisement must encourage the basic excitation to the end that the native best instrument every characteristic of himself as distinct from his fellows.

The Psychological Trend to Balance

First of the four normal procedures of dynamic horoscopy employed in the determination of astrological prediction of tendency or potential in the basic excitation charted by progressed Mars is to see whether there is any marked swing to either of the two possible extremes of immediate and practical or idealistic and mediated alignment in his nascent impulsion. In this activity-facet the contrast is between an inherent ardor for (1) the advancement of personality rather uncompromisingly in its own terms and (2) a sustainment of self-distinctiveness in common contribution and fundamental recognition by associates in familiar context. An example of the former is provided by Charles de Gaulle, and the inescapable subtlety with which an astrologer must proceed has a special illustration at this point. Is the prima donna of French military tactics and statesmanship to be seen suf-

fering from a grandeur complex as often alleged, or as
possessing the less solipsistic fervor of an exceptional dedication to his country's destiny?

The overall practical lean to immediacies in self-refinement had a particularized emphasis until 1936 when he
came into conflict with an entrenched Maginot-line men-
tality that contributed to the quick victory of the Nazis.
During the following lengthy subperiod of more long-range
orientation he refused to accept the French surrender but
gained totally inadequate support even when called to power
at the end of the war. The reins were not really delivered
into his hands astrologically until 1967, and it is too early
to venture any historical judgment. What is quite probable
however is that in ultimate verdict the enduring contribution of this controversial figure will be found to have been
accomplished under the supplementary stimulus of the long-
range extreme of psychological trend. Advisement for the
present would be difficult, and of necessity would have to
be most diplomatic if it is to help the full employment of the
native's self-assurance in the particularities concerning which
the counseling might be required. It is in the record that the
welfare of France has been a definite factor of issue to him in
the past, and the need that this continue into the future is
very obvious.

In summary, and by the selection of exceptionally
strong-willed individuals for example purposes in this activity-facet, it can be seen how delicate any astrological analysis must be at times. Charles de Gaulle has strong overall
practical slanting and his might well be a case of overemphasis of personality for its own sake and in its own way,
but a subordinate and significant stress of idealistic orien-

tation in the years of his repudiation of the antiquated military policies and then the later surrender of France to Hitler and the possibly more enduring achievements of the native's middle years may presage an ultimate verdict of self-lessly high devotion to his country's destiny.

Challenge by Progressed Station

Second of the four normal procedures of dynamic horos-copy employed in the determination of astrological predic-tion of tendency or potential in the basic excitation charted by progressed Mars is to give a particular or special attention to any station established by this significator as identifying a critical regrasp of experience needed or achieved in the activity-facet. As one of the superior planets its stations reveal the probability of exceptional accession of dimension in the simple self-impulsion of the native, and a good exam-ple of this is provided by Richard Wagner. In the instance of this quite unique giant of grand opera there is no extreme of lean in psychological orientation and indeed there are no nonfulcral testimonies whatsoever in the area of the nascent self-outreach. The highly illuminating change of direction of his Mars in the secondary directions in 1851, or virtually at mid-term in his total span of years, is in suggestive correspond-ence with the production of *Lohengrin* at Weimar under the direction of Franz Liszt in late August of 1850. The event can be taken conveniently as the turn to the peculiarly rich mythology embraced in the composer's later inspiration, and in that judgment the astrologer is able to identify the ultimate basis of Wagner's enduring contribution in his music drama. Horoscopic advisement during this period might well have been encouragement of this direction of effort which while already evident a few years before with the production and perhaps limited success of *Tannhäuser* might easily have taken another direction.

In summary, the critical regrasp of control in experience in the basic excitation when shown by a progressed station of Mars has exceptional significance because of its relative rarity in this activity-facet and the generally lessened occurrence of aspects in the secondary directions formed by the superior planets. In the case of Richard Wagner the instance of this signification standing dramatically alone, at about midpoint in his self-conscious years, reveals the overall importance of the transition in which he expanded his nascent outreach and from the operatic composer of conventional stamp as in his successful *Rienzi* became the founder of the spectacular new music drama.

Fulcrum Indication

Third of the four normal procedures of dynamic horoscopy employed in the determination or astrological prediction of tendency or potential in the basic excitation charted by progressed Mars is to give a particular and specialized attention to the squares or the fulcrum relationship that reveals the critical self-mobilization or fundamental impulsion facilitated through the natural manifestation of circumstances in some special convenience for the native's self-expression. In the case of Charles de Gaulle there is a remarkable procession of these aspects to help delimit and thereby encourage his unconditioned outreach at each given period in the general span of years coming to what may be a climactic point in his career at the time this text is prepared. Under four of these indications, or from his disablement at Verdun and imprisonment in World War I to perhaps his graduation from the Ecole Supérieure de Guerre in 1924, his character is shown astrologically as gaining the extraordinary tempering that may well account for his characteristic self-assurance. In 1939 the fifth and final signification has suggestive correspondence with the outbreak of World War II and his inevitable move from the strictly military career into a role of statesman through which his ultimate destiny is obviously to be determined.

Advisement of necessity must be on the basis of the quality of self-challenge identified by the natal planet activated, as of the aplomb of Richard Wagner when he was the toddler of four well able to strut about as he pleased. With Charles de Gaulle there can be successive distinctions in the nature of fulcral quickening indicated by the sun, Mercury, Neptune, Pluto in aftersignificance and finally Venus. Hence the counseling would be toward act or decision respectively in areas (1) of the fundamental strength or morale for the imprisonment, (2) of aplomb when resuming the army career with freedom regained after the armistice, (3) of acceptance as possessing pertinence somewhere in the renewed military training and (4) of probity with the quickening possibility of recognition seven years after and probably identifying elements of his additional studies coming to fruit with his publications that brought him an initial distinction and (5) of realization or the actual clear insight concerning the Nazis.

In summary, the critical self-mobilization required by events shown in basic excitation by the fulcrum aspects of Mars in progression reveals heightened and challenging phases of opportunity for a nascent self projection. Astrological counseling can be helpful through the identification by means of the activated planets of the times and situations concerning which a special concern or attention can produce effective results.

Nonfulcral Indication

Fourth of the four normal procedures of dynamic horoscopy employed in the determination or astrological prediction of tendency or potential in the basic excitation charted by progressed Mars is to give a special and particular attention to the nonfulcral aspects in the secondary directions. Since in this activity-facet these may be very few in number or even absent in the pertinent span of a native's life, the significance may be of far more vital sweep at a given point in the march of circumstances for him while their absence can be a broader encouragement of a self-consistency in alignment with the general pattern of character. In the years of life for Charles de Gaulle at least nine of them are formed. With a current activation of his moon by conjunction as this text is under preparation, any counseling necessarily deals with the now completely pragmatic expression of his basic excitation and should stress the definite immediacy through which he must function at this point in global adjustments. He must not reduce the dimensions of his perspective but rather must accept any enhancement of his fundamental endurance as he seeks to further his goals.

In summary, an effective fourth step of analysis of the basic excitation in the dynamic horoscopy is to determine what indication may be provided by the nonfulcral progressions for a proper recognition of whatever might facilitate the everyday outreach of the native in the general course of circumstances. With progressed Mars the incidence of these aspects is slight but their significance usually greater in consequence. Their absence means a lessened challenge rather than any dissociation or inadequate self-projection since there is the fundamental alignment in the pattern of the nativity.

THE FIVE TRANSCENDENCIES

In the activity-facets of his basic attitude and natural drive the native reveals himself as an essentially uncomplicated manifestation of his existence in any given syndrome of life or as an irreducible representation of himself in a public image he sustains for better or worse with whatever superficial refinements he may be capable of achieving and an inescapable demonstration of his particular actuality through his characteristically uninhibited pressing forward in any line of convenient interest or invitation. He also is a social creature, and from birth he must instrument his continuing existence in an environment of which he is far from an independent part. Even as a baby, in the tireless drawing to self or striking out from self in his early discovery and instinctive exercise of the powers of genuine participation in a human society, he reveals the fundamental nature of associative reality in the literal hunger and ardor that provide the outer linkage from the focal center of his being and so develop into the sensitivity and excitation that in supporting a personal mutuality are the basis of interrelations delineated in the dynamic horoscopy through progressed Venus and Mars respectively. Here at times may be little more than a self-sustaining animality, but a magnificent refinement may come to characterize it. What must be identified next in the broad simplification at this point is the further dimensional unfoldment of man's nature and capabilities, and this be-

354

comes the expanded and more truly individual continuance that is seated primarily in his conscious intelligence rather than his body. A creative plussage of selfhood now must be recognized against mere self-presence in context or the purely superficial compulsions represented by the in-pull and out-push of hunger and ardor.

The Dynamic Nature of Myth

Man definitely comes into his own with the employment of his imagination, since it is his capacity to establish and manipulate images in his consciousness that marks his psychological differentiation from the physical organism in which he still must have time-and-space anchorage for his total identity. Here are the kaleidoscopic implications or meanings that have but feeble foreshadowing in the lower orders of life. His hunger and ardor may never be less primitive in everyday actuality, as he achieves more and more sophistication as the social creature, but their enhancement in significance through the strictly human manifestation is something far beyond the primary lineaments of natural evolution. Myth as a word is in somewhat bad repute, because of its suggestion of unreality, but no better term for this area of subjective transcendence seems to be available. Man's stature is exalted in these pages by the idealized ultimacy of a myth figure illustrated sociopolitically by Abraham Lincoln and more occultly by Annie Besant. The designation is certainly of no literal fancifulness but rather is a dramatization of meanings and significance coming to total independence of prevailing limitations in thought and expectation. All men to some extent are myths both to themselves in each shifting context of experience and to others in every immediacy of pertinence in contact or relationship. Personality achieves its recognizable fixations in imagination as the various phases of itself gain identifiable point in each given situation either as participant or observer. As an enthronement of implication over mere incidence, this phenomenon reveals the emergence of motive out of a nascent dependence on simple insight or sheer accident of conditioning.

In summary, the exposition at this point moves (1) from the uncomplicated manifestation of the native in his basic attitude and natural drive (2) through his permutations of fundamental hunger and ardor as a social creature in sensitivity and excitation (3) on into a consideration of his possession of capabilities beyond possibility for the lower orders of life and in his case transcending the functions on which he continues dependent at base in the universal time-and-space reality. Imagination is now identified as the factor through which man comes into his own, and this is represented most commonly by myth or the phenomenon that dramatizes the elements of a truly conscious or genuinely motivated human adultship. To some extent every individual is a myth to himself in a myriad of differing representations, as he is no less to everybody around him, and the fact of this demonstrates the evolution of man from a basic dependence on blind instinct and chance conditioning to the dominance of meanings and motivations in a truly personal existence.

THE NASCENT CONSISTENCY

Jupiter in the dynamic horoscopy locates the fifth of ten distinct types of activity characterizing conscious individuality, and the first of five that primarily have indication in the realm of imagination or where man is able to function in complete freedom from his fundamental delimitations in time and space. Because it is the planet of the two with regular performance in superior orbit known to the early astrologers and the nearest of them to the earth and so to be conceived as the more friendly or perhaps at least admired as the brightest, it was designated the traditional greater benefic and taken to represent the most practical and in general probability the most favorable eventualities in human experience. In their premodern psychology the horoscopic pioneers saw the larger body in contrast with Venus or the lesser benefic as charting primarily the operation of a higher power or the gratuitous intervention of superseding forces in man's affairs for purposes of rescue or reward or the like. In modern realization the planet's role is better seen as the delineation of the native's mythmaking that at this point can be found to instrument his motivations or facilitate his establishment of personal meanings as a psychologically free agent in the society of which he is a part. In its progressions his nascent consistency is identified, or the factors of elective self-projection in his conscious aliveness through which he is able to demonstrate an intelligent direction of his own evolving selfhood. Thus he lays the cornerstone of his character in its ultimate stature.

The Psychological Trend to Balance

Three of the normal procedures of analysis in this essentially transcendental area of dynamic horoscopy increasingly provide little indication, but the negative significance remains important in revealing the absence of exceptional crisis or issue in a given activity-facet. In the psychological trend in the nascent consistency of character the nonindication would mean a freedom from any necessity to distinguish between the immediate and the remote in personal motivation, or an insulation for better or worse from any characteristic involvement of personal morals or prejudices in the general currents of eventuality. Such an insouciance in this phase of selfhood would permit a more effective self-refinement in other directions, as was true in the overall indication for Abraham Lincoln. Differing from Annie Besant, whose cornerstone of character involved an indissoluble tie with everyday reality and had its result in her almost blind fidelity to the Krishnamurti myth because of its promised immediacy, the American martyred president had unlimited scope for embodying the essence of the national ideal in his acts and person in both practical and idealistic fashion.

David Lloyd George, the British statesman who in many respects was the outstanding figure of World War I but who declined to accept any responsibility in World War II, is a particularly pertinent example of the mythmaking individualist. The two late-forming nonfulcral progressions in his nascent consistency testify to the overall and uncompromisingly practical trend in his psychological orientation, and he was at once dramatically alive to the human wrongs he saw around him and inclined to overpragmatic or devious methods in accomplishing his purposes. Horoscopic advisement for him at the threshold of the first world war would properly have stressed the culminating necessity for a tending to his political bridges in the immediacies of attention to his constituents that at the outset had carried him high in his career. Instead his intentness on the advancement of his own personal position of power permitted the roots of it to wither away and leave him a tragedy of indecisions.

Challenge by Progressed Station

In this second of the four normal procedures of dynamic

horoscopy the chance for progressed stations is a constant in the case of all five outermost planets of the solar system, since in the geocentric schematism they occur twice annually and hence can be encountered in better than two-thirds of all nativities for natives whose life span approaches the traditional ideal of three score and ten years. In the activity-facet of the nascent consistency the absence of indication usually means the lack of any horoscopic necessity for a stop at some point in life in order to capitalize on some phase of fundamental self-refinement of character and thereupon inaugurate a new pattern of mythmaking for the self-fulfillment. Such a regrasp of control in experience was necessitated in the career of Lloyd George in 1889, or when he was twenty-six and a progressed station of Jupiter occurred significantly close to the marriage that would endure until his wife's death half a century later. The astrologer offering advisement at the time and even in Victorian England might well have suggested a maximum of attention to wifely counsel, and that his listening to her advice actually became a fact was a very important factor in his meteoric rise to worldwide prominence.

Fulcrum Indication

In this third of the four normal procedures of dynamic horoscopy the critical self-mobilization required by events is rather crucial in connection with the rise of Lloyd George and his subsequent regression to rather complete eclipse. Speculation is fruitless concerning the psychological crisis in the consciousness of the English-born Welsh boy of six only a few years after the death of his father had left his mother destitute, but the kaleidoscopic events of 1905-8 that precipitated him into the front rank of parliamentary leadership suggest the importance of the fulcral significance of 1907.

The demands on him at that time were met by his efforts leading in essence at least to the welfare state in Great Britain, but in ultimate view it is evident that the gains were premature as far as the full ripening of his powers was concerned. He simply had failed as the unusually eloquent spokesman for humanity to establish the myth figure he had promised to be, and with no continuing influence history all too soon would be dismissing him to superficialities of indecision despite his magnificent performance in the 1914-18 armed conflict.

Nonfulcral Indication

In this fourth of the four normal procedures of dynamic horoscopy an absence of indication in the activity-facet of nascent consistency is not too common and primarily would be a testimony to an indrawn personality without much myth potential or general sustainment of any breadth in everyday life. A case is provided by Bruno Hauptmann, who achieved wide notoriety as the convicted kidnapper and slayer of the Lindbergh boy and who went to his death in the electric chair without ever breaking his closemouthed attitude or ceasing to claim his innocence. The second and climactic nonfulcral progression in the secondary directions of Lloyd George, or an activiation of his basic endurance by progressed Jupiter, is significant charting of that native's six-volume *War Memoirs* completed and published as an obvious determination to fix his place in history in his own terms and issued several years before the culmination of the aspect. In consequence his mythmaking potential had gone subjective, and with the outbreak of World War II he simply retired within himself and for better or worse rested on his laurels. Astrological advisement would have sought to keep his ultimate promise alive and directed toward the future instead of this retreat into the past.

In summary, Jupiter in the dynamic horoscopy charts the first of the five activity-facets operating primarily in the realm of imagination or conscious creativity and of the two of them comprising man's mythmaking most fundamentally. Delineated at this point is the native's nascent consistency or his characteristic elective self-projection that in contrast with his instinctive drive is the ultimate cornerstone of his everyday personality. The planet by progression provides an indication of the relative psychological smoothness of the general course of events or the lack of it in any individual instance, and their facilitation of the native's establishment of expanded meaning in the development of enduring status in his own particular world of experience.

THE NASCENT INTEGRITY

Saturn in the dynamic horoscopy localizes the sixth of ten distinct types of activity characterizing conscious individuality, and the second of five that are evident in the realm of imagination or where man is able to function in complete freedom from his fundamental delimitations in time and space. Because it is the planet of the two with regular performance in superior orbit known to the early astrologers, and of the two the most distant from the earth or the less bright and so the more difficult to note with the naked eye and thus conceived as detached or unapproachable and perhaps unfriendly and to be feared, it was designated the traditional greater malefic and taken to represent the more dissociate and in general probability the most unfavorable eventualities in human experience. Such an approach to signification, in providing with cultural advancement a convenient

and increasingly catchall comprisement of all the overwhelm-
ing or defeating elements in everyday reality, led in due
course to the attribution of the essentially frightening and
ever more elusive evils of life in successive fashion to the
three newer planets as each in turn was discovered and added
into the prevailing and superficial horoscopic schematism of
early medieval astrology. Saturn's baleful influence in the
premodern psychology was distinguished from the supposed
affliction of Mars or the lesser malefic as a charting primarily of the subtle destructive forces less easily discerned or
forestalled, and the acceptance of this proposition soon built
into the notion of fate as an inescapable compulsion. In
today's realization the planet's role is seen more adequately as
the delineation of what essentially is the mythmaking of
society itself or of men collectively as this is mirrored in a
transcendental human generality.

The Problem of Fatality

Astrologically the nature of fate is freed from all encum-
bering metaphysical assumption and recognized as no more
than the simple and enduring consensus that undergirds the
development and continuing existence of a human society.
Thus Saturn is taken to represent wisdom in psychological
perspective, and law in the codification either of social conduct or the cosmic ordering in fundamental physical and
material phenomena. In progression the planet delineates personal integrity as an obvious and necessary conformity both
to lessons learned in actual experience and delimitations established in the prevailing laws of nature at large and the
social unit in particular. Irrevocabilities exist in every commonplace moment of cause and effect, thanks to their framing in the cosmic pattern of things, but a fundamental prin-

ciple of logic is that causation cannot be taken back to infinity in an endless chain since it does not operate in any single line but always in endless ramification. Meaning in consequence can never pursue the infinite regression without diffusion to vacuity. Fate in the dynamic horoscopy is the restriction of fundamental importance in some given course that by the same token is also opportunity in some complementary perspective. Existence may shift from one syndrome of experience to another, but in a universal economy it hardly can move to its own extinction. Any special emphasis of any kind identifies special potentialities, even when they are unsuspected or improperly realized.

It must be remembered that the control of destiny is always and eventually a matter of timing of act and decision, and that time in astrology means pertinence and not mere continuance. A widespread misconception must be noted at this point. Kronos or Saturn and Chronos or time are distinctly different Greek words, but the confusion between them began early with a derivation of the former coming to mean old age or out of date and the like. When the early astrologers observed that the moon and Saturn have virtually identical cycles although in days and years respectively, they placed these two bodies at the ends of the planetary sequence known as Chaldean order or the arrangement of the planets that provided the rulership and name of each day of the week and in passing led to the intriguing possibility of a lunar and Saturnine signification for birth and death. As certifying an inevitability of life's time span in them in terms of an inescapable cycle with a heavenly measure, this was an important if unhappy step in developing the essential fatalistic horoscopy of the fortunetellers. In the more psychologically grounded practice of present times the polar opposition of these two otherwise quite disparate significators is better seen as charting the mutual or concomitant and impeachable validity or irrevocable orderliness (1) on the superficial side by the moon of the everyday intermeshing of the transitory pertinences of life and (2) on the wisdom-oriented side by Saturn of the ultimate convergence of the enduring or immutable factors of every overall potential of convenience to the native. Advisement on the basis of the progressions of the latter must therefore be directed very definitely to what individual alignment may be possible with the general scheme of things in impartial or immediate and in related personal or established reference respectively.

The Psychological Trend to Balance

This first of the four normal procedures in the dynamic horoscopy, in the case of Saturn with the decreasing chance of nonfulcral aspects to provide any indication, reflects the fact that many individuals will be shown without appreciable capacity in their nascent integrity for any critical judgment in the more transcendental areas of human evolution. This was the case with Richard Wagner who apparently was unconscious of his mediocrity as a poet in comparison with his real stature as a musician. Woodrow Wilson the American president contrariwise had a complete remote or idealistic lean in the ordering of his life in the activity-facet, and the League of Nations however truncated in its launching was yet in the pattern of his more cosmic potentials. Advisement in this area of mythmaking self-establishment should encourage big ideas of any real substance when there is positive indication, or seek to enhance the everyday culture of the nascent integrity in more conventional course if such signification is lacking. A continuing self-stimulus is vital.

Challenge by Progressed Station

In this second of the four normal procedures of dynamic horoscopy the absence of progressed station is important because the native is shown without the opportunity in the particular dimension of his effort to stop and take stock and then proceed with a reinforced self-assurance. This is illustrated in the momentum developed in this transcendental area of Woodrow Wilson's life in his altogether too smooth step-by-step precipitation into his ultimate eminence. In contrast the syndome of circumstances revealing the importance of the critical regrasp of control in experience by Annie Besant in her nascent integrity was of exceptional significance in her career as already has been noted. Advisement at this point is particularly helpful for a native entertaining any hope of a destiny of imaginative scope in his own envisionment.

Fulcrum Indication

In this third of the four normal procedures of dynamic horoscopy the diminishing chance of indication of a critical self-mobilization required by events is illustrated by the absence of it in the nascent integrity of Abraham Lincoln, Annie Besant, David Lloyd George and Woodrow Wilson where there was a wholly uninterrupted sustainment by the encompassing law of nature and science on the one hand and of human sophistication on the other. They were psychologically at home in this transcendental area of their unfolding destiny. Revealing the high significance of Saturn's fulcrum progressions however is the indication in the nativity of Sigmund Freud when he was seventeen. At that time he can be presumed to have found the means for untangling the many threads of influence of his early years, and to get down to the foundations for the ultimate import of a life career centered very epochally in the cultural orientations of motivations or fundamental involvement in subjective values or whatever might be identified as the irrevocably inbuilt sanctions of human consciousness. This would be a primary basis for his contribution. In such instances it can be seen how the astrologer may be able to counsel his client in full confidence, out of the exceptional perspective provided by the determination of the dominant elements prevailing in the background of the problems he may be asked to help solve.

Nonfulcral Indication

In this fourth of the four normal procedures of dynamic horoscopy any emphasized progressive distribution of horoscopic potentials in the basic integrity can at the best indicate a totally insulated self-confidence in any transcendental estimate of ultimate values, but at the worst a subtle complacency or tendency to gullibility. Sigmund Freud is an interesting instance of the former extreme but Lloyd George contrariwise gradually fell into a marked solipsistic ineptitude that had begun to reveal itself in his *War Memoirs*. With no indication there is no stress of imaginative outreach to values, or to the reasons and meanings of life as in the case of Abraham Lincoln. In his living years and in his deeper realization the man of log-cabin roots developed his rational powers easily and in simple response to his need for them at any particular point. An astrologer could have encouraged Freud in his unorthodox investigations and Lincoln in his reliance on his innate wisdom, and perhaps even helped head off the British statesman's surrender to his failing grip.

In summary, Saturn in the dynamic horoscopy charts the

second of the five activity-facets that operate primarily in the realm of imagination and of the two of them to be understood in terms of man's mythmaking. In contrast with Jupiter it reveals the individual's relation with cosmic law and all the ingrained values and psychological delimitations of an evolving human society. As the planet most remote from the earth in their day it seemed to the early astrologers to represent the more unreachable or uncontrollable and consequently unfavorable trends in life. To them it became the greater malefic, and was seen to differ from Mars as the lesser malefic because more concerned with an assumed irrevocability in human life. In modern view it delineates the psychological compulsions of social existence from which man may as easily profit as suffer. Through the fact that the period of Saturn in years is approximately the same as that of the moon in days, a schematism of timing has developed by which a native may be helped through astrological advice to control his destiny in every ultimate or psychological sense.

THE NASCENT INDEPENDENCE

Uranus in the dynamic horoscopy localizes the seventh of ten distinct types of activity characterizing conscious individuality, and is the first of three planets that in addition to providing delineation primarily in the realm of imagination in the manner of Jupiter and Saturn are also of great value in revealing factors of reality coming into general experience with their recent identification in the heavens. This earliest discovered of these three reveals the particularized expansions of selfhood in the industrialized and increasingly universalized or ultimately global society that is quite unique in history. Its broad correspondence with the American

Revolution points up the illimitable pioneering potential symbolized at the beginning by the open frontier, and now by the emerging economic freedom for all humanity. Thus the progressed station in infancy as a sole indication by this planet in the life of Abraham Lincoln shows that it was virtually from birth that he sought to instrument some sort of a more thoroughly equitable order of things through his efforts. A progressed station as also the only indication of Uranus in the case of Annie Besant reveals not over two years before her death how in converse fashion she was moving toward future unfoldment or a purely occult potential as the culmination of her purity of soul and the curiously persisting naïveté characterizing her from the very start. The absence of progressed indication for Sigmund Freud in this activity-facet is considerable explanation for the fact that while making so epochal a contribution to modern life he yet remained remarkably the traditionalist in every operative detail of his theorizing.

What is exceptional in origin becomes in time a commonplace, but nonetheless survives importantly in the historical significance of the achievement and in that fact continues to identify new factors of similar seminal nature no matter how small in compass. The everyday indication of Uranus of necessity is of elements of free scope in relationship, even though they are filtered down into familiar actualities and as taken for granted seem to surrender their uniqueness. Hence children or contemporaries of a genius will share his greatness to varying extent, but will do this for themselves on the level and in the terms of an entirely personal meaning. But if some tiny tot or even a total incompetent can flick a switch and flood a room with light, that fact is no depreciation of the miracle of sorts that has created the possibility. Astrological counseling need not neglect continuing factors behind any miracle-become-commonplace in order to deal with the superficial utlization of what has been achieved. To facilitate a reduction of original high potential to transient and multiplying reduplication, the keywords for the ultimate or genius-touched indication should be employed for every less manifestation even if such might seem in no wise different from what always has been evident in human experience. Advisement on the basis of the new planet to be effective can never be a matter of superficial suggestion, or a mere statement of the obvious, but instead must always offer some original or transcendental insight into the native's greater potential.

In summary, Uranus in the dynamic horoscopy charts the first of the three activity-facets in which a native to the extent of his capacity or promise is revealed in a more transcendent expression of himself in dimensions of awareness and reality above or beyond the social orientations indicated by Jupiter and Saturn, and in the area identified by this earliest established of the three outlying significators he should begin to assert some necessity of his identity as it is or can be freed from the conventional compulsions otherwise of his place in the scheme of things. These planets of recent identification gain their significance from the nature of epochal changes in human history with which their discovery has correspondence, and in this first instance the coming of a new order of life is symbolized by the open frontier of the New World. Advisement at best translates the emerging and unique ultimacies into an everyday commonplace in order to encourage individual recognition and acceptance of the transcendental opportunity in the more narrow compass where a given native can make it his own.

THE NASCENT RESPONSIBILITY

Neptune in the dynamic horoscopy localizes the eighth of ten distinct types of activity characterizing conscious individuality, and is the second of three planets that in addition to providing delineation primarily in the realm of imagination in the manner of Jupiter and Saturn are also of great value in revealing factors of reality coming into general experience with their recent identification in the heavens. This next to be recognized of the three affords astrological identification of the individual's more responsible involvement in his society of increasing global structure and unification. This next phase of horoscopic significance was established through man's deliberate attempt to level off life on a wholly socialized basis, such as had climactic punctuation in 1848, and has continuing promulgation through present-day communism. The potential uniqueness of selfhood becoming possible is taken to be, in accordance with actual developments, some signal instrumentation of the new universal or collective interests of mankind as a whole. As essentially a transcendental responsibility, this filters down in the average case to a personal acceptance of a conscious or truly experienced part in current overall eventualities if only in a most minor support of them.

In the life of Annie Besant, as has been noted, the station of Neptune and the only progressed indication in the nascent responsibility has correlation with the end of the long struggle of Charles Bradlaugh for political recognition despite the fact he was an atheist and the consequent taking of the bottom out for her in the first of the two transcendental alignments to causes of sufficient scope in ultimacy to hold her in a piece psychologically. The similar sole progressed indication for Abraham Lincoln in the activity-facet corresponds to his first election to public office, and a transition from his remarkable struggle to dignified self-reliance coming to climax in New Salem on into his alignment to the myth-figure potential and a consummation of his living years in service to his country in the White House.

In summary, Neptune in the dynamic horoscopy charts the second of the three activity-facets in which the native to the extent of his capacity or promise begins to accept an effective responsibility to the culture and age in which he is functioning, whether in small compass or large. Advisement continues competent and proper as it explains and encourages every possible alignment of the native in his genuine dedication to some ultimacy he can visualize for himself.

THE NASCENT ENLIGHTENMENT

Pluto in the dynamic horoscopy localizes the ninth of ten distinct types of activity characterizing conscious individuality, and is the third of three planets that in addition to providing delineation primarily in the realm of imagination in the manner of Jupiter and Saturn are also of great value in revealing factors of reality coming into general experience with their recent identification in the heavens. This last to be discovered of the three affords astrological identification of the individual's genuinely transcendental involvement in a modern society of increasing global structure and unification. This means on the basis of a completely equitable recognition of every other personal concern as no less essentially his own, but yet an actual participation in the collective citizenship.

The planet came to astrological significance with the Great Depression, and the total reconstitution of the world's socio-economic system, and it indicates the potential uniqueness of selfhood in the more universal divisions of labor just beginning to mark human functions. Advisement continues in the pattern of helping every native to achieve some practical conception of the universal factors now expanding all potentiality and every hope of man to the end that at least his token participation in the overall developments can have a significant and personal immediacy for him.

THE NATURAL INVOLVEMENT

The moon in the dynamic horoscopy localizes the tenth of the ten types of activity characterizing conscious individuality, and because it is the planet astronomically most intimately related to the heavenly sphere on which man has his time-and-space existence it traditionally (1) has charted the greatest spread and variety of the immediate and superficial factors of human experience in their general availability and (2) therefore has been taken to indicate any particular concentration of events of individual pertinence in their momentary significance in various given situations. As the only true satellite of the earth it has a simple approximation to regular motion in the zodiac, and this it shares only with the sun when in the geocentric perspective of astrology that celestial body takes over the movement of the terrestrial globe. In recognition of a consequent uninterrupted direct reference, these two of the ten planetary significators commonly employed by the astrologer have been set apart from earliest times and given a special designation as the lights. Basic personal identity as it persists primarily in its own changelessness at core during the course of its kaleidoscopic manifestation of itself is identified by the greater light, and the lesser light in definite complementation is seen fundamentally to reveal the endless changing and illimitable nature of the overall reality. Such a total comprisement by lunar significance may be summed up conveniently in the conception of a natural involvement as universal substance and eternal actuality in a sense facilitate any self-expression of the moment through the ready fortuitousness of pure chance or seeming accident. Here of course is merely absolute potentiality in nascent impartiality of balance with man's free will.

A superficial astrology can destroy the force of the moon's testimony in progression by reducing it to the role of subordinate significator, or considering its indication to be no more than a bringing of specificity to probable eventualities charted more fundamentally by the progressed aspects of the other nine planets. This establishment of a species of pecking order, in the transits and other techniques as well as here, is an attempt to escape the apparent problem of nonoperating predictions by requiring some subsidiary factor as a necessity for triggering the manifestation of anything to which there is principal testimony. To break a chain of causation to account for its deficiencies is the regression to infinity that must be avoided if reasoning is to remain logical. Obviously the lesser light must possess an importance fully equal to that of the greater if there is any actuality in their relationship of direct complementation of each other. Indeed and as far as the signification of the lunar orb is concerned, nothing is more vital to conscious existence than the raw and illimitable potentiality of the cosmic otherness through which individuality perforce must substantiate and know itself. Because the focus of attention in this area centers in eventualities of principal pertinence in the moments of their accentuation, the interpretation of the lunar secondaries is best in their simple time sequence.

An individual in difficulty often can have his most practical help from the dynamic horoscopy when through the lunar progressions, or the techniques particularly supplementing them, he can be given dates and periods for charting the most intelligent course through the day-by-day vicissitudes of his experience. The fulcrum squares of the moon are perhaps the most important as straws in the wind or intimations of potential accomplishment, but what they indicate is very actual in its own nature and what must be guarded against very rigorously is assuming that the delineation is of the native's state of being instead of the current and pertinent manifestation of the universal and eternal otherness in its co-operation with his efforts or its challenge to his particular capacities. A measure of psychological lean may be determined when there is a particularly marked sequence of progression by either immediate or mediated indication, but this is relatively superficial and what is revealed is not a trend of the native's consciousness but rather the relative practical or hypothetical potentiality in the transiencies with which he deals.

The nonfulcral progressions of the moon reveal the emerging opportunity in circumstances for any application of (1) general capacities of the self in the case of a conjunction or of (2) specific capacities when a sextile, and this usually can be the basis of guidance of a very fundamentally practical sort in the light of a native's actual or existing situation. Similarly these progressed aspects identify an emerging opportunity in circumstances as (3) a move or continuance of activity of more positive and broader fashion in company or co-operation with others in the main stream of events in the case of a trine or (4) the definite enhancement of participation in the prevailing flow of eventuality or of marked adjustment in the continuing relation with it on the basis of special personal skills or endowment when the progression is an opposition. The horoscopic counsel when the elements are more mediated should still be practical in the nature of definite suggestions but in a pattern of more effective involvement in the under-lying or long-range developments.

In advisement on the basis of the lunar progressions it is profitable at times to make suggestions in view of whether they are approaching culmination or receding from exactness. Fairly generous time orb should be allowed, but hardly as much as a month in either way unless there is unusual corre-spondence with everyday consequences of unmistakable per-tinence. In advance of maturity the counseling should be toward any possible advance practicing or rehearsal in act or reaction as well as in consciousness of a desired outcome. After the occurrence of the events and they have been identified in their importance or continuing significance by the dynamic horoscopy, the advice should be toward the intelligent selection of consequences best perpetuated in act and realization or what in some way would be the most fruitful capitalization on the circumstances in the light of perhaps unrealized but possible potentiality.

In summary, the moon in the dynamic horoscopy charts (1) the immediate pertinency of general circumstances in a native's life at any moment or situation of his natural involve-ment in current affairs and (2) the possibility of his effective employment of transient events in his own interest. In comple-ment with the sun's indication of his stability of simple identity, the lesser light reveals the available dependabilities in every-thing around him. There must be a rigorous avoidance of the infinite regression in which the lunar progressions are reduced to mere subordinate factors supposed to instrument the more fundamental indications of the other planets, or to act pri-marily to bring otherwise predicted outcomes to manifestation.

The moon's indications in the secondary directions are taken in chronological sequence because the attention is directed to personal potentials coming to full pertinence in relatively transient fashion. Advisement in this activity-facet is on the basis of the times and circumstances of importance in the day-by-day vicissitudes of experience.

THE BASIC CALCULATIONS

In the ideal instance the student or practitioner of astrology who refers to this text or employs the techniques here presented will at least (1) possess a thorough acquaintance with the principal horoscopic components or specifically the twelve houses, twelve signs, ten planetary bodies and five major aspects listed in the appendix as well as (2) enjoy a ready familiarity with astrological calculation in the more common procedures of erecting a chart and computing the day-for-a-year progressions and (3) have appreciable practical experience in interpreting a nativity. This is a necessary background to be built up if not possessed. In the meanwhile it should be noted that the legitimate mathematical demands at any stage in even the most comprehensive mastery of the dynamic analysis need never go beyond the several uncomplicated operations that have varied application in perhaps considerable but yet quite simple modification of themselves. The present exposition however should start from the beginning, even if in necessarily summary fashion or for review at this point. Greater detail for the neophyte is provided in the appendix.

The Natal Horoscope

The calculation of the nativity involves two steps or (1) the establishment of the houses and (2) the location of the planets in the signs at the moment of birth.

The houses are identified in the celestial equator in right ascension and this is expressed conveniently in hours, minutes

378

and seconds of sidereal time. The ephemeris shows the mid-heaven or point of balance between the rising and setting of heavenly bodies on this most immediately important of the two great circles in space (a) at the Greenwich meridian and (b) at noon or midnight depending on the tables used. The sidereal time of this astrological fulcrum point in the heavens is adjusted for (aa) distance in terrestrial longitude of the birthplace from Greenwich and (bb) difference in time of birth from the noon or midnight, and as thereupon adjusted is recognized as the midheaven of the nativity and given its notation in the zodiacal longitude corresponding to the right ascension. The other horoscopic houses that are determined in their relation to it by the terrestrial latitude of the horizon at birth are taken from the tables of houses where they are identified through the zodiacal positions of their cusps needed for the familiar form of natal chart.

The usual procedure in locating the planets in a nativity is to take their zodiacal place shown in the ephemeris for the midnight or noon preceding the moment of birth at Green-wich, and to correct this on the basis of (1) time elapsing from the given midnight or noon to the birth moment and (2) the daily motion of each particular planet in the particu-lar twenty-four hours of which it will be a proportional part. The operation is facilitated generally by changing the local and usually standard time of birth to the equivalent Green-wich hour and minute as a convenient adjustment to the ephemeris in making the calculations.

The Secondary Directions

The computing of the fundamentally important progres-sions known as the secondaries is in essence the establishment in order of a special chart for each day after birth corresponding to the years of life to which attention is to be given or is the necessity (a) to take in connection with the whole movement of each planet in a given day's span (b) the amount of that motion required for the completing of any major aspect formed with a natal planet in the course of the twenty-four hours in which this occurs and (c) to determine how this fraction part of the daily movement corresponds in terms of a date of culmination to the proportionate segment of the year of which it provides the progressive indication. Horoscopic houses in this process are of little significance, as has been explained, and in consequence are ignored. Needless computations are commonly avoided by the device of moving the birthday, after the first year, so that the planetary positions in the ephemeris then will correspond directly to a special annual date represented by the noon or midnight of the ephemeris used. This shifted birthday, of no reality except as a mathematical convenience, is known generally as the adjusted calculation date. Here of course is the simple sort of time-saving procedure already illustrated in the translation of the local time of birth into Greenwich hours and minutes for the calculation of the natal places of the planets.

In the establishment of the horoscope itself the time is known for the planetary places, but the amount of motion required for arriving at them must be calculated and added to the positions shown in the ephemeris. By contrast in the directions the amount of motion in the planet's progression to its aspect is to be seen by eye inspection or determined by simple addition but the time or date of culmination must be computed. In both these astrological procedures the locations and interrelations of the planets are at all points a phenomenon of celestial longitude, and are held rigorously to consideration in the zodiac or the ecliptical great circle in the heavens.

The determination of the adjusted calculation date can be facilitated by taking advantage of the column of sidereal time in the ephemeris, or using it as a convenient scaling in mutual relationship of days in the year and equivalent units of the circle in degrees and divisions of degree in the equatorial span of twenty-four hours. If the interval in hours and minutes of time from birth to a following noon or midnight is added to the hours, minutes and seconds of sidereal time given for the noon or midnight on the day of birth, the resulting correspondence to a date in the ephemeris identifies the artificial birthday. When the Greenwich mean time of birth is after the noon or midnight of the ephemeris used even if a following morning, the adjusted calculation date is prior even if in a preceding year, and vice versa. Twenty-four hours of course are added or subtracted in the sidereal time as necessary in this operation.

More precise computation of the date of maturity of aspects in the secondaries can be facilitated by the use of the diurnal proportional logarithms employed familiarly to gain preciseness in calculating the basic horoscope. The logarithm for the total motion of a planet in the day corresponding to the year of life under consideration is subtracted from the logarithm of the movement needed to complete the particular aspect, and the result obtained in that fashion in hours and minutes can be translated into the date of culmination by adding them to the sidereal time of the adjusted calculation date.

The Tertiary Directions

Computation of the tertiaries is very similar to the calculation of the secondaries since all the progressions are formed in the zodiac or in celestial longitude. Under the general uni-

fication of procedure to which this text is committed as a help
to the student and less experienced practitioner, and following
in line with the commonly accepted method of computing the
positions of planets in a natal horoscope from the previous
noon or midnight positions under all circumstances, consideration of tertiary progression begins with the regular lunation
preceding the moment of birth even if this should happen to
be virtually the whole month, and a first step is to count the
number of these regular lunations that in succession after the
birth correspond to the years of life up to the period of progressed interpretation to be undertaken and then to proceed
in the ephemeris to the point where the moon is in precisely
the same relation it had with the sun in the nativity and thereupon reproduces the synodical lunation representing the real
and not the artificial birthday at the threshold of the year of
life to be examined.

Under the astrologer's essential principle of equivalence or
distinction the eccentricities of the lesser light must be taken
as a prime factor in the significance of the tertiary directions.
The moon in consequence is considered in its four phases in
providing the determination of time of culmination of these
progressions as its daily motion varies in four quarters in which
the birthday year is divided. A fourth of its whole movement
in the lunar month corresponding to the year or experience
establishes the date with which each quarter begins, as this
can be recognized in necessarily approximate form by eye
inspection in the ephemeris. With the time orb that enters into
delineation in any case, the attempt to achieve a greater precision by defining the boundaries of the annual quarters by
the hours in the days of the synodical lunation that mark them
off is simply not worth while. Each of the planets progressed

in the tertiaries is taken separately in the aspects it forms with the natal significators in the course of the seven-odd days corresponding to the three-odd months of life in the same manner as in calculating the secondaries.

The Primary Directions

The primaries stand altogether apart from the other forms of progression when it comes to calculation since consideration is entirely in the celestial equator or in terms of right ascension instead of celestial or zodiacal longitude. As a first step in the employment of the planets in this technique their natal longitudinal positions as differentiated in celestial latitude must be converted into the equatorial measure, and in addition to the condensed tables for this operation in the present text there are those of greater preciseness generally available. The span in the revolving firmament from the midheaven point of balance between the rising and setting phenomena of the heavenly bodies to the terrestrial horizon that astrologically identifies personal existence or represents the practical ground of individual uniqueness is known as the semiarc, and in the case of the basic horoscope it is an even ninety degrees of right ascension. Under the time correlation that characterizes this one of the progressive techniques the degrees in the undistorted quadrant of the houses are equivalent to ninety years of life. The problem is to determine the dates of indication as the planets are moved into progressed aspect with their natal places, and this again is ultimately the proposition of simple geometrical proportion.

A complication is that the planetary significators as moved by the daily rotation of the heavens do not move in the celestial equator in which the houses are established, and hence an even degree of shift in their cases almost never will measure

ABRAHAM LINCOLN: PRIMARY PROGRESSION IN RIGHT ASCENSION (RA)

planet and quadrant	natal position of planet			horizon at 37° 40'N		planetary semiarc		RA per year	diminished RA		increased RA	
	longitude	latitude	RA	longitude	RA	diurnal	operative		1858	1863	1858	1863
	° '	° '	° '	° '	° '	° '	° '	° '	° '	° '	° '	° '
☉ SE	♒ 23 29	0 0	325 49	♊ 15 33	73 45	107 56	107 56	1 11.6	267 21	261 23	24 19	30 15
☽ SE	♑ 27 19	N 4 58	298 24	♉ 14 55	40 58	102 21	102 21	1 9.2	241 34	236 7	354 54	0 41
♃ NE	♓ 22 7	S 1 7	353 12	♋ 11 7	101 52	108 41	71 19	1 48.2	313 51	309 49	32 33	36 35
♄ SW	♐ 3 10	N 2 1	241 32	♒ 15 57	317 48	76 16	103 44	1 9.5	184 47	178 59	295 17	304 5
♂ SW	♎ 25 29	N 2 38	204 36	♑ 3 47	273 50	69 14	110 46	1 13.5	144 35	138 27	264 37	270 45
♀ NE	♈ 7 30	N 0 13	6 44	♋ 22 45	114 35	107 51	72 9	1 48.1	327 27	323 27	46 1	50 1
☿ NE	♓ 10 21	S 0 1	341 52	♋ 1 33	91 41	109 49	70 11	1 46.1	307 38	300 23	16 6	23 21
♅ SW	♏ 9 40	N 0 28	217 25	♑ 17 21	288 45	71 20	108 40	1 12.2	158 27	152 26	276 23	282 24
♆ SW	♐ 6 39	N 1 35	245 6	♒ 20 51	322 43	77 37	102 23	1 8.0	189 19	183 54	300 53	306 18

a year of life. In consequence a second step in employing the primaries is to determine the semiarc of each planet at birth in a given native's case, so that this can be equated proportionately with the time of culmination of the progressions. The familiar tables of houses can be used to find these planetary semiarcs by quite uncomplicated operations. If the planet's natal right ascension is placed quite arbitrarily at midheaven in the tables, the zodiacal degrees shown for the ascendant or the eastern horizon in the terrestrial latitude of the nativity can be converted to right ascension as without latitude and the difference from the natal right ascension thereupon becomes the special semiarc. This is not a locating of the planet in any respect but wholly a matter of a first step in determining the celestial span in which it moves in right ascension in ninety years.

An additional factor of fundamental importance is that when the horizon at birth places a significator in the northeast or southwest quadrants of the basic nativity the distortion from the norm characteristic of the structure of most horoscopic houses is reversed and the first-obtained or diurnal semiarc for the planet is subtracted from 180° of right ascension to obtain the operational semiarc that otherwise is identical with the diurnal one of initial calculation. A ninetieth part of the operational semiarc becomes the progressive shift of the planets corresponding to a year of life. By multiplication of these ninetieth segments of right ascension the progressed position of each significator is obtained for the period of living experience to be analyzed, and the culmination of the primary directions is computed in the same manner as in the other systems of the dynamic horoscopy. Here the convenient division of zodiacal longitude into thirty-degree signs is lacking, but the recognition of aspect distance does not need to be any more difficult.

A unique feature of primary directions, explained in connection with Lincoln's horoscope, is that they may be computed both clockwise and counterclockwise or in terms of decreasing and increasing right ascension respectively. 360 degrees of course are added or subtracted as is convenient.

Life Recapitulation

The calculation of the solar return involves no complication. The zodiacal distance the sun must travel on the actual day of its return in the year to be given delineation, from its previous position at noon or midnight in the ephemeris for that particular year to its place in the nativity, must be taken together with its total movement in this particular twenty-four hours, and the logarithm of the latter subtracted from the logarithm of the former. The resulting logarithm yields hours and minutes that are the Greenwich mean time for the precise moment of return. With this corrected to local mean time, the chart can be calculated in the usual manner from the given ephemeris. To avoid interpolation it is well to use diurnal proportional logarithms for which the minutes of the first two degrees are given for seconds.

The lunar return is calculated in the same manner as the solar. Consideration of minutes down into seconds in the logarithms is not possible however, and with the swifter motion of the lesser light such precision would not be significant.

A great variety of opinion and procedure is found in connection with the diurnal or ascendant return. Properly the natal ascending degree is found in the tables of houses for the geographical latitude at which the day will be spent. From the corresponding sidereal time of the midheaven it then is necessary to subtract the sidereal time of the preceding noon or midnight of the day in the ephemeris to gain the hours and minutes that with allowance for the usual corrections for geographic longitude and difference in mean and sidereal measure will give the mean local time from which the subsidiary horoscope must be calculated.

In the supplementary returns the consideration is from the prevailing chance-choice context of the heavenly stresses and strains, and these charts should be calculated for the place of current residence or primary self-establishment at the moment. The procedure is in polar balance with the evolution of indication from the birthplace represented by the nativity and its progressions.

Rectification

The calculations in rectification are merely familiar ones performed in a sense both tentatively and backwards.

appendix I

SECONDARY DIRECTIONS, ABRAHAM LINCOLN
(with page where delineated)

BASIC ATTITUDE

1812, Mar. 12	☿ ☌ ♀	58
1821	SR	49
1829, Aug. 9	☌ ♀	58
1833, Nov. 30	☌ ☿	29
1834, Sep. 4	△ ♅	33
1839, July 23	□ ♆	46
1843	SD	50
1847, Jan. 29	□ ♆	46
1852, July 10	△ ♅	33
1853, May 23	☌ ☿	29
1858, Jan. 4	☌ ♀	58
1864, July 28	☌ ♃	44
1868, June 13	✶ ☽	45

NATURAL DRIVE

1811, Feb. 10	☉ △ ♂	64
1818, Sep. 23	□ ♄	62
1822, Mar. 13	□ ♆	63
1825, Mar. 19	△ ♅	65
Nov. 17	☌ ☿	65
1830, Jan. 11	☌ ♀	66
1837, Aug. 30	☌ ♃	66
1842, Nov. 23	✶ ☽	67
1848, Oct. 16	△ ♄	67
1852, Apr. 26	△ ♆	68
1853, Mar 7	☌ ♀	68
1869, June 14	✶ ☉	69

BASIC SENSITIVITY

1823, June 30	♀ ✶ ☉	77
1825, May 12	☍ ♂	78
1827, Feb. 4	□ ☽	75
1839, Feb. 4	☍ ♅	78
Oct. 10	✶ ☿	79
1844, Jan. 23	✶ ♀	79
1852, June 14	✶ ♃	80
1854, Jan. 22	□ ☉	76
1858, Sep. 27	△ ☽	80
1866, Dec. 22	☍ ♄	80

BASIC EXCITATION

1827	♂ SR	85
1827, forming	□ ☽	87
1843, July 5	☌ ♂	88
1851, Mar. 31	△ ☉	89
1906	SD	86

FIVE TRANSCENDENCIES

1831, May 6	♃ ✶ ☽	94
1855, July 31	△ ♄	95
1870, Jan. 29	△ ♆	95
1838	♄ SR	97
1867, July 31	☌ ♄	97
1811	♅ SR	98
1834	♆ SR	100

SECONDARY DIRECTIONS, ABRAHAM LINCOLN

(with page where delineated)

NATURAL INVOLVEMENT

1857, Mar. 30	☽ ☌ ♂ 105	Mar. 17	⚹ ☉ 110
May 14	▫ ☽ 106	May 7	⚹ ♂ 111
1858, Mar. 16	☌ ♅ 106	1862, Mar. 12	▫ ♀ 111
Apr. 2	△ ☿ 106	May 8	⚹ ♅ 112
July 14	△ ♀ 107	May 25	⚹ ☿ 112
1859, Jan. 19	△ ♃ 107	Sep. 11	⚹ ♀ 112
Feb. 22	▫ ☉ 107	1863, Mar. 31	⚹ ♃ 113
May 28	⚹ ☽ 108	June 28	▫ ♂ 113
Oct. 21	☌ ♄ 108	Aug. 16	☌ ☽ 113
1860, Jan. 16	☌ ♆ 108	1864, Jan. 19	⚹ ♄ 114
Feb. 6	△ ♀ 109	Apr. 24	⚹ ♆ 116
Apr. 19	▫ ☿ 109	May 17	⚹ ♀ 116
Aug. 2	▫ ♀ 109	July 15	▫ ♅ 116
1861, Feb. 10	▫ ♃ 110	1865, July 29	☌ ☉ 117

SECONDARY DIRECTIONS, ANNIE BESANT
(with page where delineated)

BASIC ATTITUDE

1848, Oct. 22	☿	□ ♃	193
1853, Aug. 29		☍ ♀	202
1854, Oct. 28		△ ♆	203
1861, Jan. 19		△ ♄	203
1864, Oct. 20		△ ☽	204
1866, May 24		☍ ♂	205
1868, Sep. 10		△ ♃	205
1875, Dec. 4		□ ♆	194
1884, June 29		□ ♄	197
1885, Jan. 1		✶ ☉	206
1889, Sep. 29		✶ ♀	**207**
1893		SR	192
1896, Feb. 22		✶ ♀	208
1899, Nov. 29		✶ ☉	209
1900, Apr. 14		□ ♄	198
1907, Nov. 5		□ ♆	199
1913		SD	192
1918, June 28		□ ♆	200
1927, May 13		□ ♄	201
Sep. 14		✶ ☉	209
1930, Feb. 3		✶ ♀	210
1934, Feb. 13		△ ♅	210

NATURAL DRIVE

1850, Dec. 11	☉	☌ ♀	216
1852, Nov. 7		□ ☽	213
1856, July 30		☍ ♅	217
Aug. 24		☌ ☿	217
1858, May 24		□ ♃	213
1866, Mar. 19		☍ ♀	217
1868, Jan. 17		△ ♆	218
1877, July 12		△ ♄	218

1882, Dec. 23		△ ☽	219
1885, Mar. 25		☍ ♂	219
1888, June 6		△ ♃	219
1897, Dec. 5		□ ♆	214
1907, Apr. 13		□ ♄	215
Sep. 16		✶ ☉	220
1910, Oct. 22		✶ ♀	220
1916, Apr. 19		△ ♅	221
May 13		✶ ☿	221
1925, Sep. 10		△ ♀	221
1927, June 24		✶ ♆	222
1936, Oct. 10		✶ ♄	222

BASIC SENSITIVITY

1852, Nov. 29	♀	☌ ☉	229
1870		SD	226
1889, July 16		☌ ☉	229
1894, Apr. 2		☌ ♀	230
1896, Nov. 27		□ ☽	227
1901, Sep. 23		☌ ♅	231
Oct. 4		☌ ☿	232
1903, Oct. 17		□ ♃	228
1912, June 17		☍ ♀	232
1914, May 11		△ ♆	233
1923, Oct. 20		△ ♄	234
1929, Jan. 10		△ ☽	234
1931, Feb. 25		☍ ♂	235
1934, Feb. 7		△ ♃	235

BASIC EXCITATION

1860, Apr. 4	♂	✶ ☽	239
1877, Feb. 28		✶ ♄	239
1911		SD	238

SECONDARY DIRECTIONS, ANNIE BESANT

(with page where delineated)

FIVE TRANSCENDENCIES

1886			♃ SR	242
1921,	Dec.	10	☌ ♃	243
1936,	Feb.	19	□ ☿	242
1890			♄ SD	244
1926,	Jan.	5	☌ ♄	244
1931			♅ SD	245
1886			♆ SD	246
1939			♇ SD	247

NATURAL INVOLVEMENT

1875,	Jan.	27	☽ ☌ ☽	250
	Mar.	30	⚹ ♂	250
	May	8	□ ♅	250
	May	10	□ ☿	250
	June	26	☌ ♃	251
1876,	Feb.	1	□ ♇	251
1877,	Jan.	4	⚹ ☉	251
	Apr.	6	⚹ ♀	252
	Aug.	6	□ ♂	252
	Sep.	17	△ ♅	252
	Sep.	19	⚹ ☿	253
1878,	July	30	△ ♇	253
	Aug.	24	☍ ♆	254
1879,	June	9	☍ ♄	254
	Nov.	24	⚹ ☽	254
1880,	Feb.	2	△ ♂	255
	May	12	⚹ ♃	255
1882,	Jan.	5	☌ ☉	255
	Apr.	13	☌ ♀	256
	June	10	□ ☽	256
	Oct.	2	☍ ♅	256
	Oct.	4	☌ ☿	257
	Nov.	27	□ ♃	257
1883,	July	24	☍ ♇	258
	Sep.	18	△ ♆	258
1884,	July	4	△ ♄	259
	Dec.	17	△ ☽	259
1885,	Feb.	24	☍ ♂	260
	June	1	△ ♃	260
1886,	Mar.	15	□ ♆	260
	Dec.	21	□ ♄	260
1887,	Jan.	3	⚹ ☉	261
	Apr.	6	⚹ ♀	261
	Sep.	16	△ ♅	262
	Sep.	18	⚹ ☿	262
1888,	June	22	△ ♇	262
	Aug.	12	⚹ ♆	263
1889,	May	10	⚹ ♄	263
	May	22	□ ☉	263
	Aug.	19	□ ♀	264
	Oct.	11	☍ ☽	264
	Dec.	14	△ ♂	264
1890,	Jan.	22	□ ♅	265
	Jan.	24	□ ☿	265
	Mar.	14	☍ ♃	265
	Oct.	16	□ ♇	266
1891,	Sep.	3	△ ☉	267
	Nov.	27	△ ♀	267
1892,	Mar.	19	□ ♂	267
	Apr.	27	⚹ ♅	268
	Apr.	28	△ ☿	268
1893,	Jan.	6	⚹ ♇	268
	Feb.	23	☌ ♆	269
	Oct.	28	☌ ♄	269

THE ESSENTIAL PRINCIPLES OF ASTROLOGY

(1) CONCORDANCE OR CONCOMITANCE

This principle is a fundamental statement of the nature of reality, and a recognition of the eternal and universal co-operation of twin manifestations of the cosmos in (a) order and (b) flux. IN ASTROLOGY this means a concern with repetition or reduplication in either time or space and an establishment of the most basic clues to the significance of individual events in human lives. As anything in question becomes important in experience it tends to repeat or reduplicate itself indefinitely in some fashion or another, and the horoscopic measure of it identifies the most definitive orientation for the given nature of what at best protects him from any regression to irrelevance.

References in text: pp. 13, 21, 27, 28, 39, 52, 58, 62, 104, 133, 189, 203, 230, 238, 248, 308.

(2) CONVERGENCE OR CONVENIENCE

This principle is a fundamental statement of the nature of individuality, and a recognition of the status of any living organism as in effect the peer of the cosmos through an equality of functioning potential. The part in other words cannot have a nature that contravenes the essence of the whole, and the very actuality of existence must serve all the existents that comprise it. Therefore the utilization or adaptation of what-

ever is needed in order to exist must of necessity be the acceptance of a contribution rather than an inescapable surrender to
a compulsion. The corollary is that there can be no situation
in the context of reality that lacks a loophole or a potential
of exceptionality through which free will can operate while the
individual still remains basically and effectively sustained in
the universal order. In ASTROLOGY this means a realization of
the ubiquitous latitudes in all experience, and so a rejection
of any necessity that any native at any point can be compelled
to regress to insignificance. In consequence the astrologer
must avoid the Procrustean fallacy or the attempt to tailor the
life and character of the native according to any particular
presumptions of horoscopic indication.

References in the text: pp. 15, 16, 31, 88, 146.

(3) EQUIVALENCE OR DISTINCTION

This principle is a fundamental statement of the nature of
dimension in experience, and a recognition of the inescapable
significance or importance even if in most miniscule fashion
(a) of any individual personality to others than itself and con-
versely (b) of any human achievement at large to the particular individuality. Thus man in his universal selfhood is the
measure of all things, precisely as all things collectively are the
measure of man in his particularity. Uniqueness as it increases
in its manifestation, whether in the case of the individual or
his pertinent context, must have increasing emphasis that
follows from the corresponding and paradoxical infrequence
of occurrence. In ASTROLOGY this means a realization of the
balance inevitably established between (a) personal excellence
through everyday current or special historical significance in
the actualization of exceptional potentials of the horoscope

on the one hand and (b) the general tenor of events in the common matrix of reality on the other. In this way interpretation avoids identifying and accepting any needless regression to superficiality.

References in the text: pp. 14, 16, 62, 82, 83, 203, 232, 237, 266.

(4) IMMEDIACY OR RELEVANCE

This principle is a fundamental statement of the nature of scope in self-fulfillment, and a recognition of the cosmic economics through which individual existence continues. Thus any living entity in order to exist must have an inbuilt practicality that becomes the special manifestation of universal order in the essence of this particular and personal being. Supply and demand continually beget and nourish each other as the operative basis of all measurable reality, and nothing is more characteristic of man than his capacity to shape his own world or definitive context of actuality to his unfolding needs and desires. IN ASTROLOGY this means a realization that life in its make-up is opportunity, and that the horoscope basically charts an individual's capacity to grasp his own unique potentials in simple self-preservation. Delineation therefore reveals the core ongoing of the native in a sequence of logical removes in all details of his experience from his primary anchorage in the familiarities of his day-by-day existence, and what is to be avoided is the fallacy of the greener pastures at a distance or the endless and seductive regression to infinity.

References in the text: pp. 17, 21, 22, 119, 134, 144, 145.

(5) SELECTIVITY OR EFFICIENCY

This principle is a fundamental statement of the nature of

effectiveness in self-control, and a recognition of the necessity for well-grounded choice in any exercise of free will. An individual with any balance of self-expression increasingly and properly will avoid all involvement in what can only prove extraneous or unnecessary in his case and thus will be able to escape (a) the dilutions of judgment on the one hand and (b) the consequent and subtle regression toward nonentity on the other. In ASTROLOGY this means the cultivation of the analytical decisiveness often known as Occam's razor or a special care always to consider the fewer factors of greater significance in each separate detail of reasoning and thus to disregard unquestionably what might well be taken into very definite account in a different perspective.

References in the text: pp. 14, 22, 134, 144, 159, 169, 300.

(6) INCISIVENESS OF CONSISTENCY

This principle is a fundamental statement of the nature of perspective as a logical tool of mind, and a recognition of the necessity in any reliable thinking for definitive fixed points of reference or invariant canons of judgment that while perhaps wholly arbitrary in origin yet can be the basis for valid understanding as long as they are employed consistently. In ASTROLOGY this means the practical development of the stellar science as a specialized analytical language in which its concepts, symbols, verbal formulas and keywords are held to a single sharp or utterly constant meaning despite any possible connection with other meanings. Such precise channeling of the thought processes is characteristic of all competent technical insight, and is a measure of insurance against the regression to perplexity.

References in the text: pp. 15, 27, 301.

(7) Discernment or validation

This principle is a fundamental statement of the nature of difference as a logical tool of mind, and a recognition of simple contrast as an impartial agent through which all things may be used to shed light on each other. Here is the universal basis of general symbolization on the one hand and of the particular dramatization of experience or establishment of human values on the other. In astrology this means the employment of the almost illimitable spread of varying and alternative procedures for mental check and balance in reference to each other, and thus (a) the facilitation of an ultimate accuracy of horoscopic judgment as well as (b) the prevention of any final regression to resourcelessness.

References in the text: pp. 20, 27, 169.

(8) Definition or discrimination

This principle is a fundamental statement of the nature of specificity as a logical tool of mind, and is a recognition of the constant need in conscious existence to hold the elements of experience in context and to embrace all manifestations of general reality in some definite one or another of the endlessly possible phases of pertinent concern. In astrology this means the realization that the events of human life are the actuality of individual existence, or are that of which alone the horoscopic factors can be either identification or measure in any practical fashion. When astrological analysis is seen to define rather than explain man's being, or to interpret what is critical or possible for him in purely personal lineaments, there is no necessity for any regression to unreality.

References in the text: pp. 18, 28.

(9) Impartiality or adaptability

This principle is a fundamental statement of the nature of circumstances, and is a recognition of the cosmic flux as the utterly generalized potentiality in which conscious human existence is sustained and thereupon either exalted or averaged out in the mass of its kind. There is neither prejudice nor indifference in respect to man in the eternal and universal totality, and the endless stream of free-flowing natural phenomena is for him to employ or suffer entirely as he wishes or fails to concern himself. In astrology this means the realization (a) that significance is testimony to advantages the native may grasp in one way or another and thus is indication of his potential or actual adaptation of eventualities into his own pattern in fulfillment of his own promise and (b) that delineation or advisement should be consistently pragmatic if it is to achieve its maximum accuracy and escape a regression to sheer ineptness.

References in the text: pp. 13, 41.

(10) Dichotomy or identity

This principle is a fundamental statement of the nature or organism, and a recognition of the inescapable cosmic order (a) in the terms of which the human mind ultimately must operate and (b) which actually is experienced by conscious individuality if through no more than the mere continuance of its own basic or self-identifying rectitude and cohesion. The continuous interchange between self and not-self that creates and maintains consciousness as such must be instrumented through any or all awareness in every possible relationship. In astrology this means the realization of the essential and basic balance among themselves of all the factors that establish

the differing structures of horoscopic analysis. Thus delineation is made possible as a function of the mind by the characteristic employment of potentialities and actualities in mutual
interpretation of each other. It is an operation that at core
should be in the broadest possible expansion of perspective.
Facilitating the limitless encompassment is the fact that for
everything on down into the most trivial details of astrological
measurement there is an opposite of equal pertinence at all
times and in all places no matter how variantly the polariza-
tion is recognized, and the equilibrium that maintains the
individual well-being in every particular area of experience
is ultimately the factor that prevents any undue regression to
disassociation.

References in the text: pp. 19, 169.

appendix II

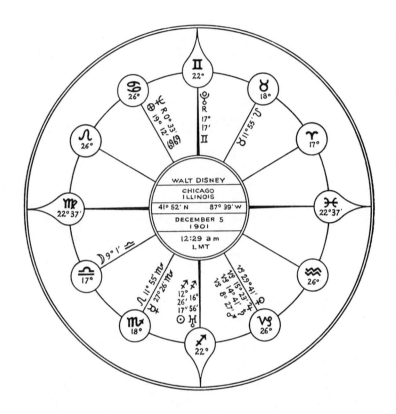

Sidereal time: 5h 22m 26s

Greenwich mean time: 6:20 a.m.

Time difference: 5h 51m

Adjusted calculation date: March 1, 1902

A PRIMER OF CALCULATION

Preliminary

The astrologer's tools for calculation are (1) ephemerides or tabulations of the geocentric places of the planets during the years in which horoscopes are to be set up, (2) tables of houses for determining the zodiacal position of the horizon or the ascendant and the other cusps of the horoscope at the moment of birth or other event to have astrological attention, (3) an atlas for finding or checking the geographical latitude and longitude of the location for which at a particular time the horoscopic chart or wheel-diagram is prepared, and (4) as a convenience or for the special niceties of computation a set of diurnal proportional logarithms. The tabulation of these logarithms usually included in an astrological ephemeris is adequate for all common operations except the preparation of a solar return, and the establishment of the sun's natal position in the horoscope if such a return is to be prepared.

In their established language the practitioners and students of astrology (1) refer to the basic wheel-diagram as a horoscope, chart, nativity, figure or map and (2) speak of (a) calculating, computing, casting, erecting, setting up, putting up or making it in the first place and then of (b) delineating, reading or inter-preting it in an analysis either of the character of the native or person for whose birth it has been prepared or of the significant factors of any special event to be given astrological attention and finally and in usual course of (c) computing progressions or directions in the dynamic analysis of the native's performance or of the actualization of his potentials together with (d) the con-

403

sideration with any necessary calculations of other and varying or supplementary techniques such as charting the transits or preparing the different returns or resorting to horary testimony and the like.

Quite properly there is a wide range of divergent astrological theory and practice, in consequence of the intellectual freedom that ever remains a veritable sine qua non of human progress. What is at issue is never the sincerity of some advocate of difference, but rather the realization that (1) established acceptance and method are the fundamental basis of reliability in human affairs and (2) any change amounting to real advancement of man's knowledge and skills tends to be gradual since it always is a small part of the whole reality of existence at any one point and therefore can seldom be assimilated into the scheme of things until there has been a continuing demonstration of its validity. The deviations at the fringe of modern horoscopy are generally slight in their modification of the long-employed techniques, and are espoused by definite minority if earnest groups. Thus as a matter of simple and practical efficiency it is best for anyone but a trained researcher to ignore them completely. There is however no escaping a rather continual adjustment to one particular divergency. This is the interchangeable use of ephemerides calculated for Greenwich noon on the one hand and for the Greenwich zero hour or midnight or the threshold of the day on the other.

In general, the tools for horoscopic calculation should be checked as follows:

(1) Is the ephemeris geocentric? It can be recognized as heliocentric if no positions are given for the sun and moon, and should not be used except by a specialist in the very deviate heliocentric astrology.

(2) Is the ephemeris based on the long-familiar zodiac established by the equinoxes, and maintained in fixed rela-

tion to them or with no adjustment to their precession? Check can be made against the wheel-diagram of Walt Disney. Unless any particular ephemeris shows the sun for December 5th in the vicinity of Sagittarius 13°, it should not be used.

(3) Does the ephemeris give noon or midnight positions? The check can be made at the equinox in late March. If the sidereal time for the day when the sun enters Aries is shown as approximately 0h 0m 0s, the planetary places are given for noon, but contrariwise if the sidereal time approximates 12h 0m 0s the tabulations are for midnight.

(4) Does the ephemeris show the planetary positions, whether at noon or midnight, in relation to the universally accepted prime meridian of Greenwich? (Greenwich observatory in London established the meridian from which terrestrial longitude has been reckoned by all countries since 1884.) Nothing else of consequence is available as this text is prepared, and the various tabulations usually label themselves as based on the 0° of terrestrial longitude. Checking is simple enough by comparison with known Greenwich positions of the moon, as in the Disney horoscope. These are later if the ephemeris is for a meridian west of Greenwich, as has been the case in the past with calculations for 75° west, and correspondingly earlier for a meridian to the east.

(5) Are the tables of houses a charting of motion in the celestial equator, as in the Placidian system that has been in long and very general use? An appreciable number of these tables established in the Campanus, Horizontal or Regiomantanus systems have an occasional employment, but they represent a theoretical or purely geometrical and so spatial division of the heavens and are a controversial distortion of astrological perspective that is best ignored

except in competent research. A given tables of houses can be checked easily by them with the tabulations in these pages of the Walt Disney Placidian cusps.

The Natal Horoscope

Before erecting a horoscope the necessary data must be marshalled. Walt Disney is used for illustrative purposes in this appendix section because he was born most recently of the example lives employed in the general exposition. Most practitioners or students making use of this text will have access to an ephemeris for 1901. In gathering the necessary horoscopic information, at the start the place of birth or event must be located on the surface of the globe with reasonable precision in terms of terrestrial latitude and longitude. This location by atlas permits the necessary individualization of the chart, and in the case of Disney the birthplace at Chicago is thus localized at 41° 52′ north and 87° 39′ west in the geographic measure.

There is nothing in common between a competent fluidity of operation and an unskilled carelessness in workmanship, whether of mental or physical nature. While an overstrain toward precision or a fetish of exactness can destroy the fine edge of every power of the human mind, a demand for preciseness of detail at every point of pertinence in any consideration of vital moment in experience is the ultimate hallmark of intelligence. If the astrologer gives his basic arithmetic the dignity with which he seeks to endow the situation brought to his attention, he continually strengthens his basic insurance of mind against the untoward and invalid or against the often unrealized leap to conclusion that is man's principal weakness as the thinking animal. In view of this overall proposition, it is well if the average student or practitioner avoids the species of shorthand notation represented by showing 41° 52′ N as 41 N 52, or in the same fashion by placing the sign of the zodiac between the degrees and minutes of longitudinal position as is done in the ephemeris but again omitting the superscript symbols. The nonmathematician in astrology needs to be reminded in every way possible that he is dealing with degrees, minutes and seconds in one instance or hours, minutes and seconds in another and so on. A hundred pennies may always make a dollar but it takes sixty seconds to make a minute, sixty minutes to make an hour or a degree, twenty-four hours to make a day, thirty degrees to make a sign, twelve signs or houses to make a circle and then there are such irregularities as the ninetieth part of a planetary semiarc in primary directions. The more the astrologer's notations remind him of the widely differing fractional elements with which he is dealing, the clearer the operations are likely to be in his own mind and in consequence the more accurate his analysis has the chance to be.

At the other pole of the matter, however, he need not pursue precision beyond his own immediate convenience. For practical purposes the terrestrial latitude and longitude can be rounded to quarter degrees, as 41° 45′ N and 87° 45′ W for Walt Disney, since this makes no significant difference in the usual calculations.

In the marshalling of needed information the concern goes next to the date, and with it of necessity the hour and minute, of birth or event. There is little protection against faulty judgment in astrology when the birthday is wrong, either by day or year. With adequate opportunity a competent astrologer by rectification can bring the hour and minute to an operational reliability, but to check the day or year can hardly be more than questionable procedure because of the enormous number of variables or shifting possibilities involved.

Mean time is established by averaging out the eccentricities of the sun's daily motion in order that clocks may function simply, and no other immediate measure of duration ever really enters human experience or requires astrological attention. A sundial shows the apparent or astronomically real time, but with no useful or perhaps even measurable preciseness. Nowadays mean time around the globe is organized in definite zones to become the standard time that virtually everywhere is the basis of clock or watch indication and of life's general schedules. This standard time, before actual horoscopic calculation, must be corrected to the mean local equivalent. In the continental United States the zones are the eastern, central, mountain and Pacific representing respectively 75°, 90°, 105° and 120° west longitude. Since fifteen degrees of terrestrial longitude corresponds to an hour of difference in time, each degree of the fifteen requires an adjustment of four minutes by the clock in correction to the local measure. It is easy to remember that where the sun gets first it obviously is later. Walt Disney at 87° 39′ W was born at about two and a quarter degrees on that side of his 90° time meridian where the sun arrived first, and so the local time of his birth was nine minutes later than the central standard. The time difference from Greenwich of 5h 51m should be noted carefully.

Daylight saving or war time is an hour later than standard in each zone, and the astrologer must find out if it was in effect at a moment of birth or event. If it was, he must deduct the hour before his other calculations. There was no daylight saving time for Walt Disney in December, 1901.

The Wheel-Diagram

The familiar wheel-diagram of the horoscope provides the eye with a combination of three fundamental elements that of themselves are quite independent of each other. They are respectively the planets, the houses and the signs. The planets in the usual practice of horoscopic diagramming are shown in the geocentric places they occupy concurrently in the two great circles described by the earth's motions in the heavens. The more immediately important one of these circles is the celestial equator. It is established by the earth's axial rotation that creates the alternation of day and night or waking and sleeping as the most fundamental cycle of human experience. This circle is divided into the twelve pie-shaped segments of the heavenly vault known as the houses of astrology, and they are shown most commonly by printed lines in the wheel-diagram. The house cusps are not taken to center, but rather to the rim of a smaller circle or globe that can represent the earth as central in all horoscopic perspective. In a sense these houses, through which the change-less sky makes its promenade around the earth every day are the actual horoscope in its most simple manifestation of itself. Through them the circumstances of man's existence and individual potentialities are scaled out initially at birth in relation to his individual horizon on the one hand and to his personal zenith of reality on the other.

The second great heavenly circle is established by the annual revolution of the earth in its orbit in the solar system as a satellite of the sun. This motion of the terrestrial globe creates the ecliptic, which is given astrological form in a zodiac comprising another and separate division of the heavens into twelve equal segments. The astrologers identify these as signs rather than houses, and take them as representation of the seasonal or summer-winter cycles of human experience. They are seen to embrace all natural phenomena of personal concern in the more generalized or more common and so less individualized functions and conveniences of reality.

The planes of these two celestial circles lie some twenty-three degrees away from each other in outer space. Since the planetary bodies used in astrology have their own orbits in their particular circling of the sun, and these with but slight deviation lie in the same plane as the earth's ecliptic, it is convenient to consider their positions in the zodiacal measure created by the earth. Fortuitously the orbit of the earth's own moon falls into the same situation, and needs no special adjustment or separate treatment on this account in usual horoscopic practice. As a further convenience each house cusp is shown in the zodiacal terms corresponding to its equatorial position, by notation in the wheel-diagram, to indicate the point where it is sweeping the sky. Visualization of each of these two astrological schemes of the cosmos must conceive it as comprising the whole vault collectively, and see each separate house or sign as a sort of orange-slice segment of the three-dimensional infinity. The established manner for showing the positions of the planetary bodies, and any supplementary elements in the astrological symbolism, is by notation in degree and minute of zodiacal sign of each location and is illustrated in the Walt Disney horoscope.

The astrological ephemeris shows the position of the zenith point of the house circle in the heavens at the meridian of Greenwich at either the noon or midnight of the particular tabulations for any particular year or day. By what the medievals presumably thought to be an aid to calculation, this position is shown in hours and minutes or in terms of the span of twenty-four hours instead of 360 degrees. What thus comes to be known as sidereal time, and often is so listed without further explanation in the ephemeris, is of course identification of place on a circle. To determine the houses for a horoscope the sidereal time for the noon or midnight immediately previous to the moment of birth or event must usually be subjected to two necessary corrections as a basic step in calculation. A rather common practice in horoscopic computations, that tends to contribute to accuracy in the mathematical processes, is to keep all operations a matter of addition as long as reasonable facility is served or as here in working always from the previous noon or midnight in the erection of a chart.

If the terrestrial longitude of the place of birth or event differs from Greenwich, the first correction must be made. Since the sun in determining noon or midnight moves approximately a zodiacal degree toward meeting its prior position once a day, an hour of clock time is a little shorter than an hour of arc in a circle and there must be compensation for this in the astrological computations. The terrestrial longitudinal difference from Greenwich in degrees determines the correction from mean to sidereal time at the rate of approximately ten seconds of time for each fifteen degrees, or exactly 9.86 seconds if taken from the table in more precise calculation.

For west geographic longitudes the correction is added to the sidereal for the previous noon or midnight given in the ephemeris, but if the terrestrial latitude of birth or event is east of Greenwich the correction is subtracted instead. Holding here to addition in preference would simply be cumbersome.

If birth or event has not occurred at the Greenwich noon or midnight of the ephemeris employed for the calculations, the second correction must be made. It is the same adjustment for the difference between clock and full-circle time. For each hour and fraction elapsed from the previous noon or midnight the same approximate ten or precise 9.86 seconds per hour must always be added to correct the elapsed time. The product of these operations is the sidereal time of the midheaven of the chart under calculation, and the total of them can be illustrated in the case of Walt Disney as follows:

Sidereal time at Greenwich noon, December 4, 1901	16h	50m	25s
Correction, Greenwich to Chicago			58
Elapsed time from previous noon to birth	12	29	
Its correction to sidereal time		2	3
	28	81	86
By subtraction of 24h, and reduction of terms	5	22	26

The Tables of Houses

With a sidereal time of the zenith point of the horoscope thus determined according to the geographic longitude of the place

CORRECTION, MEAN TO SIDEREAL TIME

Mean time	Add		Mean time	Add	Mean time	Add	Mean time	Add
1h 0m	9.86s		1m	0.16s	25m	4.11s	49m	8.05s
2 0	19.71		2	0.33	26	4.27	50	8.21
3 0	29.57		3	0.49	27	4.43	51	8.38
4 0	39.43		4	0.66	28	4.60	52	8.54
5 0	49.28		5	0.82	29	4.76	53	8.71
6 0	59.14		6	0.99	30	4.93	54	8.87
7 1	9.00		7	1.15	31	5.09	55	9.03
8 1	18.85		8	1.31	32	5.26	56	9.20
9 1	28.71		9	1.48	33	5.42	57	9.36
10 1	38.57		10	1.64	34	5.58	58	9.53
11 1	48.42		11	1.81	35	5.75	59	9.69
12 1	58.28		12	1.97	36	5.91	60	9.86
13 2	8.13		13	2.14	37	6.08		
14 2	17.99		14	2.30	38	6.24		
15 2	27.85		15	2.46	39	6.41		
16 2	37.70		16	2.63	40	6.57		
17 2	47.56		17	2.79	41	6.73		
18 2	57.42		18	2.96	42	6.90		
19 3	7.27		19	3.12	43	7.06		
20 3	17.13		20	3.28	44	7.23		
21 3	26.99		21	3.45	45	7.39		
22 3	36.84		22	3.61	46	7.56		
23 3	46.70		23	3.78	47	7.72		
24 3	56.56		24	3.94	48	7.88		

and the elapsed time from the previous noon or midnight of birth or event, the next recourse is to the tables of houses where this corrected zenith point of the house circle is identified as the midheaven or tenth house in both the zodiacal terms that now will be employed and the corresponding right ascension that will have a more specialized use in the dynamic horoscopy. Since the midheaven lies in the celestial equator, or in a plane that as created by the same motion is parallel to it in terrestrial terms, it is the same for all parts of either the northern or southern hemisphere although the cusps other than the tenth and fourth are different by necessity at any point on the globe below the geographic equator.

The individual with little astronomical background may find the celestial mechanics characterized by seemingly endless and baffling exceptions to whatever basic rules may be put down. This is a consequence of the almost illimitable irregularities in the specific components of the physical cosmos. The earth is not round nor its surface smooth nor its orbit circular. The planets employed in astrology not only have their orbits in the same heavenly plane to merely an approximate extent but they exhibit continual modifications among themselves beyond their geocentric manifestation as a result of variations of gravitational influence and the like on toward an infinity of deviation. Astrologers need have little concern with these ultimate niceties, since on very practical grounds they must work with rounded or averaged factors in order to have a common measure for the variations in mankind. Thus horoscopy uses mean time and ignores leap year. It equates 365-odd days with 360 degrees, and finds correspondences in one context that may in no wise exist in any other. Without such an accommodation to an overworld of as much disjunction as concordance, the astrological operations would be too complicated for human minds and probably even for computers held to the capacities of their human programming.

Astrology is a highly symbolical science that must at all times be recognized for what it is, and practiced with a full knowledge of its limitations no less than of its powers.

Except for a person born at the earth's equator when an equinox is at the midheaven, the horizon falls into all sorts of irregularity as can be observed on a geographic globe by moving a small card around the surface at random to represent the horizon at any chance time and place. If a pin is put through the card and kept pointed to the center of the earth as well as perpendicular to the card, it is easy to note the possibly extravagant tilting of the horizon against the norm or when birth or event is on the terrestrial equator. A card used in this way of course will not reveal the slight distinction even at the equator between the cases of an equinox or a solstice at the midheaven. The horizon is the basic determinator of the horoscope, although this fact is somewhat obscured by the mathematical primacy of the midheaven and its distribution of the overall or more general against the more individual specifics of existence. Effective delineation must never forget that the horizon identifies the very ground or functioning foundation of all personal identity.

The houses of the horoscope, defined by lines printed or drawn on the wheel-diagram, are known by number. Their designation counterclockwise from the meridian as cusp of the tenth is through an eleventh and twelfth to the horizon found at the east or left hand (astrology always reversing the compass directions of a geographic map) and there identifying the ascendant or first house. After the second and third of these equatorial mansions, the nadir or lower line of the midheaven meridian defines the fourth house and the continuing process in the western hemisphere marks out the fifth through the ninth. The older custom of printing or writing the house numbers on the chart is now generally abandoned. In erecting the horoscopic figure the houses other than the tenth are taken from the tables of houses for the geographic latitude of birth or event, and the distribution in their corresponding zodiacal positions on the one side of the circle is complemented by the inverse of these positions on the opposite side. Thus in the case of Walt Disney born at 41° 52′ north the eleventh house cusp of Cancer 26° is balanced with a Capricorn 26° cusp for the fifth, and so on. In usual practice the indication of minutes as well as degrees of arc for other than the ascendant and descendant is seldom of value, but it is well to make sure that the next full degree is always taken in case there ever is resort to the symbolization of the degrees. Thus the Disney midheaven, that will be found to be Gemini 21° 23′, is rounded as Gemini 22° rather than Gemini 21°.

Interpolation

It cannot be emphasized too often that an astrologer in virtually all his computation is making approximations, and ending up at nearly all points with approximate judgments. This is inescapable in the universal reality of chance and change, or of the freedom to be different as well as the inability to avoid some cooperative conformity to concomitant factors of limitation. In principle his mathematics must involve continual interpolation, or an estimate of fractions of value between fixed points or lines of measure, and in consequence he must remember that the fixities between which he determines any special pertinency for his immediate purpose are by the very nature of things no more than a convenience as far as he is concerned. Actually the widespread arbitrariness of all reality is a matter ultimately of logical structures necessary for the operation of human thought. The essential transience of any organization or realization of life's actuality is seen in the modern development of the metric system to supplant a primitive extemporization of units of weight and volume, or in the modification in similar fashion of the Fahrenheit in the centigrade temperature scale. The establishment of mean time to simplify the mechanics of everyday temporal indication has already been noted. The origin or rationale of many common modes of measure remains unknown, but obviously they evolved in an outgroping consciousness far anterior to any recorded history as in the highly sophisticated arrangement of 360 degrees in a circle with sixty minutes to each degree and sixty seconds to each minute. By comparison the acceptance of a Greenwich prime meridian for a globe-wide indication of geographic longitude is almost indecently recent.

Thus history is the record of man's approximations in the delimitation and enhancement of his particular context in the universal reality. At times his progress was desperately slow. The location and employment of the equator as a base for terrestrial latitude seem logically very elementary in today's hindsight, but the founding of a science of geodesy or geodetics among the Greeks provides an excellent illustration of the puttering outreach of mind at work when unaware of the entangling blind spots of everyday acceptance. Greek scholars did blunder through, and in passing lay the foundation for the horoscope. In dramatic contrast was the strange failure of the wonderfully civilized Babylonians and Egyptians to deduce the fact that the earth was a sphere, even while they excelled in astronomy and while their mental block at this point was challenged by such obvious phenomena as the shape of the shadow eclipsing the moon or the fact that when a ship approached port the masts were always to be seen before the hull. Here is testimony to the extraordinary difficulty with which any mind ever really transcends the familiar grooves of its thinking, and so to the particular necessity for an unusually fluid comprehension as a prime characteristic of the competent astrologer.

Simple interpolation is nearly always necessary in locating the houses of the horoscope through the use of the tables of houses. Employing the Dalton calculations according to the Placidian method of house division in his *Spherical Basis of Astrology,* the sidereal time for the midheaven that has been obtained for the Disney chart or 5h 22m 26s is more than the 5h 20m 49s column in the Dalton tables. Looking to the next or 5h 25m 10s column, it can be seen that the amount of sidereal time corresponding to a midheaven movement in Gemini from an even 21° to 22° is 4m 21s. It must be remembered that in calculations around a circle it is possible to add or subtract either the 360 degrees or the twenty-four hours as needed. Degrees or hours may be reduced to minutes or vice versa, and minutes to seconds or vice versa, as in all mathematics dealing with whole and subordinate units of the same scheme of measure. Thus 5h 25m 10s is reduced to 5h 24m 70s to permit the operation as follows:

$$
\begin{array}{rrr}
5h & 24m & 70s \\
-5 & 20 & 49 \\
\hline
& 4 & 21
\end{array}
$$

It now is necessary to see how much zodiacal movement beyond Gemini 21° is needed to reach and locate the Disney midheaven in the zodiac. The sidereal time that represents this is the difference between the 5h 20m 49s of Gemini 21° and the 5h 22m 26s of that midheaven, found as follows:

$$
\begin{array}{rrr}
5h & 21m & 86s \\
-5 & 20 & 49 \\
\hline
& 1 & 37
\end{array}
$$

The Rule of Three

The rule of three was once the acme of elementary or pioneer education. Thus, if ten yards of a certain floor covering costs $150, what would twenty yards cost? Put in proportion form this would be:

$$10 \quad : \quad 20 \quad : : \quad 150 \quad : \quad x$$

The product of the means (here 20 and 150) equals the product of the extremes (here 10 and x). If in the case of either pairing the product by multiplication can be known, the known partial factor in the other pairing can be divided into the known product, and the result will be the previously unknown factor represented by the "x." 20 times 150 is 3000, which divided by 10 is 300. Thus 20 yards will cost $300. Note that the elements on each side of such a proportion must be of the same order and measure. The problem at this point is to find what the ratio of 1m 37s to 4m 21s in sidereal time means in zodiacal minutes and seconds to be added to Gemini 21° for a precise Disney midheaven in terms of the zodiac. The proposition is: 1m 37s : 4m 21s : : x : 60′, and reduction to seconds both of sidereal time and zodiacal measure for sake of manipulation is necessary, thus:

$$97 \quad : \quad 261 \quad : : \quad x \quad : \quad 3600$$

3600 multiplied by 97 is 349, 200, which divided by 261 is 1337.9, and which in turn as seconds is 22′ 17.9″ to establish the midheaven at Gemini 21° 22′ 18″.

A facility with simple fractions and a reasonable skill in eye inspection can greatly shorten the interpolation process, and in astrology this becomes a commonplace in the multiple-fraction method or the use of a primary fraction plus a fraction of it if necessary and even perhaps a fraction of the first subsidiary one. Here the movement of 1m 37s out of 4m 21s of sidereal time is a case of (1) a quarter of the whole 4m 21s or 1m 5s plus (2) approximately a half of the 1m 5s, or 32s, which add to 1m 5s to become 1m 37s or the given increment in sidereal time. A quarter of 60° of zodiacal measure is 15′, and a half of the 15′ is 7′-plus, so that the total of 22′-plus gives Disney a midheaven of Gemini 21° 22′-plus in general agreement with the more precise calculation.

In the Rice tabulations of the *American Astrology Tables of Houses* each column presents an even four minutes of sidereal time in the advancement of the midheaven in the celestial equator rather than the even zodiacal degree of advance in the Dalton tables. However, the location of Walt Disney's individual midheaven proceeds in similar fashion. Its sidereal time of 5h 22m 26s is next beyond the column for 5h 20m 0s from which the calculation proceeds. The amount of movement necessary to reach the Disney midheaven from the column of reference must be determined thus:

$$
\begin{array}{ccc}
5h & 22m & 26s \\
-\ 5 & 20 & 0 \\
\hline
& 2 & 26
\end{array}
$$

Then the total zodiacal distance between the midheavens of the column of reference and its next at another four minutes of sidereal time must be noted, with Gemini 21° 43′ 56″ expressed as Gemini 20° 103′ 56″, thus:

Gemini midheaven for sidereal time 5h 24m 0s		20° 103′ 56″
Gemini midheaven for sidereal time 5 20 0		20 48 39
		55 17

The proportion then becomes:

$$
\begin{array}{ccccccc}
2m & 26s & : & 4m & :: & x & : & 55′\ 17″ \\
\text{or} & 146s & : & 240s & :: & x & : & 3317″
\end{array}
$$

Multiplying 3317 by 146 produces 484282, which divided by 240 is 2017.8 or 33′ 37.8″ to be added to Gemini 20° 48′ 39″ to show Gemini 20° 81′ 76.8″ or Gemini 21° 22′ 17″ as the Disney midheaven.

By the fractional calculation in connection with the Rice tables of houses the determination of the fractional nature of the incre-

PLACIDIAN HOUSE CUSPS IN COMPARISON

Calculations by:		Joseph G. Dalton (1893)		Hugh S. Rice (1944)	
		5h 20m 49s	5h 25m 10s	5h 20m 0s	5h 24m 0s
Sidereal time of midheaven	All latitudes				
10th cusp		Ⅱ 21°	Ⅱ 22°	Ⅱ 20°48′39″	Ⅱ 21°43′58″
11th cusp	Lat. 41°N Lat. 42°N	♋ 24°.9 ♋ 25°.1	♋ 25°.8 ♋ 26°.1	♋ 24°38′.7 ♋ 24°51′.8	♋ 25°32′.3 ♋ 25°45′.4
12th cusp	Lat. 41°N Lat. 42°N	♌ 25°.6 ♌ 25°.9	♌ 26°.5 ♌ 26°.8	♌ 25°28′.3 ♌ 25°42′.5	♌ 26°19′.3 ♌ 26°33′.2
1st cusp	Lat. 41°N Lat. 42°N	♍ 22°15′ ♍ 22°19′	♍ 23° 6′ ♍ 23°10′	♍ 22° 5′.2 ♍ 22° 9′.8	♍ 22°52′.7 ♍ 22°56′.8
2d cusp	Lat. 41°N Lat. 42°N	♎ 17°.6 ♎ 17°.4	♎ 18°.6 ♎ 18°.5	♎ 17°22′.6 ♎ 17°15′.2	♎ 18°14′.5 ♎ 18° 6′.7
3d cusp	Lat. 41°N Lat. 42°N	♏ 17°.5 ♏ 17°.3	♏ 18°.5 ♏ 18°.3	♏ 17°19′.6 ♏ 17° 9.2	♏ 18°14′.3 ♏ 18° 3′.8

ment to the Disney midheaven by interpolation between the two
midheavens in the tables is still in the sidereal time where all
factors are known. Half of the 4m between columns is 2m, and
a quarter of 2m is 30s, or together 2m 30s as adequate approximation to the 2m 26s of increment. The total amount of
zodiacal movement of midheavens between the two columns in
the tables has already been found to be 55′ 17″. Thus:

Half of the zodiacal span		27′	38.5″
A quarter of this half		6	54.8
		33	93.3
Gemini midheaven for 5h 20m 0s	20° 48	39	
Gemini midheaven for 5 22 26	20	81	132.3
or	21	23	12.3

If three fractions had been used, to narrow the approximations
of 2m 30s for 2m 26s of increment, or plus a half plus a quarter
of the half minus a seventh of that quarter:

		33′	93.3″
	—		59.1
To add to Gemini 20° 48′ 39″		33	34.2
	20°48	39	
The Gemini midheaven	20	81	73.2
or	21	22	13

Except in the case of the ascendant, the next full degree is
sufficient exactitude for a house cusp under ordinary circumstances. The midheaven usually is rounded, but its calculation
is needed to minutes. For all cusps except the midheaven a double
interpolation may be necessary, and in the instance of Walt
Disney the nearest simple fraction for the difference in cusp
location between geographic latitudes 41° and 42° north should
be subtracted from the locations shown for 42° in the tables of
houses. This fraction is taken as a sixth. Calculations for a
seventh as representing eight-sixtieths could not possibly have
more significance in this operation. For his eleventh-house cusp

by the relatively quick fractional method and using Dalton's tabulations for an even Gemini 21° on the midheaven, the increase in Cancer longitude at that cusp from latitudes 41° to 42° is .2° or 12′, of which a sixth is 2′. The 22′ of Gemini longitude the Disney midheaven has advanced from Gemini 21° 0′ to 22° 0′ can by simple fraction be taken as a third. The advance in Cancer longitude at the eleventh cusp at 42° geographic latitude from the one column to the next in the tables is precisely 60′ of which a third is 20′, or as obvious to the eye the precise 22′ can be taken. Cancer 25.1° is expressed as 25° 6′ from which 2′ is subtracted to give 25° 4′, and to which 20′ or 22′ are added to give 25° 24′ or 25° 26′. This rounds to Cancer 26°.

By the Rice tables and working from right ascension 5h 20m 0s at the midheaven, the sixth of diminished Cancer longitude for geographic latitude 42° compared to latitude 41° of 13.1′ is approximately 2′ as again the first correction. The increment in midheaven sidereal time in these tabulations from 5h 20m 0s to 5h 24m 0s embraces the increment from the 5h 20m 0s of the column of reference to the 5h 22m 26s of the Disney midheaven and it is the 2m 26s that fractionally is the half plus a quarter of the half of previous calculation. The longitudinal increase of the 11th cusp in Cancer at 42° north terrestrial latitude, from the column of reference to the next, is 53.6′ of which a half is 26.8′ and a quarter of the half is 6.7′ to add to 26.8′ and becomes 33.5′ as the second correction. The interpolation becomes:

11th cusp for 5h 20m 0s midheaven at 42° north: Cancer 24° 51.8′
                                          minus   2
                                                ─────────────
                                                   24 49.8
                                          plus   33.5
                                                ─────────────
                                                   24 83.3
                                          or   25 23

which also rounds to Cancer 26°.

A rather precise location of the ascendant is calculated generally, and it becomes very essential in connection with the primary directions. Double interpolation is usually necessary and in the case of Walt Disney and using the Dalton tables of houses the first correction of a Virgo ascendant at 42° north geographic latitude for a Gemini 21° midheaven diminishes it to adjust to 8' of this latitude less than 42° north. The total Virgo increment from 41° to 42° north is 4' or 240". Thus 8' : 60' : : x : 240". Multiplying 240 by 8 produces 1920 which divided by 60 is 32. The second correction involves the increment in Virgo longitude at 42° north at the ascendant in correspondence to the zodiacal longitude increase in Gemini at the Disney midheaven out of the even degree between Gemini 21° and 22°. The total Virgo increase at 42° north in correlation with the Gemini degree at the midheaven is 51'. Thus 22 : 60 : : x : 51. 22 and 51 multiplied are 1122, which divided by 60 is 18.7 or 18' 42". The ascendant then is:

Virgo	22° 18' 60"	
minus	32	
	22 18 28	
plus	18 42	
	22 36 70	
or	22 37 10	or Virgo 22° 37'

With the Rice tables the first correction is determined by the proportion 8 : 60 : : x : 4.6, and it becomes 36.8". The second correction on the basis of the increment in sidereal time at the midheaven from 5h 20m 0s to the Disney midheaven at 5h 22m 26s in proportionate part of the 4m from column to column, and in connection with the increase in Virgo longitude at 42° north latitude from column to column of 47' establishes the proportion 2m 26s : 4m : : x : 47 or 146 : 240 : : x : 47. The result is 28' 36", and the ascendant then is:

Virgo	22°	9′	48″
minus			37
	22	9	11
plus		28	36
	22	37	47	or Virgo 22° 38′

The Southern Hemisphere

When a birth or event takes place in the southern hemisphere the steps in erecting the horoscope need special adjustment in a single detail only. The distortion of the equatorial houses in zodiacal terms must be the inverse of what it is in the northern. This result is obtained easily by (1) adding 12h to the sidereal time of the midheaven for the purpose of using the familiar tables of houses and (2) then substituting the opposite sign on each cusp for the one shown by the tables in this inverted use.

The Planetary Places

In order to place the planets in the horoscope, their zodiacal positions in degrees and minutes at the moment of birth or event must be obtained as the basis of notation of their places in the wheel-diagram. Often the sun's position is needed in degrees, minutes and seconds. Their placement in best practice is immediately next to the cusp in the sign in which they lie whether on the one side or the other of the cusp and close to the outer circle, as seen in the Walt Disney example. Their degrees and minutes should be next to the planetary symbol and toward the center of the chart so as to be read from left to right or down vertically as may be most convenient for reference without turning the wheel. The symbol of the sign in which they lie should come next toward the center. Retrogradation or near station should have its symbol between the planet and its degrees and minutes. This general arrangement permits the eye to sweep easily around the equatorial circle in uninterrupted fashion, and thus determine the many varying but complementary patterns to be taken into account with each necessary shift in logical perspective or change of focus in inquiry or investigation. In usual practice the moon's north and south nodes, or the dragon's head and tail respectively, and the part of fortune are added to the ten planets now employed as at times a subsidiary but enlightening contribution to analysis. Complicating the horoscopic diagram with factors beyond these few of primary import may easily lead to confusion, however, by confronting the mind at some particular point with too much indication of widely varying nature or reference.

For calculating the planetary places the moment of birth or event must be expressed in Greenwich mean time in order to use the ephemerides that in general are computed for noon or midnight at Greenwich. The elapsed time from the previous noon or midnight is found in its proportional part of the given twenty-four hours, and by the rule of three this ratio shows how far each planet moves in zodiacal degrees to its horoscopic place out of its total movement in the same twenty-four hours. Mercury in the case of Walt Disney is shown at Scorpio 26° 17′ at noon on December 4th, and at Scorpio 27° 47′ the next noon. Hence its daily motion is 1° 30′ or 90′. Since the Greenwich mean time for this chart is 6:20 a.m., the elapsed time from the previous noon is 18h 20m and by the fractional method this is a half of 24h plus a half of the half plus an eighteenth of the second half. Using the ratio for the planet's motion, the half of 90′ is 45′ and the second half 22.5′ and the eighteenth a little more than 1′ or a total of approximately 69′ of motion necessary to add to Scorpio 26° 17′ and thus reveal Mercury's place in the horoscope at Scorpio 26° 86′ or Scorpio 27° 26′.

If a planet is retrograde the required motion is subtracted as with Neptune in the Disney wheel-diagram. The daily motion is 2′, and so the required motion is 1′ plus .5′ plus .03′ or 1.53′ that rounds to 2′ to be subtracted from the noon position on December 4th and place Neptune at Cancer 0° 33′.

Logarithms

The rule of three can be very cumbersome when a necessary reduction of minutes to seconds means an operation with sizable numbers, and then too with large numbers the chance of error is increased. With slow-moving planets such as Neptune the mathematics becomes simple and quick, but in many cases as with the moon the employment of logarithms can facilitate the use of the geometrical proportion through the method of multiplying by adding and dividing by subtracting. The Merriam-Webster dictionary in defining this device of working with the powers of numbers rather than with the numbers directly, illustrates its definition with the statement that 4 is the logarithm of 16 to the base 2. This suggests a possibly helpful over-simplification in taking a sequence or 2 in multiplication of itself with the powers shown by superscript number to identify the logarithms thus:

$$2 \quad 4^2 \quad 8^3 \quad 16^4 \quad 32^5 \quad 64^6 \quad 128^7$$

To multiply 16 by 8, add 4 and 3 to get 7 and find 128 as the product desired. To divide 64 by 8, subtract 3 from 6 to get the 3 that identifies 8 as the desired result.

In the astrological employment of this device there always is the proportion:

| elapsed time to moment of birth or event from previous noon or midnight | : | 24h | : : | x (degrees needed to reach planet's horoscopic place) | : | degrees planet moves in twenty-four hours |

Thus 24h must always divide the product of the daily motion and the time from noon or midnight and in consequence it has been possible to prepare the diurnal proportional logarithms, in which in a sense the division by twenty-four is precalculated. Thereupon it is only necessary to add the logarithms of the daily motion and the elapsed time to obtain a logarithm of the required movement for the planet to reach its horoscopic place. The logarithm for Mercury's daily motion is 1.20412 and for the time from noon is .11697, and by adding them the logarithm 1.32109 identifies 1° 8′ 45″ or 1° 9′ to be added to Scorpio 26° 17′ or show Mercury's place in the chart to be at Scorpio 27° 26′.

Some tables of diurnal proportional logarithms cover only fifteen of the twenty-four hours, but they can be used when an elapsed time is more than fifteen hours by using the interval to the following noon or midnight and subtracting the result of the calculation from the planet's position on the following noon or midnight. Thus the interval in Greenwich mean time from 6:20 a.m. to noon on December 5th is 5h 40m, for which the logarithm is .62688. Adding to this the logarithm of Mercury's daily motion or 1.20412 produces 1.83100 or the logarithm for 21′. This subtracted from Scorpio 27° 47′ is Scorpio 27° 26′.

It is good practice to use these logarithms always for calculating the moon's position in a horoscope, and the result can be checked by the fractional method. The moon's daily motion in Walt Disney's case is 12° 4′ for which the logarithm is .29862, to be added to the .11697 for the elapsed time already found in connection with Mercury, and the resulting .41559 is the logarithm for 9° 13′ which when added to Virgo 29° 48′ locates his natal moon at Libra 9° 1′. This can be confirmed by the fractional method thus:

Virgo	29°	48′
Half of 12° 4′	6	2
Half of the half	3	1
An eighteenth of that		10
	38	61
or Libra	9	1

The Part of Fortune

The part of fortune has a particular importance over all the Arabian supplementary ascendants because it is the distance of the moon from the sun counterclockwise in the zodiac or is the point of synodical lunation in the nativity as this has a special projection counterclockwise from the ascendant. It is calculated most simply by adding the celestial longitudes of the moon and ascendant and then subtracting the celestial longitude of the sun. Most astrologers put down the number of the sign rather than the total of whole signs from the vernal equinox, but adding 1 to all terms achieves the same purpose. The calculations for Walt Disney would be as follows:

	Signs	Degrees	Minutes	Signs	Degrees	Minutes
Moon	6	9	1	7	9	1
Ascendant	5	22	37	6	22	37
	11	31	38	13	31	38
Sun	− 8	12	26	9	12	26
	3	19	12	4	19	12
The part	Cancer 19° 12′			Cancer 19° 12′		

The Secondary Directions

The calculation of the secondary directions, in which each successive day after birth corresponds to a year of life successively, has had general explanation beginning on page 379. The adjusted calculation date for Walt Disney is determined, in accordance with the method there explained of using the familiar column of sidereal time in the ephemeris as a convenient scaling of twenty-four hours against 365-odd days, by first adding the interval from birth to the following noon in Greenwich time or 5h 40m to the sidereal time of the birthday in the noon ephemeris or 16h 54m 21s to obtain 21h 94m 21s or 22h 34m 21s as the sidereal time to be found in correspondence to the calendar date of the artificial birthday. Since birth was prior to noon on December 5th in Greenwich mean time the planets still must move to their positions on that noon, and the adjusted calculation date must follow December 5th even if into the next year. March 1, 1902 is identified as the artificial birthday since 22h 33m 25s or the sidereal time for that date provides the closest approximation to 22h 34m 21s.

In preparation for the interpretation of the secondary directions it is necessary in any thoroughness of operation to take each of the nine planets other than the moon in turn through the span of days representing the whole of the years actually lived or on beyond the present as far as concern for a living native may dictate, and list all the major zodiacal aspects it can make in this progression in their sequence. The nature and significance of the aspects has been given a complete exposition in the main text, beginning on page 21. While the moon is handled in the same way it covers too much ground in a lifetime to be tabulated for more than perhaps extensive periods of particular or immediate concern. It is not necessary in normal course to determine the dates of culmination of these progressed aspects except as they have practical significance in some pertinent context. Stations of planets in progression should be listed along with the aspects in their common sequence. These tabulations for both Abraham Lincoln and Annie Besant, and in their instance completed with date of aspect culmination, are listed in Appendix I.

Walt Disney is the example taken for the activity-facet of basic sensitivity in the more general exposition of the dynamic analysis beginning on page 333 in the main text. His Venus by progression moves from its birth position at Capricorn 29° 41' by normal zodiacal motion to Pisces 3° 21', at which point it is stationary and then moves back to Aquarius 29° 35' at the time of his decease or shortly after his birthday in 1966. Its complete performance in secondary directions therefore was as follows:

Venus progressed in	trine with	natal moon
	sextile	natal sun
	sextile	natal Uranus
	trine	natal Pluto
	square	natal Mercury
	trine	natal Neptune
	stationary going retrograde	
	trine	natal Neptune

Calculating the date of culmination of a progressed aspect is a simple modification of the process for finding the planetary places in the erection of a horoscope. The lack of available biographical information as this text is prepared is a handicap in presenting adequate illustration at this point, especially in the subtlety of the basic sensitivity, but in the basic attitude of Walt Disney the progressed opposition of Mercury with natal Neptune has dramatic correspondence to his move to Hollywood to start his own company and to put down the foundation of his career in 1923. In correlation with March 1, 1923, in his life, Mercury on December 26, 1901, has moved to Capricorn 0° 10′. In correlation with March 1, 1924, on December 27, 1901, it was at Capricorn 1° 45′. Thus the movement charting the year of life in the basic attitude was 95′ or almost an exact 8′ a month. Mercury consummated the opposition at Capricorn 0° 33′, or in a movement of 23′ requiring approximately three months and identifying the date as around June 1, 1923. Hugh Rice in the *American Astrology Tables of Houses* presents tables for the determination of maturity of progressed aspect to a more precise degree, as in this instance giving the date as May 28, 1923.

The use of diurnal proportional logarithms in determining the time of culmination of a secondary direction requires an adjustment that was summarized without explanation in the main text.

The nature of the proportion now set up is as follows:

| x (time needed from artificial birthday to complete direction) | : | 24h | : : | zodiacal movement culminating in the direction | : | movement corresponding to year of life |

To be noted is that the unknown factor x is here in ratio with the inbuilt 24h factor. In consequence the manipulation of the proportion must be inverted in employing these logarithms, or the desired result obtained by division through subtraction rather than multiplication through addition. Disney's progressed Mercury in opposition with his natal Neptune can be taken to illustrate this form of the operation.

Logarithm of 23' (zodiacal distance moved to aspect)   1.79663
Logarithm of 95' (whole motion in day indicating year)   1.18064
                                                            ─────────
                                                             0.61599

Logarithm 0.61599 identifies a span of 5h 49m out of the 24h between the artificial birthdays of March 1st in 1923 and 1924. Using the column of sidereal time as purely a convenience, the 5h 49m is added to the 22h 33m 4s corresponding to March 1st in 1923 to produce 27h 82m 4s or 4h 22m 4s which in 1923 correspond most closely to May 29th for the culmination of the progression.

The Tertiary Directions

In the ideal or precise calculation of the tertiary directions the particular day, hour and minute of synodical lunation after birth to be taken in correlation with a year of life is determined and the exact zodiacal distance traversed by the moon from such moment of synodical lunation to the next is taken and divided into four equal quarters computed to degrees, minutes and seconds of arc. Each of these lunar quarters in turn provides the

WALT DISNEY'S TERTIARY PERIODS

Year of life	Previous lunation	Synodical lunation	Tertiary periods	Seasons of indication
36th	October 9, 1904	November 3d { ☽ ♍ 6°55' / ☉ ♏ 10°19' }	♍ 6°	Midwinter, 1937-8
			♐ 14°	Midspring, 1938
			♓ 21°	Midsummer,
			♊ 28°	Midautumn,
37th	November 7, 1904	December 2d { ☽ ♎ 6°22' / ☉ ♐ 9°44' }	♎ 6°	Midwinter, 1938-9
			♑ 14°	Midspring, 1939
			♈ 21°	Midsummer,
			♋ 29°	Midautumn,
38th	December 7, 1904	December 31st { ☽ ♏ 6°14' / ☉ ♑ 9°38' }	♏ 6°	Midwinter, 1939-40
			♒ 13°	Midspring, 1940

special progressed measure for the intimate emotional and psychological involvement of the native's make-up for a corresponding one of four equal three-month seasons beginning with the one true rather than artificial birthday and ending with the next. This is extremely intricate and time-consuming procedure, and hardly justified except in connection with a depth and length of analysis similar to psychoanalytical thoroughness. Genuine illustration is impossible since whoever is able to enter very far into the sanctum sanctorum of a human soul even if a very important and superficially well-known public person?

A generalized utilization of the tertiaries is possible by calculating to the approximate day rather than down to the hour and minute of synodical lunation, as suggested and with the details of calculation given in the main text beginning on page 381 and illustrated in the life of Abraham Lincoln in the earlier section starting on page 157. The possibility that in the Lincoln interpretations, at remote view in time and with the vastly later context of present history, the delineations really could penetrate very far into the mysterious melancholia of the great American myth figure is very questionable but the nature of this analytical measure deserves at least some practical clarification as part of the general dynamic horoscopy. A specimen of tertiary calculation for Walt Disney is presented as a mathematical example.

The Primary Directions

What complicates the mathematics of primary directions is the fact that the scheme of motion that provides their base for progression is entirely independent of the actual situation and movement of the planets in their own physical orbits. It is necessary to make sure that any consideration of a zodiacal nature be disregarded completely, and an initial step in consequence is to translate the birth positions or particular horoscopic place of each of them into right ascension. There are widely available tables of equivalent right ascension from which the planetary

EQUIVALENT RIGHT ASCENSION

Latitude north	0°		1°		2°		3°		4°		5°		6°		7°		Latitude south
	°	′	°	′	°	′	°	′	°	′	°	′	°	′	°	′	
♈ 0	0	0	359	36	359	12	358	48	358	24	358	0	357	36	357	12	0 ♎
4	3	40	3	16	2	52	2	29	2	5	1	41	1	16	0	52	4
8	7	21	6	57	6	33	6	9	5	45	5	21	4	57	4	33	8
12	11	2	10	39	10	15	9	51	9	27	9	3	8	39	8	15	12
16	14	44	14	21	13	58	13	34	13	11	12	47	12	23	11	59	16
20	18	28	18	5	17	42	17	19	16	55	16	32	16	8	15	45	20
24	22	13	21	51	21	28	21	5	20	42	20	19	19	56	19	33	24
28	26	0	25	38	25	16	24	54	24	32	24	9	23	46	23	23	28
♉ 2	29	49	29	28	29	7	28	45	28	23	28	1	27	39	27	17	2 ♏
6	33	41	33	21	33	0	32	39	32	18	31	57	31	35	31	13	6
10	37	35	37	16	36	56	36	36	36	16	35	55	35	34	35	13	10
14	41	32	41	14	40	55	40	36	40	16	39	57	39	37	39	17	14
18	45	32	45	15	44	57	44	39	44	21	44	2	43	43	43	24	18
22	49	35	49	18	49	2	48	45	48	28	48	11	47	53	47	36	22
26	53	41	53	25	53	10	52	55	52	39	52	23	52	7	51	51	26
30	57	49	57	35	57	22	57	8	56	53	56	39	56	24	56	9	30
♊ 4	62	0	61	48	61	36	61	23	61	11	60	58	60	45	60	32	4 ♐
8	66	14	66	3	65	53	65	42	65	31	65	20	65	9	64	57	8
12	70	30	70	21	70	12	70	3	69	54	69	45	69	36	69	26	12
16	74	48	74	41	74	34	74	27	74	20	74	12	74	5	73	57	16
20	79	7	79	2	78	57	78	52	78	47	78	42	78	36	78	31	20
24	83	28	83	25	83	22	83	19	83	16	83	13	83	9	83	6	24
28	87	49	87	48	87	47	87	46	87	45	87	44	87	43	87	42	28
♋ 2	92	11	92	12	92	13	92	14	92	15	92	16	92	17	92	18	2 ♑
6	96	32	96	35	96	38	96	41	96	44	96	48	96	51	96	54	6
10	100	53	100	58	101	3	101	8	101	13	101	18	101	24	101	29	10
14	105	12	105	19	105	26	105	33	105	40	105	48	105	55	106	3	14
18	109	30	109	39	109	48	109	57	110	6	110	15	110	24	110	34	18
22	113	46	113	57	114	7	114	18	114	29	114	40	114	51	115	3	22
26	118	0	118	12	118	24	118	37	118	49	119	2	119	15	119	28	26
30	122	11	122	25	122	38	122	52	123	7	123	21	123	36	123	51	30
♌ 4	126	19	126	35	126	50	127	5	127	21	127	37	127	53	128	9	4 ♒
8	130	25	130	42	130	58	141	15	131	32	131	49	132	7	132	24	8
12	134	28	134	45	135	3	135	21	135	39	135	58	136	17	136	36	12
16	138	28	138	46	139	5	139	24	139	44	140	3	140	23	140	43	16
20	142	25	142	44	143	4	143	24	143	44	144	5	144	26	144	47	20
24	146	19	146	39	147	0	147	21	147	42	148	4	148	25	148	47	24
28	150	11	150	32	150	53	151	15	151	37	151	59	152	21	152	43	28
♍ 2	154	0	154	22	154	44	155	6	155	28	155	51	156	14	156	37	2 ♓
6	157	47	158	9	158	32	158	55	159	18	159	41	160	4	160	27	6
10	161	32	161	55	162	18	162	41	163	5	163	28	163	52	164	15	10
14	165	16	165	39	166	2	166	26	166	49	167	13	167	37	168	1	14
18	168	58	169	21	169	45	170	9	170	33	170	57	171	21	171	45	18
22	172	39	173	3	173	27	173	51	174	15	174	39	175	3	175	27	22
26	176	20	176	44	177	8	177	31	177	55	178	19	178	44	179	8	26
30	180	0	180	24	180	48	181	12	181	36	182	0	182	24	182	48	30

EQUIVALENT RIGHT ASCENSION

Latitude north	0°		1°		2°		3°		4°		5°		6°		7°		Latitude south
	°	′	°	′	°	′	°	′	°	′	°	′	°	′	°	′	
♎ 4	183	40	184	4	184	28	184	52	185	16	185	39	186	3	186	27	4 ♈
8	187	21	187	45	188	8	188	32	188	55	189	19	189	43	190	6	8
12	191	2	191	26	191	49	192	12	192	36	192	59	193	22	193	46	12
16	194	44	195	7	195	31	195	54	196	17	196	40	197	3	197	26	16
20	198	28	198	51	199	13	199	36	199	59	200	21	200	44	201	6	20
24	202	13	202	35	202	58	203	20	203	42	204	4	204	26	204	48	24
28	206	0	206	22	206	44	207	5	207	27	207	48	208	9	208	30	28
♏ 2	209	49	210	11	210	32	210	52	211	13	211	34	211	54	212	15	2 ♉
6	213	41	214	1	214	22	214	42	215	2	215	22	215	41	216	1	6
10	217	35	217	55	218	14	218	33	218	52	219	11	219	30	219	49	10
14	221	32	221	51	222	9	222	27	222	45	223	3	223	21	223	39	14
18	225	32	225	50	226	7	226	24	226	41	226	58	227	14	227	31	18
22	229	35	229	51	230	7	230	23	230	39	230	54	231	10	231	25	22
26	233	41	233	55	224	10	234	25	234	39	234	53	235	8	235	22	26
30	237	49	238	2	238	16	238	29	238	42	238	55	239	8	239	20	30
♐ 4	242	0	242	12	242	24	242	36	242	47	242	58	243	10	243	21	4 ♊
8	246	14	246	24	246	34	246	44	246	54	247	4	247	14	247	23	8
12	250	30	250	38	250	47	250	55	251	3	251	12	251	20	251	28	12
16	254	48	254	54	255	1	255	8	255	14	255	21	255	27	255	33	16
20	259	7	259	12	259	17	259	22	259	26	259	31	259	35	259	40	20
24	263	28	263	31	263	34	263	37	263	39	263	42	263	45	263	48	24
28	267	49	267	50	267	51	267	52	267	53	267	54	267	55	267	56	28
♑ 2	272	11	272	10	272	9	272	8	272	7	272	6	272	5	272	4	2 ♋
6	276	32	276	29	276	26	276	23	276	21	276	18	276	15	276	12	6
10	280	53	280	48	280	43	280	38	280	34	280	29	280	25	280	20	10
14	285	12	285	6	284	59	284	52	284	46	284	39	284	33	284	27	14
18	289	30	289	22	289	13	289	5	288	57	288	48	288	40	288	32	18
22	293	46	293	36	293	26	293	16	293	6	292	56	292	46	292	37	22
26	298	0	297	48	297	36	297	24	297	13	297	2	296	50	296	39	26
30	302	11	301	58	301	44	301	31	301	18	301	5	300	52	300	40	30
≈ 4	306	19	306	5	305	50	305	35	305	21	305	7	304	52	304	38	4 ♌
8	310	25	310	9	309	53	309	37	309	21	309	6	308	50	308	35	8
12	314	28	314	10	313	53	313	36	313	19	313	2	312	46	312	29	12
16	318	28	318	9	317	51	317	33	317	15	316	57	316	39	316	21	16
20	322	25	322	5	321	46	321	27	321	8	320	49	320	30	320	11	20
24	326	19	325	59	325	38	325	18	324	58	324	38	324	19	323	59	24
28	330	11	329	49	329	28	329	8	328	47	328	26	328	6	327	45	28
♓ 2	334	0	333	38	333	16	332	55	332	33	332	12	331	51	331	30	2 ♍
6	337	47	337	25	337	2	336	40	336	18	335	56	335	34	335	12	6
10	341	32	341	9	340	47	340	24	340	1	339	39	339	16	338	54	10
14	345	16	344	52	344	29	344	6	343	43	343	30	342	57	342	34	14
18	348	58	348	34	348	11	347	48	347	24	347	1	346	38	346	14	18
22	353	39	352	15	351	52	351	28	351	5	350	41	350	17	349	53	22
26	356	20	355	56	355	32	355	8	354	44	354	21	353	57	353	33	26
30	360	0	359	36	359	12	358	48	358	24	358	0	357	36	357	12	30

right-ascensional positions may be taken by interpolation according to the celestial latitude of the planet given in the ephemeris for the day and time of the native's birth. The abridged tables incorporated in this text are adequate for most normal computation. Thus if Disney's moon is taken as 187° 6' instead of 187° 5' the difference could hardly ever have appreciable consequence. In using these tables for planets with north latitude the sign of the planet's zodiacal position is found at the left for each four degrees of zodiacal longitude in the first column, and the equivalent right ascension is then identified in the proper column for celestial latitude. In most instances single or double interpolation is involved. For planets with south latitude the sign and degrees of zodiacal longitude are found at the extreme right of the tables, and the equivalent right ascension identified in the same way in the proper column for celestial latitude, but in this case 180° must be added in obtaining the correct right ascension and thereupon 365 degrees may be subtracted if necessary.

What gives the orderly distribution of progressed potential in secondary directions the possibility of a programming by the mind, as in a sense dealing with a cosmic computer and using its operations in an incisive analysis of elements of the possible and the profitable in personal human life, is the distinctiveness of each planet's motion as a consequence of its geocentric place in its own unique orbit in the solar system. What gives the same orderly distribution of progressed potential in primary directions the similar possibility of a programming by the mind, as in a sense dealing with a cosmic computer and using its operations in an incisive analysis of elements of the possible and the profitable in personal human life, is an identical logical procedure but of uniquely narrowed pertinence because established in the very immediate context created and maintained by the earth's rotation on its axis and the consequent revolving of the entire firmament around the particular world in which each individual has an existence. In this scheme of indication each planet again has its own highly distinctive path of significant motion, and this path astronomically is known as its semiarc and is considered commonly in its form of diurnal semiarc or right-ascensional distance from the midheaven meridian to the horizon. The houses of the horoscope in a fashion provide the norm of this. The turning of the heavens in the plane of the equator, or in a subsidiary plane that is surrogate for it, creates the correlation of a degree of motion in right ascension with a year of a native's life in primary progression. It is not the number ninety that is important but rather the ideal correspondence between an undistorted quadrant of arc in degrees and of human existence in equality of balance between the objective poise or harmony in the rising-setting phenomenon and the subjective balance of similar sort in the establishment and realization of personal horizon. It is in their relation to this virtually unattainable but ever desired self-integration that the planets have their special differentiation or indication in primary directions.

Each planetary semiarc or private orbit of distinctiveness in this area of dynamic horoscopy is found by placing the right ascension of the planet quite arbitrarily at the midheaven in the familiar tables of houses in order to find the point of intersection of the semiarc with the ascendant or its horizon at the terrestrial latitude of the native's birth. This is shown in zodiacal position but the equivalent right ascension can be taken from the tables of that equivalence, as here of logical necessity without celestial latitude. The right ascensional increase of this from the birth position is the semiarc identified as diurnal, and one ninetieth part of it represents the year of life in the primary progressions in the normal case or when the planet in the nativity at birth lies in the southeast or northwest quadrants of that horoscope. If contrariwise the planet lies in northeast or southwest quadrants the diurnal semiarc must be subtracted from 180° to represent

WALT DISNEY: PRIMARY PROGRESSION IN RIGHT ASCENSION (RA)

planet and quadrant	natal position of planet			horizon at 41°52'N		planetary semiarc		RA per year	diminished RA 1937	increased RA 1937
	longitude	latitude	RA	longitude	RA	diurnal	operative			
	° ′	° ′	° ′	° ′	° ′	° ′	° ′	° ′	° ′	° ′
☉ NE	♐ 12 26	0 0	250 58	♒ 27 26	329 38	78 40	101 20	1 7.55	210 17	291 39
☽ NE	♎ 9 3	S 2 57	187 8	♐ 16 11	255 0	67 52	112 8	1 14.75	142 17	231 59
♃ NW	♑ 15 23	S 0 14	286 43	♈ 29 7	27 4	100 21	100 21	1 6.9	246 35	326 51
♄ NW	♑ 14 41	N 0 13	285 54	♈ 27 31	25 32	99 38	99 38	1 6.4	246 4	325 44
♂ NW	♑ 8 27	S 1 5	279 16	♈ 16 19	15 2	95 46	95 46	1 3.8	240 59	317 33
♀ NW	♑ 29 41	S 2 37	302 26	♉ 22 6	49 41	107 15	107 15	1 11.6	259 28	345 24
☿ NE	♏ 27 26	N 1 5	235 25	♒ 5 4	307 25	72 0	108 0	1 12	192 13	278 37
♅ NE	♐ 16 40	S 0 3	255 30	♓ 4 39	336 31	81 1	98 59	1 6	215 54	295 6
♆ SE	♋ 0 33	S 1 12	90 34	♎ 0 21	180 19	89 45	89 45	59.8	54 42	126 26

438

the reversed distortion of relation with the horizon in the circling heavens in order to obtain the operative semiarc required for primary directions. One ninetieth part of it represents the year of life in this case, in differing from rather than conforming to the diurnal semiarc. As pointed out in the main text, this procedure has nothing to do with the locating of the planet in right ascension but only with determining its rate of progressed motion in these directions.

In practice a reference table of needed factors in primary directions should be made for each native, as illustrated in the case of Abraham Lincoln on page 384 and for Walt Disney at this point. The amount of right-ascensional shift in arriving at correspondence to a year of life can be shown in terms of the momentary right ascension to which each planet has diminished in the case of clockwise indication or increased in terms of counterclockwise indication at the threshold of some particular year or years of concern. Thus 1858 and 1862-3 are taken for attention in the Lincoln primaries and 1937 for Walt Disney's. Primary directions are particularly dependent on precise birth data, however, and there is no guarantee whatsoever of accuracy in Disney indication.

An inescapable handicap in calculating primary directions is the fact that consideration is in degrees around a circle with no such division as into thirty-degree signs and then of the signs among themselves by quadrature on the one hand and triplicity on the other. In recognizing and computing longitudinal progressions or natal aspects there is great and familiar help to attention and judgment. Where continual work is to be done with the primaries for any particular native a helpful device is to tabulate the unchanging aspect points of each of the natal planets in the degrees and minutes of right ascension. The Disney points can be shown by table as an example, and therefore they are presented in that form on the following page.

WALT DISNEY POINTS OF ASPECT IN PRIMARY DIRECTIONS

	TRINE	SQUARE	SEXTILE	CONJUNCTION	SEXTILE	SQUARE	TRINE	OPPOSITION
	° ′	° ′	° ′	° ′	° ′	° ′	° ′	° ′
Sun	130 58	160 58	190 58	250 58	310 58	340 58	10 58	70 58
Moon	67 8	97 8	127 8	187 8	247 8	277 8	307 8	7 8
Jupiter	166 43	196 43	226 43	286 43	346 43	16 43	46 43	106 43
Saturn	165 54	195 54	225 54	285 54	345 54	15 54	45 54	105 54
Mars	159 16	189 16	219 16	279 16	339 16	9 16	39 16	99 16
Venus	182 26	212 26	242 26	302 26	2 26	32 26	62 26	122 26
Mercury	115 25	145 25	175 25	235 25	295 25	325 25	355 25	55 25
Uranus	135 30	165 30	195 30	255 30	315 30	345 30	15 30	75 30
Neptune	330 34	0 34	30 34	90 34	150 34	180 34	210 34	270 34

A suggested regular routine is to begin with the smallest positions of right ascension coming to clockwise or counterclockwise significance in the period of attention, taking each in turn to see if it is close to any of the natal points of aspect in right ascension. Neptune is found by clockwise primary progression to have just had its opposition with natal Mercury by 43'. It is moving 59.8' a year in progressed indication. Thus:

$$43' \quad : \quad 59.8' \quad : : \quad x \quad : \quad 12 \text{ months}$$

By the proportion the primary direction came to culmination in 8.6 or approximately 8½ months before Disney's actual rather than artificial birthday or in mid-March, 1937. Neptune also and in the same general period is found by counterclockwise primary progression to be approaching a sextile with natal moon and to need 42' of motion in right ascension to consummate the aspect. Thus:

$$40' \quad : \quad 59.8' \quad : : \quad x \quad : \quad 12 \text{ months}$$

By the proportion this will occur in 8.4 or approximately 8½ months following the actual birthday in 1937 or around August, 1938.

Life Recapitulation

While few students or practitioners are likely to have ephemerides for 1809 or even 1847, the birth years of Abraham Lincoln and Annie Besant, it is probable that few do not have access to planetary tabulations for 1888-9 and in consequence the returns of Annie Besant can be used for illustration of the computation. Since interpretation of these charts often takes full advantage of house cusps and employs the symbolizations of the degrees in which significant points are found, they should be calculated by use of the diurnal proportional logarithms and this means an inverted employment for the solar and lunar returns where the x factor is the elapsed time from the previous noon or midnight to the moment of arrival of the planet to its original position.

For the Besant solar return:

Logarithm of 10′ 21″ required movement of sun   2.14342
Logarithm 59′ 5″ or its daily motion on September 30th   − 1.38690

                                                                 .75652

.75652 gives 4h 12m or 4:12 p.m. for both Greenwich and local mean time.

For the Besant lunar return:

Logarithm of 10° 18′ required movement of moon   .3674
Logarithm of 11° 47′ or its daily motion on May 4th   − .3089

                                                                .0585

.0585 gives 20h 58m or 8:58 a.m. on May 5th

For the Besant diurnal: (by the Rice tabulations)

Ascendant, 51° N (midheaven sidereal time, 18h 16m 0s)
    Aries   9° 29.7′
Half of increment, ascendant 51° N to 52° N   12.1

                                                           9   32.8
Needed increment, to ascendant of original nativity   1   24.2

                                                           10   57

The ascendant increase at 51° N, corresponding to 240s increase in midheaven sidereal time, is 2° 18.4′ or 138.4′. The needed increment of 1° 24.2′ is 84.2′. Thus: 84.2′ : 138.4′ : : x : 240s. The 147.4s or 2m 27s value of x in sidereal time so obtained is added to the sidereal time of the midheaven of reference in the calculation, 18h 16m 0s, to establish 18h 18m 27s as the sidereal time of the diurnal. The interval from the sidereal time at noon on May 9th, 3h 9m 58s, to the sidereal time of the diurnal, 18h 18m 27s, in sidereal time is 15h 8m 29s. Remembering that the correction from mean to sidereal time is approximately 10s for each hour, in the reverse correction here some 150s or 2m 30s must be subtracted from 15h 8m 29s to get the approximate 15h 6m from the previous noon for the L.M.T. of the diurnal or the 3:06 a.m. taken a little more precisely as 3:05 a.m. in calculating the day's return of the Besant ascendant.

THE COMPONENTS OF A HOROSCOPE

THE TWELVE SIGNS OF THE ZODIAC

Name	Quadrature	Triplicity	Basic Keyword
♈ Aries	Cardinal	Fire	Aspiration
♉ Taurus	Fixed	Earth	Virility
♊ Gemini	Common	Air	Vivification
♋ Cancer	Cardinal	Water	Expansion
♌ Leo	Fixed	Fire	Assurance
♍ Virgo	Common	Earth	Assimilation
♎ Libra	Cardinal	Air	Equivalence
♏ Scorpio	Fixed	Water	Creativity
♐ Sagittarius	Common	Fire	Administration
♑ Capricorn	Cardinal	Earth	Discrimination
♒ Aquarius	Fixed	Air	Loyalty
♓ Pisces	Common	Water	Sympathy

THE TEN PLANETS OF GENERAL RECOGNITION

Name	Department	Rulership	Basic Keyword
☉ The sun	Vitality	Leo	Purpose
☽ The moon	Vitality	Cancer	Feeling
♂ Mars	Efficiency	Aries, Scorpio	Initiative
♀ Venus	Efficiency	Taurus, Libra	Acquisitiveness
☿ Mercury	Efficiency	Gemini, Virgo	Mentality
♃ Jupiter	Motivation	Sagittarius, Pisces	Enthusiasm
♄ Saturn	Motivation	Capricorn, Aquarius	Sensitiveness
♅ Uranus	Significance	Aquarius at times	Independence
♆ Neptune	Significance	Pisces at times	Obligation
♇ Pluto	Significance	Scorpio at times	Obsession

NOTES: The symbols ☊, ☋ and ⊕ represent, in order, the dragon's head or moon's north node, the dragon's tail or moon's south node and the part of fortune, and are points respectively of protection, temptation and effective self-interest. Uranus is also known as Herschel. A large P with special base and a modified Mars are also Pluto symbols.

THE TWELVE HOUSES OF THE HOROSCOPE

Number	Axial Position	Area of Experience	Basic Keyword
First	Angular	Personality	Identity
Second	Succedent	Loss and gain	Possession
Third	Cadent	Perception	Environment
Fourth	Angular	Establishment	Home
Fifth	Succedent	Pleasure	Offspring
Sixth	Cadent	Sickness	Duty
Seventh	Angular	Opportunity	Partnership
Eighth	Succedent	Mutation	Regeneration
Ninth	Cadent	Consciousness	Understanding
Tenth	Angular	Business	Honor
Eleventh	Succedent	Objectives	Friendship
Twelfth	Cadent	Predilection	Confinement

THE PLANETARY INTERRELATIONSHIPS

Major Aspects and Keywords				Principal Minor Aspects	
☌	Conjunction	0°	Emphasis	Semisextile	30°
✶	Sextile	60°	Encouragement	Semiquintile	36°
□	Square	90°	Construction	Semisquare	45°
△	Trine	120°	Momentum	Septile	51°26′
☍	Opposition	180°	Awareness	Quintile	72°
	Aspect in Declination			Sesquiquadrate	135°
				Biquintile	144°
P	Parallel	0°		Quincunx	150°

THE EXALTATIONS OF THE PLANETS

☉	Aries	♂	Capricorn	♄	Libra	♃	Cancer
☽	Taurus	♅	Aquarius	♀	Scorpio	♆	Leo
☊	Gemini	♀	Pisces	☋	Sagittarius	☿	Virgo

NOTE: A brief treatment of the dignities and debilities is to be found in the author's *Horary Astrology, Problem Solving by.*

THE ANATOMICAL AND PHYSIOLOGICAL RULERSHIP

♈ Head	Brain	♎ Lower back	Kidneys
♉ Neck	Throat	♏ Pelvis	Lower ducts
♊ Shoulders, arms	Lungs	♐ Thighs	Flesh
♋ Chest	Breasts, stomach	♑ Knees	Skin
♌ Upper back	Spine, heart	♒ Calves, ankles	Blood
♍ Abdomen	Intestines	♓ Feet	Liver, lymphatics

index

index

A

Activity-facet, 15, 24
Adams, Evangeline, 173
Adams, John Quincy, 35
Adjusted calculation date, 380
Anareta, 172
Animoder, 168
Anthroposophical Society, 233
Antietam, 73, 126
Anti-Semitism, 253
Ascendant return, SEE diurnal.
Aspect (SEE ALSO BY NAME OF EACH), 22
Aspects, families of, 21, 22, 307

Aspects, minor, 22, 120
Asteroids, 14
Astrologers, early and medieval, 96, 146
Astrology, How & Why It Works, 19, 21, 301
Astrology, nature of, 15
Astrology, ultimate achievement of, 19
Atlanta, 25, 44
Autobiography (Annie Besant), 239, 253, 280, 287
Avatar, SEE Krishnamurti.
Aveling, Edward, 206, 207, 254, 259, 261, 275, 323

The index, which covers the main text of the book, should be used in conjunction with the supplementary contents and in Appendix I the complete listing of the secondary directions of Abraham Lincoln and Annie Besant (in which there is reference to the pages on which their delineations occur) together with the summary statement of the essential principles of astrology (which similarly lists the references to them in the expository sections by page).

B

Benares Affair, 221

Berry, William, 32

Besant, Annie, adolescence, 204, 212, 214, 217, 239, 272

Besant, Annie, and birth control, 218, 240, 251, 252

Besant, Annie, and British social reform (SEE ALSO, Bradlaugh, Charles), 218, 263, 265, 275

Besant, Annie, and Christianity (SEE ALSO, Buddhism, Hinduism), 204, 205, 218. 231, 251, 257, 278

Besant, Annie, and marriage. 206, 218, 250, 272, 273

Besant, Annie, as publisher. 252, 256, 265

Besant, Annie, childhood, 194. 202, 203, 213, 216, 217, 226, 239

Besant, Annie, custody of children, 253, 254, 255, 266

Besant, Annie, diurnal, 284

Besant, Annie, education of (SEE ALSO, Marryat, Ellen), 198, 203, 207, 213, 254, 256, 257, 272

Besant, Annie injury to knee, 255

Besant, Annie, internment, 221

Besant, Annie, literary effort of, 206, 274, 323

Besant, Annie, lunar return, 282

Besant, Annie, move to India, 198, 209, 324

Besant, Annie, protean nature of, 308

Besant, Annie, relative to Lincoln, 83, 84, 189, 203, 280

Besant, Annie, solar return, 280

Besant, Annie, twin strands in make-up, 206, 212, 225

Besant, (Arthur) Digby, 227

Besant, Frank, 196, 205, 214, 226, 250, 253, 259, 272, 274

Besant, Henry, 194, 217, 272

Besant, Mabel, 226, 227, 253, 254, 268

Bhagavadgita, 209

Birth control, SEE Besant, Annie.

Black Hawk War, SEE UNDER war.

Blavatsky, Helena, 192, 207,

208, 211, 214, 220, 226,
228, 229, 230, 244, 257,
262, 263, 264, 266, 267,
276, 282, 284, 289, 293,
324
Blavatsky Hall and Lodge,
198, 209, 230, 244, 265,
266, 277, 288, 324
Bradlaugh, Charles, 189, 191,
194, 196, 198, 207, 213,
219, 240, 242, 244, 247,
250, 251, 252, 254, 255,
256, 260, 261, 265, 267,
274, 275, 276
Bradlaugh (Bonner), Hypa-
tia, and sister, 196, 255,
256
Brahmanism, SEE Hinduism.
Breaking the horoscope, 324
Bright, Esther, 228
Broughton, L. D., 17, 173
Brown, John, 108, 162
Buchanan, James, 106
Buddhism, 232, 269
Bull Run, 111
Burrows, Herbert, 255, 263,
264

C

Calhoun, John, 41
Cameron, Simon, 125

Case history, necessity for,
178
Caste system, 200, 253
Cause and effect, 14, 141,
363, 374
Central Hindu College, 199,
221
Chakravarti, Gyanendra, 192,
268
Chaldean order, 363
Chance (SEE ALSO flux, free
will, concordance), 60, 104
Charlatanry, SEE fortune-
telling.
Chicago Republican convention, 109
Chinese-boxes arrangement,
17, 47, 51, 58, 203, 304
Choice, SEE chance.
Christian orthodoxy, SEE Besant, Annie, and Chris-
tianity.
Chronos, 363
Clairvoyance, 199, 203, 208,
214, 215, 222, 228, 230,
231, 234, 245, 257, 258,
264, 266, 276, 289
Clay, Henry, 25, 34, 38, 39,
41, 58, 61, 68, 72, 80, 84,
85, 89, 129, 132

Collins, Mabel, 265

Common sense, 4

Commonweal, 192

Comparison of Horoscopes, 36, 39, 51, 52, 114, 215, 220, 230, 233

Compromise, Missouri and 1850, 30, 41, 63, 129

Concordance, cosmic (SEE ALSO, flux, and principles, essential), 15

Conjunction, nature of, 21, 22

Converse directions, 150

Cultural matrix, 334

Cusps, house or sign, 120, 170

D

Das, Bhagavan, 269

Death, impact of, 26, 53, 63, 64, 202, 213, 229

Debates, Great, 80, 106, 107, 123, 132, 153, 156, 164, 165, 166

de Gaulle, Charles, 348, 351, 353

Democratic Party, 106, 110

Democrats, Jacksonian, 35

Deviation, human, 43, 193

Directions, (SEE ALSO progressions), 16, 20, 142, 157, 160, 304

Disney, Walt, 337

Diurnal, nature of, 140

Douglas, Stephen, 30, 35, 36, 37, 38, 41, 76, 80, 105, 106, 107, 123, 132, 153, 156, 164, 165, 166

Dreams, significance of, 93

Dred Scott Decision, 105, 153, 161

E

Early, Jubal, 117

Earth, astrological function of the, 147, 148, 336

Eclipses, nature of, 121, 128

Education (SEE ALSO, Besant's education, Indian education, Lincoln's education), 6

Edwards, Ninian, 39, 55

Emancipation Proclamation, 113

Empirical science, astrology as, 15

Equity law, 68, 88

Esoteric Christianity, 231

Esoteric Section, 264, 266

Essentials of Astrological Analysis, 36, 181, 332

Everett, Edward, 73

Explanations of astrology, their limitation, 303, 306

F

Fabian Society, 197, 219, 260

Faculty psychology, 300

Fatality, 362

Fell, Jesse, 107, 167

Flux, cosmic (SEE ALSO, concordance), 15

Formulas, 8, 29

Fort Sumter, 110, 111

Forts Henry and Donelson, 111, 125

Fortunetelling, charlatanry, 8, 119, 208, 258, 363

France, 113, 126, 348

Free love, SEE birth control.

Freethinker, 256

Free thinking, SEE National Secular Society.

Freethought Publishing Company, 252, 256, 265

Free will (SEE ALSO chance), 15, 19, 212

Frémont, John, 112

Freud, Sigmund, 365, 366, 368

Fruits of Philosophy, 218, 240, 251, 252

Fulcrum indication, 46, 62, 75, 87, 193, 213, 227, 242, 250, 315, 329, 341, 351, 359, 365

Fundamentals of Number significance, 307

G

Gandhi, Mohandas, 200, 221, 232, 242, 292

Genius, 19

Gentry, James, 50

Geocentric ordering, 147

Gettysburg, battle and address, 73, 113, 126, 155, 156

Grant, Ulysses, 111, 113, 114, 115, 116

Great Britain, 111, 113, 126

Great Debates, SEE UNDER debates.

Guide to Horoscope Interpretation, 83, 180, 287, 324

H

Hall, Manly, 173
Hamilton, Alexander, 35
Hanks family (SEE ALSO Lincoln, Nancy Hanks), 26, 78, 89, 129
Harpers Ferry, 108
Hauptmann, Bruno, 360
Hay, John, 110
Hermes, the astrologer, 168
Herndon, William, 42, 51, 52, 53, 54, 67, 79, 311
Hinduism, 192, 232, 269, 278
Hipparchus, 317
Hodgson, Richard, 258
Horary astrology, 20, 86, 134, 144, 148, 170, 172
Horary Astrology, Problem Solving by, 20, 86
Horizon, function of, 148, 150, 170
Horoscope, foundational elements of, 157
Horoscope houses, nature of, 303
Horoscope, limitations of, 18
Horoscope or nativity, SEE natal interpretation, comparison of horoscopes.
How to Learn Astrology, 5, 287

I

Illinois legislature, 33, 35, 100, 153
Illinois Staats-Anzeiger, 108, 124
Indian education, 192, 278
Indian National Congress, 189, 200, 221, 243, 289, 320
Indian politics, 193, 201, 234, 242
Indiana, SEE Lincoln's Indiana boyhood.
Inexactitudes in astrology, 145, 303
Infinity, SEE proliferation to.
International socialist congress, 263, 264
Intuition, 6, 119
Ionian physicists, 146
Irregularity in all human relations, 87

J

Jessel, Sir George, 253
Johnston family (SEE ALSO Lincoln, Sarah Bush), 78, 89
Jones, Marc, 330, 331, 332
Judd, Norman, 106

Judge, William, 214, 227, 228, 268

Jupiter, function of, 356

K

Kansas, slavery in general, 30, 32, 76, 106, 122, 128, 162, 308

Kentucky, Owens and Todd background, 39, 54

Kentucky, SEE Lincoln's Kentucky childhood.

Key Truths of Occult Philosophy, 331

Keywords, nature of, 317

Krishnamurti, Jeddu, 190, 193, 201, 209, 210, 211, 220, 222, 223, 226, 231, 233, 234, 237, 238, 244, 245, 289, 313, 324

Krishnamurti's apostles, 222

Kronos, 363

L

Lamon, Ward, 73

Language, horoscopy as a, 317, 338

Law and Liberty League, 220, 262

Law of Population, The, 252

Laws, governing, SEE Principles, essential.

Leadbeater, Charles, 199, 230, 232, 288

Legislature, SEE UNDER Illinois.

Leo, Alan, 287

Letters, anonymous ("Rebecca"), 72

Lincoln, Mary Todd, 39, 51, 52, 53, 54, 55, 56, 57, 67, 73, 75, 79, 89, 130, 131, 162, 163, 176, 311

Lincoln, Nancy Hanks, 25, 176

Lincoln, Sarah Bush Johnston, 26, 52, 124, 129, 174

Lincoln, Thomas, 25, 26, 31, 78, 89, 129, 174, 176

Lincoln and law, 34, 50, 67, 76, 86, 87, 162

Lincoln, as county surveyor, 29, 323

Lincoln, as postmaster, 32

Lincoln defeated for the Senate, 108

Lincoln in Congress, 30, 34, 48, 107, 175, 319

Lincoln, relative to Besant, 83, 84, 189, 203, 280

Lincoln, scholarship concerning, 83, 173, 181
Lincoln, "Spotty", 48
Lincoln's cabinet, 110
Lincoln's children, 42
Lincoln's Cooper-Union Address, 109, 124
Lincoln's diurnal, 140
Lincoln's duel, 73
Lincoln's eccentricities (SEE ALSO Lincoln's melancholy, loner), 53
Lincoln's education, 65, 85
Lincoln's engagements and marriage, 55, 61, 72, 73, 74, 89
Lincoln's "house-divided" address, 59, 107
Lincoln's Indiana boyhood, 49, 66, 76, 129
Lincoln's Kentucky childhood, 25, 63, 64, 65, 129
Lincoln's lunar return, 138
Lincoln's melancholy (SEE ALSO eccentricities, loner), 43, 99, 160, 179
Lincoln's Peoria address, 32
Lincoln's self-sufficiency, 308
Lincoln's sister, Sarah, 25, 26, 53, 65
Lincoln's solar return, 134

Little Giant, SEE Douglas, Stephen.
Lloyd George, David, 358, 359, 360, 365, 366
Logan, Stephen, 47, 131
London University, SEE Besant, Annie, education.
Loner, 17, 99
Long Nine, SEE Illinois legislature.
Loophole in jurisprudence, 87
Lucifer, 265, 267, 277
Lunar return, nature of, 138
Lunation, synodical, 158
Lunations, nature of, 121, 127

M

McClellan, George, 126
Mahatma Letters, 258
Malthusian League, 261
Manchester executions, 273
Marfan syndrome, 42
Marryat, Ellen, 191, 203, 204, 205, 213, 217, 239
Mars, function of, 344
Marx, Eleanor, 259
Masters of Wisdom, 214, 235, 245, 246, 258
Mercury, function of, 16, 305

Melancholy, SEE Lincoln's melancholy.

Messiah, SEE Krishnamurti.

Metaphysics of astrology, 303

Method, astrological, 4

Mexico, SEE war, Mexican.

Midheaven, function of, in progression, 149, 171, 172

Mind, 3, 20, 300, 305, 306

Minor progressions, 160

Minor, SEE aspects, asteroids.

Miracle-mongering, SEE clairvoyance.

Missouri Compromise, SEE compromise.

Monitor and *Merrimac,* 111

Moon, the, function of, 102, 103, 104, 157, 158, 170, 373

Mundane astrology, 154

Mundane primary directions, 150

Myth, dynamic nature of, 355

Myth figure, 16, 18, 24, 43, 69, 87, 97, 101, 114, 130, 132, 140, 190, 200, 223, 226, 243, 355

N

Natal interpretation, 19, 21, 30, 134, 138, 178

Natal interpretation distinct from progression, 134, 317

National Reformer, 194, 198, 207, 219, 250, 251, 252, 254, 256, 274

National Secular Society, Secularism (SEE ALSO, Bradlaugh, Charles), 194, 206, 207, 241, 250, 258, 265, 267, 274, 276, 277, 320

Nehru, Jawaharlal, 201, 232

Neptune, function of, 13, 370

New Orleans, 50, 78, 94, 112, 130

New Salem, 31, 34, 50, 54, 58, 72, 85, 94, 97, 100, 123, 130

Nine, Long, SEE Illinois legislature.

Nityananda, 245

Nodes, planetary, 120, 284

Nonfulcral indication, 29, 64, 77, 88, 94, 202, 216, 229, 239, 243, 244, 250, 321, 331, 342, 353, 360, 366

O

Offutt, Denton, 50, 78, 94

Olcott, Henry, 199, 214, 215, 220, 230, 268, 320

Old, Walter (Sepharial), 287

Opposition, nature of, 21, 22

Orb in directions, 30, 141, 376

Order, material or natural (SEE ALSO, concordance), 19, 20

Order of the Star, 201, 209, 210, 233, 234, 238

Our Corner, 197, 219, 257, 260

Owens, Mary, 54, 55, 75

P

Pall Mall Gazette, 220, 262

Parallel of declination, 22

Parliament of Religions, 192, 269, 277, 311

Parts (as part of fortune), 120

Pate, Samuel, 50, 76, 86

Paul the Evangelist, 302

Perversion, SEE deviation.

Planetary hours, 103

Planetary orb, SEE orb in directions, wide orb.

Planetary stations, indication in progression, 49, 62, 74, 85, 97, 98, 100, 192, 213, 226, 238, 242, 244, 245, 246, 310, 329, 339, 350, 358, 365

Planets, SEE UNDER NAMES OF EACH.

Planets, as symbols only, 28

Planets, in progressed activation, 27

Planets, newly discovered, 14, 18, 91, 189, 210, 245, 246, 247

Plato, 146

Pluto, function of, 16, 371

Point Loma community, 215

Polk, James, 48, 68

Polk, Lilian, 287

Pottawatomie Creek Massacre, 162

Principles, essential (SEE ALSO in appendix), 13

Progressed horoscope, the, 136

Progressed interpretation distinct from natal, 134, 317

Progressions, essentially the same as directions (SEE ALSO, directions), 304

Proliferation to infinity, 120

Protean, 7

Psychological trend to balance, 22, 23, 61, 71, 84, 94, 190, 212, 225, 237,

241, 244, 309, 328, 336, 348, 357, 364

Ptolemy, Claudius, 168

Pythagoras, 3, 146

R

Reality, 3, 15, 103, 119, 133, 136

Removes in consideration, 18, 20, 119, 134, 144, 145, 147, 170

Republican party, 34, 68, 106, 109, 110, 116, 164, 176

Retrogradation, 121

Revolution, American, 110

Revolution of 1848, 190

Roberts, William, 218, 273

Robertson, John, 198, 259

Romans, 302

Rutledge, Ann, 54

S

Sabian Manual, The, 332

Sabian Symbols in Astrology, 21, 287

Sangamo Journal, 72

Sanskrit language, 209

Saturn, function of, 103, 361, 363

Scholarship, Lincoln, SEE UNDER Lincoln.

Scott, Winfield, 68, 114

Secession of first states, 155

Secret Doctrine, 220, 262, 276, 282

Secularism, SEE National Secular Society.

Self-analysis, dangers of, 330

Sensitivity, meaning of, 337

Sepharial, SEE Old, Walter.

Sextile, nature of, 21, 22

Sexual perversion, SEE deviation.

Shakespeare, 3

Shaw, (George) Bernard, 191 197, 206, 207, 260, 261, 262, 275

Shelley, Percy, 196

Sinnett, Alfred, 230, 258

Slavery, SEE Kansas.

Socialist Defense Association, 261

Society for Psychical Research, 208, 258

Solar return, nature of, 134

Springfield, 38, 47, 67, 79, 97, 130, 319

Square, nature of, 21, 23, 46

Stanton, Edwin, 125

Star Camp, SEE Order of the Star.

Stations, SEE UNDER planetary.

Stead, William, 220, 262

Steiner, Rudolf, 233

Step-by-step procedure, 5

Stuart, John, 34, 39, 47, 67

Summaries, characteristic of, 8

Sun, the, function of, 326

Symbolical and mechanical reference in contrast, 19, 147

Symbolical movement of planets, 144, 172, 302

Synodical lunation, 158

T

Taney, Roger, 86, 105

Taylor, James, 50, 66, 76, 78, 129

Techniques, alternative progressive, 20, 169

Techniques wholly distinct, 20, 134, 317

Theosophy and Theosophical Society, 189, 191, 198, 199, 207, 208, 210, 214, 215, 216, 220, 222, 223, 226, 230, 232, 233, 235, 243, 244, 246, 253, 255, 257, 258, 262, 263, 264, 266, 268, 269, 277, 278, 282, 287, 288, 313

Theosophist, 258

Thousand and One Notable Nativities, A, 287

Time correspondence, 143, 144, 172, 303

Time identification by Saturn, 363

Time, obsession with the moment of, 136

Time orb, SEE orb in directions.

Time To Be Born, Accurate Birth Date of 3000 Notable Persons and Events, A, 287

Tingley, Katherine, 215, 227, 230, 233

Todd family (SEE ALSO Lincoln, Mary Todd), 39, 320

Trafalgar Square riot, 220, 262

Trent Affair, 111

Trine, nature of, 21, 22

Trumbull, Lyman, 164

Trutine, 168

U

Uranus, function of, 41, 367

V

Venus, function of, 333
Vicksburg, 113, 126, 155, 156
Victorian age, 192, 196, 200, 206, 218, 359

W

Wagner, Richard, 350, 351, 352, 364
Walters, Aunt Peggy, 173
Washington, George, 35, 114
War, Black Hawk, 32, 34, 38
War, Civil (SEE ALSO Kansas), 25, 36, 44, 116
War of 1812, 58
War, Mexican, 48, 320
War, World I, 190, 234
Warren, Earl, 86

Webster, Daniel, 41
Whig party, 34, 68, 176
Wide orb, 178
Wilderness, Battle of the, 116
Wilson, Woodrow, 364, 365
Women Lincoln Loved, 173
Women's rights, 253
Wood, Emily and family, 194, 202, 213, 216, 217, 229, 266, 274, 289
World's Columbian Exposition, SEE Parliament of Religions.

Y

Yates, William, 264, 277

Z

Zodiac, SEE signs.
Zodiac, as subordinated, 148
Zone of dynamic rapport, 151